A Barista's

LIFE*LOVE*LAUGHTER

As of 4-26-06 TXU1301345

A Barista's Life*Love*Laughter LLC

Print ISBN: 978-1-66780-809-3

eBook ISBN: 978-1-66780-810-9

A Barista's Life*Love*Laughter

Of One Enchanting, Isolated, Challenging Year

In the High Mountains of Washington State at

OUTPOST ESPRESSO

Plus 365
Pacific Northwest Daily Grind Recipes

Cynthia Marie
Michelle Murphy

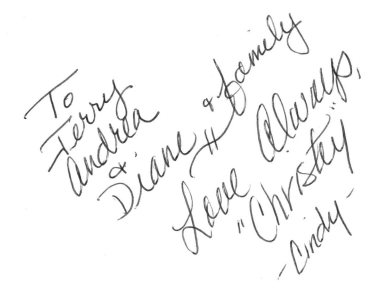

To Terry
Andrea &
Diane & family
Love Always,
"Chrysler"
-Cindy

DEDICATION

A BARISTA'S LIFE*LOVE*LAUGHTER is solely dedicated to
Mamu our Grandma. She lost her mother at the fragile age of twelve
and summoned unbelievable strength to raise her four brothers, while caring
for her alcoholic, devastated father. She taught all of us girls to…

"Just throw those shoulders back and do it!"

Disclaimer

A Barista's Life∗Love∗Laughter is a work of fiction.
Names, characters, places and incidents are the products of the
author's imagination and are used fictitiously. Any resemblance to
actual persons, living or dead, events, locales is entirely coincidental.

The authors have invested their time interviewing
espresso shops in various unique locations, along with
owning espresso establishments. This story was inspired
by the various baristas interviewed and customers
along their travels and first-hand experience.

Some true Washington landmarks may be mentioned;
all are used fictitiously.

Note: Some fictitious words, spelling and hillbilly grammar
have also taken up residence within this cover.
Fall in love with the characters along the way...

PROLOGUE

Researching Male & Female Relationships
A Bad Science Project

A Barista's Life∗Love∗Laughter was written to inspire *real* women with *real* lives! Let us set the stage: With unbelievable trepidation, Christy undertook an espresso business, animals, house, store, barn and plow, all on an acre of riverfront, isolated on a highway in the high mountains of Washington State. Customers in this foreign land are mostly mountain people; that are to say forest hermits, crusty local old-timers, clueless inbreeds, hillbillies, and then the "city people" who travel through this territory in awe. They said it couldn't be done. *She's doing it...*

Christy, a beautiful slip-of-a gal, 110-pounds soaking wet, tends **OUTPOST ESPRESSO,** juggling espresso, her animals, and customers. This book sheds Christy's light on the unique perception and truths between two beasts – male and female, and this combination is referred to as a *Bad Science Project,* in her never to be humble opinion! You will not quite be reading sexy details of being "bent over the espresso machine" by the most gorgeous guy in the world, but it comes close.

Come along for a wild ride into the retail world of *The Old-Fashioned Bartender, The Barista,* who serves the legalized drug – caffeine. This barista deals with the extreme public, in an extreme location, in the extreme times of today. Enjoy the 365 "Daily Grind" recipes which include a unique blend of beverages and desserts. Enjoy, laugh, cry, and watch out – *men*-kind…

TABLE OF CONTENTS

JANUARY

Winter is raked, pruned and plenty, as
vanilla bean glows through the pane

1-21 49° Semi-cloudy.

Cinnamon Apple Latte: 1/2 shot apple syrup, shot cinnamon syrup or powder, espresso shots, steamed milk.

8:41 A.M. Not much going on today…eeny, meeny, miny, moe…Will this yearning be satisfied with a king-size chocolate bar, a trip to the craft store, possibly a few shillings in the slots or shall I shag the next stunning, three-legged stud that walks through my doors? I think I will just sit tight, inside this cubicle, and actualize the journal, which has been rolling around in my head for far too long. Much healthier than at least three of *those* options…

I must give you some background so you can appreciate this Barista girl's solitary existence at the **OUTPOST ESPRESSO**, high up in the mountains of Northwest Washington. It is one of my reminiscing days…looking back over the years at some of the unbelievable stories in the barista business, sharing *only* enchanting, lonely, exciting, and emotional year!

My espresso and gift shop just happens to be located up in no-man's land (no normal men that is). I am that rare, single, white female, running the joint.

I live alone above my store and try to keep a handle on an acre of river front-age, along with the four powerful seasons in the Northwest.

This designated scenic highway is my front yard. I am a tiny gun-totin', mace carryin' mama, ready for war-at-all-costs gal! Doing it just to say, "I did it!" and to prove to women everywhere that if we discard our poisons (men, booze, fear, insecurity, food, pills, and lack of inner strength), WE CAN DO ANYTHING!

11:38 A.M. In the meantime, many hopeful men and male customers, daily, surround me. The two are *not* synonymous! Along with all of *them,* come thousands of different people and I shall share only the *printable* stories. They reflect the realities of men and women's issues and plain ole *life*. My doors swing open to innumerable and varied *creatures* in "these-thar-hills". I also cohabit with my six birds and a lovable guard dog. This ma 'n pa form of isolated living is on a plot of land that dates to the turn of the century and is considered by some to be heaven-on-earth!

The Bower family owned this building and some of the surrounding area cabins from the early 1900s on. It has had various owners since then, but always a small grocery store and gas station. It even boasted a restaurant until the 1950s, when it burned down, along with hundreds of other buildings in this region. It is now called MINE!

5:04 P.M. This book tells the story as **A BARISTA'S LIFE∗LOVE∗LAUGHTER.** It mainly focuses on the truths of male and female relationships, which *I* consider "*a bad science project.*" We will take a deep look into a female solely handling *retail* and *service*. My tiny town of Saratogan is the hub and depicts the lifestyle of this isolated community, along with the golden days of logging, mining, railroad lines, and brothels.

6:11 P.M. Come on along for this ride…

1-22 49° Cloudy-Only one sweater on. Nose is not running. How can this be?

> Rum/Amaretto Latte: 1/2 shot rum syrup or real rum, copy with amaretto, shots of espresso, steamed milk.

8:03 A.M. It has been thirty-two years since the Pineapple Express blew in like this! Mountain Peak Ski Resort closed *again* last Monday, and who knows if and when it will re-open! I am supposed to be selling espresso to masked, bundled mummies, looking for a kick and warmth! The Seattle Flyer even interviewed me this afternoon, along with some of the employees up at the resort. I am finally newsworthy – too bad the news is about a dusty, dried-up espresso machine and going broke!

12:02 P.M. *Good God Business Is Slow!* Saturdays have become just another boring Wednesday.

Today one of my customers surprised me with gifts from Hawaii. *Rub it in!* Believe me, these gifts at hand will cost me plenty – many free cappuccinos, and I'll end up spending even more than he did the ol' muckworm. But then again, this is the man responsible for getting me started on my writings – since one of my gifts from Hawaii is a beautiful baroque, padded journal and a note. "Go Girl!" So, I will transfer page one from bits of scratch paper and here we go...

BMW Brian is one of those Microsoft guys that cannot comprehend my life up here, even one iota. So, he *tells* me, "Get this craziness down on paper!" I normally do not listen to men that *tell* me anything.

I began this journal during a historically dead, snowless season, and **OUTPOST ESPRESSO** is located close to a ski-resort. So, instead of boring you to death, I will share some facts:

THE HISTORY OF ESPRESSO

The simple human desire-for-speed became the root of the invention of espresso. It began in the mid-1800s, when people wanted a quick and personal cup of coffee made, just for them. It became the process of brewing coffee faster. In 1901, an Italian named Luigi Bezzera patented the first espresso machine, using steam pressure to force water through ground coffee. Then along came the foamed and steamed milk idea. In 1948, Gaggia improved this system by developing the first spring-piston espresso machine. The first hydraulic machine arrived in 1956, by Cimbali. FAEMA came up with an electric pump machine, which was considered a much more modern system in 1960.

Espresso took a while to catch on in America. It intrigued the public as something foreign that sparked up thoughts of romance, mystery, and sophistication.

Espresso is a 1.5-ounce beverage that is prepared from 8 grams of coffee, pressurized under 198-degrees of steam, and forced at 9 atmospheres of pressure, with a flow time of 25-seconds. *Snappy and fastidiously flawless!*

4:09 P.M. A nice yuppie couple came in. They looked calculated. In the first thirty seconds I was not surprised to hear that he was a computer engineer, working for the Big Guy, and she a realtor. I was foaming and frothing cappuccinos while they were digesting their surroundings. "How can you live in a place like this? Got any neighbors? We see Porta Potties, forests, animals and this is so isolated and rustic, I am sure you don't dare do French Nails – are you masochistic?" "Well, I hadn't thought of this place in quite those terms, but now that you mention it…" Just then, one of the toothless locals strolled in. Perfect timing to spook these city slickers.

Next…an adorable single from "down-below" stopped in on her way to eastern Washington for a wedding. She was not pleased. "My younger cousin is gaining a husband and losing her freedom. At least that is my impression. Every old aunt is going to be on my case, poking me in the ribs with, 'Are you going to *ever* be *next*?' This is at every damn ceremony. Make my drink a double…no, a triple!"

5:53 P.M. Early close. Slow day. May as well save the electricity as the highway is hollow…

1-23 50° Clear.

Rum/Amaretto Latte: A ½ shot of rum and amaretto syrups (or real liquor), shots of espresso and steamed milk.

8:01 A.M. *All-in one-half hour!* My daughter, who lives in Alaska, has a baby. How did I get to be a forty-five-year-old grandmother, who still gets "carded" for buying beer? I found out today that she is getting a divorce, via her cell phone from a bar. She was sitting outside smoking and spitting, under the year-round heat lamps, trying to get a word in edgewise, as I was crying and screaming, a mile a minute! She was so engrossed in our conversation that when she turned her head to spit, it accidentally landed on a comely million-aire from Pacifica, Washington. Obviously, they got to know each other pretty well in the next few minutes. She insisted that he meet her mother! He jumped right on her phone, "I'm coming down to the lower 'forty-eight' next week. Let us get together for some dinner!" He suggested Valentine's Day… UGH. Doesn't he have a life?

A client stopped by for a large supply of my chocolate-covered espresso beans. She informed me that her cheating husband was a *doll* this weekend while visiting *their* home, so she was now packing up her life and the kids to re-join him at his *relocation* site on the other side of the mountains. I figured that was probably right next door to his latest missy! She emphatically explained, *again,* that he will get no more chances! No wonder she inhales espresso beans…

Just then, a gentleman walked in and pulled out one of my historic railroad postcards. He pointed to himself in the photo, "I'm the guy in front of the touring steam engine," as he stood in the same pose with railroad pride all over his face. His name was Derek, and I am sure I'll see more of him. He left feeling famous! *All in only one-half hour…* Believe in coincidence? There is no such thing in my opinion. Those are the daily miracles, which are meant to be gifts – in one way or another.

12:00 P.M. I was supposed to be taking a fly-tying class today, but just cancelled. I have one of the most popular fishing holes right here in my back yard. Hundreds of fly fishermen have thrown their lines in throughout the years. My visitor today was a famous editor of an international fly-fishing magazine. We exchanged one of *those glances.* So many men, so few hours…

2:02 P.M. A crazy one, stepped in…one of the locals with *maybe* four snags for teeth. He wanted a triple espresso shot, two muffins, and ten chocolate-covered espresso beans. Now, the espresso and muffin I could understand, but how would he chew the beans? I guess he just enjoys sucking the chocolate off, swallowing the beans whole and just praying for good luck.

4:32 P.M. Saratogan is an old logging and railroad town. The tracks line the highway where I live. Twenty-three trains thunder by every day. Our town's population today is approximately two hundred people. Back in its heyday there were thousands in these hills and still today we have some of the local families that date back three generations. Why on earth are they still here? *But then again, why am I?*

6:24 P.M. I am done. No more energy…

1-24 48° Clear.

Malt Mocha: 1 tsp. malt powder, shot of chocolate syrup, espresso shots, steamed milk, whipped cream.

7:47 A.M. Snow gods, where art thou?

It is so easy to *not* write a book, simply for the fact that it should have been written long ago. All those stories lost… *Not* writing it at all would be the shame. Throughout this diary, I will go back and touch on some of the unique experiences that *must* be printed, to heal my guilt of neglect. Most diaries, and this one would be no different, are chock-full of the past, present, and future fantasies.

8:23 A.M. Here comes my first Harley of the winter. This weather was so uniquely warm, breaking records right and left, maybe I would keep track of how many Harleys pulled in compared to the number of cars totin' golf clubs. The Harley guy complimented me on having the cleanest Porta Potty on the entire highway! Restrooms are a luxury up here in these mountains and most of the others on "down-the-line" are frightful.

Last year was a different story! We had normal snowfall, normal winter temperatures and were terribly busy. Unfortunately, the Porta Potty company would not service these impersonal, disgusting, you would not-catch-my-butt-out-there amenities if it was snowing or the glop had frozen! Three weeks passed last season without a service call, during the busy holiday vacation in December. The stew rose and rose. One day an astonished gentleman could not believe his eyes. He just had to have a picture! He grabbed his camera, all the while describing the sight in detail to me, and to the rest of the customers that were here, who had not yet run for the hills. He was so proud! Was it going to become his Christmas card photo?

Saratogan history as promised:

THE HISTORY OF SARATOGAN

The City of Saratogan was founded in 1893 as a railroad town for the Pacific railroad. The town was supported by rail, timber, and mining. It was named after the Saratogan natives meaning "sparkling place." The tribe's territory was along the Saratogan River, but most of their villages were further downstream near Tillamook, Crag Rock, and Snow Peak Mine. The natives mainly used the Saratogan area for temporary campsites for hunting and berry picking. The Euro-American settlers came to this region in the 1850s and introduced smallpox and other diseases to these tribes. This depleted them considerably.

The Pacific Railway was built from St. Paul, Minnesota, to the Pacific Northwest in the late 1800s. In 1890, engineer George Bass explored the area around Swift Creek and carved "Mountain Peak" into a tree. That was to become the area for breakthrough. Paul Manning quickly staked a claim, realizing that many men would now need supplies, housing, and a post office. The whores arrived by the droves. Thus in 1893, the community was named Saratogan.

Saratogan became the point where trains switched from steam engines to electric engines for the trip over Mountain

Peak. Later, they built the 7.8-mile-long Kodiak Tunnel beneath Mountain Peak. It opened in 1929, replacing the old three-mile tunnel.

The population back in the 1920s was nearly 8,000. Today the population is just 200-250. What still stands is the Saratogan Hotel, boasting success over the many years. There are still ghost stories about one of the prostitutes named Suzanna, who, in the 1920s, was supposedly murdered by one of her customers in room 13.

In 1909, Saratogan became incorporated. In 1970, the Pacific merged with the Illinois Railroad, North Coast Railroad, and Squire Railroad and became the North Coast Northern Railroad. Extraordinarily little else has changed in Saratogan to date! People became more interested in our area for weekend get-a-ways and thus Mountain Peak Ski Resort was founded.

5:01 P.M. I am people hungry, conversation starved, and my cash register's bones are showing. Is there *anything* I can do to encourage snowfall…?

1-25 51° Sunny. -Three blooms on my primroses. What is up with that?

Chocolate Mint Latte: 1/2 shot chocolate and mint syrups, espresso shots, steamed milk.

8:43 A.M. I have owned this building for seven years now, but it just so happens; I lived in one of the apartments upstairs twenty-four years ago! My first husband (No. 1) and I lived upstairs for a summer, while he worked on the railroad gang for North Coast Northern Railroad. It was a busy gas station then, with an old *grocery* store. To be back after all these years was my "Circle of Life!" *Coincidence? – I think not!* Something about Saratogan draws its folks back.

You will not be reading too much about the barista being bent over the espresso machine by *The Man*, but it comes close. I will share my truths, both mental and physical incorporating PTSD & OCD, in dealing with the bizarre public, in a unique location, in these outrageous times. Everything you have only thought (even in church!) and wanted to say to idiots throughout your lives is written here for fun and enjoyment. I have included a drink (or dessert) recipe for every day of the year, with some of them being my originals!

This book goes *beyond* espresso. It winds through every aspect of every life with a prejudice slant, here and there. If you get bored along the way, then you must have allowed yourself to get too hungry, angry, lonely or tired. Just remember, *we* choose to rise out of our beds and so-and-so's arms, at all hours, to continue our lives, as *your* barista!

I grew up in Bellevue, Washington, back in the '60s and '70s, before Microsoft infused it with millionaires. Thankfully, Microsoft did emerge to save our state just in case Boeing got pneumonia again. I remember the famous sign well – Will the Last One to Leave This State, Turn Out the Light!

Both Bellevue and Saratogan have such beauty, sprinkled with timber, rivers, and lakes. We lived the good old-fashioned lifestyle back then, which still exists up here today, in an inbreed sort of way.

MICROSOFT INVADES SEATTLE AREA

William H. Gates discovered an interest in software at the tender age of thirteen. Bored, he ditched college to join a childhood pal, Paul Allen, in a new venture, hopefully donating funds to their personal bank accounts. Their energies were directed toward Microsoft, a computer company they began in 1975. It was his belief that the computer would be a valuable tool on every office desktop and hoped this feature would spread to the home front. His foresight and vision reached revenues of $39.79 billion for the fiscal year ending June 2005. Thankfully for Seattle, Bill Gates grew up in the Northwest and selected the City of Redmond, on the eastside, for his headquarters. His campus has exploded to numerous high-rises, beautiful grounds, and an employee count that skyrockets our real estate market. We love Microsoft!

5:43 P.M. I am going upstairs to bathe and shave, while dreaming of the why…

1-26 51° Sun & rain mixed.

Kahlua Cream Soda: Ice, 2 shots Kahlua syrup, milk 1" from top, finish with soda water.

8:07 A.M. My daughter signed those messy divorce papers today, at the tender age of twenty-two! Both of us with pen-in-hand – I hopefully get a "yes" on my re-finance today also!

My best friend called in tears – again. Her boyfriend, who was also the father of their child, was leaving her for another woman, after twelve years. No wonder I had given up on the mess of relationships. Seven divorces later, I am fine up here in the sticks, alone. Or was it eight? I may have caught up with Liz Taylor's dramatic record – or beaten it! Do you get paid to be in 'The Guinness Book of World Records'? The eligible bachelors that try and coerce me into an eighth walk-down-that-aisle, find me happily solo, plowing, plumbing, tending animals, and doing all the chores I love. No *aisles* for me! Now give me back my shovel and hit the pavement!

9:40 A.M. My customer wanted to talk mathematics while I was frothing and stirring her espresso with two-flavors. "I got married about six months ago, for the third time, and I think I finally figured this whole damn thing out: A smart man plus a smart woman adds up to romance. A smart man plus a dumb woman equals an affair. A dumb man plus a smart woman totals marriage. And finally, been-there – done-that, a dumb man and a dumb woman equals pregnancy. This time I think I have snagged me a good one, only time will tell…"

My furry beasts consist of a Husky dog, five birds, and a macaw. My macaw, Mister, was a gift from a customer. At only ten years old, he has a vocabulary of forty-some words. His swear words from his previous life had ceased…finally. Course, he may pick up some new ones around here.

1:11 P.M. Sold lots of cappuccinos and lattes. A couple of spilled ones and a few customers stayed way too long with nothin' to say. Not the most exciting day on the Richter Scale.

2:05 P.M. Another *boring* customer meandered in – it took him thirteen and a half minutes to decide between a latte and mocha! Then he started to get fresh and began leaning on my counter. It looked like *this* one may take a bit of my *ever-ready* rudeness to push him back out the door. He was wearing a wedding ring. Mark this as my first asshole of the day. They come in threes, so I had better brace myself. I sometimes wonder if the moon had something to do with it all. Loads of horny, married men walk through those doors, starving to be *heard*. "Take home a flower someday and note the difference in her attitude." Sorry, married misters, listening and caring are not *My Job*!

Sure enough, the next jerk that asked me out was married with four kids at home! "Did you forget you were married, or just forget to take the gold band *off*?" Sheepish was not even the word for it. He closed the door…silently! Still waiting for No. 3 asshole.

My grass was re-appearing, and it is January. Goodbye to what was supposed to be winter…and profit…and much more exciting times. Sniff…sniff…

5:56 P.M. I wondered how easy it is to get food stamps. Did it cover animal food? How about make-up…

1-27 49° Partly sunny.

Raspberry Breve: Shot of raspberry syrup, espresso shots, and steamed Half & Half.

8:43 A.M. Well, my regular and friend Dennis, a U.S. Navy serviceman, Harley biker turned local logger, finally got laid this weekend! It had been two years or something obscene (his words) like that. He was a thirty-eight-year-old strapping man, which made it hard for me to believe that he had so much difficulty getting a gal. What grotesque personal habit was he not telling me about? Unfortunately, on the fourth date, that new Godsend told him she was involved with a boyfriend! Just needed some excitement in her life. What's new! This day 'n age, those #%*&# crazy-making-relationship-games were mind-boggling, and I wanted no part of it. He still had a smile on his silly face…I would have grabbed a bat!

2:00 P.M. A lady with breath like the bottom of a crap-can came in and was waaaaay too close. I jumped over my counter in one swift leap. She complained about a humongous hangover. She needed caffeine and she needed it quick, hot and strong, "I hardly ever drink but last night my sis and I celebrated her fresh divorce and my man-less life. We dissected them all and burned each tiny morsel in effigy!" Gals after my own heart – minus the booze.

3:44 P.M. A regular came in for a frappe. Oh God…not another disgruntled man who was tied up in wedded horror. "I've heard Christy that married men lived longer than single men do, but in *my* opinion, married men are much more willing to die!" This attitude was from someone who could not be fifty years old!

Where was that phone call from my re-fi man!

4:06 P.M. My daughter called for a phone hug, I swept the parking lot, I cleaned the aviaries, and I set up a bargain sale table.

5:39 P.M. And as I locked up, I tried to invent a new craft that I can do right from this location, to kill the time and increase revenue. Got it! I could paint hourly rates for counseling on my windows. HOURLY RATES: Customers married and still looking - $1,000… Applicants married and happy – Free… Single clients looking for a one-night-stand – only $50 per quarter-hour (as most of these are right here standing in line) …

6:11 P.M. Now for my own personal fees…

1-28 52° Clouds with blue.

Cherry Cream Americano: Shot of cherry syrup, shots of espresso, hot water within 1", Half & Half.

8:08 A.M. Oh my God! I just survived the all-time *worst* experience with a customer, *ever*! If you have a weak stomach, pass on today…or just leave for the weekend. If *I* could, I would!

Jack and Merle, two if my wonderful elderly regulars, came in for their semi-weekly *fix*. Merle, the older of the two, walked in and promptly jetted toward the back of my gift shop, practically knocked an astonished lady off her feet. I thought to myself, maybe one of those guys is finally going to purchase a gift. Well, he knew *full well* where he was going and knew *full well* not to even ask. Or did he even have time for that? He was aware that I had a private, hidden toilet of my own! That room was *also* my legal commissary kitchen. Fifteen minutes ticked away, and I asked Jack where Merle could have gone? He headed off in search of his friend and returned immediately for a roll (or three) of paper-towels. He *ordered* me to stay put and glared at the other customers. He was on a mission to help a friend in need. Suddenly, a beyond-belief stench started drifting through the store, eliminated all oxygen from the building. I began to panic!

Jack said Merle had problems! *No Shit!* Human feces, excrement, bodily waste, poop, shit – there is just no nice word for it – was *everywhere*! It started along the store carpet, down to *the room,* where it covered just about every square inch. *Please - please - Health Department, be busy on the other side of the world!*

Bleach and tears, here we come! My chant: *"It's no different than diapers; it's no different than diapers…"*

It smelled like chlorine the rest of the week! That was the *worst* in eighteen years of retail! Poop Patrol!

6:07 P.M. Maybe I should have been a secretary. Goodnight…

1-29 52° Clouds with no snow.

Mt. St. Helens Volcano: Triple shot of espresso with loads of whipped cream!

7:42 A.M. My customers are all concerned about a single gal, completely isolated up here – with no life at all. It may look lifeless, but I have approximately one hundred neighboring cabins hidden in the woods behind my property - named Treetops Loop. It is an incredibly unique combination of cabin owners, from ex-cons to Microsoft execs, living (peacefully?) side by side. With that sort of combo surrounding me, I have only had to call 911 a half-dozen or so times, and that usually was over strangers (customers) with bad tempers, unhealthy moods, or split-second ideas about robbing me. I began to worry for a minute that maybe this was really scary with only lil' ol' me, all by myself… But it is worth it, and I am determined to win the gunfight.

I live upstairs, behind three locked entries. The foolish and uninvited that would even think of intruding would be looking down the barrel of a 20-gauge shotgun and into the beautiful ivories of my huge watchdog.

11:36 A.M. A few hikers moseyed in for their soy. The Pacific Crest Trail goes through this area, but the *normal* PCT schedule had their hikers through during the spring from the south – *not* the dead of winter! The weatherman said it is supposed to snow on the pass but still no skiing this weekend. The season-pass holders coveted worthless pieces of paper. They might as well hang them up as wallpaper, along with their old lotto tickets and concert stubs. But there *was* talk that maybe they would honor them next year.

HISTORY OF THE PACIFIC CREST TRAIL

The Pacific Crest Trail winds its way from the Mexican border to the border of Canada, experiencing the greatest elevation changes of all scenic trails in the USA. It takes its hikers from scorching deserts to rainforests shaded by old growth trees. It is an expensive journey, and most hope to have their jobs waiting when finished. Strap on your four pairs of hiking boots since you will wear each of them out over your five-month journey and its 2,650 miles.

12:41 P.M. Another lady stumbled in. It was a freak-ess, walking around browsing and mumbling away on her drug-of-choice. Crack. Meth-heads all looked alike and they were downright ugly.

2:00 P.M. I bought another parakeet. Figured two was a crowd and the newest member would calm down Mr. Bossy Blue. Now he was confused as to which feathered pal to dominate first. He is so ornery; he will figure it out in about 3 seconds!

I also have my two cockatiel brothers named Dude and Dudette. But Freddy is the most famous among my customers. He is a twenty-year-old cockatiel who thrives on head scratches, almost shoving his little skull through the bars when he spots a human being. Course I have warning signs posted: Freddy Loves Scratches! Likes To Chat! Hates Children! Bites Big Time! You've Been Warned! No Litigation – Freddy's Broke! Then, there is Mister, my newest child, a macaw. HE runs the joint.

A very l-o-n-g winter and spring, if the white fluffy did not dump on us.

Saratogan is starting to boom. Our population included VIPs from Microsoft, huge developers, doctors and lawyers who are building their beautiful vacation homes. We would eventually outgrow our stagnant ghost past and start exploring the possibilities of joining the 21st century. With one of the finest ski resorts around, colorful history, raging rivers, and year-round waterfalls, could the grandfathers really ignore the fortuity of becoming a large tourist village – forever? Did those locals really enjoy our non-booming, one-block-long-empty-shell-of-a-town? Where the graduated senior class never topped a half-dozen? Where a new face in the local pub caused cardiac arrests?

5:55 P.M. A family stopped in to get a snack and drink. They had two of the unruliest teenage brats I had ever seen! When they did not get their way, they would stomp their feet! And those were not two-year-old's! I never knew MO-THE-RR-RRRR was a four-syllable word. Was I the only one noticing?

6:25 P.M. I'm done with customers and will attack my email…later…

1-30 47° Raining.

Nutty Yummy: Shot of chocolate syrup, shot of hazelnut syrup, espresso shots, steamed milk.

8:39 A.M. Could this rain by any chance mean some snow at the resort?

9:48 A.M. Well, I survived my two appointments today. The first was an interrogation by the appraiser for my re-finance. I needed the value to come in *high*! The appraiser was around my age, fit, and quite pleasant. We ended up gabbing the last hour about antiques, relationships, and memories of younger days. He was also a native Seattleite, who grew up down the street from Kurt Cobain and some other musicians that were not so famous. "The whole neighborhood voted Kurt the most likely *not* to ever amount to *anything*. So much for all that playground childhood gossip!" We argued about whether or not the 'Heart Sisters' went to my school or his – our No. 1 rival.

People are buying décor items, not just drinks! Hallelujah! Gifts are my *bread* – espresso is my *butter*! I hoped the days of "lines out the door" were not history.

12:26 P.M. Scanner: Someone was having a heart attack in Stonewall. That explained the helicopter I heard off in the distance. If you were to have a health emergency up here, you must plan ahead!

It takes two hours, minimum, from incident to hospital bed. We only have a volunteer system in "these-thar-hills" so don't be surprised if you smell beer on the guy who has your life in his hands. The nearest clinic is forty-five minutes away, without traffic. Thus, airlifts are common, landing at our itsy-bitsy, grassy airport.

A guy from Calcutta dropped by for refreshments. The conversation was extremely interesting. I learned my lesson for the day, as he shared the flip side of the coin. "When foreigners of any color hang with whites, we call it 'Hanging with skiers,' whether or not you even ski!" He also informed me, "You whites all look alike too." I handled that opinion.

3:03 P.M. The rich dude from Alaska called and reminded me that I had agreed to go to dinner on Valentine's Day. Oops, forgot. No! Just remembered! I never said one way or the other! But I'll cancel shortly with a phone call and hopefully get voice mail. I wish I had his email and could skip calling. *Deal with it, Christy!*

5:42 P.M. Our sheriff just stopped by the drive-thru, just to make sure I was still "alive 'n kickin'." He was a welcomed regular. One of my competitors dropped in. She got a big bang out of all the flamingo merchandise for sale. She had not sold them, but decorated her whole espresso building with that shocking pink. Copy-cat-r-ratter! I had sold pink flamingos for years - the love/hate stories kept me selling that particular venue. Flamingos started back in the 1950s as a social status thing. People would post one in their front yard, bragged about the fact they had traveled to Florida. They sold like hotcakes!

6:17 P.M. No more for today. I needed to go stare at my bare refrigerator and figure out dinner…

1-31 42° Overcast

Peach Cappuccino: Foamed milk, shot of peach syrup, espresso shots, lightly stir.

6:38 A.M. Could not sleep, opened early, and had been sitting here for two humdrum hours. Could have been *that* busy between the sheets upstairs, alone! Had not seen another human being, except for the men that harassed each other out at the Porta Potty. I had one *john* and there were three men! I hollered out the window to draw straws and asked if they had seen any new snow at the pass. "No," and they continued wrestling...

11:40 A.M. I just emailed my slick, sexy, once-boyfriend. He was the kind of guy we all wished we could *rent-out* by the ¼ day...because he was charming! But I think I've given up on guys – completely. It's all pretty simple; really... there are three categories of men: passive, asses, or a combination of both. Women, on the other hand, aren't that simple, and could easily send a guy's psyche into the "*tilt-mode!*"

Another twenty-five minutes had passed – no bodies. That challenged my disposition.

1:00 P.M. OUTPOST ESPRESSO is a gift shop, with a walk-in/drive-thru espresso business. The coffee business was the portion that seemed to create that *soap opera* called life. It entails dealing with sweet old people, darling couples, well-behaved kids, pets galore, the rich and the underprivileged – TO – jackasses, bitches, perverts, drug dealers, brats, and robbers! Baristas put up with it all, while standing behind a counter; as though being behind the bar at a local pub across the USA. Baristas' lives are like bartenders when it comes to *harassm*ent.

I will not only open people's lives here in print, I also open up my own. This book will cover all my marriages, no-name exes, mistakes and faults. Hopefully, it all boils down to giving insight into the behavior of humans, the rights and wrongs of decisions. Most of all, I am writing to give women more strength than they ever knew existed, especially if life had overpowered them. Walk with me through the truth of women's failures and strengths that make us unique – gallop into the world of harassment, flirting, cheating, and all three bundled into one bigger, physically stronger, hairy-bodied being...man.

WHAT IS A BARISTA

Whether it is in the USA, the Netherlands, Australia or Italy, the career as a barista has become one of the most popular professions in the coffee industry.

A barista is a person who has been trained in the art of preparing and serving espresso. Anyone who serves coffee products in a coffee shop is a barista. The word means "bartender" in Italian.

2:32 P.M. My scanner had added some excitement this year. I had a front seat to car accidents, robberies, bad guys, fires, and injuries. Mine was connected to the Washington State Patrol, sheriff, fire and ambulance. All the local happenings, along with some State Patrol from "down-below."

I just finished putting an anti-harassment order against one of our locales. I do not mess around. Harassment can come in many forms: aggravation, annoyance, bedevilment, bother, disturbance, exasperation, molestation, nuisance, persecution, perturbation, pestering, provocation, torment, trouble or vexation. But whatever form it takes – it is wrong!

3:34 P.M. I was knitting away, my winter sport, waiting and waiting to make drinks! A young couple came in. Held hands, tossed around numerous adoring glances, practically glowed. Oh…those memories. Then, he ordered a latte for himself, with whip. I was just about to give him hell for ordering *his* first, when I realized he was finished ordering period. But not because *she* was not thirsty. Because he was a bad-mannered pig. She shyly asked, "Pretty-please, could I have one too?" "Oh yeah, babe. Throw her one will ya, hon." Now…I took him on! "You are a rude little SOB, and I won't hand you yours or make your lady-friend's until you ask, please!" Smart-mouthed me at first, but I did get the "P" word outta him. Being self-employed rocks! I would have been fired for that one! His poor little girlfriend never took her eyes off the floor. She was exactly the type I am trying to reach! I had been there, done that – BUT NO MORE!

This book will also keep a silent score card for both males and females, where points will be deducted for moronic and wrong behavior by either. It is based on purely black and white thinking, with gray being no doubt, the stupid and cruel actions.

I sat here imagining… Sometimes I wished I were a Starbuck's gal; much too busy to chat, which was a great escape-hatch from lingering men. Must be a bummer though, when Mr. Perfect walked in and you could not even look long enough to take it all in.

5:42 P.M. Yes! Two couples in a row stopped for chai teas and vanilla mochas. That sale would pay for my computer energy wattage.

6:07 P.M. Last customer of the day. Doors were locked, only drive thru was open – and I was about to nail that shut for the next twelve hours…

Up drove cutie-pie. She was a chick from "down-below," most likely a rich bitch, in a Mercedes. First, I had to suffer through her finishing with the lipstick. Re-check in mirror. Then the squirt of 'Beautiful' that caught the wind exactly right and ended up my nose and in my mouth. Finally, she was ready… "I'll take a tall, sugar-free vanilla soy latte, with only a half shot of espresso, and please, only a quarter shot of the vanilla that you would normally put in. I would like only two drops of chocolate syrup but only Hershey's if you have it. Leave room for whip and, please, make this only room temperature. No straw, no bean."

Thank God she was finished because both my pencils were out of lead!

6:17 P.M. Could anyone blame me for being finished for the day…

FEBRUARY

Men have settled for warm winter women,
yet with china cups in hand, women sip
away their glance

2-01 38° Sunny.

White Chocolate Raspberry Mocha: Shot of thick white chocolate
and raspberry syrups, steamed milk, espresso shots.

6:00 A.M. eBay was exciting and I am enthusiastic! I slapped some new stuff on the site, and I'll be damned, they sold in one day! That makes up for *Echo Highway!* I could not sleep, so I was on the road before the birds and worms. Took that mandatory sixty-mile drive just to do some shopping. We were talking *real, normal,* shopping. Good ol' Wooly's, open twenty-four hours a day. Then on to my espresso supply house opening at 7:00 A.M. and those necessities at Costco. Finally, to the post office for the ultimate disappointment that my appraisal results were still somewhere in transit.

11:00 A.M. Returned just in time to catch a local. He spent a lackluster morning up at the ski slopes, doing the hike up by foot and down by board. The resort was not open, so unless you were actively into abusing your body vs. enjoying the real sport, you may as well just stay on the job, at your desk. His scowl said it all, "I'm going to California, where there *is* snow." So far, it seemed they hijacked all our white flakes; what…they can't be content with all the sun, surf, and sand?

11:32 A.M. Scanner: A fifty-five-year-old lady was experiencing chest pain in Treetops Loop. A few blocks from me!

I just had a guy order a Kahlua latte. He had every color of paint splattered over every inch of clothing. "That goop on your bod had better be dry or be ready to run for your life!" He nodded saying he just finished a big sheet rock job and asked me if I needed any done around here. "Yes, my whole house!" He wanted to see it and give me a quote. I skipped taking this stranger, a 6'3" dude upstairs without a bodyguard. I was tempted…but not stupid. "Next time."

I loved it when a customer walked in and would stand there just glaring at me. Like they are the phone police, and I am not supposed to be using mine. What if my doctor was on the other end, giving me "The News"? Why couldn't those customers chill for ten seconds and allow us baristas to hang up our damn phones when we were good and ready, without the evil eye? Then the *darling* customer only wanted directions to somewhere *else*! Fuck. She bought nothing, used my amenities outside, and demanded personal, immediate service, as if she were going to spend her paycheck here!

2:05 P.M. I have spent an hour on the phone, trying to talk my daughter into staying in her marriage. Me…the *worst* example! But then again, the *best* example of what *not* to do!

2:58 P.M. Sold my third latte in three hours. It was a start. Wouldn't want to wear out the ol' espresso machine now would ya, Christy? What a half-baked justification for no business that wasmy life. It has been full of self-inflicted disasters with multiple divorces, seventy-three moves, heartbreaks endured, and heartbreaks inflicted, lost time with children, alcohol abuse, a father's abandonment, sexual abuse, and a shit load more. Seems all too common and sad these days. However, all these make for an awesome barista, who could offer daily counseling to hundreds! We, who have lived hard, have a lot to share with those who come from a more sheltered presence in this world of ours. When the shit flies, they duck for cover; we grit our teeth and raise our dukes. So, come on in, pull up a stool, and drink until your heart's content. I've seen it all and it is always nice to hear your story.

4:00 P.M. A couple came in from Santa Cruz. They could *not* believe that I lived, "Way out here! Where do you get food?" The most asked question once again. "The first grocery store available is a thirty-minute drive down the hill. But their prices are sky-high. The next decent, normal grocery store is another twenty minutes "down-below". Forget pizza or *any* delivery service. Even our milkman quit. He couldn't get enough business to justify the gas. So, there you have it." I smiled as they pondered....

Someone just ran over my flamingo display out front! Bent their legs and bruised their bodies. I used some Liquid Nails, a little bright highlighter and stuck them back out. Those crazy creatures drive customers my way, and now maybe more will have some sympathy for *crippled* critters...

5:44 P.M. I am giving customers a few more minutes – to *storm* the doorway...

2-02 38° Sunny.

German Chocolate Cake: A shot of chocolate syrup, shot of caramel and coconut syrups, drop of hazelnut syrup, espresso shots, and steamed milk.

7:00 A.M. Could not sleep. I will share my solitary life at **OUTPOST ESPRESSO** as a mountain woman barista, up in "these-thar-hills":

THE HISTORY OF MY BUILDING

This building was built in the 1920s. The Bower family was the original owner. It was a gas station and grocery store. The garage, that still stands, was an auto repair shop. A restaurant was also located on this property, on the west end, in the 1930s. It was called Bow Down Diner, but the building is long gone. The Old Mountain Peak Highway wound behind me along the river. The Bowers owned all the cabins in Treetops Loop and the compound was named Bower's Camp. People from all over would come and rent cabins for the weekend, to fish and swim in the pond. In 1939, the main store building burned. I still have remnants down in my basement. It was rebuilt in 1941, using cement blocks. Prior to my ownership, it sadly had become an abandoned flophouse for skiers and snowboarders alike. There were overcrowded living conditions and a banquet of drugs. Mice were literally falling from the ceilings. Today it is once again a proud piece of real estate, displaying the finest of travelers' rest spots in the region.

9:00 A.M. I cheated and took a drive up to the ski resort this morning, opening a tad late. I had to see it for myself. With Snowburg and Mount Pearl also being closed, the record for a late opening goes back fifty-four years! No wonder we may all go down the toilet in one mutual flush! On my drive back down, I saw three bald eagles in trees.

Speaking of *Lines*. We have our local, single and married guys, still dreaming of the lifestyle of the 1800s, when all the men lined the railroad tracks in front of the brothels. Thus, the phrase "down-the-line". The grand Saratogan Hotel, the most famous of the brothels, still stood today displaying framed photos of the *women-of-the-night* lining its banisters. Men today call those *the good ol' days*, where the miners, loggers, and railroad men all took their turns with these ladies. The locals today still have *their* women "down-the-line", thinking that we still lack communication. I was engaged to one of them last year. I am *not* proud to say that that was my *only* engagement in my numerous nuptials. I never took time for that vital threshold; I always got married NOW…or walked. He was one of our third-generation chaps. I was absorbed in a turning-back-the-clock sort of mind game, trying to recapture a cleaner, honest way of life. I soon met the others, "down-the-line", alias railroad tracks; I awoke with a punch that dreams like that are only in print. Most of the men were the *exact* opposite of what I craved.

5:59 P.M. I will end today with that. I'm depressed over my stupidity…

2-03 53° Sunny and warm.

Chai Tea: Fill the cup half full of liquid chai tea. Fill to top with milk. Serve hot or cold.

8:15 A.M. OPEN.

3:22 P.M. I think I will knit another hat. A man and six women stopped and asked if I had indoor seating. I said, "I'm so sorry, but no. The county won't allow me to serve tables without indoor restrooms." The man said, "Well then, we will have to continue on down the highway because we just finished dispersing a relative's ashes and we would like to sit down and have espresso together." Shall I grab my broom and dustpan? T.M.I.!

4:26 P.M. It was almost dark, and this was when I stepped outside and walked the length of my parking lot. It is exactly 350 feet long. I shut down various signs, put my dog Butch into the side yard and locked gift shop doors, leaving only my drive-thru window open. It was a ritual now, and a little exercise. Being chained to my desk and counter gave me a tiny hint of what it must feel like living in a cellblock.

The flavor of customers immediately changed after dark. It was 100% predictable and my police scanner proved it. My eyes were always re-checking the locks on my doors.

5:30 P.M. Scanner: Someone on a ferryboat in Seattle just stole two bikes and tied them onto their car. On the ferry? The culprit is unbalanced!

Some "regulars" stopped and asked if I would like to own their conure named Mildred? I said, "Sure, what's another chirp in the air?" The hubby had to sleep on it first. That would make eight birds in here. Would I get busted?

6:14 P.M. A local friend Boone from Stonewall called. He must be lonely. He lived seven miles from me, and we went to dinner this last October but only once. During the meal, while swallowing his whole, he undressed every gal with his eyes that walked by. I do not believe he looked at me thrice. He allowed me to pay for my dinner and graciously waited for me to get some of my wine down. A point was taken off the men's column for such disgusting, loutish behavior, that was not so uncommon these days. So, there were no more dinners with Boone from Stonewall. He was a fascinating Harley owner with silver-streaked black curly hair, green eyes, and a perfect body. Oh…and in love with himself! That evening, after the *unromantic* dinner date, he brought me to his place. My idea was to leap from his car to mine. But stupidly I went in.

Lonely much? True to form with these conceited *me* guys, he had his clothes torn off before I could even consider reaching for my boots. They stayed on! The additional wine did not work. No wonder he called. He didn't score.

7:05 P.M. Off to rest…

2-04 49° Raining.

Coconut Mocha Latte: A shot of thick chocolate syrup, shot of coconut syrup, espresso shots, steamed milk.

9:03 A.M. My computer was down again. Dial-up was our choice up here.

11:28 A.M. I went ahead and dusted my million gifts and vacuumed.

My girlfriend, with the cheating boyfriend of twelve years, called sobbing. The jerk physically moved out of her house today. She should be celebrating! He even left his payments due on her desk. He packed up his crap in a flurry and left her home in a holy mess. That is what twelve years will getcha. He is a typical jerk on a rainy day. Another point off, boys. But don't worry; we'll screw up too.

3:06 P.M. Another gal friend, who packed-it-in on a cheating husband a week ago, just came in on her way to his new home away from home. She claimed, "I said I would give him one more chance. But his goodness and sweet behavior normally only lasts for a couple of days." My advice, "Dump the moving truck idea; go mooch off him for a month, *with the kids*, on his turf and see if he was for real. They can't fake it for more than thirty days if you already know them well." She left with a fist full of chocolate-covered espresso beans.

BROTHELS & MORE
Along the five miles just east of me, the area lined itself with five brothels; three of them were named The Primeria, Red Mandolin, and Blush Farm. The transient railroad workers frequented these brothels.

There was another prostitute camp up here. It was called the Railroad Rest. This one serviced the men that were working on the Rail Man Line and the Kodiak Tunnel. Another was located up the Frothingham River Road. Today it is an expensive piece of acreage, owned by a state trooper, and they call it The Fortress.

In the town of Keystone, where only a dozen cabins stand today, John Santos built the Keystone Hot Springs Hotel in 1904. It could house a hundred guests for a soak in the springs or a mud bath. The Saratogan Indians would visit these hot springs for the rich ocher deposits used as a sunburn preventative. The hotel was mentioned regularly in the Seattle Mail Flyer. Guests could fish, hike, dine, or play billiards, lawn tennis, handball, croquet, and basketball. The new owner today plans to rebuild under new county zoning laws. This old hotel burned down in 1908. The guests all survived but everything else was lost. Santos was seriously burned while trying to save collectibles. It re-opened in 1909 with a Swiss lumberman's design. The train stopped only three hundred feet away. In 1927, there was a major prizefight held there between Sonny Lund and Al Perry.

5:37 P.M. It had begun to thunder and lightning...

2-05 34° Snowing a tad!

Latteccino: Espresso shots, steamed milk, top with foamed milk.

9:07 A.M. I had never seen a customer glance at the bottom of a soda can. Were there prizes posted there too? I thought not. So, I asked her why? She told me, "I am checking the date. Diet sodas die *fast*." She ultimately would not buy mine because it was packaged two months ago! Excuuuuuuse me! I offered to open a new case from the back room and rushed to rip open the box. I sliced my finger on the cardboard. The date on this case was bottled only a month ago, so she accepted it…grudgingly. She walked out with a look of distain still wrinkled on her pointy nose! Women! Oh well, learned something new today. More picky-ass rules that now extend to soda sales! Then I laughed – I think I left blood on her can.

11:20 A.M. I have had six drive thru customers! It is snowing like crazy here now; probably three to four inches and people are roaring up the pass just to *see* white! *Smile, barista!*

2:32 P.M. Boone from Stonewall stopped by. Still lonely. He was a fantasy. He was adorable! All bad boys are. He said, "I just had to come by and get a handful of some ass." A portion of his bear hug was a squeeze on the tush and then I slugged him…it was our little ceremony. Boone's theory, "If I'm visiting you, the town already has us frolicking in the haystack, so we may as well!" The answer was, "No, Boone, but you get an E for Effort!" And I got one of those wonderful hugs.

Plenty of snow hats walking in for lattes and children's hot chocolates. Tea and those hot chocolates are a barista's highest profit items. Our little tricks…

5:00 P.M. This whole hill is praying for this white shit to accumulate.

6:40 P.M. Let us hold that thought…

2-06 36° Looks snow-ish.

Honey Espresso: Espresso shots, 2 shots honey, and hot water.

8:56 A.M. One customer. It was Super Bowl (Super Idiots) Sunday. Business would be *anything* but a touchdown!

My freshly dumped girlfriend, with the abandoned bills left on her desk, called again panicked. She claimed she would never be able to make her mortgage on her own, her mobile home would fall around her ankles (suddenly today?), she felt fat as hell (men can do that to ya) and was destined to be a spinster for life!

I knew exactly how she felt. None of this was true in real life, but when we have relationship troubles, somehow, we immediately pole-vault into that dark, sordid, twisted part of the brain, reserved for allowing men to gain squatter's rights. We go beyond stressed. We think we are helpless, which only magnifies our panic! I reminded her, for the 93rd time that the jerk never paid for a damn thing when he was there. The worthless mobile home she was referring to sat on a very valuable acre of land, that she had already managed to pay off, and that anyone with naturally blond curly hair down to her waist would neverbe a spinster!

11:41 A.M. Today was busier. Mom came by and visited with her pal, Roger. It was great to see them. She brought shrimp and cocktail sauce for munchies, one of my (our) favorite treats. You will find us counting them out *equally*! YUM!

3:48 P.M. Praise be! Snow clouds were rolling in, temperature was dropping, so my *prawn-company* had to head-out – no snow tires, no studs, no chains, and a hundred miles before they were home sweet home. Drive safe!

4:10 P.M. I had to be rude to one of the local guys. He stopped by to *visit*, right before dark! What gave men the idea I wanted them to stand there and talk about nothing for an hour at any time of day? I would have seating if that were my plan. The idea here is: Order a drink, pay, tip, and re-hit the pavement. Also, fifteen minutes is max for those with a fence-post personality. All he did was block the aisle for new paying customers. If you had not gained access to my behind-counter-chair, by invitation only, order-pay-tip-and-split!

Maybe this called for another new sign...

Well, here was the first point off the women's column! Damn! My married gal friend spent the night with her boyfriend! Shit! By tomorrow, I expected to hear that he was great, spectacular, unbelievably wonderful, and she could not live without him. The husband had been demoted to a dirty, lazy dog! Point off.

4:52 P.M. Locked doors, too dark, too scary.

5:42 P.M. And then there is nothing...

2-07 36° Icy out and clear.

Asian Iced Espresso: Ice, 1 shot espresso, pineapple syrup, water.

9:00 A.M. Went to the bank first thing. It was a joy to drive around and see a little bit of fresh snow up on the mountains.

10:10 A.M. I was back and open. Had a couple from Texas come in and he rudely admired my *excessive* watchdog! He said, "A 12-gauge works well too!" I told him, "I wouldn't *consider* being here without my barking, fang-bearing dog!" He believed that the NRA was full of liberals who wanted their own social club and *men* do not have to get their guns registered. He also started mouthing off about my macaw and if that feathered body were his, he would have already introduced him to the 12-gauge. Nice. When his wife caught my reaction, she stepped up to the plate, "My husband is noise-sensitive." *Shotguns are quiet?* My solution? "Let's lop off his ears then!" She loved it. He didn't see a bit of mirth.

1:03 P.M. Called my ex-fiancé, Buck, the third-generation guy, and told him that snow tires needed to be put on my truck. He'd do it for little, ol' me. In the beginning of our *relationship*, we did the *friend* thing for about five months. Talking for hours on slow days, writing notes, chatting on the phone till the wee hours and not even holding hands. The next six months were *hot n' heavy*, doing the *wild* thing, and it filled a real void in both our lives. Until…his old girlfriend, who was supposedly out-of-state, out of mind, came waltzing into my espresso joint with her teenage kids one evening. She laid it on me. *They* were as *friendly* as he and I were – at that very moment! She *had* been seeing him for the last four years, without a break-up in sight! I about shit my britches! "Upstairs, all of you. I have a twelve-inch stack of letters, three *gigantic* baskets of potpourri from I don't know how many dozen roses, and more!" She claimed to have the same stack. So, I plunked cutie-pie and her kids into some chairs in my kitchen and dialed his number. I could not have dripped with more sugary schmaltz, telling him to come over *now*, "I miss you sooooo much, I can't stand it, honey darling!" We did not have to wait ten minutes. He booked on over in a flash, picturing massage oils, lit candles and a darkened boudoir. The five of us greeted him at the door. He got the frigging shock of his life. It was a ghastly hour!

Now, I don't claim to be perfect – or even very brilliant – but being thick-headed I invited him to do *favors* around the place, even after that. I was the idiot that allowed the relationship to continue.

Buck had a ton of brawn, but not much brain, when it came to women. I am done with all of them! Since I dated some city slickers over the past months and played *their* fucking games, this *ex* was a gem.

2:40 P.M. Since I owned this high-speed-direct-cable-small-town-gossip-ma-chine, **OUTPOST ESPRESSO**, I found out every philandering thing Buck did, practically before he even did it! That included just about every male's life up here. Back to business.

4:30 P.M. Served up a vanload of Japanese tourists. They all ordered mochas! They loved the birds and it was now time for me to lockout any potential rapists.

5:00 P.M. Later…

2-08 24° Clear.

Vanilla Steamer: Shot of vanilla syrup, steamed milk and stir.

8:19 A.M. Boxed and taped up my Internet sales, a sign of our times. I have served up a few customers. My loggers came by for their coveted granitas. Said something about towers being moved and how working with Hispanics ain't easy. They did not clarify. Thank-you! I am sure it goes both ways. It was still *very* racist up in these woods. Especially with the old school guys, the product of many, many generations of this type of stinkin'-thinkin' and training.

3:17 P.M. Some of my regulars stopped for their mochas, with their little puppy in tow. It was a Pomeranian named Bear. I could not wait to get my hands on him and immediately he peed all over my jeans. Luckily, I love animals. His tail was so tightly wound it could pierce his back.

4:22 P.M. I'm locking the doors with a note "Find and Seek" and headed out to the back acre to burn my personal, shredded trash. I started the fire with a little diesel, which was nice and slow burning. Butch, my killer dog, adored having me out in his yard. I swore he had a grin on his happy face. I relaxed out there, especially because biz was slow, as he ran from east to west, alerting me of customers – or prey. Speaking of fire:

OUR LOCAL NATIVE AMERICAN HERITAGE

Due to the hostile winters, there were never any permanent Indian tribes that lived year-round at Mountain Peak. They came here to hunt around the north fork of the Saratogan River and did their berry picking up at Mountain Peak. The Saratogan Indians were like the Makana Indians. They had a potlatch village along the north bank of the Saratogan River, near the junction of the north and south fork, where Crag Rock lies today. Locals from Crag Rock have found many arrowheads in the area, due to past floods and changes in the river pattern. Bands of people lived further up toward Saratogan, near Frothing Ham River, and were called "Feather People." There is a cave-like dwelling that still exists – just about 1/32 of a mile from where my store stands. Many artifacts have been found right here, within a stone's throw of my building.

5:41 P.M. Upstairs to sit by the heater to enjoy another red glow…

2-09 28° Freezing ass cold and clear.

Apple Pie Latte: Shot of apple syrup, shot hazelnut syrup, sprinkle cinnamon, shots of espresso, steamed milk.

8:35 A.M. This ancient building got colder and colder as each day passed, I swear! It seemed like the weather compounded inside these cement block walls! Getting dressed in stiff clothes was an experience.

I just heard that after the couple with the puppy left my building yesterday, their car crashed down a cliff! Airbags came out on both sides. The husband was fine, but his wife had a broken back! Bear, the Pom pup who had whizzed all over my lap, survived it all – even after being squished between the airbag and the wife's stomach. Gosh – how quickly life changes!

12:42 P.M. My Navy buddy, Harley Dennis, came by today, just in time to serve a customer and grab tools for me. I constructed a new cockatiel aviary and was high up on a ladder, wedged behind wire fencing. It was practically, "Ya want some Joe…get it yourself!" An idiot strolled in and I had never seen him before in my life; he hit on me. Right in front of my friend. "Nice butt, want me to carry that beautiful bod down from there?" Dennis *could* have been a boyfriend or even my husband, standing there serving his espresso! Some guys are absolutely clueless!

3:50 P.M. More faxes to my appraiser along with a silent prayer for the strength to ward off verbal mastication and attempted murder before this situation was resolved! Forget anything flattering I may have previously mentioned about that appraiser guy – he is the No. 1 slacker in my life today! One of those *just-licked-the-stamp* liars!

Bear and his daddy stopped by on their way back to Sunbird, where mom lies in a hospital bed, wrapped in a cast and pain pills.

5:49 P.M. Upstairs to pet my dog…

2-10 40° Still clear. Raw cold.

Hot Buttered Rum: Shot rum syrup or real rum, shot butterscotch syrup, espresso shots, steamed milk.

9:00 A.M. My toes were freezing! Even with two pairs of wool socks and snow boots. I had a pellet stove installed last December. This building had not seen heat in twenty years. But the cement floor did not seem to change even one degree. It is a thick bed of concrete – originally it was the area where cars parked to get their gas pumped. The overhang above is the second floor – upstairs bedrooms. We wondered just how many trucks *didn't* make it under the roof and gave the owners an earthquake-style wake-up-call! I've since remolded and enclosed the space for my walk-in/drive-thru espresso business.

I am bored, so I'll digress…

Several months ago, I had an affair with a man who owned an international fly-fishing magazine. Tossing that line in the water did lead to something after all. He inspired me and called our tryst "A

Secret Poetry Night." That will get me every time! This particular evening consisted of heading off to a secret five-star hotel in Seattle. We brought our personal composed poetry, other poems we both admired, along with forty candles, wine, and bath bubbles. The backdrop, the twinkling lights of the Seattle skyline, surrounded us. I had not had a drop of alcohol for over a year at that point. But forget it! It was such a glorious and over-the-top night for this country bumpkin. My first mental complaint, though, was the hotel room lacked the romantic accoutrements of a whirlpool tub and fireplace.

That guy insisted we carpool from his pad, so I dropped my car off at his house. First, we went to a movie, then stopped and bought Demousse chocolates. At the hotel, we popped the cork, added plenty of bubbles, plenty of nudity, and plenty of our own flames! The morning called for eggs benedict down at Pike Place Market – a tradition for all Seattleites, *especially* those who had just had a one-nightstand. The minute I woke up, I was sorry I had not driven my own car. My choice was *not* to stay for breakfast, but it was not my wheels! We arrived at his home after the meal and I promptly left 2.5 seconds later. An experience I will remember for a long, long time. I only heard from him once after that. *What category does that put Mr. Fish-Man in?*

What made me think of this memory was that he just contacted me today via email. Asked if it was time for another *prose* evening. Was I his calendar fuck for February? I emailed back just that! He responded, and it read: "No, sweetie—just been thinking about you and the crocuses have come up early in my yard and the sun is shining as brightly as your smile." My reply: "Okay,

Mister, we'll call it spring fever, a new rank for you. Forget it! My new demands would be a romantic *weekend!* With both a hole for burning wood and a bathtub with lots of jets! And plenty of notice! And stop by in the meantime. And call *several* times."

He wanted to discuss orgasms prior to our previous date over the computer. My replies then: "Leave it alone, Mister!" His reply: "Common…whatcha got to hide?" Okay…here ya go, sportsman: "Of course I fake from time to time and ALL women do! We have to, to protect men's fragile egos." Back to me: "No way! I can tell! It has never happened with me! Girls are *always* satisfied!" Do men know that they all said this? And I still participated that night? Live and learn, Christy!

3:40 P.M. According to my finance officer, the appraisal amount would be announced tomorrow. Hello…hello…is that a recording?

5:18 P.M. I served my last drink, not even an espresso, only a hot apple cider. "Would you at least like some freakin' caramel added for a little excitement in my life?" Even customers were getting the humor; they knew there were very few cars on this highway and absolutely no snow.

6:13 P.M. I have measured cars…there was 5-minutes between the last two. Goodbye…

2-11 29° Sunny.

Skinny Sleeper (Why Bother Latte): Decaf espresso shots and nonfat steamed milk.

8:50 A.M. I was glad I left the sink dripping again last night! I learned my lesson last winter when the pipes to my espresso machine froze. Froze *in* the commissary, froze everywhere *inside* the building. I had to hike down the rickety old stairs to my *haunted* basement. I never, ever, *ever* head down there, unless it is an absolute dire, burning emergency. Old, dark, musty, cobwebs for curtains! A hundred feet of pipe had to be connected and I drilled through beams I could barely reach and *could not* see. I had to feel along the lumber with frozen hands. Then it was time for the "heat tape." &#∗%@#&∗ and fuck, fuck, fuck!

1:46 P.M. A lady stepped in to relax after driving over Mountain Peak Pass. I made her a chamomile tea. She needed it! She was not just another pathetic female driver. She had hit a strip of black ice and slid seventy-five feet, before softly nudging into a snow berm. I congratulated her on the courage to continue. She stood up straight, with a new sense of nobility.

4:05 P.M. An email response again from Mr.-Glutton-For-Punishment-Calendar-Fuck. I could not believe his persistence. Email: "Yes, Yes, Yes! How about a beautiful 5-star Bed 'n Breakfast somewhere? We will lie under toasty blankets, in front of a roaring fireplace, while the icy-cold outside envelopes the less fortunate. I will feed you chocolates and peeled grapes, while you read me your new poetry. After that I will make long, slow, passionate love to you, all night long." Ladies, I will take this one by one: The *somewhere* concerned me…couldn't be near *this* peering town! We did have a fabulous B&B down the road that Ms. Nordstrom used to own. I did the chocolate scene with him already – gave me zits. Will you be peeling the grapes with your fly-line cutter? I cannot peel – nails are stubs. And no new poetry – been writing a book instead. The lovemaking scene? That man, in his early fifties, overestimated himself. Viagra much? I emailed him back *politely*: "No, but thanks for the nice offer. I would sure love a fly-fishing lesson though, next time you want to drop a line in my fishing hole. Don't be a stranger." Think I'm nuts, ladies? Want his telephone number? It is 1-SEX-FOR-FREE!

Just the *thought* of Nordstrom made my mouth water and wallet slimmer. We brag up here in Seattle, and rightly so, Nordstrom originated in our fair city:

NORDIES
Although it was only a shoe store in the beginning, started by John W. Nordstrom and his partner Carl Wallin, it was beautiful, classy, and became a legend. Mr. Nordstrom was able to stake his claim to this partnership with $13,000

he earned from another stake, a gold mine in Alaska. Just twelve years earlier, he arrived from Sweden to the land of opportunity with only $5 in his pocket. By 1993, with both men retired, Nordstrom was owned and run by the three sons, Everett, Elmer, and Lloyd. Nordstrom's Philosophy: Exceptional Service,

Selection, Quality, and Value. We do not so much like Nordstrom – as crave Nordstrom!

5:58 P.M. I'm dreaming of shoes in the latest fad...

2-12 36° Raining finally. Warmer finally.

Snowy Mountains: White chocolate syrup, espresso shots, steamed milk, topped with vanilla powder.

8:21 A.M. Maybe throwing out a snowy recipe will induce some positive thoughts to start off the day. Flakes! Now! Dammit!

Just served an Americano, a huge mocha, and three Italian sodas. I am wealthy!

10:30 A.M. Valentine's weekend. Last night my ex-fiancé snuck into my home for some fun. Did not want to start the gossip tongues a waggin', so, Buck drove his truck up along an old logging road and I picked him up in my Jeep. No lights. We came in around the fencing, through two locked gates, down the dog run, along the side yard, entered the locked back door, up the flight of stairs, and unlocked my house. Prior to leaving to give him a ride, I turned off all of the floods and outside lights to my fortress. I even deducted a point off the women's column beforehand, knowing you were probably having delirium tremens at me right now, over my pure stupidity. Premeditated ignorance!

We had fun catching up on local happenings, laughing, washed his clothes, and played kissy face. He had the most luscious lips in the land! *Down girl!* It was good to see him after all those months. He is an earthy kind of guy, true to his roots, which can be both good and *so* bad! Still smelled of diesel and wood sap. We somewhat behaved like angels. So, no smut. Yet...

11:45 A.M. I heard from my daughter and today. That always made a mama happy!

3:33 P.M. I do not think I have mentioned my *bum* I named BOO. He lived up across the railroad tracks, just above me. I could see his campfire lights tonight and the smoke billowed up through the trees. Was he warming himself or cooking dinner? Maybe cat? I called him BOO, as I had never seen him – ever! Could he spy on me from his vantage point? All it would take were a pair of binoculars, as I am totally out in the open. *He is* buried in fir and cedar. I wondered if he had ever actually been in here. Nobody seemed to know him. Maybe even ordered an espresso from me? Creepy!

Reminded me of one-night last year... I took my dog and ran errands.

We returned home around 10:00 P.M. I put Butch in his dog run, when I noticed that the gate wire was bent down. I was the mother of a teenager, so of course I immediately blamed him. He forgot his key again, I was sure of it! I will kill him! I just started to unload when my son came around the side corner of the building. "Hi, mom." He had just stepped off the bus from his job up at the ski resort. I bitched about his key and the fence and the contorted wire and...yadda, yadda, yadda.

"I swear I didn't do it!" At that very moment, a man stepped out of the cab of my plow truck – parked within five feet of me! He had been in there watching me the whole time I unloaded my shopping supplies! My son screamed obscenities at him while dialing 911 on his cell. I ran into the store and grabbed my gun and flipped on the floods. The jerk headed toward my son, mumbled something about getting hit by a car and could not walk. I faced the burning question that had plagued me since I bought this place: Could I pull the trigger and shoot someone? He seemed to walk simply fine as far as I was concerned. He stopped dead in his tracks after he saw my weapon and me.

5:07 P.M. The 911 call brought a local, who happened to be a cop from another city. The aid guys showed up quickly too. They got rough with the slime-ball. Then our local sheriff arrived and carted him off to the police station "down-below."

I have a concealed weapon permit and always carry my gun with me.

Speaking of shopping and unloading goods, here is a little info on Costco. I cannot live without that warehouse and it appeared no one else could either:

COSTCO

The first location opened in 1976, under the Price Club name and the original warehouse was in a converted airplane hangar in San Diego. Choosing a new name in 1983, a second warehouse, called Costco, opened in Seattle and was touted as the first company to ever grow from zero to $3 billion in sales in less than six years. The two companies merged in 1993, calling themselves PriceCostco and have grown worldwide, with total sales figures in recent fiscal years exceeding $40 billion. Their Merchandise Motto: We guarantee your satisfaction on every product we sell with a full refund. Their Membership Motto: We will refund your membership fee in full at any time if you are dissatisfied. It worked. They continue to enjoy astounding growth. Their headquarters are in Seattle.

6:25 P.M. Reminiscing at the end of another day in the life of a solitary barista…

2-13 32° It's snowing!

Vanilla Chai Tea Iced: Ice, shot of vanilla syrup, and fill cup full with liquid chai tea, top with Half & Half.

7:03 A.M. I was awakened by DOT plowing snow on the highway! I thought I must be still in a sweet dream. Sure enough, there was a centimeter of white! I immediately thought of all those Valentine sweethearts driving home from our resort at Icicle Town. Hopefully, they all needed a *caffeine-kick* after being up all night, doing *whatever*. Drive safe!

There were still some old-timers that remembered putting this highway in, covering the gravel with asphalt. I know one of them, Big Sam, a super color-ful man. For a total of forty years, he held such positions as sheriff, city police officer, fire chief, and judge and had his own ambulance service. In the good ol' days *(his words),* he used to head up the hill to Mountain Peak Ski Resort during storms. He did the roundtrip in twelve minutes (*normally it took twenty-five*). He had zero accidents in all those forty years!

HISTORIC AMBULANCE STORY FROM DAYS GONE BY...

A local's rendition: "There we were, flying down the road in the 1969 Chevy panel ambulance. Mom was the only one who could fit between the bench and gurney. We had to go get a dead logger. He got loaded just before dark. There was a slider window between the cabs. Dad would have to turn off the rear light or the headlights would dim. Then we hit a bump in the road. The dead man's hand slid out and hit me on the knee. I about jumped out of that rig! I was a young lad, and I was scrambling to get to the front of the truck, yelling, "He's alive! He's alive!" My dad yelled right back, "Get the hell back there, goddammit, and NOW!" I had to stay in the back with the stiff. My body was hanging halfway out that slider trying to get as far away from the corpse as possible! Back then the coroner would have to break their joints to get 'em in the boxes. And slice the back of their calves to drain 'em like oil from a car."

10:11 A.M. One more fact about those small towns "down-the-line". We live in an area where two counties merge. To this day, the towns do not have their own police force, because of major past corruption! All our law enforcement officers are either Emerald or Makana County sheriffs.

12:40 P.M. The ski resort had three new inches and dumping! *Hallelujah!* It was hysterical, looking out at my pink flamingos, displayed on the white fluff next to the highway. I will leave them out there for only a little while, as they would either be eaten by the snowplows or covered up by the berms.

1:27 P.M. A guy walked in for a triple espresso, with whip. He was a cute one, about my age. Turned out he was from Bellevue, my old stompin' grounds and we probably met at some drunken bash in the '70s. We started reminiscing about the *party days* out at *Eighty Acres*, which was now The Microsoft Campus. In the late '70s, he worked at a BMW dealer and had to deal with the rich, young, spoiled brats who came in for their oil changes. *They* seemed to be able to re-direct every conversation to brag about their Microsoft stock. Back then, George the oil-change-man did not know a thing about stock, much less Bill's company. He constantly got bonuses from his manager at the BMW service station *because* of these guys. He could *always* talk these computer geeks into a not-needed air filter and more. Of course, who really had the last laugh…they were most likely retired multi-millionaires now, driving Lamborghinis, with a manservant taking care of that bothersome auto-servicing business!

3:50 P.M. Bear's parents dropped by. The wife, who was in her early forties, was out of the hospital, but in a full body cast. Her hubby was totin' the walker for her. It started snowing again while they visited, and you could see signs of mild panic on her face. Bear ran around the store, peed and pooped on my carpet, anywhere he damn well pleased and drank some water out of my espresso cup. *What is this, pit stops for animals?* I just smiled and grabbed a throwaway rag and a can of Lysol. *Health Department Inspectors keep on drivin'!* Between you and me, girls, I am a dog lover to the max. *If* a man even *thought* about making a mess like that in my store, he would be dead meat! I wished them well on their trip.

4:20 P.M. I got my Valentine early. My BMW biker, named Brian, came in and gave me a bouquet of flowers, a chocolate teddy with a love heart, more chocolates and sweetheart cookies just in case the chocolates didn't work. I'm on a diet… I gave him his usual free cappuccino, as he was always gift laden. He was one of my not-invited-back-stage, as my friends call it, to the computer stool.

That authentic over-stays-nice-guy always cost me an hour of quality time. Why could I not fall for the good guys? Why is macho – marvelous?

5:05 P.M. Speaking of macho. Harley Dennis just came by in a tank top, showing off his tattoos and biceps, on a snowy, freezing evening. Now that's balls! He wanted to take me to a Valentine dinner tomorrow night, *as friends only,* he said. I learned a long time ago *exactly* what that meant! "As friends" meant, "I'll sleep on the couch, you take my bed" – or – "Let's share the bed and we'll keep our clothes on" – or – "I won't even touch you, just kisses" – or – "I won't let you drink too much" – or – "I know where you stand, and I wouldn't want to ruin a friendship." The best one ever, "We will be strong!" All the get-laid lines that men acted out were such bullshit – and not a foreign language to me anymore! It is English – loud and clear!

8:26 P.M. It was a twelve-hour day, which was plenty. Let us shut down this joint...

2-14 30° Dumping snow on Valentine's Day!

> **Peppermint Swirl: Shot of peppermint syrup, shot of white chocolate, espresso shots, steamed milk.**

7:40 A.M. I will start from the very beginning. No electricity in the entire building. So, it was get dressed in a flash – or freeze. My house had all night to get into the high twenties. Today the make-up mirror was God's light at the window. I stepped outside into a foot of snow! I checked in on the birds in my store, they only had two hurricane lamps for heat. I accidentally broke one of those! Glass was everywhere! I threw some pellets in the stove then remembered the damn thing wouldn't work without electricity! My hands were as cold as a whore's heart!

8:30 A.M. Since I could not sell espresso, I started up my plow. That was a lot of snow to move all at once – plus, it was so damn wet and heavy. Great for getting stuck. Each swipe had to be done at just the right *angle*, keeping the trucks rear-end from getting sucked into the new snow berm I created.

10:30 A.M. Back to open the store – they *had* to get this power on – it is Valentine's Day for God sakes! I hand-shoveled all the walkways and gate areas and brought my dog through the store to his acre out back. I totally forgot about the broken glass on the store floor until I saw red snow. Butch had cut his paw. Being that my dog was a Husky, he could be very difficult to deal with when there was an issue, he wasn't pleased about addressing. The vet was 1.25 hours away – the bill would resemble its twin…$125!

So, I used the mountain-living-emergency approach. Duct tape! My Life's Rules: You need only two tools…WD-40 and duct tape. If it doesn't move and it should, use WD-40. If it moves and it shouldn't, use duct tape. I checked out his paw as best as he would allow and completely wrapped it, much as a cast, and put him in the Jeep.

11:40 A.M. The power just came on. Back in to open the store and get online to answer more legal questions for the f-ing re-finance company.

3:00 P.M. Was it really Valentine's Day? Well, I guess I will just be in love with *life* today! So, a Happy Valentine's to all you lovers out there, who *really* love each other, *unconditionally,* if there was such a thing… And to the rest of *us* – better luck next year.

7:00 P.M. Good night to y'all. I truly had a minimum of 50-75 bodies, mostly sweethearts returning home from heaven. Sold too many espressos and crap food to count.

8:39 P.M. I will sleep well tonight…

2-15 22° Clear and writing in the evening.

Valencia: A shot of orange and chocolate syrups, espresso shots, steamed milk.

8:40 A.M. What a day! Refinance signed this morning, those thousand and three papers. Took a drive up and over to the east side of my mountain, just to de-compress after the long, long wait for that money. The mountains were covered in snow and the sun was out. It was brilliant – a WOW Washington day – a photo shoot opportunity! Mt. Crag Rock was spectacular on my way up!

SOME CRAG ROCK HISTORY

Crag Rock and Saratogan were the only two towns that remained and stayed permanent fixtures along the west side of Mountain Peak. All other "temporary locations", were railroad and logging camps, left behind, as men moved on to a new site. In 1890, news of this rich land could not be kept a secret any longer. Minerals and trees were expansive, and the prospectors rushed in. People would wagon train from Crag Rock to Saratogan along

Barklett Road that still stands today and is even partially covered in asphalt. The east starting point of Barklett Road is only one mile west of my store. Gold, silver, copper, lead, and iron sulfide were prominent in these mountains! Ore was getting $58.70 per ton in 1895!

12:12 P.M. I ended up tootling on down to Seattle after my mountain fix and was the only snow-covered car on the road! I loved showing off on a workday. Eight or so inches brought looks of surprise…then admiration…then envy. I put some of the city slickers into a trance, dreaming about their possible ski weekend ahead.

I got a kick out of all the BMWs and Mercedes everywhere you looked in the Microsoft, Bellevue, and Redmond area. They were doing their usual tailgating in the fast lane. I would have laughed my head off if the eight inches of snow had flown off my roof onto their precious, polished, cars! It would have made quite the two-second snowstorm!

I visited some of my wholesalers and I found more flamingo wares to sell. I also did the Costco errands so that I did not have to leave my secluded paradise for another week. I'd better be home soon to tend to my injured dog, demanding parrot, a plugged-up espresso cart sink, and a busted pellet stove handle.

7:24 P.M. End of a full day – everything is handled and repaired...

2-16 22° Sunny.

> Mocha Cappuccino: One pack of hot chocolate or a shot of chocolate syrup, foamed milk, stir, add espresso shots.

8:38 A.M. I walked out my gate to open my store and I saw a sheriff's card taped to my gate. Greeaaaaaaaaat. But as I read further, it had to do with some papers they tried to serve. Whaaaaaaaaaat! I had no idea. Maybe I was being considered a witness to the robbery and drug bust that happened up here awhile back.

Oh well, in the meantime, my dog caught a bird despite his crippled paw. Over the last couple of days, every time I saw him limp, I had felt so bad, like *I* had deliberately jammed a glass shard up his pad! Just maybe he had been trying to make me feel worse than he did, getting more treats than usual that way! But if quicksilver Butch could catch a bird and drop it at the door for praise, then I was over my guilt!

2:05 P.M. Was I sitting? My local sheriff just came by with the papers. Consider myself *served*! My No. 1 husband, from way back in 1980, had me served with an anti-harassment order. Lately, he had been extremely nasty to our daughter in Alaska. Maybe he did not like my family-wide email sent over this divorce mess and his meddlesome behavior. It did trash his ass! Now *if* he wants to play hardball, he had better watch just how hard he throws the pitch at me! I could and would exploit his past and it could and would get really ugly, considering his precious government position. Like I said before, I LOVE hardball! And this little body would be happy to take on his big, fat, overweight buns in a New York minute!

3:18 P.M. Scanner: An injury car accident at milepost 52. Aid was in route. I ran a flare out front since I was at milepost 50. I tried to aid as best I could to get those idiots to slow down for our volunteer aid guys.

ANOTHER HISTORIC AMBULANCE STORY FROM DAYS GONE BY...

So, these volunteer firemen had to watch over the "stiffs" (dead people). At the station house, they had to lay them between the fire truck and the wall, on the cement floor. One of the newer guys, with a super ego, was walking around the station. They had one of the 'stiffs' in there. The stiff was an old guy with brand new, shiny blue ski boots on. This old guy had died up at the resort from a heart attack. One of the station's old-timers wanted to play a trick on this new smarty-pants, so he told him to get some supplies out of the fire truck garage, knowing how dim the lighting was out back. This rookie saw the boots immediately and thought to himself, "Gosh, they must have gotten a full-size manne-quin in for our CPR classes." He tapped the body with his boot and a leg flopped out from under the blanket. He ran to his car and flew home and was never seen again. The old guys ripped a gut laughing and they are still telling that tale today!

3:41 P.M. A lady walked in with her baby for a twenty-ounce mocha. "Can I change my baby's diaper in your bathroom?" What bathroom? I explained that there was no such thing in the building and unfortunately, she would have to change the rag in her car. "Well, I'm willing to purchase a mocha so that you would allow me to use the restroom!" Okay…let's try that again, "There - Is - No - Can - Inside - This - Building!" Not surprising, she left in an angry huff.

5:10 P.M. Pitch black and over it…

2-17 23° Sunny.

Peaches & Cream Italian Soda: Ice, a shot of peach syrup, a splash of vanilla syrup, soda water and topped off with Half & Half, stir.

9:02 A.M. Mountain Peak Ski Resort opened today! This will be a super weekend! God…I am jazzed!

10:00 A.M. Scanner: A sixteen-year-old male with a concussion. He was stable and alert, requesting a medic. I love to ski but it is not worth the gamble of losing life and limb.

1:23 P.M. Scanner: A forty-two-year-old female with a leg fracture at the resort.

AND ONE MORE HISTORIC AMBULANCE STORY FROM DAYS GONE BY...

Great-grandfather Big Sam, who originally started the ambulance business up here, got an accident call in the 1940s. He jumped into the ambulance to check out the casualty, and there at the top of the summit he saw his own son, lying pinned under his car. Great-grandpa Big Sam had to jump back into the ambulance, tear back down to his station and grab the tow truck to go pull the car off his son's body. Then he raced back down to the station to get the ambulance again. Back up the mountain, he loaded up his son into the vehicle and sped to the hospital, forty-five minutes away racing his speed. The son was pronounced DOA, and probably had been at the accident site. But great-grandpa Big Sam could not consider trying. There were no extra helping hands to be found that night. He did it all by himself – in the snow.

2:16 P.M. I told Buck today that we were not having any more secret rendezvous. He left. It was a boring day. The skiers in Seattle do not believe, or had not heard, the slopes were open. The main Seattle television stations do not cooperate with our mountain, only the resort closer in proximity. What is that all about? Are we chopped liver?

Just got a call that my re-finance does not close tomorrow as planned. They made a goddamn, fucking *typo* on my docs. Taking off work the other morning was just a tease, just a waste of precious time and gas! The receptionist gingerly called and said that they would be happy to FedEx the correct documents, as *they* were responsible for the delay! I informed her, in a voice at least seven octaves above my own, that we do not have *overnight FedEx,* or anything else up here!

It was going to be one of those nights exactly right for a good movie – but we don't have any video stores up here either. I guess it will have to be chocolate therapy and my measly eight snowy TV channels…

2-18 24° Sunny.

Orange Nut Latte: Shot of orange and hazelnut syrups, espresso shots, steamed milk.

7:52 A.M. They sure do get off on the little bit of power they *do* have. A beautiful day and I had to deal with men "stuck-on-stupid!" If they did not have us out-muscled, men would be *toast* and women would *rule!* They were absent-minded and dotterel and had major selective hearing. They never heard for the last week and a half that the grass has grown taller than the front porch, but can recite, verbatim, the last baseball scores of the century! They are unorganized, cruel, controlling, cheating, lying, SOBs. That had been scientifically proven, I am sure of it! In case you had not noticed, my blood is boiling at my No. 1 ex! This anti-harassment business had ticked me off – royally! And more than that, when he hurts our daughter, I am like a mother cub and would rip his testicles off if I had to!

10:10 A.M. My package delivery guy stopped in today and we chatted about relationships. He told me that he was appalled, but a guy he knew had been married *seven times* and that *had* to be a record. "Should be on one of those crazy talk shows! I feel so sorry for this poor guy to have run into so many horrible women." "Sorry, bud, you horse's arse, but certain movie stars and certain baristas you know are ahead of him. Read occasionally, dingbat. Keep your ears open and pay attention for a change! So, you do not have to come in here and start spouting off about multi-marriages, like we should be sent to a leper colony." As Mr.-Once-Divorced-Deliveryman headed out the door to retreat from my wrath, he almost absolved himself with his parted quip, "Instead of getting married again, I'm going to find a woman I don't like and just give her a house."

Guys do suck, though. They hate strong women and spend their whole lives trying to crush us, until they finally hit the grave first. Those stupid monsters love mentally weak women and marry needy, drugged, fat, skinny, ugly women…or pretty and perfect, in which case they still strive for control. To put it simply, *just in case I have not gotten my point across*, they love women that would wait years for a measly crumb. Especially true back a few decades. Women waited and submitted themselves, orgasm-less, for years, for that new Sears & Roebuck catalog dress! Waiting till that glorious day would come when *he* decided that *she* deserved it. She pulled the ribbon from the box, lifted the lid to gaze at her earned treasure and mindlessly believed the honeymoon has started all over again. It is just a crumb. Of course, the damn dress stayed in the damn box because he never took her to any damn place to show it off! That was most men – in all countries.

I had been trucking in and out of Mexico for years, buying merchandise for my store. I would have been the *last* woman raped, for the simple fact that I drove the truck and was in charge. The men actually put down their burritos for a minute, to run out of their shacks, just to believe what they saw. A woman driving a BIIIG truck. NO WAY! She must be part man. They hollered and slapped their knees and pointed. I had become a prime example of a liberated American woman. And I meant to stay that way! One of the factory owners down in Baja told me, "My woman had better not get a glimpse of you!" Screw you!

3:33 P.M. My girlfriend, with *his* overdue bills, called. The boyfriend contacted her to say that he and his new *honey* were so happy he would be staying in Colorado. Forget about the mother of your child – forget your son? Her next statement just slayed me, "But he may return to me if things don't work out." OVER MY DEAD BODY! I wish I could get inside her head and wring it out! I felt so helpless.

3:50 P.M. Busy day at the store and I wanted to strangle every two-legged male beast that walked through my doors. I could conceivably, or may possibly, and almost certainly, be having an over-reaction to dealing again with my ex and the court date – *and* the re-fi *male* assholes. They told me today that this transaction cannot close without a septic inspection! They just realized that today?

It was afternoon now. I had lots of customers inside the store. My dog's foot was bleeding again. Could I delete today?

5:04 P.M. Tomorrow would be a new sunrise and I would welcome it with open arms! And I am going to get out of the *other* side of my huge, empty bed... just for luck...

2-19 20° Ass freezing!

> Crème de Cacao Latte: A shot of crème de cacao syrup, a splash of mandarin syrup, espresso shots, steamed milk.

8:40 AM. A new day. I needed it. I wore a new shirt I picked up at a thrift shop in the city last week in honor of this new dawn! I indulged in nine hours of sleep and I really felt like a new woman.

Now that my brain is fresh, I will tell you the news about the septic yesterday. It was the last straw, and I bawled my eyes out and completely ignored two sets of customers. They looked shocked to see a storeowner in such a state of sheer abandon and they twirled around on the balls of their feet and scurried right back out the door! Great customer service, Christy! In that negative-man-mood, I had sent emails to potential guys to tell them to stay-away-from-me-completely.

11:20 A.M. Scanner: A sixty-year-old man was having chest pain at the resort.

A father entered with his two-year-old. "Do you sell apple juice?" I showed him my little cans of the stuff. The kid had so much snot coming out of his little nose that I could not help myself. "Would you like a tissue to wipe his nose?" The dad looked at his kid as if seeing him for the first time and said,

"Ohhhhhhhh, sure. Hadn't noticed." I noticed from the parking lot and I also noticed him wiping his snotty nose with his hand and grabbed at my biscotti! How would I disinfect cookies?

4:05 P.M. I was spent now. Stresses will rip-ya-a-new-one! I had better pay attention to my health. Forced myself to gleefully anticipate my healthy salad tonight. Mixed greens, artichoke hearts, blue cheese chunks, bacon bits, soup crackers, and Caesar.

5:55 P.M. I am closing. I can tell another good night's sleep will not hurt a bit…

2-20 24° Sunny

The Scotchman: Two shots of butterscotch syrup, espresso shots, hot water, and a tad cream.

8:56 A.M. I had decided to go fight the anti-harassment order. How could I not? The jerk should not be able to get away with this! Maybe *he* was exactly why I had extreme dislike and distrust of men. So, Wednesday was the court date. I will keep you posted. He tried to throw me a curve, but I knew the rules of the game too.

Fun, mellow customers so far, except for the couple in my drive-thru, who were most likely in the middle of World War III? He snapped and cranked at her; she whined and picked at him – making them both rude to this barista. Go home and kill each other and leave me alone.

10:42 A.M. Was the sun ever going to turn to snow? Winter had even amazed itself. Records continued to break – more entries in the books! I might as well add some more historic records:

SOME HISTORY OF SARATOGAN...

In 1900, the Saratogan Hotel was built. It burned down in 1902 but was quickly rebuilt into the four-story structure that still stands today. In World War I, Saratogan was in high demand for its wood products, producing and shipping lumber and cedar shingles by able-bodied men who were not drafted and worked in these mills. Saratogan boomed. In the 1920s, many businesses thrived. Including Steve Sandefier's barber shop. Marcus Thompson bought it sometime in the 1940s and still lives around here at the ripe old age of ninety-two! Peter McCaster's Saloon, Saratogan Hotel, Manning's General Store, Andersen's Drugs, Jeff Little's Dairy, Livingston's Dairy, The Loco Theater, which now houses the sheriff and state patrol offices, Medford's Auto Camp, and Stopher's Apiary, were the major players.

Mr. Livingston bought the White-Water Hotel, which still stands today. The White-Water became the center of town, where the wealthy businessmen and perfumed ladies would meet. With all the success in Saratogan, the streets were rough and tough and lined with cows.

5:54 P.M. Let us try that prescription again…sleep…

2-21 24° Sunny again.

Espresso Kiss: 1 shot each of coconut and pineapple syrups, espresso shots, Half & Half, splash of grenadine.

8:27 A.M. I was so ho-hum blasé; I had decided to play matchmaker and against my better judgment! My best girlfriend, with the cheating swine boyfriend who split for Colorado after another skirt, needed to be introduced to my brother. They lived in the same city, had lots in common, liked mates who had left for greener pastures. Both were single parents. They were on the same page. Hope, hope, and hope. Down deep, I believed relationships could be wonderful, just rare, and may not be in the cards for everyone – me!

10:22 A.M. Scanner: An airlift helicopter was on its way to retrieve a young guy who took a bad blow to the stomach with his snowboard.

I just dealt with a group of unruly punks. There were eight guys and one female. I was on guard. I definitely didn't have enough bullets for that many bodies! I got a little tense under circumstances like those – outnumbered to say the least. And you never knew what those kids were *on!* What I would really like to have done was paddle each one of them.

2:33 P.M. What was it with cowboy hats? If men could wear them 24/7, they would all be hunks and I would go after every damn one of them. Did the old westerns get to us as little girls? The same goes for Harleys, construction tool belts, sports cars, and uniforms. Who conditioned us to be drawn to certain looks? A guy changed his tire in my parking lot, and he was decked out in tight britches and wore a black cowboy hat. I had no idea how old he was, or if his face looked like it had been run through a knothole. I could only see the backside and was drawn to those fitted jeans and that damn hat. Watch…with my luck, it would turn out to be a woman!

Some new customers broke my concentration, "You have sugar-free smoothies!" Yup, I did. "Oh God, oh God! Honey get you're tush in here and see these choices! Mama Mia, I'm in diet heaven! What else do you put in them?" "Half & Half, ice, and that's about it." "Half & Half? Well, shit, that blows it for me." They left with their heads down. I hate to tell y'all, but there was no such thing as cream-less ice cream or cream-less smoothies. Those dieters had not quite decided if they were on no-carb or no-fat diets.

4:01 P.M. Scanner: A two-vehicle non-injury car accident at milepost 45.

5:05 P.M. It is dark and I will leave now…

2-22 24° Hello! Ditto! Sunny!

Espresso Alexander: Ice, 2 shots of crème de cacao, espresso shots, top with Half & Half.

7:58 A.M. No. 5 hubby was here and graciously attended to my honey-do list. Everything became too overwhelming for me, especially having to deal with the septic system for the appraiser. The inspection of the buried poop box was scheduled for today and did I frickin' ever know where the damn thing was? Not! And could I have dug a massive hole in frozen earth? No way! Could I deal with the shit down there? Or the fucking inspector? No way in hell! I did know that part of the tank was under the fence! That was the crucial finale for my loan! So, thank God for wonderful exes. Not terrific odds, but one out of seven was a gem! I wondered how Liz Taylor's odds stacked up to mine.

I am going to sleep for a week when this loan was completed! And when the check was cashed, all involved would hear what I thought of their service: all the delays – all the broken promises – all the non-assistance! *But mum's-the-word, till the money is in the bank!* I have learned you do not deposit an escrow check – you cash it and simultaneously deposit the greenbacks. There was that teensy, weensy, little window of opportunity for the funds not to clear.

The two men were in the yard inspecting that antique system. *Please septic, hold together…just for today! No flushing toilets…just for today!*

I was babysitting the inspector's Pomeranian. This store was a magnet for fluff-balls on four legs. I wondered what type of biohazards the downy little creature carried – his master inspected s–h–i–t, for God's sake! I was ready to shoot either of those men if they even *thought* of touching a doorknob. They had been told to stay outside until the job was done. They could whiz in the woods. Or use those classy Porta Potties! I do not care; they won't be getting through my door! I would hand out any drink they wanted at the drive-thru window!

2:50 P.M. They finished! A good report! We passed! Re-fi, here we come!

Now…boys. Pretty-please, fix my landscaping, backfill the dirt, set the decorator rocks where they were…then leave! The shower was nice and warm at your own house! I'd washed my hands a hundred times today just thinking about it. The inspector bailed, but my ex put everything back like nobody was even here today. He knew me. Why do we chuck the good ones who are so trainable? Do we need nasty challenges for entertainment? I needed my head examined!

2:57 P.M. The Bio-Pom left and the couple with Bear walked in. What timing. Bear was not the least bit cute to me at that moment. Juggling dogs, men, "real" customers, espressos, and hand washing – it was time to close. I was over it.

The topper of the day – and we are still talking *toilets*! My daughter just called from Alaska. One of her guy friends broke up with his long-time girlfriend. The gal was not happy. She called him saying, "We need one last good screw for the road. I just bought a bunch of new sex toys and I'm horny as hell." He rocketed over there; told his buddies he was going to *use* the hell out of her one more time. The guys were all hysterical – she had asked for it, right? He arrived at her home and she wanted to tie him up. He was wide-eyed with excitement over her new kinkiness. Now she had him right where she wanted him. She returned with a butcher knife and whacked off his member! (*Bobbitt!*) Then she flushed it down the toilet. But there was so much blood, she panicked and rushed him to the hospital. The doctors alerted the city and they somehow found the evidence in the sewer system and were trying to re-attach it. My daughter once had this poor guy for a boss. The real facts are in the City Public Records – that was how it was told to me. *My* sewer day did not even compare…

6:30 P.M. Signed off…and headed for a good, long, soapy shower…

2-23 24° Sunny again.

Headlines Read… *"Northwest residents stare at the sky!"*

Screwdriver Latte: Shots each of rum and orange syrup, espresso shots, steamed milk.

8:42 A.M. Should I, or shouldn't I? That was the question of the day. Go to court to fight the lying bastard No. 1, or let him slap a year's anti-harassment order onto my record? Okay, but the key was not to look at him…even once! Today was D-Day. Off I went, grinding my teeth…

2:55 P.M. I am baaaaaaaack! I WON!!!!!!! Had heart palpitations, but I kicked his embarrassed ass and *he is* the one in the political scene with the slimy gift-of-gab! We women must not be afraid or intimidated by those bully-men! Physically or verbally! Praise the Lord…today! NO espressos served. I am resting.

BULLY-MEN FROM DAYS GONE BY…

1972. Volunteer firefighters here in Saratogan were having their annual fireman's picnic at the ballpark. They suddenly heard the town siren go off, so they all jumped into the trucks and headed for the station. There were no decent radios or cell phones back then. They thought, maybe the town was burning down. Fire was not the problem at all. The Hell's Angels were in town! They were in the historic Saratogan Hotel, planning on robbing it and causing a ton of trouble. A few of the firefighters, loggers by day, came in the back door to surprise these bikers. And sure enough, one of the local eighty-year-olds had his double-barrel shotgun up against one of their throats! Shaking like a leaf but holding the "Angel" dead still. I was told you could hear a pin drop when the others arrived from behind. Don't let these old-timers fool ya. Some of them can still pump 450 pounds.

The fire trucks started blocking the three exits out of town until police arrived. The Hell's Angels wanted to leave but could not. The firefighters sprayed them with their hoses every time they attempted an exit. Some men stayed in town to protect it. Most returned to the picnic and got drunk.

7:00 P.M. I was only killing time down here at my desk, thinking back on my big win. Downed a cookie and pranced back up to my ivory tower…

2-24 24° Sunny again and again and again.

Straight Espresso: Shots to your heart's content! Splash of sugar, cream or both.

8:17 AM. I felt in a daze today – so did my customers. Full moon? Snowboarders were still going up and down the mountain. How on earth had the resort made inches of snow last for weeks? Were they importing?

Butch's foot had healed.

My brother was out with my gal friend on their first date.

1:40 P.M. Now what do I do with myself when it was this slow and lifeless? Had not served in hours! I could do a striptease out on the highway. Or send another worldwide email regarding fat-fuck No. 1's failure in court. Start building a guesthouse out back? God, why couldn't I just sit still and contemplate my navel? PTSD and OCD do not allow such. Sad really.

Oh…that perfect wife I had been to dear No. 1. I did everything, which included chucking my make-up, burned all my albums (I did sneak Elton John, Supertramp, and John Klemmer from the fire), and cooked every meal from scratch, even quiche! Had his baby, kept a beautiful home, knitted, embraced his Christianity, and whatever the hell else he demanded. Did it get me anywhere? Make me happy and content? Make me feel loved? HELL NO! We even attended a marriage encounter weekend, where he about fell out of his chair when a magnificent lanky Swede slinked into the room. We never made it to Sunday or the ceremony. We went home – both wrapped and tied up in a bow of anger.

The whole thing was, most wanted a mistress, not a wife. Point made.

4:44 P.M. Two male species stopped for mochas and survived.

5:09 P.M. I am going to leave now, before I think of amputating some guy's favorite third leg…

2-25 25° Clear.

> **Silky Breve: Shot honey, shot anisette syrup, espresso shots, foamed Half & Half.**

8:38 A.M. Well, I waited by the phone for the re-fi officers to call, now that I had been assured the septic report was in their hot little hands.

My brother called and he was insanely in love with my friend – already.

1:51 P.M. A couple of Harleys stopped. They always needed caffeine and lots of it. "Great predictable weather for a ride and we are enjoying your scenery and thanks so much for the excellent drinks!"

4:25 P.M. It was dark out and my drive-thru was the only service open. A chap stopped, wanted me to call Washington State Patrol because a guy with a backpack was walking along the highway – at night. I told him that was normal – we had transients, hikers, and crazy guys with skis, trolls, and bums all the time – that walked along this road! It was just another pitch-black night on the ol' Mountain Peak Highway.

Weary, no more eBay, no more customers, thought it was time for a breath of fresh air.

WAIT! Butch was barking his fool head off! I grabbed my gun, shoved it in my back pocket, and cracked the door open. A grungy man walked toward my building (the bum the customer mentioned?). I hollered, "Doors are locked, come to the walk-up window." He ordered a 16-ounce mocha and as I turned around to make it, he gasped at the butt-of-that-baby sticking out of my pocket. He laid the money down, did not wait for change, grabbed the drink, and *hightailed it!*

5:48 P.M. All was well…now a real goodnight…

2-26 26° Sunny.

Granola Bar: Shot honey, shot molasses syrup, shot coconut syrup, splash of hazelnut syrup, espresso shots, steamed milk.

7:00 A.M. It is so pretty and fresh out.

11:37 A.M. A whole troop of Boy Scouts and their leaders came in for drinks on their way up to camp in what little snow there was. Sorry, fathers, no sleep tonight! I asked if they had their "S'mores" makings. They had forgotten all about that – apparently mom had not packed for them. Polite little buggers and the dads snuck some candy bars for themselves. Too cute.

I had somehow gotten busy. Great! One of the customers was a state trooper *needing* a latte. He must have been 6'8"! The troopers allow me to give those discounts – but the sheriff –NEVER! The sheriff's department was so aware of the past corruption, that they had very harsh rules. No acceptin' nothin' from nobody, worth any kind of value, without *full* cost paid in return, or it was considered bribery! It is hard for me to charge those high prices for espresso drinks to any of our law enforcement officials or firemen. Too often we must depend on them for our very survival up here. But laws are laws, rules are rules…I guess…

6:07 P.M. Eleven hours on the job was quite enough! I felt mesmerized. Goodnight, journal…

2-27 27° Tad warmer, still sunny.

Licorice Latte: A shot of black or red licorice syrup, espresso shots, steamed milk.

We were supposed to have rain in Seattle this week; would that mean snow at the pass? I stepped outside to see if my bulbs were coming up…sure enough… and frozen solid!

9:50 A.M. Scanner: A young man was being rushed to our little airport for an airlift. Head injury at the resort.

My brother and his love spent every waking moment together. I was happy for them.

While watching the Oscars tonight, I would sew up a couple of nine-foot fleece snakes and finish knitting another white purse. Anything *white* sells! Where was Paris Hilton when I needed her? She just must buy *one* and I am off and runnin'!

10:51 A.M. Scanner: A seventeen-year-old female skiing has a hematoma of the left eye. Airlift was requested!

11:14 A.M. Scanner: Someone was unconscious up at the resort.

3:45 P.M. Today was super busy. Fun people and wisps of clouds moving in. The temperature soared to forty degrees – almost felt balmy compared to the last three weeks of dry and biting.

5:55 P.M. Oscar night would be my television *date…*

2-28 36° Warm rain.

The Rich: Heavy shot of chocolate syrup, espresso shots, steamed Half & Half and tons of whipped cream.

9:00 A.M. MY RE-FINANCE HAD GONE THROUGH! I'M HEADED FOR THE BANK! Customers could come back tomorrow – I'm busy!

I won't come back after the bank. I could just feel a runaway day coming on. Do not know where I'd go, or with who, or when I'd be back. I'll leave you with some tidbits about our town:

SARATOGAN FACTS

In 1853, the population in Saratogan was approximately 175 people. In 1881 it dropped drastically to about 155. Then by

1900, it jumped to about 320, with all the inter-marriage within forty families. Told ya! Tony Swin-ko-mish was appointed as the sub-chief of the Saratogan Native Americans in 1856. The berries being picked were wild huckleberries. The animals hunted were mountain goats, deer and bear. The tribe sought healing powers at Mountain Peak and Lake Hazel. The Saratogan tribe signed a treaty in1855 and moved to Swinoot and became part of the Makana tribe. They melted into this tribe so deeply that they had to fight aggressively for their identity as Saratogan Indians and won their long court case in 1965...

MARCH

Ice cracks under cream as his breath
passes by the crystal's rim

3-01 37° Partly sunny.

Espresso Viennese: Shot of vanilla syrup, hot water halfway up, espresso shots, whipped cream, sprinkle nutmeg.

7:48 A.M. I felt like Snow White, awakened by the handsome Prince and rescued from my cold coffin. Yesterday seemed like a beautiful dream as I floated in and out of activities. After I hugged every teller in the bank, it was chocolate on my mind, and I wasn't stingy with myself. Looked at clothes, spent $17 in a casino, stopped to hug mom, checked out the new additions at the animal shelter (just looking!), visited a friend, blew in and out of an AA meeting to meet and greet old friends, came home to tend to my critters, and fell into bed. What a day – what a night's sleep!

8:48 A.M. Opened to people talking about golf and fishing. Unfortunately, they were supposed to be discussing winter and such sports like – falling and breaking legs on slopes, chair lifts stuck high above hard ice, the exorbitant cost of food at a resort, and which fight for a parking spot was the bloodiest! Where was I? Mother Nature has forgotten about our Northwest corner!

First early-bird guys ordered cappuccinos, bought hand-knitted ski-caps (maybe for next year?), and helped me move a huge buffet in my antique store.

1:47 P.M. I do not wish to reach for melodrama, but I just found out two new espresso businesses are opening up, just two miles down the road west of here. One is a new drive-thru – the other is a walk-up window at the only gas station within thirty miles. They will be within 150 feet of each other! What?! Do they think I am getting filthy rich off espresso? Do they covet working 12-14 hours a day? There just flat-out are not enough cars to support three espresso businesses up here! We are not living in Seattle, for bloody hell! Survival of the fittest! I am the only one on the north side of the highway for at least thirty miles, so this place will catch all the westbound drivers at least. I guess no biggie. Progress in a ghost town – how special! I gave the locals, all those small-minded gossipmongers, no more than thirty-six hours to fly through these doors with the negative news. This will be a highlight in their narrow lives.

3:07 P.M. I have had nothing but colorful hippies in today. It is guaranteed they will order tea, chai tea or soy drinks. I guess there is a craft fair going on in eastern Washington. They even dressed crafty. Dyed clothes of every color, dreadlocks, more adornment than our local jewelry store and lots of black nail polish and lipstick. I've often wondered about dreadlocks. How are they created, and do they smell downright awful?

Maybe had twenty-six customers this whole damn day.

5:22 P.M. Signing off…to take turpentine to my thoughts…

3-02 37° Sprinkling.

Tuscany Mocha: Shot of chocolate syrup, splash of orange syrup, espresso shots, steamed milk, whipped cream and chocolate sprinkles.

8:29 A.M. Boring morning, so I was glad my hilarious, comedian neighbor, Rosie, came in for an iced mocha. Her cat got fixed and she was on her way down the mountain to pick it up from the vet. She was describing the difference between males and females and the pain and suffering female felines endure. "The damn cat's own fuckin' father was trying to procreate with the poor puss. I was caught in the middle, between the bastard and this yowling, scratching, biting bitch, fighting for her virginity. I have got the scars to prove it! And, Christy, I have some relatives like this! Now, following her surgery, will this keep happening? I don't think her damn dad will even know if she's fixed or not – or care – the bastard." Sounded like ordinary life here in Saratogan…

She and I added up all the espresso possibilities within fifty miles of my store; indoor seating, booths, and separate lone stands. Geez – there must have been twenty! Is this a drug or what!

I was reduced to watching the clock.

5:32 P.M. I could stare at that circle with two hands just as easily upstairs, in my home. So, later…

3-03 40° Sunny! Here we go again!

California Sunshine: Shot of pineapple syrup, splash of rum syrup or real, splash of coconut syrup, espresso shots, steamed milk.

8:00 A.M. I was feisty today. One of my neighbors illegally parked her semi-truck across the lot from me…again! I have named her "Trucker Bitch." This gigantic rig blocks my store, right at a dangerous curve in the road, and I lose business. And she gets off on it! Apparently, no one around here, or at Emerald County Code Enforcement, gives a rats-ass about laws! "You are too far out of town for us to deal with such nonsense," they told me. "Well, then, turn this isolated strip the hell back over to the Makana County office, you lazy dolts!"

It was the same with the drug dealers. Not enough cops. Not enough money. Laws too lackadaisical for any searching. Yawn… In the meantime, methamphetamine dealers were driving around in bright red, shiny new sports cars. Marijuana junkies were opening new businesses. Drug dealers were spending money like they just lifted the winning lottery ticket off some comatose customer. Bums living like kings in their cabins in the woods. It gets old – screw it! All these sub-humans continue to flourish without jobs. Makana would kick our county sheriff department's butt up here! I was married to one of those cops. They do not mess around! We need some freakin' muscle, with eyeballs open!

12:16 P.M. Well, speak of the devil! The sheriff just stopped and served me papers! What the hell! Could it possibly be No. 1 going for a second strike?

Nope. It was from Trucker Bitch, the slime queen! Damn, how did I allow her to beat me to the punch? She has served me with anti-harassment papers for calling-the-cops too many times about her illegal truck parking! Life and justness are antonyms in my book. Just doesn't compute in the brain sometimes. I had legally proven my codes and safety points regarding this elephantine-fucking truck to the satisfaction of the county, DOT, sheriff, and Treetops Loop Association. Who is in charge of our plat of land up here? They have told her numerous times to cease and desist and now she served me! This "Hatfield and McCoy Feud" has been going on for three years. So...let us get it on – woman!

I just realized this is the second mother f-g court serving within weeks – and the only two in my entire life! It's preposterous! The sheriff will start thinking *I'm* the evil one!

4:49 P.M. Finally...a little levity in my day. A few customers, all in one van, stopped in for triple lattes. They sure were not planning to bed down early! One was on the brink of orgasm over the chocolate-covered espresso beans. Another was lost for greater eloquence than, "Wow, man," over his first bite of my pink, cream-cheese-frosted cookies. And a third could hardly contain himself, just thinking of wearing the pink-flamingo briefs he just bought. They were all more fun than a free amusement park!

5:54 P.M. I will say goodbye now and go for a walk to try and get semi-trucks, semi-automatics, massacre, and carnage off my mind...

3-04 47° Sunny.

Spiced Apple: Shot apple syrup, shot cinnamon syrup, espresso shots, steamed milk.

8:33 A.M. I was thinking of giving two chocolate-covered espresso beans with each drink, to out-do the new stands down the way. But I am too frugal!

11:06 A.M. Scanner: A vehicle fire up at the summit. Flames were visible. Occupants were standing by.

HISTORIC AMBULANCE STORY FROM DAYS GONE BY

The 1965 Ford Falcon that was used as our ambulance for many years had a glass window that lifted, allowing the tailgate to go down. There was a car accident up at Mountain Peak Pass in a snow blizzard. The big problem with this aid call was that the injured man was seven feet tall! The volunteers were concerned that this guy wouldn't fit into the back of the ambulance. They slid him in, but his feet were hanging out the back – over a foot! "How we gonna close the door, guys?" They put the glass window down but had to leave the tailgate out flat. The volunteers took turns putting hot packs on his feet for the long ride "down-below." Great-Grandpa Big Sam started this ambulance service after seeing a horrible head-on accident right out in front of his tow-shop. The injured man's body was just lying on the highway, in the deep snow. The decision was made, a brown '65 Ford was purchased, and Saratogan started their volunteer "Aid Service."

3:32 P.M. The comedian was back. Rosie came by to have me be a witness to her new resolution, "I swore off watching TV during the days! 'Soaps' are my life, whereas getting off my butt and doin' chores *should* be. I was doing okay when my old, upstairs aunt-in-law lost her hearing aid and now the volume is turned up so high, I'm still fucking enjoying my soap operas!" A drink, and she was back out the door, shored up mentally for the grueling life-style-change task ahead…

5:18 PM. Scanner: Another nut case on Mountain Peak Highway, shooting off a gun. He started in Pacifica and did not even make it to Alpine, which lays thirty miles down, before he was caught. Thank you, Sheriff, cuz he was heading this way! I love my scanner!

It's Friday night – big deal – makes-no-matter-to-me! I'm *not* heading upstairs to perform major surgery at my make-up mirror. I just don't go out anymore!

Buck just dropped off some of his mama's homemade macaroni and cheese – yum! She makes the *crunchiest and cheesiest,* best-in-the-west!

6:17 P.M. My Friday night date is a bowl of carbs. Bye…

3-05 42° Sunny, sunny, sunny. -Boring, boring, boring.

Espresso Mandarin: Shot of mandarin syrup, espresso shots.

8:42 A.M. It is probably the very last weekend they can possibly squeak out some skiing. It has only been open a total of about twenty-one days. Reminds me of my "Why Bother" recipe.

11:18 A.M. Another Tupperware of macaroni salad – this time with tuna, and this time the container appeared on the hood of my Jeep, along with $400 in cash. I could smell logger money from across town! His greenbacks were always scented with the mixture of cedar and mildew. It was a bribe from Buck! I had to send it back. I didn't have to get laid (yet) for money, thank you very much. Business was slow and he knew it all too well. But, gosh, golly-gee-whiz, a little sex for four hundred big ones wouldn't hurt now, would it, gals? Yes! Would hurt my pride, morals, and who knows what else!

2:09 P.M. Sold a 20-ounce mocha to a customer who complained that mine was twenty cents higher than in Seattle. "Go the hell home then! Where do you live anyway, the slums? And how much did you say the gas cost to get you all the way up here?" Gave directions to another couple for a local campground. Had several Porta Potty users and abusers. Some people were such complete and utterly disgusting pigs – makes a person wonder if their own bathrooms have legs!

6:01 P.M. A lady just came in and ordered her very first espresso, ever! They left Tennessee more than two weeks ago. I said, "What? No Starbucks down yonder in your entire state?" There was, but not in her wee town. And I thought *my* life was boring.

Starbucks-Schmarbucks. If I heard this once a day, I heard it thirty times. This popular espresso chain had even invaded my dreams. My major competition – keeping me on my toes:

STARBUCKS COFFEE COMPANY
Starbucks opened its first location in Seattle Pike Place Market in 1971. At first, they were satisfied with raves from customers, but in 1982, Howard Schultz joined forces with this little business as a "marketer" and concentrated on providing fine coffee to fine restaurants and espresso bars. This new coffee bar culture was designed after bars in Milan. Development of product, locations, and new roasting facilities (the second one ever was in Kent, Washington,) and this FIVE STAR coffee company, called Starbucks, exploded across the U.S. mainland and ultimately signed international contracts.

6:58 P.M. To hell with customers, competitors and logger's money...

3-06 44° 90% Sunny, 100% skiing is finished!

Royal Flush: Shot of orange and lemon syrups, espresso shots, some steamed milk, some foamed milk, whipped cream and a cherry on top.

8:33 A.M. There must be *boulders* popping up through the snow at the resort by now!

I just served three Americanos and one iced mocha latte. That was a long list these days. Four drinks! Hoo-hah!

Swept more of the parking lot. Wheel-barrowed the rest of the snow-muck and dumped it across the highway. It was the DOT's plow-gravel-muck, but who is keeping track. This year, I did not get to have my bitch session with DOT. Usually, they were here on a daily basis, flying by way too fast and blasting customers, cars, and my windows with tiny rock pellets and snow while plowing. They always slowed down for the tongue-lashing.

1:45 P.M. Drinks galore, hot and iced. Food. Gifts. What's up?

Bear and injured mom and dad came in. Her back brace was off – without the consent of the doctor! "I'm so over it, Christy! But I won't go into it." Bear stayed in dad's arms. Thank you. My carpet was just cleaned!

Another cool couple I had not seen in ages just got married. She demanded the honeymoon first! Why hadn't I thought of that? "I thought it was a good idea to check-out the Prone Ceremony before the Vertical one." She requested New Zealand for this pre-nuptial trip.

4:00 P.M. Scanner: A vehicle injury accident at milepost 67. Three people were injured; one of them was lying on the shoulder.

5:48 P.M. No wolves at the door today.

6:00 P.M. Little Red Riding Hood says goodnight…

3-07 45° Sprinkles.

Mystery Espresso: A shot of any flavor, espresso shots, foamed milk, a sprinkle of cinnamon or nutmeg.

8:54 A.M. A big delivery day in the Gift-Merchandise-Department. I call these MAN-DAYS! Tons of lifting, re-arranging, unpacking boxes, moving furniture, and stacking shelves. Handling 1,500 square feet of gifts and an espresso business can get overwhelming sometimes.

11:42 A.M. A new weekend homeowner just came in for the first time. Introductions yack-yack, double-shot espresso. This reminded me to tell you about his new neighborhood up here, called Rockfish River Estates. I will call this short stretch Groovy Street. The guy, who is building the newest one, brought his sister in to meet me the other day. He is most definitely the No. 1 Bachelor of Seattle. Okay...I'll admit, I could easily be "caught" again, if this one threw out a line! He is a catch-'n-a-half! The real reason he brought her by was to tell me that she had lived in one of my apartments upstairs, twenty years ago – four years after I rented here. Back then she was a rebel – skier-party-girl! She worked up at the Mountain Peak Ski Resort and hung here. We both were oohing and aahing about how our paths almost crossed. This building has touched so many lives. Makes me wish I had a record of all the owners and renters. I'll have to go take a peek at this new bachelor's pad soon! He bought a giant bag of beef jerky for his dog, Burt. And he loves dogs. Oh my...trouble Christy.

4:06 P.M. Customers were spunky today. Spring is about springing. Makes ya almost want to mimic the birds and the bees and have a little sex!

The blended mochas and fruit smoothies were doing their nice-weather comeback.

Where was Buck? He had not bothered me for a few days, only leaving food and funny money.

5:43 P.M. Oh well, nobody loves me. I guess I will just go eat dirt...or pound sand...

3-08 35° Sunny.

Long Pour: Pour 2 shots or water through a shot of espresso.

10:42 A.M. No customers and I wanted to run away for a day. The radio just confirmed. Mountain Peak Ski Resort closed. In March!

2:41 PM. Escape! I could take a hike on Blue Bear Trail and maybe learn some history:

HISTORY OF THE BLUE BEAR TRAIL

Where trains once thundered, volunteers are now construct-ing a historic recreational trail. This trail reaches the historic site that once was the town of Westson. The story of Blue Bear dates back more than a hundred years ago, when the last spike of the Pacific Railway was driven, completing one of the most remarkable engineering feats of the nineteenth century. It was the mark of the crossing over the Cascades at Mountain Peak, which helped open the Pacific Northwest to settlement and trade with the rest of the world –through Seattle and Pacifica. The establishment of the Mountain Peak Historic District in 1976 recognized this remarkable feat.

The Kodiak Tunnel, completed in 1900, by-passed the switch-backs. Several snow sheds were also added for safety, but snowy winter conditions still presented serious hazards. Trains were often stopped for days at Westson waiting for win-ter storms to pass. Once, a huge section of snow on Stark Mountain broke loose and caused an avalanche, knock-ing both trains off the track and into Rockfish Creek below. Rescue efforts were quickly organized, but over one hun-dred lives were lost. Westson was one of the worst railway disasters in our nation's history.

5:03 P.M. Enough of this madcap, riotous existence for one day…

3-09 42° Finally raining.

Macchiato: Espresso shots, top with a layer of foamed milk.

9:04 A.M. I drove through a couple of local neighborhoods this morning. It always made the drug dealers nervous when people poked around. Lazy leaches. They get really torqued-off, thinking *we* all need permits to enter *their* county roads. Tough shit, ya bums! I wanted to check out the new Microsoft employee cabin – the second one to sprout up on Groovy Street. We were told it is our very first million-dollar vacation cabin! Up frigging here!

My first customer ordered a German chocolate cake mocha. Made the whole building smell so yummy – as though grandma and her white-starched apron were at it again! This was Ms. Gossip No. 2's regular order. Where she gets the *moola*, I will never know, since the kids all have holes in their knees and shoes. But espresso and French Nails were much more important. She told me that she was sick of husbands, kids, and life! "It's only the time of year, darling. Chin up!" Silently…better you than me.

12:45 P.M. Just had a guy in for a peppermint mocha. He grew up here and walked through my doors today to share. I considered these visitors gifts!

He went to school up here in Saratogan. A few of his grades were held in the old four-room school building until they built a new one in 1936 and it still stands today. He was one of twelve kids in his class. He also knew the Bower brothers, who originally owned my building, "Back then it was named 'The Bower Camp.' It had a pond out back and was a favorite necking spot for us hellions. I actually dated Lee Bower's daughter, without him ever knowing. We both feared for our fannies if anyone ever squealed!" He had three paper routes, delivering the Seattle Star Flyer. It cost patrons sixty cents a month. There was a prostitute in town, named Ms. Janey. She always paid her bill from coins saved in a tin cup and she was one of the few who always paid him on time. The late paying customers would trade him for scrap-iron, beer bottles, and other treasures. He waved me goodbye and walked out, dreaming back…

5:47 P.M. A few more dribbled in and out. It was dark now. Doors locked. Still on eBay.

6:04 P.M. American Idol was on tonight, causing me to feel a sudden, intense sensation…

3-10 42° Sunny.

Soymilk Latte: Espresso shots, steamed soymilk.

8:36 A.M. There was ash in Yakima from the most recent Mount St. Helens blow.

11:21 A.M. A creepy looking guy just stopped by in a beater van. "I make Southwest Native stuff, like dream-catchers, etc." "No thanks. I import mine through China." He was not paying a bit of attention and headed out the door, throwing words over his shoulder, "I have a few dream catchers and things in my van. I'll bring 'em in." I watched him through the window wondering why it was taking him so long to grab a couple of items. Next thing I know, he marched in carrying a big bundle of whatever, wrapped in deer hide. I noticed what I believed to be the butt of a gun peeking out of a slit in the hide. My adrenalin started pumping and I was ready to grab my metal! He saw my distress and hurriedly started talking about the weaponry pieces he had in the bundle, as he whipped out an enormous, fucking machete! "Dream-catchers are not made of hard shiny metal; they are made of soft yarns, leather, and feathers! Pack up and get the hell out of my store – NOW!" The fucker smirked, hesitated just long enough for me to move closer to my gun. Then he gathered up his roll and left. I think he was truly disappointed that I did not cry or faint. God, I was mad. Then, this nervy bastard came back in to say, "Goodbye." I yelled, "I hope none of my neighbors saw that or the posse will be here in a jiffy."

4:10 PM. It's 62°. I've sold a *few* espressos – but a *load* of furniture today. A cabin owner just furnished his whole rental house in my rustic treasures from Mexico. "I love you."

5:21 P.M. Cannot do another minute for sanity…

3-11 45° Sunny.

Best Tea: Black tea, six packs of raw sugar, cream.

8:39 A.M. The North Cascades Highway Loop opened this weekend – the earliest ever! More record breaking! Even Good Morning America was commenting about us every other day.

9:47 A.M. Here he comes, galloping across his acre. My dog literally hates the Porta Potty pooper-scooper man. It must be the mixed scents. How can anyone do this job? Sure enough, Butch jumped high, trying to scale his fence. He could catch the top lip of the Porta Potty hut, hold on by his teeth and shake the crap out of it. His front paws balanced him on the top rung of the fence. It is hysterical! It is a weekly ritual. I have told this man to run for his truck should the dog ever get out. I have not seen fur stand up on my dog's back like this – ever – and then I began to wonder if any of my customers get the "shake, rattle, and roll" routine?

We have tons of bats around here and they are going to have a heyday this summer. They dive-bomb bodies in the evenings, barely missing heads. They never crash right into you, but it's eerie! I don't mind flying rodents until I think one is going to get stuck in my long hair.

One-night last summer, lugging boxes of Costco groceries to my second floor, I got stuck in the stairwell between the door to my home and the outside, downstairs door. There were several of these accordion-winged, yellow, beady-eyed, pointy nosed varmints. Close up, they were adorable. I electrocuted a couple of them on my outside Christmas lights over the years and that is how I got close enough to take a good look. Big eyes, little ears, and cute little faces… kind of like kittens. That evening, I somehow got the food in, with the bats circling the *entire* time – and me screaming the *entire* time.

4:44 P.M. I had two new perverts in my drive thru. "Two double mochas, double cupped, double straws, double good, by a double cute gal." UGH! Today I asked them if they wanted to pay double. No response. No humor. I tried to swallow this bothersome talk from two ugly, old farts and addressed this differently today. So, I was behaving (me!) like a good little waitress. A big smile…a slight blush…a bat of the eyelashes, for a tip. GAG! Cannot do THIS again! Even though there was a new wrinkled ol' $5 bill to pop in the tip jar.

5:00 P.M. Enough…

3-12 42° Sunny.

Sunset Soda: Ice, shot of peach and raspberry syrups, shot of pineapple syrup, soda water, splash of cream.

7:33 A.M. Just brewed my first tea. I'm gonna clean.

3:33 P.M. One of my locals came to tell me the latest. He said he may have to think about his espresso purchase today, since it may be a waste of his hard-earned money. He shared that a local bank "down-below" had posted a sign in their lobby: DON'T THROW YOUR HARD-EARNED MONEY AWAY ON DAILY ESPRESSOS! GIVE IT TO US! Attached to this bizarre sign was a poster explaining that the average espresso drinker spent $212K on these legal drugs over a twenty-year span. The base was around $96K, and if they would deposit this money in a nice fund, the value would rocket to over $200K! Continuing, the median priced home in Seattle was rising approximately $52K a year; invest your extra espresso in real estate and sit back and sing to your empty *99 Bottles of Beer on the Wall.* Cute. I may have to sue them. Laughing, he ordered a triple. Seriously folks, add cigarettes and liquor to that figure and other fun mischief, not to mention *illegal* drugs! Mind-boggling…

4:58 P.M. And that was about it for customers today. I sure couldn't/wouldn't live up here in this backward locale if I didn't own a store!

A contractor stopped by for an espresso smoothie, he is working on a cabin in Treetops Loop. As I was handing his drink through the window, I heard a loud crashing sound and metal debris was flying in the air. OMG there was a head-on crash right in front of my store! I dialed 911, then I practically threw my fire extinguisher at him and screamed, "Go and use this on their engine" My heart was pounding so hard as I ran outside towards the scene. I watched the man die in the driver's seat inside the crumpled Jeep. There were kids screaming from the back and an injured woman in the passenger seat. I was nauseous but determined and the other driver in the Subaru was a woman and she was also dying. There were no other passengers in her vehicle. Air bags were deployed in both vehicles. Everything was a blur, the contractor was using the fire extinguisher, which I later found out did put out a flame. I ran to my barn, screaming on my phone to mom that I felt as though I was going to have a heart attack. I grabbed all my moving blankets and ran back to the scene, now dialing Gossip No. 1, "Please come up to my store. There has been a head-on and people are dying. We need help." I could see people running from the third car which was a van full of people in the same party as the Jeep occupants. They were, with unbelievable strength, tearing the doors off the Jeep and getting the injured kids out.

The next thing I knew, the angels were arriving from various cars that were abruptly stopped by this scene and some were nurses and a doctor or two. Ambulances arrived and the scene was surreal. I sat with children one by one as they laid on my blankets crying in pain. I was sick, dizzy, frightened.

Once the scene cleared, the news stations started showing up to camp for hours while we waited for the coroner to finish the process.

8:00 P.M. I will go upstairs now, hug my dog, say some prayers and wake again tomorrow…nightmares are on their way…

3-13 44° Sunny.

Tahitian: Shot of coconut syrup, fill halfway up with hot water, espresso shots, whipped cream, and chocolate powder.

6:00 A.M. I took a stroll the length of my parking lot, picking up various debris from the wreck, taking in the peculiar smells of automotive liquids and just horrible scents. I decided that I would plant flower seeds along my grass bordering this dangerous highway.

8:22 A.M. Good news about the Trucker Bitch who blocked my business! Treetops Loop Association decided *not* to renew her lease on the *bogus-lot* next to me. She could no longer park her piece of shit semi there…starting in four months from today! Yes! Yes! Yes! There is Justice. I am still waiting for our court date.

The sheriff arrived asking me if I was okay from the crash, and did I need to talk about it. I was still numb. He then shared that he had heard that Trucker Bitch could no longer park next door. With *this* great news and a couple of stories about recent arrests: drunkenness, abuse, and drug dealings. Remember, we only have a little over 200 residents in this fair locale. He said, "This place reminds me of the Old West on the Western reruns!" Speaking of colorful characters:

BOOTLEGGERS

Hunter, here in town, is known for miles. He owned our gas station and a huge tow business up here forever and sold out years ago. He still lives here and is perched up on the highest piece of real estate in town, watching over everything like the buzzard, he is. This is the story of yet another old-timer, who beat his multiple wives to a pulp - in his garage! He forced them to join in his planned orgies. He was in jail for many short stints for the spousal abuse and imported some of the most violent criminals he befriended while doing his time.

His grandfather was known as Grandpa Hunter. He was one of the biggest thieves in the valley. The biggest bootlegger around! He took care of all the "boys" on the railroad, tunnel, and logging crews. "Kept 'em all from be'n too thirsty." Well, since he was also known as a thief, the crews would hire him to guard the work camps to make sure no one "stole stuff." They figured they had the biggest thief right where they wanted him, so, they were safe.

5:29 P.M. Just another sterling local…

3-14 38° Sunny.

Black Americano: Espresso shots, hot water.

9:00 A.M. Another MAN-DAY! So far today, I removed the plow from my truck. It weighs about 800 lbs., I am told! Each side of the plow had to be jacked up by sliding bricks under the frame for support. I prayed a lot and I used to be worried about my nails! Now I am just worried that I might lose an arm. I jumped the rider-mower's battery, which for some reason wouldn't hold a charge…later I'll attack that problem. Then I spread six wheelbarrows full of bark and set at least a dozen boulders into place. Still must go to the dump! I also must get the riding mower into the bed of my truck…somehow. Wednesday it needs to be taken down to the dealer for repair. This is *not* going to be giggles. I then dolly some huge, heavy ramps from the garage, across gravel, and out to the truck. Jump the damn mower with my Jeep again. Then, gingerly, drive the mower up the ramps, without falling off the slats. I am overwhelmed.

1:18 P.M. Done! Just counted and still had ten fingers. I have been serving espressos in filthy clothes, on demand.

Next customer practically overheated me with the longest yawn ever. When the mouth finally shut, he slowly slurred, "Now I can hear again!" Apparently, his ears had been plugged from going over the Mountain Peak Pass. Whooooooo cares!!!! Cover the mouth.

3:00 P.M. My muscles were wiggling. It was downright dangerous to be a woman sometimes. I wondered if I would end up front-yard-mincemeat for the critters, or news for the scanner today. Made me think back on all the pioneer women who did what I do, times fifty! Like some of our local pioneers, as in one named Marge. Old Marge was supposedly a large, handsome woman and sharp as a tack. She owned both restaurants up here at the same time. She raised two wild children and kicked her husband's girlfriends off their front porch, at all hours of the day and night. Even carried him back from the local bar downtown, up a flight of stairs, and bedded him down after another drunken grandstand. She also made time to cook for various elderly local men, who had previously lost their wives. Often, she would shove her son outside in the snow to make the rounds, seeing to it that so-and-so's porch had fresh wood for heat. She was a member of every association. Then somehow, she found even *more* minutes to play nurse and jump into the ambulance and save lives. She had incredibly strong moral beliefs and was strangled and locked into a long-term marriage. She died, but many years after tending to her sickly, controlling husband. One of the thousand women who certainly paid high dues – our pioneers of a time not that long ago. There were a handful of these courageous, hard-working, abused wives-of-the-good-ol'-boys left, but I heard a couple of them were triplin' the salt on their ailing husband's dinners…

4:17 P.M. Gosh family and friends from the crash victims are showing up to the scene to pay their respects and let the tears flow freely. They have been stepping into my store to ask me all the questions, to reenact what had happened. Breaking my heart, all of them. My contractor came by and told me he was going to take a couple of weeks off, "I'm extremely effected by what I saw." Poor guy, me too.

5:55 P.M. I tip my espresso china cup to them all…

3-15 38° Sunny and ice crystals.

Skinny Mocha: Shot of chocolate syrup, espresso, steamed non-fat milk.

7:32 A.M. It is a day early, the roads are a little icy, but I must take the mower to the dealer "down-below" anyway. Tomorrow it is supposed to rain, and I just cannot face the "tarp-thing." And I'm sore, sore, sore! Picked up some espresso supplies and a new sink faucet for my cart. Mine had been dripping for days. The birds were going to mimic that drip if I did not get it corrected. Then…I will definitely go coo-coo!

Court is tomorrow, to fight the Trucker Bitch! I noticed she is home, but her truck is motionless somewhere else. Wonder where she's hiding it?

2:05 P.M. A man walked in and was looking for cowboy this and that. I made him his 20-ounce vanilla latte and pointed to my plaster cowboy statues. He was looking for *antique* - saddles, bridles, hats and boots. I had none.

Back to plumbing. Something from my childhood inspired me – lefty-loosy – righty-tighty. Okay, all the parts were on the floor. I was jammed inside the cart cabinet. My hammer was heavy. The flashlight was dying. I needed my glasses. They were upstairs. I realized I was trying to remove a *lock*-washer! No way, José! I called the mechanic Buck and he snuck over and dropped off a bucket of tools I could not even *lift*. So, I carried one piece in at a time, while winding myself back into the cabinet to break the washer loose. I had to use some sort of huge fifty-pound nut-tak'r-off'r thingie! The rest was a piece of cake. New faucet – no leaks *anywhere*! WE *CAN* DO IT. When fear is right there, staring you in the face, face it!

4:00 P.M. A guy strolled up to my window with a huge walking-stick and started twirling it around Kung-Fu style. I watched this for a full minute, and he wasn't ordering. "And your point is?" "Oh, sorry, I twirl this subconsciously – past training to let everyone know I have a weapon on me!" "Well, sir, just FYI, I have several aces-up-my-sleeve in here too!" "Loud and clear, ma'am – may I have an Americano?" This place is plain – strange! More sad family members down at the scene. I am still traumatized myself. Hugs!

12:00 Midnight. Get some sleep! Tomorrow's a big day. A 10:00 A.M. date with a courthouse, and it is down the hill again…

3-16 30° Snowing!

Toasted Coconut Cream: Shot of coconut and hazelnut syrups, splash of toasted marshmallow, espresso shots, steamed Half & Half.

5:11 P.M. I LOST THE COURT BATTLE! I CAN'T BELIEVE THE WHOLE THING! I'M BEWILDERED, PISSED, AND HURT – ALL AT THE SAME TIME!

But as the judge and everyone else said, "You both won." We *each* got an anti-harassment order against one another. *Ahhhh, togetherness…* Absolutely no contact whatsoever! The judge felt I had harassed this <u>LADY</u> (*his word – not mine!*), by calling different government agencies about her semi-rig, over and over, for three years! The Bitch even brought some screws in a zip-lock bag saying I stuck them under her tires. That lying sack of shit! She proceeded to tell him that I loosened her oil filter. *Now, let's get serious!* This is a *gigantic* semi-truck – I would practically need a ladder to get *in* the damn thing. And who-the-hell would know where-in-the-hell an oil filter is? Go to hell, you Bitch… You lied Under Oath!

I was poker-hot-mad and drove around aimlessly for a while. I even stopped at a casino and made $3.75. Makes up for at least *one* of the mochas missed.

9:55 P.M. I am hittin' the sack, before I vent somewhere I shouldn't…

3-17 40° Raining. St. Patrick's Day.

Luck of the Irish: Shot of chocolate syrup, shot of Irish cream syrup, espresso shots, steamed milk, whipped cream, white chocolate powder.

6:10 A.M. I am leaving for the day.

4:10 P.M. I'm back home serving espressos. Jack and Pete came in. Merle no longer can visit with the guys. His bowel problems had escalated. He was in the proper place – a rest home – and not in my concession kitchen! They both got some lattes and asked if they could park an RV down on my river road and leave it there. You mean move in? No way, you cute lil' ole lechers you. I *love* old people! Always have but *give me a break!*

Today I am in overload. Court. Retail. Men. Travel trailers. I need a cruise…

4:57 P.M. Closing…period…

3-18 41° Rain.

Caribbean Blend: 1 cup of milk, 4 shots espresso, 1 tbs. sugar, 1 cup ice, blend and top with toasted coconut.

9:17 A.M. I had a court-crazy-concoction hangover. I jotted down evil thoughts, ran far away after I slammed the door hard enough to have reached the neighbors.

I have become a member of the 'White Trash Society' and will leave you with the newsletter:

ANOTHER ISSUE OF THE SARATOGAN WHITE TRASH NEWSLETTER

Hi y'all,

I jus becum a member of the White Trash Society of Saratogan, Worrshington. I jess got a Anti-Harassment Order agenst me. Ain't that grand! I will let y'all know the date of the recep'shun. It'll be in my front yard, by the Porta Potties, jus in case ya wunna come! Reception will be wunna of them thar B.Y.O.W. kind, so start gatherin' up yer lady-foke.

Yup, my asshole, white trash neighbor *out spun* me 'n court. I have lerned wat that means now. I guess tellin' the truth don't werk too weel theez daz. If the dang dummies just red their dang codes, we wudn't had this problem in da ferst place. But hell, a reason fer party'n! So y'all, cum on down, ya heer!

5:43 P.M. Home. It is time to look at maps and cruise brochures…

3-19 35° Sunny.

French Vanilla Latte: A shot of French vanilla syrup, espresso shots, steamed milk.

8:54 A.M. *I'm letting it go*! I feel like a new person. And I do believe in that "What comes around, goes around" stuff. I am going to forget this week ever happened. Buck came by with $1,000 and said he just wants *one* over-nighter. Shit.

No. 5 just called and needed me to sign off his van title. Three years later…still connected. Shit.

3:07 P.M. Scanner: A woman was slumped over the wheel of her car at milepost 60. The R.P. (Reporting Party) claimed that she appeared to be unconscious. Aid in route.

HISTORIC AMBULANCE STORY FROM DAYS GONE BY...
AGAIN

The old ambulances had an intercom system inside of the vehicle so the front passengers could communicate with the back. One night, they had an injured drunk in back, flailing around and trying to beat up our volunteer. They stopped the ambulance and handcuffed him to the gurney. He had been in a car accident and his head was leakin' like a stuffed pig. The driver told the volunteer, "Take off the guy's gauze and let him leak awhile and he'll stop fightin." He did calm way down from the loss of blood. A couple of blocks away from the hospital, the driver told the volunteer, "Go ahead and plug up them holes with some more bandages – he won't perform very well, two quarts low."

Back then they also had one-man gurneys, where one volunteer could handle a call alone. It could be spread out flat on the ground; then the volunteer would lay the patient on it. He'd lift one end up, with the patient's head pointing down and feet up in the air. Lock that in place and go around and lift the other end and lock it up. The volunteers back then had to search for bodies in the dark, without flashlights or lanterns. They would follow screams, moans, and groans, in blizzards.

5:58 P.M. Great day, great income, I will sleep like a babe tonight...

3-20 39° Raining.

Espresso Romano: Shots of espresso, a splash of lemon syrup.

8:46 A.M. BOO built a rip-roaring fire this morning, trying to stay warm and dry. I have been told the county was going to be logging the trees up in that area, running alongside the railroad tracks. But I just learned recently that this has been BOO's home for six years now! I would still love to meet the mystery hermit, who has never caused a lick of trouble for anyone. I sure hope he announces himself if he ever comes in for espresso or decides to leave.

1:15 P.M. Bizi as a Bee. No time to talk, type, pee, think, eat!

2:44 P.M. A *classic* 1968 Cadillac was in my drive thru. Stats: Immaculate, 514 under its exquisite hood and it was all stock! The lady driver was only the second owner. She used to be a barista too, until she was robbed at knifepoint in Lake Stevens! Yeeeeowww! Scared her so bad, she could not work *anywhere* for over a year!

5:00 P.M. Lots of customers, 100+ espressos! Not *one* gift sold all day! Doesn't *somebody* need some nonsensical *something* for *someone*?

LOGGING HISTORY FROM DAYS GONE BY...
Loggers in the old days didn't like longhaired guys. So, hippies were on their hit list! But one of the loggers that worked up here temporarily had a ponytail. One day, they were

wrapping the cable around the drum and his ponytail got caught-up in it and, "It fuckin' killed the guy! And back in those days, the crew was shut down for about fifteen minutes was all," my logging visitor said.

5:48 P.M. Closing, happy, tired, and looking forward to another relaxing evening and sweet, sexless dreams...

3-21 36° Hailing.

Highball Soda: Ice, shot of lemon syrup, shot of mint syrup, soda water.

7:10 A.M. I got up early to drive down the mountain to pick up my riding mower. Murphy's Law – they are closed on Mondays. "Crap...I knew that!" Did some errands.

1:10 P.M. I was back home to reality after using up $20 worth of fuel for basically nothing!

3:11 P.M. A very clean-cut married guy, new to the area, just lost his dogs again. I baby-sat them once before for him, overnight, in my fenced yard. But he *keeps* losing track of them. "Not great thinkin' with all the bobcats and cars out here!" Just about an hour later, some charitable soul dropped them off. I called this Mr. Hunk Wyatt and he picked them up immediately. I got another look at this "eye candy." Oh my...

My mom just emailed me another lady's room joke. I staple these on the adjoining Porta Potty's fence and the folks in line just howl. This one hysterically describes the "women's stance." Using thigh muscles, never getting close to the porcelain, and trying to aim. You women *all* know what I'm talking about! I frankly do not know why they even *install* seats on the public toilets in the women's restrooms! We sure as hell don't use them! Our mothers screamed our whole childhood: Sitting is forbidden! Germs jump! These bacteria are lethal! And by God, if there isn't one of those purse hooks, you had better fig-ure out how to hold it between your knees, while standing!

I sat and wondered why all the hunks that walked through these doors in their camouflage and boots, fishing poles and SUVs, were married. Every last one of them. Damn.

6:32 P.M. Just closed the drive thru. Off to dream about a *single* Prince Charming…

3-22 38° Sunny.

B-52 Latte: A shot of B-52 syrup, espresso shots, steamed milk.

7:44 A.M. Down again today to *really* pick up the mower this time. I had been off the mountain so much lately, I felt like a city slicker. I will probably start Egg McMuffin withdrawals when I'm stuck back home. The mower bill came to $349 – this damn machine better be good to me for *years*! I think I will mow the field tonight, since it's one of my "look-like-hell-and-don't-give-a-shit" days. Might as well spray my greasy hair with grass clippings.

11:42 A.M. My espresso machine maintenance man was due any minute and I knew this repair was going to take hours. I called up my wild and crazy Rosie and told her she had to come over for a debate – from A to Z. I will need the company! Even the customers who came in and found the machine down didn't care. They just hung out and listened to her. They left howling at the antics she described about her old man! Rosie was the female impersonator of a bar hopping, truck driving, Cinderella who never found her Prince. She entertained us all by describing Ex-Con as a lazy slob of a controlling, asshole husband. "My hubby is *such* a couch potato that I wish I had a spatula large enough to flip him over once a day. His socks are *so* dirty that when I open the washing machine lid, they race through the house to be the first ones in the tub. His ears are *so* dirty – who needs bees? My old man plans for his future by buying two cases of beer!" We all laughed and cried for her at the same time.

I handed her a free iced 24-ounce mocha with whip for the show. Any talent scouts out there?

12:19 P.M. Scanner: There was a shooting in Crag Rock over a property line dispute. This was down the hill only twelve miles but sounded like something that would happen in "Wild-Wild-West-Saratogan." I could just see the headlines now: "Newcomer male slays old-timer female resident, who won't budge ¼ of an inch for the new fence he is erecting – on *his* property!" I was sorry to report, though, he did shoot her in the chest and killed her!

I drove the mower off the pick-up, along the same wood slats, while I still had a few people here in the store poised over the phone, ready to dial 911! Now I am back down to earth and safe!

5:00 P.M. Yard work time. "Y'all have to leave now" …

3-23 28° Sunny.

Peach Pie Latte: A shot of peach syrup, espresso shots, steamed milk, and sprinkled cinnamon.

7:04 A.M. Could not sleep in. So, I headed out early for a scenic drive up and over the North Cascades Highway Loop. I thought I needed a break. I got about fifteen miles from home and had to turn around out of guilt! *I must get a life!* Guess I haven't *survived* Catholicism after all…good thing – sold ten flamingos and lots of hot and iced lattes.

1:11 P.M. I had a gal come *on to me* today. An hour later, so did a guy. Whew! I was worried that I had finally gone over-the-top, with my jeans, boots, and all that body-toning manual labor. Then add days without make-up.

6:10 P.M. My yard looks delightful. I finally took a break and laid my body down on the picnic table, staring up at the sky. I watched the bats zooming about, with Butch right at my side. He loves it when I do that. He is such a pal. I closed my eyes and tuned into the sounds of the river, the distant birds chirping, and the occasional train. Butch nuzzled me now and then with his wet nose as if to say, "Come on, mom, get up and get back to work, so I can chase you around."

I sometimes wonder how I can enjoy this existence. I remember when I used to look at this yard with such panic and confusion; I could not even spend two minutes out back…alone. Without the kids' screams and giggles and the confidence of a husband within 150 feet, I was lost. I could not imagine lighting a fire and getting any enjoyment out of it. I thought it would kill me to even try and smile, while the flames gave me warmth and dried my constant tears. But, golly, here I was alone now, and I could not imagine it *any other way*. With only God as my partner, this had become my peace. I no longer had to prepare those gourmet hot-dog dinners, devoured in five minutes, as the kids all ran off on their pre-planned excursions. I was more alone then…in a deeper sense. I would love women to see the beauty, peace, and serenity in solo existence, until Mr. Perfect falls from that star-filled sky.

7:45 P.M. And a goodnight to all…

3-24 36° Sun.

Mexican Mocha: Two bags of Mexican hot chocolate, espresso shots, steamed milk.

8:29 A.M. Clouds are moving in now.

3:01 P.M. Another slow day; only a few espressos and its late afternoon.

3:41 P.M. Fuck, I was almost robbed! My email to our sheriff read: "I had some real scary folks in this evening. Two cars drove up. Two tattooed non-smiling, big men came in looking for pit bull or rooster items, "For symbolism," they said. What in the friggin' hell does that mean? Didn't sound good! I told them that I had no paraphernalia of that sort but go ahead and look through the store. Then the second car unloaded, and a stoned-to-the-gills white gal stumbled in followed by a Hispanic man. All of them spread throughout the store. I did not leave my desk. The last one to enter went back out and moved his car about six feet closer to the store, angled so that I could not read the plates. He returned and they all started bringing items up to the desk. I was ringing up the register like mad, giving them discounts because of the volume. I had been told to just rattle on about nothing, keep up the conversation, while I dialed some of the local's telephone numbers. Shit! No one was home! The druggy handed me two $100 bills, knowing full well I should not have that kind of change. But between the register and my purse, I just made it. They all left, and I locked the doors in a flash. One of them came up to the drive-thru and said they need to get back in for the restroom. I tell him, "Sorry, we're closed now," and I pointed to the Porta Potty. He was not pleased. They all tried both doors.

I was weak in the knees! But finally got a chance to dial 911, and the dispatcher stayed on the line with me until they were out of sight. They had the merchandise and were coming back to get *their* money and more of *mine* and any additional merchandise that pleased them. I am sure of it!

6:12 P.M. I am really going to hate the day I must shoot my gun, other than at Coke bottles! But I will…

3-25 42° Partly sunny.

Mocha Shot: A shot of chocolate, espresso shots, steamed Half & Half.

8:42 A.M. Three huge, 250-plus lb. men came in today. They went directly back into the gift shop. No chance to really check them out. One came back and said they had a question and would I follow him to the back room. I checked out their wheels and they were pulling a boat, with a nice enough SUV and it *seemed* like they were sporty fishermen. I do not usually go where I can get trapped, especially when I am outnumbered, but I took the chance. They just *felt* normal. And that is all I've got most of the time…my woman's intuition! I told them that I had some freaks in last night and they had *better be* on the *up-and-up.* They felt bad for scaring me and just wanted to buy two big pots from the back, espressos, and then be on their way to their favorite "hole."

Jumpy me today. I will be on *high alert* for about a week, after something like that happens. It's not real common, thank God.

Here is a story from the days gone by, regarding a thief who visited this place.

BOWER'S CAMP STORE ROBBER:

A man walked in to rob the Bowers' one night in the 1940s. He pulled out his gun and pointed it at Luke Bower. Mr. Bower was ready to hand over the cash when suddenly, the cylinder fell out of the robber's gun and onto the counter! Luke grabbed the cylinder. Then he grabbed his machete and just about lopped off the thug's left arm. That robber didn't get too far with a gash like that! He is lucky...the shotgun would have been next.

4:55 P.M. Enough for today, or I am *guaranteed* nightmares...

3-26 40° Pouring, soggy, and cold.

The Leprechaun: A shot of Irish cream and crème de menthe syrups, espresso shots, steamed milk.

8:00 A.M. It is sopping wet out. It is Easter weekend. Some tourists stopped for refreshments and had lots of questions about the area and especially the unique, abandoned Saratogan Hotel. I explained that a nice, married couple from Wisconsin bought it for $500K. The new owners could just imagine a classy Bed & Breakfast with a high-end restaurant. They were willing to put $1.3 million into their dream. This dream turned into a nightmare – since the building was unfortunately on the National Historical Register. They had not been informed of this during their escrow. The real estate agent was hiding out in the hills. Dealing with the city, county, and Historical Society eventually destroyed their vision, and all their plans were shot to hell...along with their marriage.

So here it proudly stood – like some hallowed ghost.

12:07 P.M. Buck came by. "I need an emergency hug!" What the hell? No! I did give him a free iced white chocolate mocha instead, because I wanted to grill him about the Crag Rock shooting over the property dispute. He said that the woman was in her late forties and she had lived there for like seventeen years. The guy was a weekender, who had just bought his place and she was giving him lots of shit about inches here and there. He threatened her and finally *that was it*. She flipped and got her very own posse involved, all the old-time residents in the same development. They burned down a dilapidated old shed on his property and then he really flipped out. Walked over and shot her dead, point blank. Wow.

MORE RAILROAD AND ROUGH TOWN HISTORY

Paul Manning was the founder of Saratogan. Saratogan became an especially important switching yard in 1890. The town was the deciding factor on whether they would attach the helper steam locomotives and allow the trains to continue east in the ferocious weather. In

1894, there was a Saratogan depot, machine shop, round-house, coal chutes, and a water tank. The town was plat-ted, by the Mannings in 1899. Manning was the first town postmaster. Saratogan then opened the Saratogan Lumber Company, where railroad ties, lumber, and snow-shed timbers were built for the Pacific Railway. In 1897, Peter McCaster engineered the first passenger train over the switchbacks of Mountain Peak. But he soon lost an arm in a railroading accident. He was the culprit who first opened our large saloon— the Train Blow Tavern. It still stands today, with the same name, and still serves a humongous amount of alcohol. It was and still is a real whistle stop!

Some of the Manning offspring have also walked through my doors. My daily view is looking up at Manning Mountain.

Back in 1981, I purchased my first package of buffalo burgers from Manning's store. And I did not die...

5:57 P.M. Another day and another couple of bucks...

3-27 40° Raining. Easter Day.

> Raspberry/Blackberry Mocha: Shot raspberry and blackberry syrups, a shot of chocolate syrup, espresso shots, steamed milk.

8:49 A.M. It stopped snowing on the pass – completely. The roads were not slick and icy anymore and it should help save lives this holiday weekend. We heard a Good Samaritan was waving to cars to slow them down because of the icy conditions on another summit, Squillene Pass, last night. He was hit by a truck and killed. A trucker didn't see him in time and spun out of control.

It is Easter.

11:33 A.M. I have been working right through Easter and Christmas for a couple of years now. People need me and there are hundreds of thirsty and sleepy drivers who need espresso!

Boone from Stonewall, who has been trying to get another date with me, came in for a boy-girl talk. He is dating and sleeping with a gal right now, "I'm really not into her. She has a great ass but not my type, really, and is taking up my *whole* damn weekend!" Excuse me, fucker-mister, "*You* are *exactly* why I'm not dating! *These* women lie next to your buck-naked body. *You* whisper sweet nothings, gently stroke skin, pound it home, sweatin' like a pig, then immediately fall off and fall asleep. And all the time you are thinking to yourself, 'She's not my type'!" "But it wouldn't be like that with *you*, Christy!" I rolled my eyes. "In a pig's eye!"

4:40 P.M. Everyone is at their destination – dinner, resort, relatives, or such. It gets a touch lonely – so thank God I am busy.

6:45 P.M. And, yes, I am still here. What else is there to do? Buck brought me a care package – a heaping plate of his mama's Easter dinner. That was so kind! I handed him some butter rum lattes, with sprinkles of nutmeg, for the whole household. Shit…now that I think back, I did not even do that for any of my *husbands*.

7:55 P.M. Goodnight, Easter Bunny…

3-28 40° Raining.

Cherry Cream Americano: A shot of cherry syrup, shot of Half & Half, espresso shots, hot water.

8:22 A.M. Late last night, I decided to go to the bank with my weekend's funds! I was getting into the truck and going to drive it down fast and get back quick. Right then a light flashed across the railroad tracks – across the highway. I changed my mind – I was not going anywhere! Took my purse back upstairs, put the pistol in my back jeans pocket, and grabbed my two-million-candle-watt flashlight. I went to the other end of the property and beamed up into the trees. Long story short – the troll and I played flashlight games. I think it was BOO. I called Buck and he arrived in two-shakes to put an immediate end to the "beam-game." He will alert the Forest Service tomorrow, just to make sure some escaped criminal is not watching my every move. Plus, the loggers will fall those trees soon and then no one would be able to camp above me again. Freaky! Hurry loggers.

OLD LOGGERS FACT

For all of you that have wondered just why loggers cut the bottoms off their pants legs – a true explanation for this hill-billy-looking style – and I quote: "We had ta. Fer gettin' goin' if the highball whistle went off and ya had ta run like the wind….or run like a deer through the brush cuz that damn seam'l get caught on a Y in a twig. That's when the log 'll run over ya, 'n squish ya and smear ya like a slug."

2:30 P.M. I'm outta here. Can't sit doing nothin' for one more moment…

3-29 35° Mixed rain with snow.

A Racehorse: Not a quad! Five shots of espresso and steamed milk!

8:59 A.M. Another slooooooooow day. Had a *terrific* time organizing supplies. Espresso cart re-stocked after the crazy holiday. Refrigerator is full and clean, and I'm thrilled. Cupboards tidy. Counters bleached. Equipment washed.

2:31 P.M. The sheriff came by to see how I was doing. He told me that the driver of the Jeep was a well-known gym rat. He had many friends. The passenger was his girlfriend, and the kids in the back were her sister's. They were all severely injured and went through various surgeries. The lady in the Subaru had fallen asleep at the wheel after camping with her husband and son in eastern Washington. The van behind the crash was more family of the Jeep occupants and they were on their way to going camping together for the weekend in Lake Chelan. They had just left our gas station in Saratogan, and two miles later dead. Wow, this will haunt me for ages.

4:55 P.M. I just had a group of idiots in who could not decide between hot or cold drinks. None of them had minds of their own. I started tapping my fingers…an awfully bad habit. They didn't seem to notice or care, so I took the cue and decided not to either. I sat back down to eBay. That was when their minds started working in overdrive, like every damn time. Sit…start computer work or grab a telephone and their brains become crystal-clear and pissy! First, the one blond (sorry gals) had to get rid of her gum before her brain would work. So, I started with one of the males. He began the whole process of guiding this group of sheep, "I go off cliff…you go off cliff." They all voted for hot, which cooled me down a bit with the less manual labor needed to create their concoctions. And the "irritants" were finally gone. Took twenty-four minutes to serve four drinks! Broke a record!

Tonight, I swept and straightened outside. BOO wanted to play "flashlight" again, but mine stayed on my dresser upstairs. I just hope he is the hero-type and will come and save me should I ever be in serious danger! And who knows...I am still *hoping* it is him...

6:57 P.M. I want no playing tonight, so goodnight to BOO and all...

3-30 38° Partly everything!

> **Borgia: Two shots crème de cacao, espresso shots, and whipped cream.**

9:00 A.M. ABSOLUTELY NOTHING GOING ON – STILL – AGAIN. VERY BORING, so I will give you some of my wedded-bliss history. *Everyone* asks me about this! Liz and me...

MARRIAGES 1 THROUGH 7!

No. 1. We tied the knot in 1980. It lasted four years and produced my lovely daughter. Post-partum blues, PTSD and the long, dark days of Alaska, along with his abusive, chauvinistic behavior, took care of this one. I was mentally *toast!* I wanted the prince to save me.

No. 2. Six months later, I rushed to the altar with my high school sweetheart. He had heard that I had gotten a divorce and telephoned me from Texas. He flew out to San Diego where I now lived near family. We said, "Hi," got married, and moved to Texas. It lasted a month and I returned to California. He loved his drugs and alcohol. Again, PTSD & OCD caused me to panic and rely on him to make me happy. Save me...

No. 3. Six months later, I married a genuinely nice man. I got pregnant immediately and had my son. Post-partum blues pretty much ate through that one too. I turned into a complete groundbreaking, maniac – half-cocked in all directions – to keep out of the depths of depression! One and a half years later, I ran out the door. Running from me, myself and I. The voices in my head, chasing me.

No. 4. Two months later, while working in a bar, I decided the bartender was awesome. Unbeknownst to me, he was into booze, drugs, and women. Of course, if I have given the relationship some time, maybe a few hours, a few days, this all would have been revealed, during a normal dating period. This marriage involved my first 911 call with him showing up late one night on something like PCP. He was going to kill me and tried to do just that, first in the house and again in the middle of the street. An angel in a suit with golden blonde hair to his shoulders took him on. Saved my life. It lasted for one month.

No. 5. A year after I had sworn off marriage, completely, I met my fifth husband. This one amazingly lasted twelve years! Great guy with a fucked-up wife. We were wonderful business partners, but that was the only partner I was capable of being. I was the controlling, abusive, manic mess this time around, while he kindly allowed it. I made him pay for all the previous abuse I endured through my lifetime. PTSD in reverse with my OCD spilling out into my home, children and husband, No one could do things perfect, clean perfect, be perfect.

Intermission: Is this truth just too colorful – married five times before the age of thirty! But I am so happy, happy today, that this is *history*! No. 5 and I are still good friends and I made amends from my heart.

No. 6. Within six-months of that crushing divorce (call it mid-life crisis to the max!), I married shortly again to my second round of 911 calls. I was choked, kicked, forced into slave-sex – from love to hate – and landed in divorce court once again. I was diagnosed with OCD (Obsessive-Compulsive Disorder & PTSD). No shit! This idiot and I lasted 1.5 years. Still running for my life, from life, from myself and the entire world. It all scared me, and I felt unique in a strange way. I was wondering what I was doing here in the first place. Why was I born in a world that made no sense to me? It was dirty, wrong, frightening, unreliable, untrustworthy and plain foreign. I knew I just needed to get back to work and forget about everything else.

No. 7. I swore off men completely! And I meant it this time! Then, three months later, I ran into "The Knight," with the armor of a sheriff's badge! *How much safer can a marriage get?* A whole different world and breed this time...but my third round of 911 calls. We married in Las Vegas while we were on a buying trip for my store. It lasted a year. It was the seventh time for both! I needed a lobotomy! I surely wanted one...

So, I have hopefully answered all the questions as to why I am this single, white, female, business owner, isolated up in the sticks and unable to carry a very high opinion of most males – yet... And now with sharing my past of seven men and seven marriages you may understand why I live with my furry and feathered creatures and fight off the male two-legged creatures...My mantra these days: *May each moment create wisdoms unknown...loneliness can be golden...and solo is special!*

5:00 P.M. Still, a slit-of-an-eye-out for Mr. Perfect...

3-31 38° Partly sunny.

Vanilla Kahlua Breve: A 1/2 shot of Kahlua and vanilla syrups, espresso shots, steamed Half & Half.

8:28 A.M. The sheriff came by today responding to my "Robbers were here" email. "Yes, Christy, that last scary group of four *was* probably going to rob you! And put that damn second gun away. Or buy a new one. You have said it jams sometimes anyway! And *sometimes* is a pretty *crappy* word when it comes to describing a gun!"

I also got the scoop on BOO: He is in his fifties, short, trimmed hair, clean-shaven, and used to live the life of a normal citizen here in Saratogan. "Cody" was married back then and had a job. Now he lives in a nice (?) campsite of his own, with free flood light from my property, a fabulous river view, does not pay taxes, and gets to stare at me all day long. No one has ever done a background check on him and he lives "Clean and is accepted." The homeless Mission in Pacifica accepts him with open arms on extremely cold nights. I suppose he just jumps the train to get "down-below" those fifty miles. My son and I walked the tracks a few years ago, just for fun, from Saratogan to Snow Peak Mine. This was a thirty-five-mile trek, and it took us nine hours. We were walking along bridges that were over one hundred feet high, with wobbly railings. You could hear a regular North Coast Northern Railroad train coming by putting your ear to the track. It had a whistle to it. But the Pioneer passenger train is on top of you, lickety-split. One of the bridges in Crag Rock that spans the highway did not have *any* railing at all. We were in the middle and could hear the Pioneer coming. It was either we run for it or jump down thirty feet to the highway, where possibly we would get squished by a car. We ran and survived.

4:26 P.M. Just heard – THE SKI RESORT IS OPENING BOTH SATURDAY AND SUNDAY! I will be so busy! Hot damn dog!

5:33 P.M. Buck came by for his promised haircut. I chickened out. Couldn't touch him. Mustn't touch him. Just don't touch men period, girl! Leave them the hell-in-hibernation! You know how much you love your clean sheets!

6:00 P.M. Two customers in two hours and both families wanted cough drops… Later…

APRIL

The waves lap the shores in this cold, as
we cup and drink coveting warmth

4-01 38° Raining.

Sugar-Free Raspberry Mocha: A shot of sugar-free raspberry syrup, a
shot of sugar-free chocolate syrup, espresso shots, steamed milk.

7:48 A.M. A gal working at Mountain Peak Ski Resort, getting it ready for the
weekend, came by with a five-drink order in hand. Espresso booths must not
be open on Employees Only Day. It was exceedingly difficult for the ski resort
to re-open like this and get *decent* help. With our snow-void year, the good
employees went to other resorts around the country and/or got real jobs. She
said the skeleton crew needed some caffeine to get their *butts-in-gear*. Most of
the employees were stoners and couldn't get moving without a pick-me-up-
drug of *some* sort!

9:44 A.M. Buck stopped by. He kissed some railroad ass and was able to hoist
– lift – well, sorta steal, some free railroad ties and dropped them off for me to
sell. All the favors he's done for me, I guess I'll render him one back. I've got
the highway exposure for selling anything! He was lustful today, or at least is
pretending to be an old horn-dog. He was pointing to all the rips in his logging
pants – especially in the crotch region. He didn't believe in underwear (damn
hillbilly) and so he was proudly trying to show off major (his words) tools.
"Look at these peek-a-boo holes!" "Immediately!" I bowed, with a scowl and
smirk. But…as he is bending over to unload the railroad ties, his wrinkled, old,
silly balls were hanging out the slits! Cars pulling in from the west could easily
see this vision. In my opinion, these cullions were a grotesque sight on their
own, in bad lighting! All kidding aside, these railroad ties were good to have
on site – looked like I had a man around the joint!

3:00 P.M. My loggers came by for their usual granitas and they may be doing the logging job across from me. I hoped so since these guys were mostly married and appeared educated. They flirted a bit here and there, but all-in good fun and they were always in a hurry to get home to their sweethearts. All loggers seemed to know Buck. "Oh, that scraggly guy that drives an old dump truck?" Yup.

5:00 P.M. I am closing and heading down to give that promised / cancelled / promised / cancelled haircut to Mr. Buck, scraggy. He has a bright, lit kitchen with no curtains – the whole town can watch. Course, I don't need customers lined out my espresso doors tomorrow for a shaggy hair trim! Cooties thrive up here…

4-02 38° Cloudy.

Carmelo: Plenty of caramel sauce, espresso shots, and steamed milk.

8:02 A.M. Skiers were roaring up to Mountain Peak Ski Resort for their "surprise" weekend.

11:17 A.M. When I first awoke this morning, there was an abandoned car in my parking lot. Should I or shouldn't I call my tow company? That was the question. Could I use it as decoy car to pull in more customers? I had signs posted everywhere: TOW AWAY FOR NON-CUSTOMERS! I delayed the phone call and was glad I did. It was a customer who found me closed and decided to take a walk – waiting patiently for this damn female owner to get her war paint on and get her butt down and serve him espresso! My macaw, Mister, was blasting customers' ears out. Birds get in moods too, and he had a feather up his nose today. Buck must have had a nasty *ingrown* up *his* nostril last night too! God, he was humorless! And I was cutting his mop as a favor! I was determined to survive emotionally and kept my mouth shut, though I gave him two choices. One: This will be the very last free trim – or two: unless you shut the hell up, you will be sad to see one side two inches higher than the other.

He recently inherited more historic goodies from his neighbor's place. The old man was being shipped off to "The Home." Buck reveled in showing me his newly acquired antiques, knowing I was turning pea-green inside. He knew I'd do just about *anything* to get my hands-on multi-decade collectables from around this area. He showed me a copper kettle, some antique ashtrays, and an old salt and pepper set. He wouldn't part with any of these goodies without some goodies from me. The shit can burn…

2:58 P.M. Four "happenings" today - four coincidences (?). First, two customers came in, in a row, and bought a "bear" item from the very same spot in this jam-packed, warehouse-sized gift shop. Then, two families in a row asked for licorice. Two groups came in and asked for mochas with orange flavoring.

Following these flukes, my scanner went off two times in a row, alerting the ambulance of two separate local residents having heart problems! Double-Day Saturday.

What is next? Maybe two princely men arriving wanting to whisk me off on two separate white stallions?

5:35 P.M. No thank you, gentlemen. I am busy with a barista life…

4-03 36° Partly sunny. Daylight Savings Time begins!

White Cow: A shot of chocolate syrup, shot of vanilla syrup, espresso shots, steamed milk.

7:43 A.M. No excuses for not walking and exercising, ya lazy, old broad! The evenings are light now! This body needs some firming! I am open and the highway is full of cars, heading to the slopes.

12:11 P.M. My eBay pooped out. I was trying to revise items and reduce some prices, but this computer and server were slower than tacky turds!

1:53 P.M. The drive-thru was full, with three cars waiting! Two sets of gift buyers were standing in line waiting for me to ring up the register! "People… please slow down a bit…let me catch up! And you gift buyers, here's some newspaper; can ya please wrap your goods yourself?!" Steam espressos, ring a sale, take an order, squirt some whip, wrap more gifts. Here and there, hither and fro – in a whirl. Lovin' it!

6:37 P.M. Mom invited me to dinner. Three hours roundtrip and I was bushed. Next time…

4-04 38° Raining.

A Wet Cappuccino: Wet foamed milk and espresso shots.

7:18 A.M. I heard at least two customers stop while I was still upstairs getting dressed. My birds tell me when someone is near, then the dog and then horns of these impatient lunkheads. Drives me crazy, and I immediately started rushing and could not get the right foot in the right hole of the jeans. I have counted now – missed five cars. But what can a girl do? Cannot run down and serve half-naked!

8:03 A.M. I had to rush to the post office before even opening – did not know how many more paying guests I missed – and didn't want to! I had to mail a *leg*. One of my eBay customers called saying that his two white flamingos arrived today with only three legs. I remembered putting all four in the box, but, oh well…customers are always right…unfortunately. Okay, just in case anybody is chompin' at the bit for a piece of useless information, I mailed it in an old dozen-red-roses box, left over from Buck and it only cost $1.52 to ship the two-foot-long kitschy thing.

I have had a few customers today so far…Espresso, cream, sugar, foamy, no-foam.

3:08 P.M. Scanner: Aid response at 310 Sugar Lane; a fifty-five-year-old female with chest pain. That was another *local* heart call. What is in the air?!

ONE MORE HISTORIC AMBULANCE STORY FROM DAYS GONE BY...

A 1942 Chevy 6-cylinder fire truck, which held 500 gallons of water in case of fire, could only top 40 mph. On sharp corners, they would have to let up on the siren button, since it dimmed the needed headlights. This was a beast of a rig and it was anyone's guess if it would even start when needed. Volunteers would all jump in their cars and race to the station, dust-a-flying, using hand signals for show. They were called in on the old ringer phones and each guy would write all the information on a chalkboard during their rush. People would come out on the sidewalks to watch this show, every time. There was one man who would always come out to the intersection, where these speeding vehicles would convene. He nominated himself "Traffic-Control." Hunter would show up with a wrecker, hook a chain onto the fire truck, and drag it forward to help give the "starter" a little momentum. Then once it got started, the wrecker would get behind and push it. Even with the weight of the water, sometimes they could get it up to 80 mph instead of the normal 40 – depending on the seriousness of the emergency.

6:08 P.M. Long day. Upstairs for din-din; I think there is a can of tuna and some eggs. The excitement of it all...

4-05 36° Partly sunny.

Almond Steamer: A shot of almond syrup, steamed milk, lightly stir.

7:33 A.M. My brother is still in love with my best friend. I have told them both that if either one pulls any shit on the other, I will personally settle the score with a merciless vendetta! Playing cupid with two people you care about is foolhardy. I am trying not to second-guess myself. They were so miserable when their mates left them that I HAD to intervene! Didn't I?

1:10 P.M. An Army rig stopped in. This was very unusual in this neck of the woods and I hoped that these boys had their sexual harassment training. Eight of them stepped in and I offered my military discount. Four of them ordered quads! Quad mochas, to be exact. "Long drive to Yakima today and we have a hell of a weekend of 'play war' ahead of us. We are trying to ramp-up early with these." Another big guy ordered a 32-ounce cherry Italian soda. A gal (I believe it was a gal anyway) ordered a 24-ounce blackberry smoothie, "With the works." The last two only wanted hot chocolates. Great sale with very well-behaved troops. "Thanks, gang, for everything you do for this country!"

5:10 P.M. Buck stopped in for his usual white chocolate mocha. He point-blank asked, "How can ya go this long without sex? Come on, Christy. Tell the truth this time. Who are ya doin'?" Sigh… "Buck, are we going to have to re-enter that 'fuck-you' argument again?"

6:17 P.M. I'm so *over* this stale subject…

4-06 36° Sunny and strangely muggy.

Irish Mocha: A shot of chocolate syrup, a shot of Irish cream syrup, espresso shots, steamed milk.

8:00 A.M. I *had* to take off. I am *sick* of this place.

My first stop was at an office supply store, to get copies made of a historic photo of our Lumberman's Restaurant. I snagged it from Buck's antique frame – without handing over any favors! In my car again and it was deadsville! It would not even consider starting! Luckily, Schueller's happened to be just a shopping center away. I did not want, or need, this to be a major repair bill! At the counter, "Lady, can ya tell me what kind of a sound it was makin' when ya turned the key?" I embarrassingly attempted. "Is it like a Tick. Tick. Tick. Tick?" He smiled, "It's probably only a battery, ma'am. But I have bad news, we no longer install for customers." "Perrrrrrfect! What am I supposed to do?" He suggested I could first try their jumper box, which wasn't any lighter than carrying a new battery the two blocks! I got to my car, popped the hood, and quickly hooked up the black to black, red to red.

A lady walked by with an amazed look on her face, "Gosh, you know how to do that?" I smiled at the city slicker and told her, "We women can do ANYTHING when we HAVE TO!" Left and returned the box.

11:11 A.M. Next stop was an alteration shop, run by an exceedingly kind Korean lady. "I need my bra rebuilt!" She looked at the bra, then at me, and her awe turned to sorrow. She suggested out loud in her broken English, "Buy new one." I explained that this particular model wasn't available anymore, "You just *have* to understand, lady! Four boob jobs later and a lawsuit against Dow, I have finally found the perfect heavenly bra and *need* it for life." "Solly, lady, *nothing* can do with ragtag mess!" Tonight, I will be sewing.

5:55 P.M. I am home and for some reason opened. I've made nine espressos. Thank goodness my Jeep got me home. I have an old 1995 Jeep with 195,000 miles on it that still runs. No complaints.

6:39 P.M. Just another day as an Isolated Barista…

4-07 38° Partly rainy.

Lemon Cream Cappuccino: A shot of lemon syrup, foamed Half & Half, espresso shots, lightly stir.

8:48 A.M. Back at it and just in time to welcome Jack and Pete. "Christy, we're sure glad you hit the lottery and can go cat'n around willy-nilly as you please, but you have obligations!" They stopped by yesterday with me not here. Jack's wife just informed him that she was leaving, divorcing him. I fucking knew it! He had a stroke awhile back and while he was bed-ridden, she began selling all their rental houses, under the pretense of lightening his load. That is a royal point off the women's column. Served a few mochas, Italian sodas, and a couple more Americanos. I think I will take a long shower and clean my house tonight.

6:49 P.M. Upstairs…

4-08 38° Sunny.

The Cow: A shot of chocolate syrup, shot of almond syrup, espresso shots, steamed milk.

7:41 A.M. A driver of one of those snowboard-racked cars stopped in for a double mocha breve. "Hey, I almost bought this place ten years ago or so, back when it was $60K!" "I bought it for a cool $55K," I bragged. I pulled out some of the old photos to show him before and after. This guy still standing and sipping now owned one of our Trout Creek Estate lots up here in Saratogan, about eight miles west of me! Going backwards, he lived in Redmond for twenty-five years, long before it was Bill's domain. I screamed, "I grew up there also!" He spent the rest of his life in Poulsbo, a darling resort town, requiring a ferry, on the west side of Puget Sound. I spent seven long years there, in the 1990s, trying to eke out a living and get the kids raised. He said shakily, "I'm so blown away by all of our similarities, I gotta leave before it gets really spooky!" I laughed because similarities and small world situations walked through my doors constantly. And were considered my gifts.

9:55 A.M. The sheriff cruised by to do a business check. He had a civilian in his cruiser as a "rider" for the day. I used to love doing this with No. 7. Once you are married to the cop, the fun is over (for more reasons than one); the precinct does not allow *spouses* to ride with their *master*.

2:33 P.M. A fellow flew through the door – he needed a *hit* right now! He left home about two hours ago without food and forgot his coffee! He ordered a quad espresso with a touch of cream. I was compressing lots of grounds while he admired my macaw. He was in the service in Honduras where macaws were out in full force. His platoon ended up with a pet – Hank the macaw. He recalled, "He hung around the barracks and would attend our formations. He eventually would perch up on the porch as a bystander and shriek, 'Fuck you' over and over, as the sergeant bellowed orders! It was nearly impossible for us hob-nailed-boots to keep a straight face and Hank caused many a bellow, 'Drop and give me 50'!"

5:26 P.M. Left to do laundry and pitiful things like that. No "locals" even loved me today…

4-09 37° Sunny.

Sugar-Free Blackberry Italian Soda: Ice, 2 shots of sugar-free black-berry syrup, soda water within an inch, top off with Half & Half.

8:17 A.M. A lady strolled in for a sugar-free vanilla cappuccino. She had heard about my espresso/gift/bird store and wanted to know if I would be willing to adopt her Quaker parakeet. Yes! Again, it would be competition for my macaw, Mister, but he seemed to adjust quickly and stopped trying to bite off my nose in a week or so.

The Health Department is going to think they have come to the wrong place. This is becoming a zoo! I will pick up the Quaker next time I am down this hill.

1:31 P.M. BOO lit three fires today. He must be freezing up there in his woods. Probably cooking up squirrel. *Will we ever know?*

2:27 P.M. Buck came in looking spiffy. Said he came by to give me a hug before he headed into the woods for a firewood hunt. Yeah, right! Fresh clothes, shower, shave, and mousse in the hair for a little bit of sawing? Sprucing up for the pitch and sawdust group? Well, he was not believed or getting a hug here – on his way to get *more,* somewhere else. I had bet my life on it. He is such a poor liar, and that was the part that bothered me the most – NOT the other woman! And you men out there…just *try* and explain him out of this one! Even you guys know that he is heading over to the girlfriend's house to *snatch* a little *snatch*! I really believe women hate *lying* more than they hate *fungus*!

I planned to sew this evening – alone. I will attempt to repair my tattered bra. Could this pitiful little thing even *handle* re-construction? If not, was there another solution? Even Nordstrom could not handle this patient.

4:01 P.M. Finally, some levity to the day! A darling, handholding senior couple came in for lattes on their way over the mountain for a weekend of golf. The husband asked if he could tell me a good one. Sure! "Three couples head off on a two-week spree, but unfortunately they were all killed in a disastrous collision. Up in heaven, the first husband is standing at The Master for his interview. "You didn't make it. All you thought of your whole miserable life was money, money, money. You even married a woman called Penny!" The second husband sheepishly heads towards the throne, where he also is told, "You can go no further; all you ever thought about the entire time you were on earth was hoochand moonshine! You even picked a wife named Sherry!" The third husband steers his wife toward the exit – "No sense us going through the drill, Fanny."" I caught him giving his wife a little pat on the patootie as they left my store.

6:34 P.M. Closing and dragging upstairs. Not from the work but the *lack* of it…

4-10 35° Sunny.

> **Moose Milk: A shot of rum syrup (or real), a splash of almond syrup, steamed milk.**

8:36 A.M. I changed my espresso water filter on my cart last night. Thank goodness for certain tools – like oil filter wrenches!

2:47 P.M. I needed to work on some new cart signs. Mine were looking shabby. All baristas had an array of signs plastered on their cubicles. I did not believe the customers could ever read them all, even in several visits, but there *was* a reason for posting each and every one: WE MAY REFUSE SERVICE TO ANYONE * SUGAR FREE FLAVORS * REGULAR FLAVORS * MENUS * SPECIAL FOR THE DAY * NO SMOKING * NO PETS * NO RESTROOMS * TIPS HERE * ICED * BLENDED DRINKS * HOURS OF SERVICE * TRASH CAN HERE * SNACKS * SODAS * PET AREA * PARKING * NO PARKING * SOY * RICE * TEA * ETC * ETC * ETC *

6:00 P.M. I need to paint one more in fluorescent electric blue: NICE, HONEST, FUNNY, HAPPY, COZY, SINGLE MALE WANTED FOR AFTER HOURS... wearing a cowboy hat...

4-11 38° Cloudy.

Turtle Truffle: A shot of chocolate syrup, splash of caramel syrup, splash of praline syrup, espresso shots, steamed Half & Half.

7:56 A.M. There must be a rainbow out there somewhere! Buck braved the rains just to come in and check up on me. Earlier he almost caught me sneaking off with Boone, my gorgeous local Harley buddy, who offered to go with me to unload a truck full of two-week old, disgusting trash. I told Buck to stay away, once again. He is coming around too often lately, trying to sweet talk (*BS*) me into another trip-to-the-sheets. *NO!* He is minimally seeing his old gal friend. Lately, he has been a barfly too. New act.

11:33 A.M. Two firemen from Florida came crashing through the doors; firefighters just seem bigger than life! One of them bought some extra chocolate-covered espresso beans for his latte. The other one, a wimp-decaf-drinker, heard my scanner and immediately got on my case! He called me a "media spy." I explained, "I am alone here and get all kinds, from all over the world, on this scenic highway. It is nice to get a warning of what's coming and going around here, before a full-blown surprise barges in. So back the heck off!" We smiled.

1:34 P.M. Speaking of firemen, I have sure had some strange ones in here! Fireman No.1 was from Seattle and right before his retirement had participated in 9-11. He was coming around regularly for a while and was extremely interesting. Then the flirting started. Soon the bringing of gifts and offering to be my handyman began. He asked me to dinner four times in a row, but he was one of those guys who were divorced but incapable of moving out and taking care of himself – or simply was still married and wanted to play! I kept him at bay. He always paid $20 for a double mocha and some extra chocolate-covered espresso beans! One day he came through the drive-thru instead of coming in to visit. He started giving me a hard time, "Look what I just dropped out my window!" When I bent down to look over the windowsill, he suddenly took a fist-full of my hair, pulling my head down. He was hurting me! I reached up and grabbed his wrist and told him to "LET GO - NOW!" Luckily, a car drove up at the same time and he dropped his grasp immediately. I didn't even want to think about how long he could have kept up this sick-o-hideous-game! "You-are-to-leave-this-very-moment-and-if-I-ever-see-your-face-again-I-will-call-911-AND-report-you-to-your-old-station!" He apologized with that wicked smile that said, "Gotcha, gal – and that's for turning me down so many times!" I slammed the window and he never returned. Unfortunately, you young men and women out there, this abusive psycho is still a part-time trainer for firefighter recruits!

2:21 P.M. No. 2 Fireman-slash-customer was a regular and had a cabin in Icicle Town. His claim to fame was that he was a model for the firemen calendar! He seemed to be a nice enough person and we'd had some good conversations about all of life- 'n-limb. One day he had new news: "I'm going to try out for the calendar again, I miss all that hoopla!" He had already emailed me a full body shot of himself, at his home, in some stupid damn thong-thing. Sorry, gals, I can't insert photo – lawsuits, attorneys, etc.! I told him I forwarded the email to all my of my single and married gal friends and they ALL wanted his phone number! I was being sarcastic as hell, but he was such a conceited cock he could not even recognize bullshit. He said, "Hey, I have that same under-wear on today. See..." He proceeded to pull his shirt up and flex for his audience – me. Then started to unzip his pants and dropped them to his ankles! I about shit! What if a customer walked in? They would think I was running a sex for lattes business! I screamed for him to get dressed! He did and was laughing, not really "getting it!" I blasted him with an email that night – he got my drift now! Hadn't been around since, either. And I thought <u>cops were kinky!</u>

7:02 P.M. Monday night. Just prior to closing, Harley Dennis came in for his Americano. He was thinking of trading logging for driving trains. The North Coast Northern Railroad had hired him. "You are a *dead man* if you honk that horn in the middle of the night." He was down these days; the latest chick had flown the coup. His words, "We all have needs. Sex is a necessity. And yes, even if I don't really like the '*skirt*.' It's for me to just use and enjoy – uncomplicated sex is supreme! Beats the hell outta getting beat-up in a close relationship." And I quote! Pigs.

7:33 P.M. Upstairs – and definitely alone now. Celibacy was reconfirmed for me today...

4-12 39° Partly sunny.

Tall Two Percent: A 12 oz. cup with espresso shots and steamed 2% milk.

8:55 A.M. The ring-ring broke the silence – and my whining. It was Clint 15 calling me back. Why in the hell did I dial his number when I was bored senseless the other night? Damn! He was just too appealing to completely eradicate from the brain, I guess. My mother and her girlfriend almost fell off their bingo chairs when they met him! He is definitely not settling for just anybody. We talked about having a fling again and of course it was tempting. I toyed with this prospect for a minute or two but got my brain back in gear and remembered the conversation just last night, with Harley Dennis professing to be using 'n abusing gals, men's favorite past-time! "No thanks!"

2:20 P.M. A huge hailstorm just blew through! Came in a flash, was gone in a jiff! I have a real date tonight – American Idol and my fluffy, furry Butch.

4:14 P.M. BOO has a fire going right now. Really do not like to picture what he is having for dinner.

4:26 P.M. Scanner: A local seventy-five-year-old male DOA, cold and stiff, on Rail Line Avenue. I wondered who had departed. Could it be one of my customers? My old local guys probably had poker parties with him that were quite the big past time down in the jail's basement in the years gone by, along with lots of whiskey and fights.

6:48 P.M. And closing. It was starting to snow and its April 12th. Luck 'o the Irish...

4-13 36° Sunny.

Orange & Brandy Latte: A shot of orange liquor, a shot of brandy (real), espresso shots, steamed milk.

8:00 – 11:00 A.M. I ran errands for hours. Ten minutes after I opened, a married *Christian* logger stopped in for a granita. He was loaded to the gills with trees. I asked if he wanted whip. *I still haven't figured out a safe way to ask the whipped-cream question; you wouldn't believe some of the answers I've heard from all the perverted men out there! I understand from other baristas that this is a daily issue for them too.* This God-fearing man was not any different. His comeback: "No, thanks. Whipping cream is for one thing only, sweetie. I call it navel cream and will lick it out any day." I wondered how his wife would feel if she heard that one? And his godly pastor? *Hypocrite!* Did these types of men really tickle their egos thinking their quips are *original*?

12:00 Noon. I have an eighth member of my bird family. The Quaker parakeet is mine! I picked him up from his owners this morning and it will take all day to get his cage cleaned and situated in this menagerie – this zoological garden.

1:59 P.M. A local drug dealer on his motorcycle-drug-taxi just zipped by. He has passed me twice. The sheriff's shift starts at 2:00 P.M., so they were in a hurry to get their drugs safely to their destinations. These druggies had the sheriff's arrival and departure times clocked to a science.

6:44 P.M. Mr. Clint 15 called again today and wanted to come up here on Friday night for a "backrub." Uh huh. I think under the circumstances, this may fall under the bogus "I promise to behave" bullhoagy lines category. I do revert to intellect…eventually. Backrubs should just be called coitus and get it over with – whose fooling who here? Reunion – NOT.

5:07 P.M. Some fun single gals came in and of course we were discussing hook-ups and liaisons within the first five minutes. Lattes, cappuccinos, and chai. One of the gals had a real date last night, "You know the kind…when they pay for dinner, enjoy dancing or at least pretend to, you laugh a lot and they drop you at your door with a bear hug and a little smooch, requesting to see you again. It was so refreshing and comfortable. I thought he might be my brother in disguise!"

7:00 P.M. Well, I saved the best for last! I got laid last night! Didn't get to sleep until 3:00 A.M. Buck! It has been five to six months! I know – I know…I swore I wasn't going to even *think* about getting tangled in the sheets, especially with him! It was glorious! It truly was! And I don't want to hear any flack about it! Didn't YOU ever make a mistake? Of course, this morning I felt eighty years old! It felt like a bad hangover when I didn't get my beauty sleep! Now you ask, what about the bar flies? (*Stupid Christy, stupid Christy!*) Something about "these-thar-hills". I must have been way *beyond* desperately lonely. Who used whom?

9:06 P.M. Maybe…*just* maybe…it was only a dream…

4-14 33° Mixed snow and rain.

Cream de Mocha: A shot of chocolate syrup, espresso shots, foamed Half & Half, whipped cream a must!

7:49 A.M. This will be a fabulous weekend! Mountain Peak Ski Resort gets to end their season with a bang! Last night I had to venture out into the night again, with no make-up, no bra, a flashlight, and a gun. I looked frightful – but didn't give a shit. An animal was being brutally killed down by the river. I searched and searched to no avail. Whatever it was, it took off the minute it felt my presence. Maybe an owl was getting a cat? A bear brutally attacking a deer? Those were violent, agonizing desperate screams! Ran chills up my spine. Butch and I could hear it from upstairs. I finally had to get back inside but my dog was still going nuts. Someone or something was close by…

I remembered the night I was awakened by my pygmy goats getting killed. It was here in the yard and the attacking animal had to be *huge*. These were no small, lightweight pets and they had been dragged quite some distance. Their wails were blood curdling and the memory stuck with me for months! In the morning we found one dead and the other one barely alive. No. 5 had to do the shooting. Our pet goat looked up at him with those sweet, adoring eyes, just at the moment he pulled the trigger. This haunted *him* for a long, long time too. I couldn't have done it.

2:00 P.M. My new Quaker bird is a doll. He would like to eat one of my fingers for lunch, but I'm smarter than he is – so far! He has a huge vocabulary, and the customers love him. More "BITE" signs installed on the wire mesh.

3:19 P.M. And *maybe* ten drinks! Boooorrrrring espresso day. I got out the binoculars to see if I could spot BOO. But all I could get a focus on was a piece of plywood and a black tarp. A neighbor stopped by. "Whom in the hell are you peeping at? Have you finally gone desperately *mental*, isolated up here for so long? Looking at railroad workers?" I asked her if she heard the animal murders going on last night. Nothing. "But two nights ago, one of the other neighbors told me that two of their cats were killed. The killer left both tails behind." Hungry BOO or a cougar?

6:24 P.M. I am going to keep the binoculars, flashlight, and gun handy tonight…

4-15 42° Raining.

Cafe Hot Chocolate: Two packs of powdered hot chocolate, espresso shots, steamed milk.

8:04 A.M. Neon's say OPEN.

11:43 A.M. My Quaker bird was out of his cage for the first time. I have come to realize a lot of people are petrified of a bird in flight, especially inside of a building! I've had a few seriously panic! Watching too many movies like Hitchcock's "The Birds?"

2:10 P.M. I just gave my "lay" the other night the ax. By the time we are over forty, you would think we would have men figured out. I must be twelve! They do not change! Buck was coming on strong again with his possessiveness, glaring at male patrons, wanting another one-niter! He wanted it now! I need my head chopped off! I'm sorry, gals, for my pure stupidity. Point off the women's side!

3:28 P.M. I sometimes wonder if my customers are stopping here for my espresso or my Porta Potty and which was most urgent.

I was hungry and I started thinking about what I was going to add to my homemade spaghetti: Gobs of rotisserie chicken, tons of parmesan cheese, salt, pepper, butter, and garlic. A feast meant for *porking*! Alone! With three movie rentals to choose from! Just in case I got an obtuse wild hair, I bought some new fabric to make my giant flamingo creations. No more male crap for a coon's age! I will make myself swear! And cross my heart!

6:56 P.M. Keep tryin', girl…

4-16 42° Raining.

Foamy Mocha: A shot of chocolate syrup, espresso shots, foamed milk.

11:03 A.M. A lady parked her car on the east side of my store, walked around the entire building, through the west door. Dripping wet and pissed! She was too upset to know or care that I did have two doors. Her umbrella went inside out in the wind. "I need this (gigantic) thermos filled with drip coffee." "Sorry, I don't do drip but I can offer you an Americano, but the price will be quite high for the amount you are requesting." More furrows in the brow, "Forget it, then, and just give me a maple bar!" "I'm sorry I don't do donuts – only some pastries and muffins." Major scowl! Third, she had to go to the bathroom and asked if I had a restroom? I pointed her back outside to the Porta Potty, which was precisely where her car was parked! She was mumbling and shaking now. Then she handed me her smaller travel mug and wanted it filled with whatever! Politely, "Can you please remove its lid, I'm not allowed to touch personal container lids – Health Department, ya know." By now she was spitting nails! While I was making her Americano, she was back out in the storm, fiddling with the Porta Potty handle. She slogged back through the door and looked like a kitchen sponge! Immediately she knocked over a large basket of wooden snakes and they all went flying.

Another sweet customer started helping her pick up the toys and they bumped heads! I swear this is all true! By the time she left my store, she was laughing so hard, she was crying.

Or was she sobbing…

1:44 P.M. Scanner: Some sort of fuel spill on the highway, west of here. It is an enormous concern up here, since the highway runs right along the Saratogan River.

2:07 P.M. Scanner: A fifteen-year-old boy had a snowboarding accident. He had a broken ankle and a laceration above his right eye.

The *leak* was a tanker-truck losing fuel, which may have spread over a thirty-five-mile stretch! They caught him in Alpine. I would hate to have to pay his gargantuan fine!

5:47 P.M. Time to go upstairs and be a good girl again and again and again…

4-17 46° Overcast.

Butter Pecan Creamer: A shot hazelnut syrup, shot of butterscotch syrup, espresso shots, steamed Half & Half.

7:49 A.M. A fine day with Boone in bragging about his recent "chick use." Great way to start off the day…hating men.

5:23 P.M. Awesome busy day! And I was pooped. Sold lots of gifts today and two sales on eBay. Have not sold my sixty-five-inch tall, home-sewn flamingo though! It's a wild piece!

6:04 P.M. Rosie came in for 1.2 seconds. Snuck out with some loose change for an iced mocha before asshole got back from wherever his ass was. We couldn't even get a laugh or two in, dammit.

6:36 P.M. I am utterly thankful I am not she…

4-18 42° Partly sunny.

Cuban Espresso: Straight espresso shots in a shot cup.

8:39 AM. Ran errands…

2:30 P.M. Opened and I could tell our water was turned off in this area, so I suppose I had not missed a thing by being gone. Guilt subsided. No water equaled no espresso, which equaled no customers. Minimally, they arrived and left pissed. The pipes throughout my store and house were spitting brown and sputtering up a storm. I had better bleed 'em all so that my espresso machine doesn't get all clogged up with foreign gunk.

Everything was put away. The 800 lbs. of supplies from the car – to the store – to the back storeroom – and up the stairs. Took down all my half-dead Christmas lights; they were probably still burning their fifty watts each section! Put new trash bags in the outside receptacles, swept every walkway, hauled branches, bagged pinecones. Had my work out for the week – I can eat *hordes* of chocolate fudge brownie ice cream tonight!

4:06 P.M. Buck was here, the sweet talkin' junky. It was quite late in the day and he was probably on about his sixth snoopin' stop. "Where was my sweetie today?" "Go fuck a stump!"

6:49 P.M. And my very last customer was Rosie. I adored, needed, and loved her tales. Today, she told her hubby, Ex-Con that she wanted to recite a little tidbit she learned at Bible study. As far as he knows, she has never even been within the same *city block* as a church. He was all ears. She said the teachings were as follows: "God created MAN first and considered it His trial 'n error prototype. Then God created WOMAN and considered that His masterpiece!" He promptly headed for the couch where he has been snoring all damn day. He wouldn't get up for the dinner that she had slaved on for two hours. So, she walked out and came here for her triple 24-ounce iced mocha, with the works, and left his portion of supper burning on the stove. She had a big, toothy smile on her face. No wonder they do not eat together or have sex these days.

7:03 P.M. With the late-in-the-day marriage gossip, I headed upstairs *alone –* *thrilled* with the prospect...

4-19 48° Sunny.

Chocolate-Covered Cherry: A shot of chocolate syrup, a shot of cherry syrup, espresso shots, steamed milk.

9:08 A.M. It is becoming one of those "glad it's a dead" Tuesdays. First off, my macaw bit the crap out of my finger again. I put a butterfly on it, but it could have used a stitch or two. Brat! Then the UPS guy dropped off the imported walnuts I ordered for this cruel bird. Return to Sender!

11:30 A.M. A phenomenally successful gent I knew, who has a store in Icicle Town, stopped by to flirt. He wanted me to close shop and go with him on his deliveries – a two-hour drive each way. "Well, with such a fabulous flirtatious invitation – from a wedded father of three daughters – just how can a girl resist?" This was his very first (and last) overture and he now has placed himself on the asshole list! Toward the top! Point off men, since he was married!

5:44 P.M. Buck dropped by to give me a three-page love letter, "This is just to let you know that I am buying you a ring and proposing to you next month. I understand that you may say no unless I give you a 'rock.'" I laughed so hard he could not get out the door fast enough. This guy, like so many others – with the girlfriends for four years, other baristas "down-the-line" and 101 refusals from me – what ARE they thinking? I don't believe there are any men left out there worth marrying, especially for an eighth time. Or would it be the ninth? I will forever be confused...

6:12 P.M. I will take my confused, happy, single-self upstairs for an evening of solitude...

4-20 50° Sunny.

Grasshopper: Ice, a shot of crème de menthe syrup, a shot of crème de cacao syrup, soda water within 1", top with Half & Half.

9:06 A.M. Slow day. Mow day. An entire acre!

4:07 P.M. Toward the end of my workday, I filled my Quaker bird's food tray with zillions of new seeds and he promptly grabbed his dish with his beak, sending these miniscule morsels flying everywhere! Thank goodness for shop-vacs!

Before I was half done cleaning, a gal came in for a banana smoothie and she suggested we put some vodka in it. We chuckled. She headed out to her classic car, a '48 coupe, and in a minute or so was back. Needed a few napkins. She informed me, "Vodka goes very well with banana!" I thought I smelled booze the *first* time she walked in! And now she reeked – and they say you cannot smell Vodka! HA!

5:00 P.M. And speaking of getting wasted…wasn't today (4/20), *The Marijuana Holiday*? If you had teenagers, like I did, you knew these things.

I'm also ultra-sensitive, ever since one of the local available bachelors conned me into a glass of wine at his place last year – during my two-month relapse. I brought my own wine and we chatted from across the room and all were well. Until he brought out the hard booze and orange juice. A couple of drinks later, I could feel myself suddenly losing control, that black cloud that hovers, and in a panic, I realized that I had been drugged. I started screaming for my keys, as he cackled like a male witch in the distance. He was dangling my keys from his long fingers and somehow, I was able to grab them and run out the door to my Jeep. I drove the half-block to Buck's. I crawled inside of his house and threw-up for hours and hours. For all of you out there, NEVER, EVER trust anyone with YOUR drink ANYWHERE! If you feel faint, call 911. And if anyone appears as sick as I was, dial 911. Don't ever play nurse, since I could have died that night. Buck was an EMT in his days and he knew I was in trouble. Why he did not take me to the hospital, I'll never know. Another lesson learned. That guy's plan was to drug then rape me! I am sure of it. These locals suck and are sneaky because they all know I would tell them to go fuck themselves if they even thought of asking for sex. This was a new lesson for me.

6:49 P.M. Physical work outside – slumber. Cannot beat that combo…

4-21 46° Partly sunny.

White Chocolate Caramel Mocha: A shot of white chocolate syrup, a shot of caramel syrup, espresso shots, steamed milk.

9:00 A.M. I went to the bank and then on down to purchase my long-awaited new CD! While driving home I cried through two of the songs and got the chills on four more. Soft music is a Godsend.

Then I got a wild hair and picked up Buck. I asked him to show me BOO's camp. We went up the logging road and got out and wound through bushes and trees to where he lived – the plywood and tarp shack. Buck knew where it was all right. Even the sheriff could not tell me the exact location of BOO's camp – or how to get there, all the while insisting that BOO couldn't see my place from his vantage point. Bull-Puck he couldn't! Perfect bird's-eye view for six years! So creepy!

2:06 P.M. I might as well go lay out on Mountain Peak Highway today and try to get a suntan. Fifteen minutes are going by between cars. Ugh.

4:32 P.M. Ohmygod! My sheriff No. 7 just called! He is retired now, with long hair and a beard and drives a semi-truck. That makes three ex-husbands in the last two years who have begun long hauling! *What are the frigg'n odds?* He called from North Carolina and thanked me for talking him out of police work. Wanted to have dinner next time he was in town. Shit, what a trip that unexpected phone call was! Makes ya feel kinda good, like maybe somebody missed ya, anyway. It might be fun to see the big man again.

6:00 P.M. I have not even had a *handful* of people in here today. I'm closing! I will also write another letter to Buck telling him no and *leave me alone.* No ring, no nothing. Why can't he understand the word f...r...i...e...n...d...s... h...i...p? And believe me, I've spelled it, I've yelled it, I've crammed it down his throat. Why does he pretend to have selective hearing? Why do all men?

6:12 P.M. Upstairs to have a *real* conversation...with Butch...

4-22 54° Sunny.

Hammerhead: Two shots of espresso topped with drip coffee.

8:42 A.M. It is going to be a hot one today! Maybe 75°. And that is plenty for our Northwest thick blood!

Three frightening guys just stopped in. They were in a big, two-ton beater truck full of crap. They said they were going to park and leave it here because it was breaking down. "Yeah, right! In a pig's eye you are! Does this look like a flipping truck stop to you? Get lost and leave now!" They did! It never ceased to amaze me what this little frame could accomplish! It must be that glint of steel in the eye...

11:50 A.M. Scanner: Old two-ton truck leaking possible hazardous waste at milepost 48.

Two miles down the highway! I called 911 immediately and informed them that these guys were trying to abandon their old dump truck here! Who knew what the hell they had in there! I was so glad they were caught. They wouldn't be messin' with any of us too soon again, up in "these-thar-hills"! Turned out they were carrying aluminum dust and the driver of the truck had flown the coop! Two state patrols just flew by here. Kinda got a gal's knees a'knockin' to think they were just in my store not thirty minutes ago and I was my cocky, belligerent self! What a cover! One of these days...

1:11 P.M. Harley Dennis just stopped to visit. He was sportin' his Harley tank top, showin' off those huge arms. God, I love summer!

6:58 P.M. And what shall a single, free as a bird, female do tonight...

4-23 45° Sunny.

Orange Amaretto Latte: Shot of orange syrup, shot of amaretto syrup, espresso shots, steamed milk.

9:09 A.M. We are supposed to get rain today, but you wouldn't know it by looking at the lovely blue skies. Clear as a crystal ball. I think even a two-year-old can see there is no rain in sight. Our poor weathermen: they are always getting the berries from the citizens. Our Japanese currents make our area extremely unpredictable and almost impossible to properly forecast.

I wandered down to my river this morning and just drank the whole scene in. The sun was streaming through the trees, glancing off the ripples in the rushing water and up and over the boulders. I skipped a rock. A fish jumped. It was a breathtaking reminder of why I work here. We *can* be happy alone.

2:00 P.M. Thank goodness, this highway is the gateway to the most popular areas in the state for tourists, skiers, snowmobiles, boaters, hikers, beaches, desert, and Washington State's No. 1 tourist attraction, Icicle Town. Here is a bit of its history:

ICICLE TOWN

In 1892, the Pacific Railroad came upon a small town with log structures. Shortly after that, The Buttemont Investment Company platted a new town site and named it Icicle Town. They built a railroad depot, a roundhouse, coalbunkers, and a mill that hired up to seventy-five men at a time. With the beautiful alpine setting surrounding this dying town, investors got together and agreed on a German theme for a tourist mecca, since there was so much traffic going along this highway. Today this town boasts festivals of all kinds that have become world-renowned, following closely in the footprints of Germany. They hold the famous Christmas Lighting, Autumn Leaf Festival, May Fest, Ice Fest, and several Art in the Park weekends. It is a trip over Mountain Peak Highway worth taking!

5:00 P.M. Should I close and take the drive? Or hang out for more miniscule revenue...

4-24 49° Sunny

Sugar-Free Boysenberry Latte: A shot of sugar-free boysenberry syrup, espresso shots, steamed milk.

9:02 A.M. The most beautiful, flashy, 2002 Maserati sports car just drove up and the guy bought two plastic pink flamingos! Go figure? Just didn't match the image! He laughed as he loaded the flamingos into his hood trunk. He mentioned that he could give me great advertising if he just mounted one on each side of his car. "Sure...and paint my **OUTPOST ESPRESSO** on the side doors while you are at it!" He drives 140 mph up here all the time and has even given the state patrol guys a couple of rides. Hmmmmm, it proves once again, it's not *what ya know* - it's *whom ya know* and *whatcha got*! He used to own Lamborghinis but became tired of them. He bore no ring and I found out he is single.

Twenty or so bikers just pulled in. Bikers are some of my best customers; fun, happy, order big drinks and tip the same way. They are welcome anytime. I have even had some Banditos in. They were tough but well behaved. Love you – mean it!

2:15 P.M. A gal just came in for a white chocolate mocha. She lived here, in Saratogan, about thirty-five years ago. She went to grade school here for three years, in our teensy schoolhouse with three to four combined grades in a single room. She remembered that the school basement always flooded, and the teachers had to shoo the pre-school and kindergartners upstairs to the big kids' classrooms. She also recalled the Manning Store, where kids would go and get their penny-candy and sodas. She was full of fond memories. Her mom managed the motel down toward High Valley when it was still a family stay. That was long before it was closed. The last owners got busted for having hourly rates and hidden cameras in the rooms. Unbeknownst to the guests, they would be watching their X- rated movies and the owners would be watching them "do their thing"! Many of the guests were the elite Bellevue cheating spouses. They figured it was super-safe and never dreamt they could be caught in such a rat-hole sixty miles from home!

5:55 P.M. Now the challenge is to stay *happy* through the isolated evenings…

4-25 62° Sunny.

Café Con Leche: Two shots of espresso topped with foamed milk.

8:55 A.M. I strolled down to the bank this morning. The snow was about gone, even on the highest peak, Mt. Crag Rock. Oh boy, it really *is* summer.

12:32 P.M. Scanner: A rafter at Delusion Falls with a shoulder injury. Love 'em or hate 'em, cell phones save lives, especially in the wilderness.

1:27 P.M. I was peacefully sitting on the pot when I heard a loud, "Yoooo Hoooo!" GOD! I hurriedly pulled up my jeans, knowing my undies were jammed up my crack and stormed out. Right on the other side of my bathroom door, a guy was smiling broadly and this room was at the far back of my store! I had never seen him in my life and he was behaving as though we were old pals. With my head thrown high in the sky and my shoulders back, ramrod straight, I headed for my cart out front. When I got to my espresso cubicle, here was another smiley buddy. What was with them? Were they light- 'n-the-loafers? They ordered two iced mochas and left, still grinning like Cheshire Cats!

3:06 P.M. A total of *three* customers. If it does not pick up, I may *rot* in this place! Or run an exotic career from these four walls.

A man stopped for a triple. He just got through purchasing an old silo in S.E. Washington, on eBay. He was slowly going to dismantle it and auction off all the old wood. He saw a big beam on eBay go for $9K! I always knew there was big money in this old wood business.

The female founder of this eBay Internet business sure *hit it big* with *this* dream! The computer hula-hoop! I just heard recently that Meg Whitman, the CEO, was traveling all over the world for meetings in her many offices, via one or the other of her private jets. She said she just hates to leave the comfort of her mansions. My heart goes out…

8:10 P.M. Haggard, hungry, happy…

4-26 70° Sunny and hot!

Banana Split: A shot of chocolate syrup, shot of banana syrup, splash of strawberry syrup, espresso shots, steamed milk, whipped cream.

9:03 A.M. My beautiful antique copper arrived! I hadn't been able to locate this popular product for years. It was out of Turkey and had always been such a great seller. I had people in Crag Rock wanting six or more pots. This one sale would pay for the whole bloody load.

2:55 P.M. A couple of gay guys dropped in and bought piles of gifts and 32-ounce blended drinks. Gay people love this store and all its kitschy fun. That was a damn good sale on a dead day.

It is funny…we baristas can tell, right off the bat, who would be the good tipper, and who would leave no tip, feigning blindness. "What jar?" It was usually the look on their faces, or their attitudes. I just had a customer qualify to be a number-one-100%-non-tipper. He came through the drive-thru, ordered, and was quite friendly. Then he wouldn't even *look* at me when I handed him his espresso. These customers always suddenly pretend their cell was ringing, or they were having an emotional breakdown, etc. They went through life with imaginary personal problems available, to act out in a split-second. I had seen this in bars and restaurants – I'd seen this in hair and nail salons – everywhere that tipping was the norm. It was quite the physiological moment between the server and the customer. The *Barista-Tip-Dance* I called it!

A little tidbit on Tips: A phrase coined in 1688 in an English coffee house. The sign read, "To Insure Prompt Service." A "TIPS" card was placed by a cup and those desiring prompt service and better seating threw a coin into a tin. What wonderful wisdom they had back then!

"Stinky" was in today. This old guy lived in the woods. He got his nickname from his condition. When he walks into my store, everyone *chooses* to clear out! He brought me a *treasure* once from the dump – a new metal trash bin. I was amazed he even knew what it was for! He leased a car every couple of years and he and his three smelly dogs lived in it. When he turned the car back in, the stench *had* to make the salesman's eyes water! One day he fessed up and told me, "Not *that* many years ago I was a real estate millionaire in Seattle." Go figure…

5:28 P.M. Reminds me, I need to close and take this truck full of "stinky" stuff to the dump tonight. Our dump *used* to be fun. Years ago, we all named it the Saratogan Kmart. All of us, from all walks of life and incomes, seemed to grab that choice piece-of-something that we carted home from there. Our quaint, little, was-free dump now had gates and cameras. Half of my house was furnished from the dump! We, the Dumpster-Divers!

7:07 P.M. I am back and lost my appetite spending an hour and a half with sewage and slop…

4-27 57° Overcast but will be a scorcher.

Natural Vanilla: A shot of vanilla syrup, a shot of honey, espresso shots, steamed soy.

8:40 A.M. Three businessmen, decked out in suits and ties, just stopped for iced lattes. One of the fellows told his partners that he was going to buy a sombrero and wear it on his head all day! They challenged him! We found the sombrero – just the right size – loud and colorful. He paid and pranced out of the store with it planted squarely and firmly on his head. These mountains, so far from the hustle-bustle of corporate life, brought out the *goofiness* in people, I swear! Must be why I stay...

11:22 A.M. I also had a chat today with some elderly people from Bozeman, Montana – nice, friendly country types. They were telling me, over mochas, about the movie stars who had their 2nd/3rd/4th homes in their area. They were pleased with the dollars this had brought to their sleepy area and the boom in real estate, but they were only one of the few happy with it all. The rest of the Montanans could shoot 'em. They stayed here and visited until the mochas were gone.

The loggers were at it again today, logging the whole side of the mountain, just across the highway from me. I could hear the trees falling and hitting the earth and could feel it in my chest! Saws, whistles, thuds, truck tailgates, and the crashing of trees. Deafening trains still flying right by, just a few feet from the men.

4:09 P.M. I got a call from the new owner of Lumberman's Restaurant two miles west of me, another one of our National Historic Landmarks. He was going to remodel in the next year or so, keeping within the organization's stringent guidelines. But in the meantime, he had rented out the apartment upstairs. He asked me to *please* do him a favor. He could not leave his other numerous other investment ventures in Seattle and wanted me to check on the tenants whom he could not contact. No damn wonder! They had split and literally left their shit! This building would probably get slapped with a new sign *'QUARANTINED'* like in the days of the plague if the officials got a whiff of this! I *seriously* could not even step foot inside the door. I called the owner back and told him, "It should really be burnt to the ground, and then you could happily collect on the insurance policy."

5:40 P.M. Shower and clean clothes right this minute...

4-28 47° Partly sunny.

Praline Madness: A shot of praline syrup, espresso shots, steamed milk.

8:56 A.M. I needed to water my outside plants. We do not have the luxury of outside spigots here in Saratogan, as freezing temperatures existed half the year. Filled buckets, carried buckets, from inside to outside, repeatedly, for a span of about 350 feet. Car washing was a real treat too! Buckets of warm water thrown on car – then the soapy bucket – wipe down with a rag - carry several more buckets to rinse. By that time, there was no more warm water left for the commissary, espresso machine or kitchen. Cars stayed dirty most of the year!

12:00 P.M. You know when a man is mad! Buck stuck a nasty note into a chunk of my firewood, with a surgery tool. I didn't even know what kind of stabbing tool this was, but I will hand it all over to the sheriff.

4:27 P.M. The comedian was back. Riotous Rosie, my witty neighbor, disgusted with a 40-hour entrapment under the same roof with her beefy, blimpy, bulky, burly husband. "The slob won't go and get us some propane. I haven't had hot water in a fuckin' week, Christy, and he expects me to wash his damn clothes, cook, and live without a shower. He's a bastard." For sure. "He's stomping around the house like a griz and ranting about the dishes in the sink. I told him to fuck off and go get us some propane. He's the ass with the dough and wheels." Bastard for sure.

5:49 P.M. Marvelous out. It was time to take a walk and put some oxygen in this head…

4-29 47° Overcast.

Hazelnut Hot Chocolate: Two packs of powdered hot chocolate, a shot of hazelnut syrup, steamed milk.

10:49 A.M. Lake fishing opened this week, and our nearby Fishline Lake was a favorite.

I just had some beer drinking, young punks in my drive-thru, expelling gas in 8-second belches, like a contest, for my enjoyment. "Burps like those could give me a reason to refuse service! Plus, I have other customers in here that overheard you." The driver apologized for the gang and then asked for the caramel macchiato, for God's sake! That was a Starbucks signature drink that baristas struggle to create to the exact taste. There have been many arguments in espresso stands regarding the ingredients of this yummy, fattening caramel treat! Even ex-employees of our entire major competitor differed when they tried to pass along the recipe – how it was made and in what order! I simply asked this young man if he would like light or dark chocolate. In the past I have been asked for both, either or none. Customers didn't seem to have a clue either, but thought they knew. He asked for white chocolate and lots of whipped cream and little caramel "swirlies" on top. "Roger!" I made his drinky-poo as fancy I could stomach and as I handed it out, "I wanted it iced!" TOO FUCKING LATE, I wanted to scream, but didn't. I grabbed a cup, slammed some ice in, slopped his hot drink over the damnable ice, added more frigging whip, squirted a couple new caramel drops through the lid hole, and practically threw it out the window! He took a sip and claimed that it was still warm. "Do you want to hold out your hand and try 'n catch some more ice, cuz I'm sure as hell not making a new drink!" He sneered. I thought they were on their way. Just as I closed the window, I heard, "Ma'am! Maaaaaaaaaaam!!" Now, I've had it! Punk go piss up a pipe! Again, and only because of the other patrons around, I kept silent. I whipped my head around and he handed me a dirty old cup and wanted more ice. I obliged. With that he got ready to lead-foot it away and said, "Sorry I've ruined your day!" I hollered back, "You haven't even come close! And if I was a guy, I would have already ripped your head off and sold it to the next shitty customer!" Everyone in sight gulped…and ordered doubles! Sometimes it is Very satisfying to own your own business!

5:28 P.M. Scanner: Vehicle fire at milepost 62. The Forest Service cop was already peeling rubber.

6:00 P.M. Calm down, Christy, so you can digest your dinner…

4-30 46° Sunny.

8:29 A.M. Where is my cowboy? It rained all night, so the flowers were very perky this morning. We had another brutal cat murder last night. I hurried outside again and tried to see something, anything, with my flashlight and gun and about tumbled down my flight of stairs! This flight consisted of nineteen steep stairs with a concrete landing and a metal door. I would have killed the dog and myself, as Butch was sitting peacefully just inside the bottom door waiting to escape. We flew out the door, could not see a damn thing but could still hear the screams. I hoped it was not BOO trapping cats for dinner!

My mama and papa birds were back to build their nest in my steel pillar. This was just outside my drive-thru window. There was a hole in the pillar that appeared to have been put there just for birds. They came every year and after hatching, I could hear the babies screaming for their food. My indoor pet birds will go nuts when it gets to that stage. It's fun to watch the parents building the nest, as they try and get both the ingredients and their bodies through the tiny hole.

Well, last night I rebuilt my favorite tattered ole bra. I covered the whole thing in rainbow fleece and **taa daa**…a new bra, which will hopefully last another six years! Some of you may have been through the implant *removal* hell. A good bra is a Godsend! If you have not been through it, don't ever go there.

12:00 Noon. Okay…THE subject again. There is a big problem running the demands of retail as a sole employee/owner: I am back in "my" personal bathroom, sitting on "my" personal throne and the dog starts barking frantically. A customer. Oh God! Grunt, squeeze, hurry, wipe, yank pants up, and *forget* about fixing undies again. Get belt buckled and there is no time for freshener. Grab some milk or *something,* to give me a legit reason for hiding out, and run through the gift shop, trying to look poised for this new customer. Hoping against hope that the last piece of toilet paper isn't trailing from my shoe, or worse, from my waistband. ALL baristas who work alone can relate. At least I have the dog's warning!

Lunch is another story: You stand there *helpless* with a full mouth, my-lips-are-sealed smile, and that useless, speechless look on your face, hoping they can appreciate that I am <u>not</u> enjoying my bite at all, and may choke to death before their very eyes, as I swallow the entire damn chunk – whole! These customers, who I have never seen before in my whole life, glare at me so impatiently from the other side of the drive-thru window, it makes me wonder if they eat. Oh, the woes of retail...

1:11 P.M. One of those firemen, who had more on their minds than saving lives, asked me if I would like to own *his* very own fire pole – and then har har har, as he tickled himself to death with his own double meaning. "Okay, all kidding aside," he said, "we have an *extra* fire pole out in the back forty, behind our station, and you could make some *extra* money at night!" And he doubled over again with his own quick wit. Do they measure IQs in the fire department, or just stamina?

Two train conductors came in for espressos and asked if I would deliver drinks down at the crossing, just about a ¼ mile away. "Sure thing, fellows – fix the drinks, lock up the store, hide my outside wares, pull signs, unlock my car, drive down the hill for you, and come back up to start all over – for $6.25 plus the usual 25-cent tip." *Dream on...*

3:33 P.M. BMW Brian came by with *more* gifts. He brought me the most *perfect* man too! This man was pliable. Didn't talk back. Doesn't mess up the house! He was in a box. He was a *real* GUMBY! Included amongst these gifts was a POKEY. Both were inside of a GUMBY and POKEY mini lunchbox. I think I will have to build a "Brian Shelf" here for all of his gifts to me with a sign attached: STILL NO.

5:03 P.M. Tonight, a celebration of my lifestyle with Gumby....

MAY

Flowers have risen while she ponders over lattes and lilacs

5-01 42° 100% sunny.

Bravo Mocha: 1 pack of Mexican cocoa, 1 pack of regular cocoa, espresso shots, steamed milk.

8:00 A.M. Happy Birthday to **OUTPOST ESPRESSO**! *Music, Maestro…please!* For seven years, this place and I have been residing as one. Time just zips right by when you're having fun all by your lonesome…

12:12 P.M. A gentleman just crashed through the door yelling, "Smoke!" I called 911, as the puffs were right up in the hills here, toward the pass. I heard my address over the scanner, stating the location of this call. I called our fire station (*and someone answered – amazing!*) and told them that some more ladies just stopped and claimed to have seen the same smoke. They were on it!

1:40 P.M. Just heard that a local elder Mason passed away last night. He was very much a major player in the building of the Blue Bear Trail, a re-router of the Pacific Crest Trail and was the Mayor of Saratogan for about ten years. I heard about his passing on the scanner. Gasoline is now up to $2.55 a gallon! And the government is supposed to be trying to *help* the small businessman? Retail dies off to computer sales. Maybe that's Big Sam's plan. Keep us all in our little boxes.

6:44 P.M. I had a Harley riding couple come in to get a "kick" for that last leg of the trip. They decided to drive the 110 miles from Seattle to Icicle Town, "Just for some espresso." I couldn't imagine the hundreds of espressos joints they passed on the way up – but they rode for the joy of it and the weather was perfect.

8:00 P.M. The next two riders were frozen solid! Navy Harley Dennis came in with a new buddy for warmth and a steaming cup 'a Joe. I remembered his buddy from last year. Small world. He was riding double with a gal friend who he said was now loooooong gone, thankfully. "She was high-maintenance to the max and broke up with me the day she broke a nail trying to get the tangles out of her wind-blown hair." They hung around for less than the norm for their safety and my tongue.

8:23 P.M. Still open. Cash register still singing. This day has been a yummy taste of summer.

9:46 P.M. Exercises and stretches tonight or I will be crippled-stiff tomorrow. I am dead…

5-02 47° Partly cloudy.

-P.S. My first bare-chested male for the season!

> **Fruity Tooty: Ice, splash of each: watermelon, coconut, pineapple, and mint syrups, soda water and a splash of Half & Half.**

7:55 A.M. Took off early for Wooly's and to get espresso supplies at my whole-sale places. I felt flu-like and that was not me. I was coming down with something. I had been achy for a couple of days, so I thought I would stock up now, before the next crazy weekend hit.

12:13 P.M. Back and barely open when Jack, who had a stroke and now his wife wanted to leave him, stopped in to visit. He was going to take off to Montana after he sold off his "stuff." He said she was sort of getting cold feet. Too bad baby…cuz he is going off to set up a new life…withoutcha! Gosh, I hope he will be okay. He is my friend now – not just a customer.

An eighty-three-year-old did not get off the bus in Tillamuk today, so our sheriff had to chase after the bus, all the way to milepost 88. That was only ten miles before Icicle Town, about fifty miles away! Turned out the old gent wasn't even *on* the bus, so the family had to put out a missing person alert.

Well, it is called, "Work it off." Sometimes it is better to continue life as though the nasty flu-bug is nowhere to be found! I cleaned, vacuumed, and even did that pesky edge cleaning with the vacuum hose nozzle, rearranged, organized, and re-priced items.

3:14 P.M. Our sheriff paid a kind visit. I told him that someone around here was listening in on his radio, a frequency the rest of us could not get. He said that it would take 800 megahertz. "Well, *someone* has one because that person knows and hears things, I'm not aware of and it's not a matter of missing things or just stepping out of the building. I'm here way too many hours to have missed all that she's blabbing about." That got his curiosity perked up a bit. Mine too.

Speaking of sheriffs, I had not heard from No. 7 in a few days. Maybe he smelled "backbone."

6:10 P.M. Buck tried to dump off some huge planks tonight. "I want ta buildya a dream. A covered walkway to a deck an' a hot tub out back. And these planks 'r worth a fortune and cud start the project." They appeared to be half-rotten to me and I do not "do" the word "start." "Done" was my motto! Not accepting these boards kicked him into high gear. "You are screwin' so and so – and so and so's 'Big Root' and I'll git wind of it too." Women could care less about roots, dude. We women need tenderness, backrubs, and help with the things we can't physically accomplish and then we love to reward you when things get "finished!" Men know nothing! Who taught them?! They are stagnant.

Give us biceps any day…the root can wait.

8:44 P.M. And in my case, wait…and wait…and wait…

5-03 52° Overcast.

Mimosa: Ice, 1 shot of orange and apple syrups, soda water, (cream).

8:02 A.M. A very sad day here in Saratogan. I just found out that our part-time postmistress, only forty-seven-years-old, died. Sunday was the last day of her four-month fight with cancer. She and I had shared many conversations about our precious daughters over the last three years. She left behind a loving husband and all of us. God bless you, girl!

12:22 P.M. Buck came in for his iced white mocha and laid down five $100 bills and asked if he could see my back. My back what? He said that he loved my back, and he would pay me this money to partially disrobe. Jesus! Get lost! I tried shoving it down his shirt and accidentally ran my hands along his rock-hard chest. Now he was really amped! He threw the bills back at me with a huge grin like we just copulated. I addressed an envelope and told him it would go to the P.O. tonight! God, no wonder people swipe mail! Then he offered me $48,000 a year to have sex with him twice a week. That was so bizarre, I wondered if he was "bugged?" The longer I live, the more I hate men. Damn, I forgot to ask if this salary would allow me to have a boyfriend on the side.

7:03 P.M. American Idol with popcorn on the menu. Fingers crossed – I am beating the bug…

5-04 49° Overcast.

> **Strawberry Smoothie: My original!** Cup full of ice into blender, 2 shots of strawberry daiquiri syrup, 1 pack of fake sugar, 2 inches of cream and blend.

7:55 A.M. Okay, okay. I heard you. The dang alarm is such a nag! I just woke up from nine hours of sleep…still droopy. My brain was screaming for Mexico and California, with the sun beating down on the back of my neck, sitting under beautiful palms. Will not happen… God, I need a vacation! Will not happen…

3:10 P.M. A guy came in, "I'm thirsteeeee. What is good and cooooooold?" That was my most hated question – customers wanting my personal advice on what their mouth was craving. I do not think so… I considered this to be "Super Service" and I wanted to respond with, "I am not your mother; now get off it and think of something!" The question was always enveloped in that pathetic whine. I obliged though, and told him I had soda, water, Italian sodas, iced espresso drinks, and smoothies. He pondered and sighed. That's death! And then he just couldn't quite decide between a smoothie and water…I wanted to tell him, "I could have knitted a scarf with my computer dust by now – snap it up!" It had been over two minutes, but who was counting? With another whine and sigh, he finally decided for water. "One dollar, please." It took this slug thirty seconds to exit, and the door was only ten steps away. His poor wife…

3:41 P.M. The loggers across the way were making their way further down toward me. I guess the Forest Service warned BOO. I wonder where he will go. I saw his smoke and heard his hammering lately. Maybe he was breaking down camp…

Finally, some excitement for the day! Thank God Buck was here visiting! Another ugly truck full of creepy guys slowed down and started to pull in. Then they noticed Buck parked in my drive-thru and decided to continue down the highway. Buck left a few minutes later to follow them and just called me. The fire chief flagged him down, just about a mile from here, at the old, deserted gas station. The guys in the truck had just broken into that building! Broke windows and were stealing stuff! Holy shit! I would have been robbed for sure, maybe worse, if Buck had not accidentally come by for a drink.

4:12 P.M. Scanner: They were dispatching another sheriff up here.

4:18 P.M. Scanner: A state trooper was being dispatched. He called in that he was closer to the scene. I knew how they hated playing sheriff, but up in our desolate area, they had to. A little bit more news: Another old-timer, the kind you don't mess with, stopped to help the guys with these thugs. In fact, there were many old-timers, both male and female, that you did not dare cross. It just might be number one on your list of the worst days in your life! The fire chief told dispatch that he had plenty of back up now and would just hold the truckers right there. I guess Buck had to shove one of them up against their truck. He said, "The guy was thinkin' of leavin'." The sheriff was still racing up, code red, from forty-five miles away.

5:30 P.M. Well, all three men were handcuffed and in the back of the squad car. All three had warrants.

6:00 P.M. I am closing to go watch TV and all the crimes and craziness *elsewhere…*

5-05 54° Overcast.

Caramel Cream Soda: Ice, 1 shot of caramel and vanilla syrups, soda water and top off with Half & Half.

8:45 A.M. Ms. Gossips No. 1 and No. 2 came in, to chat; always loved playing *dirty linen* over some espressos. Great fun! I could tell when they had shenanigans on their beady little minds – they kind of lay on the counter together, like they were planning on spending two or three days. These two could get *real* down and dirty. "Mrs. So-and-So fell off the bar stool again at the Train Blow Tavern last night. Her newest boyfriend was rushing her to the hospital when hubby got wind of the fall. He stopped in the stinky saloon to raise an elbow or two and nobody's eyeball was meetin' his. Finally, he socked it out of some fella and by the time he caught up with her car and beat the shit out of 'the new honey,' two people were admitted to Pacifica General!"

Then, Mr. Blank-Blank was fucking Mrs. Blinkity-Blink, who used to mess with Mr. Uppity, on the City Council. "And speaking of the Town Council – at the last meeting, they discussed requiring hardhats once again, since Coke bottles were flying through the air as usual!" I didn't dare go near these meetings. I'd be the one chucking the Cokes! Well, both these women were sick and tired of their hubbies. They got stoned together this morning and are off to lunch. Where and with what money? They were both broke-to the-bone; half the time they looked like rag-tags, and always had to carry a tab with me. Big Macs on the agenda?

3:14 P.M. Just heard that our postmistress's funeral is set for tomorrow. The valley mourns.

7:10 P.M. Buck was hornier than hell today. He looked like he had a couple of beers in him and was coming down off a drunk. I remembered that "down."

Women get depressed, overtaxed, and could care less about the male species. Men, however, even with a beastly hangover, are always rippin' ready!

Tomorrow is Friday. People would be roaring east for the big, festive Cinco de Mayo, Mother's Day, and Apple Blossom weekend. It was like when Fat Tuesday dragged on through Sunday, and Mardi Gras was celebrated for at least four days in Idaho. Any excuse for extending merrymaking and booze.

10:23 P.M. God I am lonely. PTSD fears are bothering me tonight. Worried about everything...past...present...future. Money, loneliness, germs, people, and the whys of why I feel this for no reason. I have always worried and been a perfectionate germaphobe which causes me to be a workaholic. Seems to mask it most of the time. It is hard to hush the voices in my head, that sound like a city of people is crammed inside of a small room talking in monotone voices, but I can't make any of it out. I guess I pray to make it go away. I believe there is a God, even with my foul mouth and short temper. Even those traits seem to give me the impression that I am strong and safe. Yada, yada, yada, Christy. Nite, nite…

5-06 50° Sunny and muggy.

Crèmes Over Ice: Ice, a shot of crème de cacao and crème de cassis, top with Half & Half

10:51 A.M. My normally hilarious neighbor, Rosie, just walked by, crying! I yelled out my drive-thru window for her to come in. Her left cheek was so, swollen I was shocked! "I don't have any money for gas and need ta get ta the hospital. I have to walk down the two miles ta the gas station to call my dad for a ride. My asshole, Ex-Con won't take me." POINT OFF the men's column! I handed her $20 and told her to go get gas and get to the hospital - NOW! As soon as she was on her way "down-below," I emailed the sheriff about her jaw – just in case. I'd been abused and knew how it felt. And I was familiar with the look of those bruises.

Buck came in and threw a hundred-dollar bill onto my counter. Still wanted to see my back. I should have just pulled my shirt off and shown the damn thing to him and got it over with. I had my groovy, fleece rainbow bra on anyway, so who cared. "Christy, just keep the money for all the white chocolate mochas you've made for me in the last couple of weeks." Now we were *talking*! I kept it.

12:05 P.M. A young guy, Wayne from the feed store "down-below," came in again to visit on his day off. He drove all the way up here for a $2 short latte. He handed me a five'r and told me the change was for a tip. "Thank you!" I could tell by his nervousness that he was going to ask me out. He had probably been losing sleep. So, I mentioned my son was graduating from college and that I just talked to my grandson this morning. He was dazed; this age thing knocked him upside the head. It usually did. He left in a hurry. Hee-hee. And I am not *into* young men. God...at that point, they had not even *started* their crap.

Now, three guys came in and introduced themselves, first and last names. What? Baristas were supposed to remember their *handles*, seeing them *maybe* twice a year? Thousands of dudes fell in these doors between *their* visits. "Just worry about remembering MY name, since I'm the one feeding and watering you!" They loved the smart mouth!

4:38 P.M. I just shared some fresh strawberries with my macaw, but mine had whipped cream. What a delight! I got them the other day at one of those road-side tent-markets. I was so excited about this treat, I plum forgot to get ice. So, I must head down to our gas station after I close to grab some bags.

5:03 P.M. I try and not take my life for granted. I live on a river in the most beautiful place in the world. I do not have to punch a clock or stare a boss in the eyes and fetch coffee. It gets tough and my ribs show some during slow months, but I am grateful.

6:34 P.M. I will not forget my prayers of gratitude tonight...

5-07 48° Overcast.

Raspberry Vanilla Cream Soda: Ice, a shot of raspberry and vanilla syrups, soda water, topped with Half & Half.

11:37 A.M. Retail brought in a whopping $5 in three hours – and just now I sold over $400 in just a few minutes! Wow, that was a rush! A fantastic fifteen minutes!

I just had a mom and her two daughters in. One daughter had blue hair, blue eyes, and a blue shirt. As the blue-haired young gal stepped out to the Porta Potty, the mom and other daughter discussed whether "Blue" had fresh heroin tracks on her shoulders. She had road maps of life down both arms and legs. She almost died the night before last, and they were taking her to a rehabilitation/mental facility while she was willing. They were hoping her acceptance would last the rest of the journey. It was so sad; when "Blue" ordered her espresso, I could see she was filled with anger. She glared at me with unmasked hatred for not having espresso shakes with real ice cream. My heart went out to the mom. I would have loved to make her one if I could. Good luck, girl! It is a long, hard road – to happiness.

3:20 P.M. Our sheriff just checked up on Rosie to make sure her face was an abscess and not a domestic. It was the former. That's kinda too bad though cuz it would have been a great opportunity to lock up the bastard Ex-Con again! I believe she lied.

A vacationer in one of our cabins just called to see what time I opened tomorrow. They were going to walk up in the morning for their *fix*. That was almost *too* organized for me. I told them, "I open when I open, but tomorrow I shall have a schedule, by George."

6:32 P.M. Will it be deliveries soon? …

5-08 46° Overcast. Mother's Day.

Soda Sunrise: Ice, a shot of mandarin and orange syrups, a splash of grenadine, soda water, and cream.

7:42 A.M. Happy Mother's Day! I felt as though I was the "mother of birds" this year. Kids were scattered 1,300 miles in two different directions. If you know what is good for ya, you'll give me a call today! Where were my flowers and See's Candy? Life changes…

One 16-ounce iced mocha with whip, so far. He forgot to say whip, so I had to waste a flat lid and replace it with a dome. A waste of thirty seconds and 5 cents.

His bod was back in town. Andrew, my closest personal male buddy finally called to share a story about his father. This older gentleman owned and ran a grocery store for thirty-five years. NEVER missed a day! Got robbed a few times and shot once, since it was in the "Projects" in Omaha, but he never gave up. Today, I thought of him as I looked out my windows – inside these walls twenty-eight days out of thirty. These were my *windows to the world*. He had only *one* small window all those years to watch the seasons change. The trees are my barometers of life.

12:44 P.M. Scanner: A family of ducks, trying to cross a busy highway "down-below," caused a four-car rear-ender. I had seen this before; they were so adorable, running as fast as their little legs could carry them.

2:00 P.M. I am hyperventilating. No. 1 Bachelor in the whole Seattle area asked me for dinner. I am shaking. I sure wish I could just send my body out to eat and leave my soul peacefully at home! Oh God…I accepted but I know I am going to chicken out. He is good looking, loves animals, is outdoorsy, a fisher-man, has cabins all over the place, and says he doesn't sleep around. He has the new cabin on Groovy Street. Perfect? *Too* perfect. Isn't it funny how we paint them in the beginning? We see no evil, smell no rats. He probably has a gal in every one-light town, has his cabins named after conquests. Forget it, I ain't going; it *was* going to be my first Argentinean restaurant. I have three weeks to catch the flu as an excuse.

I just sold one of my hand-sewn nine-foot snakes! What a *trip* to sell some of this nutty stuff.

This is probably a typical barista day in the city, but good God…I am swamped!

3:03 P.M. Still pondering No. 1 Bachelor when BMW Brian came in with a bunch of posies, arranged in a flowered teacup and a sassy saucer. Adorable. Then Buck showed up while BMW Brian and I were discussing his gift and handed me a plant for Mother's Day. This began to get embarrassing. These two were sizing each other up. The scowls were hysterical.

3:13 P.M. Jack and Pete came in and almost busted out laughing, seeing that these two had just showered me with vase'd hopefuls. Jack's wife was still planning to screw-him-over in the divorce; Pete just had emergency quad-bi-pass surgery and pulled his shirt up to show us his ungodly scars, my second bare chest for the season.

5:43 P.M. BMW Brian wants to go for a car ride together, No. 1 Bachelor wants dinner, Buck wants sex. I want peace and quiet!

8:14 P.M. My day is about over. I loaded up a paper plate full of fresh strawberries and banana chunks drizzled with chocolate syrup and a mountain of whipped cream. Now, *that's* the way to get your Government Recommended Daily Allowance (RDA): Fruit for vitamins and minerals, cream for calcium, and chocolate for such exceptional nutritional qualities as theobromine, stimulating the central nervous system, tryptophan, which is serotonin, the stress reliever, and anandamide, which mimics the effects of marijuana by giving us a mild high.

9:00 P.M. Kids finally called. They knew we couldn't have a *real* conversation when I'm "Open For Business." "I love you more than you love me," kiss-kiss, big hugs, and we caught up, quickly.

9:53 P.M. Now, I will have sweet dreams…

5-09 50° Overcast.

Root Beer Float: Ice, A shot of root beer syrup, soda water, cream, topped with whip.

8:43 A.M. The cutest couple came in. They were genuinely nice looking seventy-year-olds. They both had lost their spouses to cancer and someone introduced them to each other eight months ago. That was just about how long they have been married because he proposed on their second date! He was proud to say, though, that he *did* talk to her for a *whole* week on the phone prior to the dating. Come to find out, she lived here in Saratogan some fifty years ago. "My dad was a logger, so I attended the small-fry school. My three sisters and I, who were four years apart in age, all sat in the same classroom, in one building, that housed K-12. We are going to take a drive through town right now so I can show my new husband the school and the store." I added, "The store is no more but the school is *exactly* the same."

4:07 P.M. The sheriff just stopped. BOO must leave the woods tomorrow! I wondered where he would go. In a way I will be relieved that he is gone, but in a way, I felt sadness. I felt like offering him my chapel out front as a new home. I knew he would miss this location, just ¼-mile from where the train slowed down, and it was easy for him to hitch a ride. Poor BOO. Goodbye BOO.

5:00 P.M. I want to turn a page in my book and see where it takes me…

5-10 50° Overcast.

Coconut Granita: My original and skiers are addicted! A cup full of ice in blender, 2 shots of coconut daiquiri mix syrup, 2 inches of Half & Half, one pack fake sugar, blend.

10:51 A.M. I just had an older gal in for a toffee mocha. She came from eight siblings that were born and raised in Winthrop, Washington, which is now an Old West Tourist Trap. When they were young, they would come and stay with family friends in their cabin, right here in Treetops Loop! This was forty some years ago! All eight of the kids were still alive! She was a fun lady, and we had a great conversation.

No. 7 just called from the road. He wanted me to come and ride with him for a week around the country. Must want a trapped sex-slave for a week. Dream fricking on!

Buck showed up last night while I was unloading my espresso supplies, hounding me about some guys he swore he had seen me with and blah, blah, blah. "Get over yourself and go bother someone else! When in the hell do I have such luscious free time?" My gun was in my back pocket for unloading in the dark and the butt felt so reassuring in my hand. He definitely had been drinking.

5:22 P.M. I just came in from picking a bunch of weeds. One of the batches concealed a snake. I called Butch, my dog, over but the *slither* got away. He sniffed everything in sight for hours like he could not believe his blunder! He has caught three so far this spring. I knew because he couldn't wait for me to come outside and see his proud displays. He literally foamed at the mouth when he bit them. They must give off some sort of a vile repellent that causes this.

5:59 P.M. Dreams of oceans and palms…

5-11 67° Sunny.

Almond Iced Latte: Fill cup with ice, in a separate cup mix a shot of almond syrup and espresso shots together and stir this. Fill cup with milk but leave room for this mixture.

4:00 P.M. I had been gone all day, buying more stuff for the store. I was stocked for the summer crowds.

5:24 P.M. I thought I looked like shit *yesterday*; well today I looked like shit-on-a-stick. Figures, since I ran into a hunky Italian that opened a new store in Marysville, Washington, and happened to have bought property up here only ¼-mile from me! I guess the make-up rules are for a reason.

I stuffed myself to the hilt with delicious deli-food from the "city." OH…and I bought some *security* items. Door chimes and even a Panic Emergency Phone Dialer, with a *one-button*-911 caller. What an added relief: Guns and now panic buttons, then rescuers. I wouldn't mess with me if I were you!

6:00 P.M. American Idol tonight so, see ya…

5-12 50° Overcast.

Iced Eggnog Latte: Ice in cup. Put a shot of eggnog syrup and espresso shots together, stir. Fill cup with whole milk, leaving room for the shot's mixture. Sprinkle nutmeg.

7:49 A.M. I went "down-below" again this morning to get a new muffler on my plow truck. It was guaranteed for life and since my truck and my butt would be firmly planted together for 107 years, which was a good thing. As I was patiently waiting for them to get the muffler done, I stepped next door into a Starbucks. I realized quickly that I did not know how to even act at a Starbucks. I felt as though I was in the middle of a lion's den or equally as miserable, in a Nordstrom make-up department. This Starbucks happened to be in the middle of a cow town called Makana. This old western town had slowly turned into a successful Antique Capital of the Northwest. It has become mildly snobbish compared to Seattle. I was dressed more like a local farmhand than an antique shopper from the city. There were some disapproving looks (in my mind?) and it was not terrific for my self-esteem. I ordered a decaf frappe (double the price that I could get for this drink – but I guess they had to pay for the fancy décor somehow – nice couches, cozy fireplace, granite, indoor restrooms, etc.). I stuck to that, just in case my pronunciation of the fancier ones was not quite cricket. Damn, I should have ordered that damnable caramel macchiato any-way and watched to see how the friggin' thing was constructed! I also pur-chased a soothing CD for my store but was surprised to find that they did not carry books in Starbucks! Holy crap! I had better get snappy with this book and market the hell out of it. These espresso joints need espresso books. People needed more entertainment than just people watching. And in these chichi locations, they did not get the colorful gossip like I got in my joint. Aren't people curious about the lives of a barista – after the apron comes off? Let's see… over 8,000 Starbucks…hmmmm…oh my God! Don't panic, Christy, go feed your animals and stay hooked to earth!

2:00 P.M. Slow, slow, slow. Why did I come back? I have only had four customers – total! I should have stayed in "farmland" and checked out the antique stores, just for the heck of it.

3:18 P.M. A couple just pulled up to my drive-thru in their classic Coca-Cola Show Car, with a matching '50s towed Coke trailer! Coca-Cola *everything*, including their clothes, caps, and her espresso cup! I took photos and even displayed flamingos on the front of their car for the photograph. It will appear on my website. I offered them free drinks to just sit-tight, right there – for a year!

6:39 P.M. I may be back down to Makana tomorrow…in the bread line…

5-13 50° Sunny.

Peaches and Cream: Ice, 2 shots of peach syrup, soda water, topped off with plenty of cream.

8:37 A.M. Last night Oprah mentioned "giving up men for muffins!" For those who are *allergic* to men like I am, even against our wishes, we eventually end up trading our men, and Sex Lives, back in for our Self-Worth. YES! Oprah is *one* of the *three* shows I watch on my *eight* channels. She is my teacher and my reminder.

2:17 P.M. Three neighbors just came in, in a row, asking why S.W.A.T. was up here in town, along with a bunch of sheriff's rigs. I checked to see if my scanner was plugged in. Yes – and nothing. We all hoped it was a drug bust!

Speaking of security, the door chimes were in and I was wearing my panic-button necklace. A whole new look and style! It sure feels good to be protected, to the best of my ability. The huge, famous auto swap meet is going on this weekend, in Tillamuk, Washington. This is forty-five minutes "down-below" and brings mostly men from all over the USA and Canada. Grease monkeys. My son graduates from grease-monkey-college today. I am so proud of him! He is still a kid of eighteen, so he's excited that diploma day is Friday the 13th.

3:44 P.M. I saw a tall, fit guy trying to get in the entrance door I just locked. I yelled out the drive-thru window, "Can I help you?" He walked up in camouflage pants, a black tight tee, camouflage make-up, and a fucking gun! My finger was ON my button! He *casually* ordered his mocha! He did not introduce himself, so I prayed I was correct on this and asked, "Are you part of S.W.A.T.?" He calmly replied, "Yes, I am." "Well, sir, you are the only one in this group of two that is unruffled!" THANK YOU TOO DAMN MUCH, MISTER, FOR TELLING ME THAT UP FRONT! Will you please dial 911 so I can continue my fainting spell? "Have you looked in a *mirror* lately? You scared me to death!" I got the teeniest upward curl to the corner of his mouth. Was this their training? Be mute, scare the hell out of the folks, and keep everyone on-guard and alert. Well, you cannot very well stay alert in a crumpled heap on the floor!

I gave it 1.5 minutes for the locals to come out of the woodwork for the story on *this* visitor. Sure enough, in a flash I had four residents asking, "What was he all about? What did you do, Christy? We were too scared for you to come check it out." "Thanks, loads!" I pried a drink out of each of them, with shaking hands, before I gave-it-up! "Yes, he was part of S.W.A.T. and they were looking for a suicidal guy with a weapon up at the Blue Bear Trail. God, I hoped it wasn't BOO!" It turned out the team never found the guy and was within a mile of tracking him. I thought maybe this guy was a militia because we have plenty of them hiding out in the mountains around here. Just another scare in the life of this Solitary Barista.

4:01 P.M. My neighbor came in my drive-thru and ordered his sugar-free hazelnut Americano. I showed him some of the new canes I had for sale. He suffered a stroke awhile back and accidentally left his cane in Alaska. He shared, "My mother started falling a lot in her old age. I finally recommended that she lay a blanket, a book, and a lantern down in the various places where she usually took a spill. That way, she would be comfortable and entertained until someone showed up. And it saved her sanity a couple of times!"

8:01 P.M. And I am burned out. No personality left…

5-14 54° Misting.

Iced Mocha: Ice, milk within 2" of top, mix separately a shot of chocolate syrup and espresso shots, pour over ice and stir.

7:53 A.M. I was going to try to find out the identity of the suicide threat yesterday. I hoped again it was not BOO. I felt like we were long-time best friends and I had never even met – or seen – the hermit!

It's cute when customers order their drinks as follows: "My cousin would like a caramel mocha, blended. My aunt would like to order…" Okay, which one is which, and I sometimes write *their* descriptions on the lids – always am *more* than complimentary and I catch them looking, laughing, and loving every minute of it!

It was a beautiful, clean spring day with a light mist. I was having a clumsy day – this time black and blue marks *will* appear, turning my thighs into relief maps. A few days ago, it was dropsy.

9:08 A.M. I just got word that it was not BOO. The father of the suicidal man just came in asking me if I had any flares for sale. They wanted to use them in today's search for their son! I handed them three large flares and wished them all the luck in the world. "I hope you are successful in finding him safe and sound. How traumatic for you!" "S.W.A.T. won't come up to help today," he said sadly. The father stuffed a five-dollar bill into my tip jar and would not take it back. I tried. I am a parent too! Next, the mother came in, crying her eyes out, and sobbed, "Do you know anyone up here who could assist us in our hike, so we don't get lost?" Their son was only thirty-two years old and had been suffering from depression for the last year and a half. I got on my phone, in between customers, and called every male I knew on this mountain. None were home. The difficult issue was that the son had a gun. That was why Search & Rescue was not able to assist this family. Weapons changed the whole picture. I kept my eyes peeled, just in case he meandered through this area: this highway was the only road, in or out of town.

10:22 A.M. I just had a young family come through the drive thru. They had been getting their decaf lattes here for three years now. I realized, when looking at their kids in the back seat, I was watching people's babies grow up – right through my window. It was a real awareness for a barista. Means we were aging too – and it is *flying* by!

A gal I know who is in Iraq as a civilian worker emailed to tell me about all the antique planes that were still being used to *taxi* these civilians. She claimed that bullets and bombs were at the bottom of her fear list, compared to flying in these rust-buckets! Today the pilot took three stairs at a time to replenish the oil in the left engine! The pilot's girlfriend was sitting there repairing the cockpit upholstery. How nice.

An elderly couple in the drive thru ordered a decaf mocha and a regular mocha. It came to $6.50 and he handed me three fives! You wonder how they get by sometimes – and who takes advantage of their aging difficulties.

10:30 A.M. Well, that totaled five lattes, a chai tea, three flares, and some Kleenex sold so far today. Not bad for having the doors open for two hours and twenty-three minutes.

11:29 A.M. Scanner: A male gigolo "down-below" wearing a black dress was sitting on a picnic table with another male, trying to flag down more clients. Buuuuusssted!

A Yahoo Internet dating couple came in all smiley and holding hands like they never planned to let go. They claimed, "Internet dating is the *only* way to go. Instead of having maybe six people to consider in a dim, smoky bar, we each had about two hundred choices. You can just sit home in your PJ's, drinking a brew, and snag a bunch of *willing* partners. Computer chairs are much better than bar stools!" Not for this kid.

And, speaking of dating…I am not going out with No. 1 Bachelor of Seattle. His presence will just intrude on the plan I live by these days: Build Peace and Harmony from Within!

3:40 P.M. Scanner: Another DOA, five miles up Mollson River Road, right here in Saratogan! He was cold and stiff and apparently a suicide by carbon monoxide poisoning. Could this be the son of the worried parents and the subject of the S.W.A.T. team? I have got to change the subject!

ESPRESSO HISTORY

The first espresso machine was made in France, in 1822. Dr. Illy created the first automatic machine. In 1946, an Italian named Achilles Gaggia created the espresso machine that we are familiar with today. Gaggia created the first high-pressure espresso machine.

5:50 P.M. I am going to go clean and shine mine…

5-15 50° Misty.

> **Iced Chai Tea: Fill cup with ice, fill halfway with liquid chai tea, top with whole milk.**

9:25 A.M. I have already lost count of espresso sales! Cranking! I arrived through my last gate to enter my workplace, and there stood two good-looking guys who just exited a huge black truck. They both had big friendly smiles. I yelled jokingly, "You guys are stressin' me. I'm not open and organized yet." It really *is* pressure for a barista to have people waiting and watching and sometimes pacing while we scramble with milk, beans, ice, cash, alarm systems, and lipstick…in seconds. Those in search of a "fix" are not the most empathetic and patient people on the planet. I scrambled while these guys laughed and flirted, making it much more pleasant.

11:11 A.M. One of my regular gals stopped and explained that she yanked out her husband's flowers this morning…accidentally. She was trying to be helpful in their new garden and thought she would do some weeding. Well, she yanked all the flowers he planted – by the roots! She was not the least bit interested in returning home.

Harley Dennis came in. He is still bugging me for a dinner date, "You practically *owe* me one for my birthday, but my treat, of course!" I *reminded* him, "It's still No Thank You." "You'll break one of these days, Christy." Tell No. 1 Bachelor that.

4:58 P.M. So many dazzling men through these doors today – so little time! The lakes have opened for fishing, so that must be the reason. Gets a gal tempted to once again believe in them. A few were busted for searching below my chin and that is an instant write-off in my book. If they will do it here, and I'm definitely not the biggest tits on the tarmac, they'll do it everywhere!

5:45 P.M. My grinning morning guys just stopped to harass me some more. I lost track of time and thought their visit was yesterday! Busy much? The single one begged me for a date but my usual answer, "No way," satisfied him for now. I used the old grandma trick as he was only thirty-eight years old, but he took a punch card, so he will call. Good for my ego anyway.

6:10 P.M. The phone rang. First, he said his name was George, then Rick. It was the guy who took the punch card. Fast worker!

9:02 P.M. Closed...

5-16 49° Raining.

> **Iced Soy Latte: Fill cup with ice, fill with soymilk within 2" of top, and add espresso shots.**

9:36 A.M. I was having one of those days, where I went to grab the shop vac out of the refrigerator. I went in the back room and could not for the life of me remember why. Couldn't find my register tape and I had at least a case of the damn stuff, picking up the phone and not having a clue who I was attempting to call. That is how my *medulla oblongata* was working on this fine morning!

Second day of rain. Evenings have gotten a bit nippy. Too bad for me…because I was not shutting those prehistoric, tattered windows until fall. Opening them involved every tool in my junk drawer and some loud karate noises! Summer will come…summer will come…our mystic meditation. It was my own fault for getting so excited, so early, when I heard the first southern bird chirp!

1:19 P.M. Scanner: Motor vehicle accident, two miles down. Car flew into a tree or a residence.

10:00 P.M. And I still had my drive-thru open. Computer work was keeping me awake…

5-17 45° Off and on rain.

Raspberry Mocha Breve: A shot of chocolate and raspberry syrups, espresso shots, steamed Half & Half.

7:00 A.M. Temperature outside meant my house was *also* 45°. I sleep like a baby, though, in this "camping air." TV tonight, so this cold living room ought to be incredibly challenging. Windows still jammed open, but it wouldn't make a hellavalotta diff! Next year I think I will wait to open them until at least June 1st.

1:20 P.M. I wished the sheriff would stop in – I was still waiting to know if the two suicides over the weekend were related.

3:22 P.M. Jack and his shadow Pete stopped by. Of course, we were discussing the "M" word and the light bulb just came on, as we all came to the same conclusion at the very same time: between the three of us we have had twenty marriages! That is a (sick) crack-up! How much misery can three people handle?

5:17 P.M. A seventy-year-old lady just came in (*she looked fifty*) and she was up here reminiscing about the years she lived right here in Treetops Loop, from 1980-1983. She worked for the Forest Service and was also a teacher at our tiny schoolhouse. She remembered this store being open; back when it was a gas station and grocery store. In the winter of 1981, she believed, the snow was so deep, she had to snowshoe to work, and the two miles along the railroad tracks seemed like ten. In those years, all she had were those old, webbed, wood antiques, which looked like big tennis rackets.

She just returned for her goodbye espresso, after a two-mile hike up at the Pacific Crest Trail. No wonder she looked fifty years old! She exercised routinely and was so aware and full of life! "The flowers are breathtaking, especially the patches of glacier lilies," she related. I have been asking for two years and finally she was able to tell me the name of the blue flowers scattered all over across the highway from me. Forget Me Nots.

10:07 P.M. I commanded myself to leave…

5-18 49° Off and on rain.

> Iced Mint Cream Mocha: Ice, mix espresso shots and a shot of crème de menthe, fill cup within 2" from top and pour espresso mixture in.

8:44 A.M. The county sheriff just popped in for a mocha and caught me up on the mountain happenings. The attempted suicide did happen on the Blue Bear Trail. We already knew about the other guy found dead in his car up Mollson River Road. And now there was another dead fellow on the RR tracks! Three dead men in the same weekend – all three ON Friday the 13th, and all three suicides! Uncanny and creepy! The bizarre thing was that one guy was named Mollson and he died up Mollson River Road. One man was named Marcus and he died on the RR tracks, near Marcus Road. The third has (had) the same birthday as our sheriff! This all gave me the willies! Him too!

11:00 A.M. I think I am going to break my own *isolation* record this week. I may survive eleven days in a row without leaving the mountain, except to the gas station two miles away for milk and ice. Will my sanity stay intact? Has it already left me and I am the last to know?

My neighbor, Rosie, came in to get her iced mocha and decided to hang out and talk. *Then*, she told me that she had an awful nasty cold. Sure, come on in and take a seat, while I massage your neck and you cough in my face! Seriously? Get the hell outta here, thank you, and wipe the germs off the doorknob before you leave! I could feel panic settling in. Bacteria freaks me out 100 percent.

My local German customers came in (*copper buyers*) and she screamed to her husband, "Look, how she is cutting the strings off her shirt!" I guess I was holding the scissors some foreign, contorted way that we learned when there was nobody within miles to help us. Never thought anything of it.

6:18 P.M. Maybe I *have* lost it…

5-19 50° Raining.

Mocha Cream Cooler: Ice, mix espresso shots with a shot of chocolate syrup, a shot of soda water and top with Half & Half.

8:19 A.M. When I opened this morning, I saw someone had thrown a big beer can out into my parking lot. Reminded me of the day we bought this place in 1998. We counted over 2,000 beer cans scattered around the property, parking area, and out in the barn. The barn had been converted into a teenage hangout. Somebody set up a half-pipe skateboard ramp. There was a big loft area high above the main floor and they would jump off and do their flips, twists, and turns in mid-air. I heard that between all the kids combined, every bone breakable had fractured or shattered right here. Rumor had it that doctors and lawyers with luxury homes on down to laborers in cabins, all skated on this ramp. *They* were getting drunk and stoned right along with the teenage skaters and *they* landed in the hospital too, in beds next to the punks. The entire ceiling was wallpapered in beer case covers.

This property was virtually abandoned for more than fifteen years prior to my purchase. A handful of skiers and snowboarders became unlawful residents every winter. They would haul up old mattresses, apple boxes, and ice chests. I guess the stories would write volumes. One year, they had pool tables lined up in the main store and there was so much beer and piss, it was dripping through the old wood plank floors into the basement!

The day we bought it, there were marijuana starter plants everywhere. The commissary and basement were filled with mountains of garbage, floor to ceiling. It took us twelve U-Haul truckloads to clean it up. The stench was past ripe! The squatters could add up to a total of one-hundred bodies at times; sleeping bags were sprawled everywhere, and - no heat – no fireplace – no nothing. It must have felt remarkably like the old-style prisons, with the thick cement walls, dank and filthy. One guy wrote in felt pen on a wall: It's fucking cold in here. I can't sleep. I'm leavin'. That was how it was, but most of these kids and some adults came back each year for more abuse and hilarity. Many still had fond memories. Band equipment, melted candles, weed, used condoms, booze, skateboards, rats, skis, cigarette butts, snowboards, sex toys, pizza boxes, broken flashlights, party favors – a real commune existence, up in "these-thar-hills".

2:22 P.M. Just sold a halter-top and a German chocolate cake latte to a very pregnant woman. I was just thankful she did not model it for me!

3:05 P.M. Scanner: A vehicle fire five miles up.

It was stormy today. I grabbed Butch and put him under shelter because it was wildly windy out there! Huge branches were falling from my grandpa trees out back. I did not need to find an unconscious dog.

I just had a heel! The fucker pulled right up in my drive-thru, parked his old beater, got out, locked it, and started walking away! I opened my window to ask him what the #&#X*%X he wanted. He reached over, touched *my* window and flipped it open all the way. A HUGE NO-NO! Never, *ever*, touch a barista's window! That is *her* space and she and *only* she, decides how much access a customer is going to get. And I did not open it all the way for a *reason*. I got *instantly* pissed off. Then he promptly went berserk when I said, "YOU TOUCHED MY WINDOW! Do you touch a banker's window? Consider it one and the same! And you parked and locked up your car in a drive thru. Drive-thru means thoroughfare. Now take a hike!" We had a fairly good rumble there…

4:19 P.M. Scanner: Caller claimed a man was bouncing a basketball on the roof of the car while driving on I-5.

5:05 P.M. I ended on a smiley note…

5-20 55° Partly sunny. Finally!

Mixed Fruit Smoothie: My original! A shot of each: raspberry, blackberry and banana thick daiquiri mix. Throw in blender with a cup of ice, a pack of fake sugar, 2 inches of cream and blend.

8:43 A.M. BMW Brian called from his road trip, whining over situations that I would consider extravagantly glorious! Like it being too hot to have his convertible top down on his sports car and how he was only surrounded by California cement, along with sand, surf, red dirt, and palm trees! Here I sat with record rainfalls and, yes, beautiful ferns and firs, but with two sweaters *and* a turtleneck on. He called for *sympathy*. He has been highly misinformed. He cracked me up, since this was the same guy who couldn't *step foot* onto his balcony in an exclusive upscale high-rise in Hawaii because of his fear of heights.

I just sent a nasty email to a lady on eBay – who sent me a defamatory one first. People buy things without really reading the words and descriptions that we sellers have *carefully* written. Then, they bitch about the item as if they were tricked. Tarnation! I have quality, clean, unique items and I do not need sales bad enough to mislead the public. Negative feedback will put you under – fast!

I had turned down my scanner and a bunch of cars suddenly flew past toward the west and I heard a helicopter. I think I missed something juicy!

1:01 P.M. I had an original old-timer in today! He brought a huge gift to me – more history stories! He claimed that someone could write a book solely on the characters that lived or passed through this town. I knew that a lot of towns had their colorful stories, but people agreed Saratogan was equivalent to

Alaska when it came to rough, tough, women, hard-working men, and booze. His stories are in my history clips.

Harley Dennis just called from his new railroad job. He really likes it.

The feed store guy, Wayne, came the twenty-five miles up to get *another* short latte. He was so nervous his hands shook, so I behaved and was nice, since this one was sensitive and probably nice at heart. Did I say just that?

2:39 P.M. A semi-truck deliveryman dropped off my latest order of merchandise – a seven-foot-tall pallet of flamingos from back east. Buck, where are you, you muscled creature. This driver hung around and talked for half an hour about his wife going through mid-life crisis; they had four kids, three houses, boats, cars, etc., and she had taken to barhopping, nightly, until 4:00-5:00 A.M. "Dude, the bars close at 2:00 A.M.! There is something wrong with this picture." Point off ladies.

Suddenly, the black clouds were rolling in. What the hell was I going to do with the mountain of flamingos out in the weather? Murphy's Law – nobody anywhere in sight! I ran outside, cut the plastic wrap, and started running box after box to the barn.

7:05 P.M. I am sick. I received an email from someone who heard the following statement on some disgusting medical channel: Blowjobs and swallowing can actually reduce breast cancer! I always had a suspicion that those scientists were *male*! I personally would trade a boob any day to *never* have to suck on one of those again! Or at the very least, choose to die a little sooner if that crap prolongs life! I am totally sharooshed!

Wish I had gotten a chance to ask Buck to grab me a pizza next time he went "down-below."

7:55 P.M. I have had it. I'm starving. Goodnight...

5-21 48° Overcast.

Iced Espresso: Ice, pour espresso shots over ice then add more ice.

8:50 A.M. I knew I would hear screaming for this, and my mother would kill me, but I straightforwardly cancelled dinner with No. 1 Bachelor. I emailed and told him just the *thought* of dinner made my *feathers fall out*.

Today was my 9th consecutive twenty-four hours up in "these-thar-hills". Last night I opened a can of green beans, sliced a hunk of cheese, and poured a glass of juice. Fine dining! The pop-top cans of dog food were starting to look fairly good about now! They swore they had *real* meat!

12:00 P.M. The Treetops Loop meeting is happening right now. Bet it is juicy! I know they are discussing my lawsuit with Trucker Bitch – and *both* of us are absent. Would I *kill* to be a mouse-in-the-house! I was starting to understand into which category baristas fell into. Men were so frustrated with this NO Sexual Harassment Law that it was stifling their natural "hunt" instincts. Men were created to stalk and go in for the kill, it was their natural order of survival; women had been their primal prey from the start. So, what were they to do with all this extra energy, which could/would land them jobless or worse – in jail? They found various safe avenues: waitresses, barmaids, baristas, massage parlors, topless joints, dating services, chat rooms, and more. These areas were considered safe for harassment and their obnoxious "hunt" behavior. They will be exploited in this book! It was not just for me. Almost every other barista I'd talked to would and has backed up these facts and were continually being harassed by men on an hourly basis. Unless they were ninety or looked like they'd been rode-hard-and-put-away wet; even then, if they flashed some knockers, the men were right on schedule. Maybe we should all agree to post signs at our various establishments that read:

DANGER ZONE! ENTERING A NO SEXUAL HARASSMENT AREA. BEWARE OF HIDDEN CAMERAS FILMING BEHAVIOR. YOU ARE BEING RECORDED AND WILL BE REPORTED TO THE PROPER AUTHORITIES, NOT EXCLUDING WIVES, PASTORS, EMPLOYERS, RELATIVES, AND MISTRESSES.

5:23 P.M. Well, Buck's and my friendship is over for good. He is drinking again and getting verbally abusive. Of course, he had to come by one last time to say goodbye (*pout*). So, now no BOO or Buck. They were my daily companions.

5:43 P.M. Scanner: A car was shot at on Mountain Peak Highway, in the High Valley area. Three male subjects ran into the woods. That was approximately nine miles west of me! Our sheriff was on his way down. He knew *all* the punks around here and the victims were waiting for him at the High Valley Store. Should I lock the doors? Yes!

Mr. Clint Gorgeous 15 just stopped! Holy shit, what a surprise! Although he was a self-centered rascal, he was a beautiful sight for sore eyes. He was the type that considered himself "*all-that!*" Sugarcoated compliments and sexual innuendos dripped from his luscious lips. Damn him! Stay focused, Christy!

5:59 P.M. Scanner again: More news about the High Valley shooting first car was just shot an hour earlier. Maybe local guys after all. Pull up your jock-straps boys, real tight, you are going to jail! High Valley sat down low, between two mountain peaks, and was flanked on one side by the Saratogan River. It was extremely hard to be on-the-run in High Valley! Dead ends…everywhere.

Just had a new customer buying a hot chocolate. He was traversing across the entire United States by car. He was retired. He sold his homes and bought each of his three kids a new house, with the understanding that he could stay with each of them, on opposite ends of the continent, a couple of times a year. He just bummed around, seeing new sights and visiting friends and other rela-tives. No motor home for him; he wanted clean sheets, a huge shower, and good food at night. Pretty nifty setup, I would say!

6:40 P.M. I had some newlyweds just pull up to the drive thru. Both ordered an iced latte with a splash of almond Roca. They were such a mismatched couple. You would not believe their matching outfits of fluorescent green. The age difference was at least twenty years, with the woman being the eldest. *Both* wore wild make-up, and her boobs were hanging out. He had a Mohawk and pencil mustache, almost too thin to be real – eyebrow pencil much? Were they dressed for some freaky sex?

Mister, my macaw, greets people in the drive thru by banging his beak on the window. Then he screeches, "Come in!" Kids want to steal him!

Someone sighted one of the shooters up here in Saratogan. My doors were locked. Cops were still on it. There went the train; maybe they hitched a ride when it slowed at one of our crossings.

I had a couple of drugged guys in earlier, just long enough for one to mention he was dancing in some tulips on *his* trip! They were higher than hell. I served up two mochas over ice. "Do you take food stamps?" They were *idiots* and they were in orbit. I wrote down their license plate number for the sheriff, right before I threw them out.

8:14 P.M. Cleaned my espresso machine and kept an eye peeled on every window. Not much longer, and I would be safe upstairs…

5-22 45° Raining.

Iced & Spiced: Ice, a shot of simple syrup, a shake of cinnamon powder, dash of nutmeg powder, add in espresso shots.

8:00 A.M. No customers. I could pluck my eyebrows, I guess.

9:55 A.M. My drive thru customers hope to score big on mushroom hunting today. This must be the most clandestine sport I know. No one will tell *anyone* where their secret, coveted patches are located – the tiniest hint does not fall from their lips! There are several varieties of these puff balls: the fruiting bodies, often referred to as *ground clouds,* consist of the cuisine variety from psychedelic to poisonous. They are looking for the expensive cooking shrooms.

10:22 A.M. More customers in who had triumphed with a grocery bag full of Murrells, over on Mossyrock Pass, in only fifteen minutes! This man had a friend who picked mushrooms for restaurants and got fat on $25 a pound! Next season he will collect wild huckleberries and sell those to the dining houses for $40 a gallon! Maybe unemployed people are flusher than we think.

11:18 A.M. A man just walked in with a Starbucks cup. I asked him, "What the hell is imprinted on your friggin' cup?" Belly laugh, "It says, I started miles ago and had to stop for espresso." His wife was a bitch and *slammed* my store door; maybe our little laugh got to her?

12:53 P.M. I just had some Texans in. Had to give them the espresso cram-course. They settled on flavored mochas. They returned to Seattle, from their seven-day Alaskan cruise and were headed to Icicle Town.

A damn espresso bean just fell down the drain of my cart sink, which plugged it up immediately! This meant that pesky putrid plumbing pursuit for Christy. Again! Later! This bloody well happens twice monthly.

5:47 P.M. Clint 15 just tried to stop in on his way home from his property in eastern Washington. Just late enough for an invite upstairs for din-din? Take your expectations "down-below," I thought while peering out my window at his presence! No phone calls *ever* and he expected to be entertained after doors were already locked. Bonehead! So, as I was on the phone with my sister, I hid in the back room and watched his desperate peering in the windows. Every damn one of my OPEN signs was still blaring. "Christyyyyyyy? I want to get laaaaaaaaid." "Too baaaaaaaaaad! You know I don't do boooooooooty caaaaaaaaalls!" My sister thinks I own a funny farm. "Just another dippy day at the ole **OUTPOST ESPRESSO**," I told her.

9:02 P.M. Another day and enough dollars…

5-23 52° Overcast.

Ice Cream Mocha: A shot of chocolate syrup, espresso shots, steamed milk and a scoop of vanilla ice cream dropped in, whipped cream.

7:01 A.M.

I awoke to find a guy in his motor home enjoying my park. He must have spent the night out there. Guys sleep here one-way or another! I prefer the "another."

I let Butch out, knowing he would bark ferociously. By the time I was dressed and got some eyes on, he was long gone, so I didn't get the "story."

7:52 A.M. Number eleven day of isolation! I was getting sort of used to it. I'd be going "down-below" later today but would be back again for eight straight days. Memorial Day weekend was coming.

I did dog, bird, and people poop control, emptied the huge outdoor trash cans, and all was caught up, except for trimming up my acre when the sun came out. All our properties and yards look like white trash this time of year.

9:48 A.M. I just tromped across the highway, up the high bank, over the railroad tracks, and through the nettles to take an elevated photo of this place. Just as I finally arrived at a great vantage point, I saw two sets of customers pull into my parking lot. Shit! Ran back through the bush, catapulted off the hill, using a cedar branch as a rope, darted across the highway lanes, and breathing like a marathon-sprinter, tried to gracefully greet the first large man. He asked how I liked it up here in "these-thar- hills." "Beats the hell outta horrible traffic, horrible prices, and sitting behind a horrible desk all day!" He ordered his frappe and wanted to know what we called "people" down in Metropolitan Seattle. "We call *you* everything from 'big-city-heads, townies, city-jokes, urbanites, bête noire' – but mostly city-slickers."

The second carload only wanted a potty break.

1:31 P.M. Scanner: One of our local fifteen-year-old girls was having a major seizure at the school. She had them regularly but this one was severe.

A hyperactive train-buff dude ran in to get a quick double mocha. He was racing back up to the train tunnel where they had been halted for two hours due to repairs on the other end. This buff was so excited to be able to take photos of these trains, one right after the other, emerging from the tunnel, he was about to lose control.

5:29 P.M. I'm gonna choo-choo off...

5-24 54° Mostly sunny.

Chocolate Smoothie: My original! Cup full of ice in blender, a shot of chocolate syrup, 2 packs of cocoa, 2 inches of Half & Half and blend.

9:08 A.M. No more considering those cans of dog food for dinner! I shot "down-below" last night. I was so hungry that I couldn't decide who, what, when or where to eat. So, I settled on a fried egg sandwich and fries. Shopped till I dropped. I could *vaguely* remember when *that* used to mean *malls*!

12:11 P.M. My two garage doors are all falling apart at once. I tried to Liquid Nail the smaller one and now it will not shut at all. I'm pissed. "BUUUUUCK!!!" Sprinkled salt on my weeds, but I needed about nine more bags. Great for unsightly slugs too.

I drove by the mission down in Pacifica. Lots of men roaming around the perimeter. Wondered if BOO was there.

A lot of cars were parked at milepost 39 to behold Rushing Falls. There was a wide shoulder for people to park and a short trail down onto the worn rocks. Many lives had been lost within such beauty as people were perched upon the rocks overlooking the spectacular waters. Last year, a family purchased a new vacation cabin in Crag Rock. The very first weekend, enjoying this new venture, their son took off with a couple of his buddies and started rafting down the lazy river. Unknowingly, they were right above the falls. Homeowners were out on their riverfront porches, screaming at the top of their lungs for them to stop! But the boys were having fun and couldn't hear what was being said. They were flipping-off these folks. Shortly after their sign language antics, two of the kids saw what was just up ahead and jumped out, barely surviving. The son went over Rushing Falls to his death. Someone died there every single year. The wilderness can be magnificent, but deadly.

2:11 P.M. Sheriff finally came by to do a long-awaited espresso drink. The three boys shooting at cars were all caught and toast! More good news, a local meth lab got busted!

2:48 P.M. Just had one of those couples in who had that afflicted *inbred* look. She was covered with hickies on her fat neck and didn't have a tooth in her mouth. She was admiring my chocolate-covered espresso beans, "Can't buy theez cuz I got no teeth." I carefully replied, "Well, at least you don't have to go to the dentist!" She replied, "Gone only once in ma whole life an' they pulled 'em all out." She had a nice big diamond on her hand, though. Must have earned it with all those hickies. The guy was gross too – and smelled! She ordered a caramel macchiato! How in the fuck did she know about these expensive treats? I guessed on the recipe again and she loved it! I take turns… dark chocolate syrup, white chocolate syrup, no syrup, vanilla, and caramel, whip, no whip and everyone loves them! It is a crack up!

8:19 P.M. Goodnight. Running upstairs for a *real* meal…

5-25 55° Sunny.

Blended Soy Latte: Cup of ice in blender, 2 inches of soymilk, espresso shots and blend.

8:44 A.M. Summer is coming, school is out, everyone travels, vacations and getaways = customers!

9:56 A.M. I am feeling generous right now (*for some unknown reason*) and going to give the man-column three points back! There are three *true, courageous, courteous, fair, gallant, gentlemanly, polite, valiant, and honest* men out there – I can attest to the trio, personally! And all of you are aware now that I view men with a powerful magnifying glass! No. 1: is my No. 5. No. 2: Our sheriff (married, unfortunately). No. 3: Our power company guy (married too). End of story. They are all wonderful. I would trust them with my body, my heart, and more importantly, my soul even out-of-sight! These guys are true to their wives, behind closed doors…mine. I forget where I was going with this…don't mind me. I also forgot to put my flamingos out this morning. I am getting absentminded and just plain flummoxed.

4:11 P.M. Do you remember Bobby, the pushy guy that Dennis served that day while I was trapped in the aviary? He strolled in late this afternoon. Bragged about how clean he was for a man – while cookie crumbs were falling out of his mouth, all over my counter. Bragged about how rich he was, but never left a tip, and how forty-two-year-old babes are after his sixty-two-year-old bod. Braggart is his name, alright.

10:06 P.M. A good night for stretching…

5-26 60° Complete sun.

> **Smith and Kerns: Ice, a shot of coffee and crème de cacao syrups, Half & Half and a shot of soda water.**

7:51 A.M. I hadn't heard from Buck in days. Must have gotten immediately hooked-up when I gave him the *real* ax.

Harley Dennis called, "Hi, I'm just ringing-up my favorite brunette. Piss-on-it, Christy, and get your ass over to Fishline Lake this weekend. Some of my guy friends and I will be there. I have a new tent, a new queen-sized airbed, and a brand-new sleeping bag! I'll even go so far as to bring clean sheets!" "And your point is, Dennis? I've explained that I have to stick around and guard this fort with all the 'city slickers' coming through." Did he *seriously* think I would consider mummying-it-up with him? Shit.

3:34 P.M. My very-English regulars came in. They were graciously invited to their daughters for the weekend. They were happily anticipating a wonder-ful "family-get-together." Until they got the *second* phone call telling them the visit would entail babysitting their granddaughter, Miss Bossy Brat, the hell-on-wheels four-year-old. They had their usual Americanos and asked if I could possibly have a gin and tonic ready for them at the end of this harrowing stint.

A tiny, old couple came in to visit. The first trip back in our area since 1964, when they used to ski the hell out of the hill. They owned one of the elite lodges up at Mountain Peak Ski Resort, which still stood today. The area was separate now and gated. I was unaware of these. They used to have to hike in a mile back then; it was accessible by road now. Apparently, ten couples owned the five lodges and the total consisted of thirty-four beds. These were never on the market or I would surely know the place. Instead, every one of these locations had been handed down to their children and the children's children. "No matter how fierce the weather was, we all celebrated New Year's together. One-year there was a terrible blizzard. It took us two hours to go the last two miles to the summit, while taking turns sticking our heads out the window to make sure we were still on the road! Another year, we even hired a band and chef, from the notable Olympic Hotel in Seattle, to handle our feast! We were livin' large. Do you ever get lonely way out here?" (Second most asked question). I replied, "No. How could I, with nice customers like you and all of these stories walking through my doors?"

4:07 P.M. No. 5 just stopped here in his semi rig! He stayed an hour and behaved, not taking the lid off the *reminiscing box.*

My neighbors were all overheated from mowing and stopped here for drinks.

6:40 P.M. Closing. It is 92° and will be 92° upstairs. Ugh. Ice cubes for dinner…

5-27 65° Sunny.

Iced Eggnog Latte: Ice, eggnog (or eggnog syrup and milk), espresso shots.

7:31 A.M. It is supposed to be 92° again today. Memorial Day weekend. Cars are flooding the highway going east! My insane days will be on Sunday and Monday. I adore insanity!

Ms. Gossip No. 2's husband got into a rollover car accident yesterday, on our perilous Mountain Peak Highway. He was all right, some bruising, but their car was totaled.

My old guys, Jack and Pete, came by. We had some good laughs for about an hour. Pete, who had *only* five marriages, said he would love to catch up with

Jack and me. He loved to tease us about this. Down deep, he said he was keen on being married, but if the wife wanted him out, then he would just leave. He had been known to load up his truck with what would fit, in fifteen minutes, flat, leaving the rest. "I just go back to fucking work. Don't need any more pain staring me in the face and I don't do couches very well," he said. That simple. If the next wife gave him any shit at all, he'd follow the same pattern.

10:17 A.M. Scanner: Five-alarm fire at our school. False alarm, just minutes later. It was only a faulty sprinkler.

The ants are marching in! We are talking about one inch long, three-part, black carpenter ants. This area is riddled with these disgusting bugs, yearly, but only for a couple of weeks. My dog *semi kills* them in the house. He paws them half to death and then just watches them wiggle, helplessly. I cannot get too emotional over this well-maimed torture, because if they aren't destroyed, they will literally fall from the frigging ceiling, and you can *hear* their shelled bodies hit the ground. Or feel them hit your head!

3:50 P.M. Bear and his parents came in. Mom was walking *on her own* without the walker and looked adorable. A new hairdo makes a body feel a lot better. But she will not be able to stand for more than three hours a day...for the rest of her life. She needed major back surgery but was passing on it for now. Bear, the Pom, was just too adorable. I had to stop letting him have the run of the store, as he peed anywhere, he darn well pleased - still. They also brought in their Goffin cockatoo. What a doll! Mister fell in love with her immediately! Angel was pissed!

7:23 P.M. It's too damn hot in here to write, serve customers, sit, move or breathe...

5-28 65° Sunny and already hot.

Brown Cow: Ice, shot of each: coffee, crème de cacao & vanilla syrups, espresso shots and milk.

8:00 A.M. Two train engines are pulling a ton of train-track repair equipment, eastbound.

11:30 A.M. Scanner: Sounded like river rafters were stuck somewhere in the middle of the Saratogan River. Rescue crews were on it.

12:25 P.M. Harley Dennis called from the Fishline Lake Campground, describing every tantalizing morsel, every night, on the grill – steak and prawns, sautéed mushrooms, baked potatoes, garlic bread – all done on the barbi. Brat! He knows I live on popcorn, Top-Ramen, chocolate, fruit smothered in whipped calories, pizza, and eggs. He does not know about the coveting of dog food.

12:37 P.M. Scanner: A water rescue down at Trout Creek Campground (five miles west of here). Swimmer in the water! Probably jumped off the bridge as a summer lark. My older male neighbor just stopped by after hearing his scanner. "That's how we clean out the dumb-ass gene pool!" It was a male in his thirties that fell in the water, but now he had been missing for twenty minutes. The water moved so swiftly there that you got dragged down to Rushing Falls! An hour later, they found him…alive. He was a lucky idiot this time. Lots of taxpayers' money spent.

The baby birds hatched, and I could hear them in my steel post. They were screaming for more chow - Ma and Pa were frantically bringing them worms.

6:41 P.M. Drive-thru only. Some bikers stopped and one of the gals bought a clay moon she eye-spied through the window. She also noticed Mister tapping on the window and knew that he was a macaw. She had a cockatoo but lost hers in a custody battle with an ex-boyfriend. He got the bird – she got the bed. Well, shortly thereafter, he beheaded it and left it on her front porch! God-awful story. He would be missing waaaaay more than a hea all right if it had been my bird! Point off!

8:11 P.M. Just had a van full of Seattle hippies. They ordered elaborate drinks, for up here. First drink was a white chocolate, crème de menthe latte (*he even pronounced the 'th' in menthe*), with a splash of vanilla, with the emphasis on *splash*. Second drink was a kiwi, peach, and strawberry Italian soda, no whip. Third drink was a hot chocolate, please, preferably with milk, not water, and with almond and Irish Cream flavors, and absolutely no whip. "Yessiree-bob. Comin' right up," making two other cars wait much longer than normal behind them…

5-29 56° Cloudy.

Sunset Strip: Ice, a shot of orange and cherry syrups, a splash of lemon syrup, soda water to top.

10:32 A.M. Scanner: Vehicle fire three miles west of the summit.

Fifteen Veteran Brotherhood Harley riders just pulled in. They were a little upset with the cloud cover. I learned a new word today: Nimbi – meaning opposition by local residents to construction, intrusion, and facilities, which are intended to serve! In other words - Not in My Back Yard! Sounds *exactly* like a Saratogan motto in this *"No Progress"* hick town.

9:57 P.M. I did a fourteen-hour day. I figure, you only live once, so might as well stay awake as many hours as possible to enjoy all the opportunities. I am stocked and ready for tomorrow.

10:13 P.M. Drug dealers are running their stuff tonight! Shit-for-cars going in and out of Treetops Loop and then, like a flash, running their dope to the next selling point. Like we are all clueless. Wish I was a cop. I'd spy from a tree like a bird and I'd *never* let up.

10:33 P.M. Now its fourteen-plus hours. The legs are begging for a prone position…

5-30 56° Cloudy. Memorial Day.

Decaf Iced Caramel Latte: Ice, mix caramel syrup and decaf espresso shots, fill cup with milk within 2 inches, pour decaf mix over milk, stir.

9:00 A.M. I just had a guy pull up in my drive-thru, didn't give me *two* seconds to get to the window, didn't honk for service, just peeled out all pissed off. Have another drink, bubba, and start working on tomorrow's hangover! Bite me! My first bastard for the day and it is only 9:00 in the morning!

Another car pulled into my parking lot. A lady crashed through the door and was furious that I was on the phone with my mother. "Excuuuuuuse me, ma'am!" I hung up and dealt with the bitch. Oh boy…today was going to be full of stories. People were returning home from the holiday to clouds, empty pockets, hangovers, and sick of their kids! Moods!

9:41 A.M. Scanner: Another car got shot at on Hwy 522 – this time with a pellet gun. Were video games getting too boring?

Gosh, the brother-in-law of the thirty-two-year-old that committed suicide on Blue Bear Trail just walked in to return the flare that was left in his car that I had supplied that morning of their search. He came in to thank me and to ask that I pass the same along to all the law enforcement that helped them. I told him that I was deeply sorry about the news of his brother's death. The victim had recently been diagnosed with schizophrenia.

1:40 P.M. And a real jerk, after my body, just came in for the *second* time. He was an old fart that just got angry with me for calling him a *customer*. "Sir… you are ONLY a customer and nothin' more!" Didn't finish with, "ya silly, old, fat fart!" I will stay on guard with this one. I had seen this madman twice in my whole damn life, and he was going possessive and weird on me? Buck was here the first time he came, when his behavior was a little bizarre and told me to give him a call if he showed up again. He would be in the truck and up in a sec – to call me honey-babe and plant a great big, wet smacker on me, right in front of this freak. He finally left.

I had to do an emergency fix on my blender and refrigerator today! The blender was leaking, so I quickly tore it apart and a strawberry seed from my smoothie mix was the culprit. The refrigerator in my commissary was freezing my milk – solid. Not a terrific element for a busy weekend. I searched and found the temp sensor had fallen off. I put everything back together with duct tape and all was well. Women can do *anything* in a pinch! Just try to put us in a vise and watch out! Everything is either A, B or C. Men, however, see things as B, Z, F, G, R…shit B again, maybe M…screw it until tomorrow.

5:05 P.M. A lady just took a header, inside my store, with a full cup of chai tea! It was everywhere! She was covered! I make her a new one while a man helped her try and clean up a little. He bumped into a tray full of merchandise. It went flying and glass broke everywhere. In the meantime, she was screaming that he touched her breast while he was trying to help her mop up. He threw up his hands and looked at me helplessly. I got everyone calmed down and appeased. Wonderful few moments in the life of a barista.

9:40 P.M. Traffic is dying down. Thank you, patrons, for yesterday, today, and all days ahead, even though I can't *stomach* another one of ya, for another *thirty seconds…*

5-31 50° Raining.

French Cooler: Ice, a splash of each: crème de cassis, rum (real), coconut, pineapple, French vanilla, soda water and Half & Half.

8:49 A.M. Well, I lugged heavy buckets of water across my acre, several times, to water plants – and then it rained.

Sold a robust fellow a 20-ounce white chocolate mocha. He was in his twenties and reeked of weed. Then he returned asking me for a paper clip. I gave him that motherly, evil eye and asked what he needed it for. He rambled some BS about his car and bogus parts and…I just stopped him mid-stream and informed him that I raised two kids. "Could it be a roach clip you need by any chance?" We laughed as he left…empty-handed. Then he was back behind his wheel on Mountain Peak Highway, stoned. Swell.

2:02 P.M. My English couple arrived following the dreaded babysitting weekend. Their daughter and son-in-law took off for Vegas. I apologized for not having their gin and tonics ready. They settled for espresso and chips. I saw her steal her husband's chocolate-covered espresso bean. She needed a "kick." He caught her this time, before they had headed to the door, so I coughed up another for him. She tried to swipe it again, but he was too quick for her.

4:00 P.M. A brainstorm! Leave and get to the bank, pick up a pizza, ice, milk, and a few movies. Second option: settle down and relax. The traffic has died off. I'm goin' for it!

8:17 P.M. All those errands are run. Tomorrow I will be ready...

JUNE

Hummingbirds flutter for sugar,
as our teapot whistles us home

6-01 49° Raining.

> Chocolate Mud: Ice, Half & Half, add in a mixture of chocolate syrup
> and white chocolate syrup.

8:55 A.M. I left for the lumber/hardware store. I had to face the music, no matter how sour the note was. My storage barn needed a new garage door and that is all there was damn to it! After all, this was the "house of merchandise!"

Saratogan was thick with thieves – trolls, drug dealers, and addicts, who would all sell their mother's underwear for a high! How warped was the door, you ask?

The sales gal informed, "You need a good butt-marker!" Who doesn't? "It's the tool needed to mark the areas where you have to chisel out for the hinges." "Chisel? Okay...I'll take one of those too, I guess..." I stood there pissed off and overwhelmed and feeling broke again. I went for a damn door and the sales gal was blackmailing me into believing the whole damn building would be condemned unless I purchased a butt tool, chisel, handle, lock, hinges, screws, something to hit the chisel with – and – a first aid kit for the smashed finger! So, I finally left with only the door, hoping I had enough crap in my little "girl toolbox" to handle the job – I did: A rock to use as a hammer for the chisel, which was soon replaced with a metal fingernail file. The old lock and spring hinges would suffice, and there were always screws lying around on the ground. Their yard-boy couldn't be found anywhere! He was off smoking or hiding somewhere. So, I had to strap the heavy solid door to the top of my Jeep all by my lonesome. Miraculously, I got those tight bungee cords on and off the car without putting out an eyeball, once home. This door-thing reminded me of buying your kids a $2 gerbil at the pet store. By the time you actually arrived home, with that cute little fur ball, you owned a cage, food, feeder, wheel, and toys; you actually had purchased a new member of the family! Well for now, the door is for *later*! I will call Buck and tell him his hair looks like shit. I'll offer to cut it. He has tons of tools! Hmmmm…

2:30 P.M. BMW Brian returned to his corporate world after driving around, solo, for two weeks in his new convertible sports car. "I'm back to reality. The stack of work is so high I cannot get my arms around it, much less my mind. I didn't enjoy the trip, but it was better than this!" "You are hopeless – your glass has *maybe* a splash in it; just about the same amount as when you tell the bartender you would like a dirty martini with the teensiest drop of olive brine!"

6:00 P.M. I was sweeping my walkways and looked around just in time to see the Papa bird feeding his babies. He set the worm down on the asphalt, bit it into pieces, so those little beaks could ingest. What fun to watch.

9:00 P.M. Tomorrow just must be juicier…

6-02 52° Cloudy with a tad of rain.

Iced Chocolate Coconut: Ice, stir together espresso shots, a shot of coconut syrup and chocolate syrup and pour over milk and ice.

10:57 A.M. Not one espresso! Where's summer?

11:16 A.M. A famous bird veterinarian came in, gave me his card, and admired my flock. He grew up in Washington, but now worked for the best vet in the USA, down in California. He offered to give my birds a free check-up at his clinic. "My feathered friends may be one of the most important parts of my life, but a veterinarian visit to California might be just a tad over-the-top. Now…if you were a famous plastic surgeon, that just might be a different story!"

3:00 P.M. My sis called and cracked me up. Her kids were sick with colds and so was her hubby. The sick husband was the icing-on-her-cake, and she was in the middle of that monthly hormonal insanity to boot! They were re-doing their kitchen and all she wanted to do was peacefully paint baseboard trim. Between nursing? And noses? And medicating? And feeding? And watering? And changing channels? Impossible! She called to vent to the sister that had never nursed a man in her life! Especially husbands! I had been known to throw a box of Kleenex, a jug of Vicks Vapor Rub and the car keys at 'em and informed them that they were welcome back when they were well! Her hubby was yelling from his bed, "Be sure and clean the paint roller thingy – thoroughly!" The last word got her – she was over it! The roller thingies cost 99 cents new and she'd been cleaning them out for weeks with $50 worth of solvent, which had trashed her hands and put holes in the cheap plastic trays. Not to mention the fumes were ruining her lungs! "Today, I'm going to use as many of these fucking, fluffy, round, titty-pink tubes as I damn well please!"

4:22 P.M. Some miscreation of the male species was out teasing Butch. He appeared to be in his twenties, about 6'4", and should have known better. I hollered out the door that if he didn't quit this shit, I was going to unlock the dog's gate. I thought that would take care of the situation, as I had many "BEWARE" signs posted about. It didn't. He just flipped me off. I was so gosh darn mad I went back inside, grabbed a phone, and came out with my gun in my back pocket. "Hey, mutant! I have a permit for the metal in my pocket and if you don't leave these premises, right this instant, I will dial 911 and pull my gun! You are trespassing!" "You are a flaming bitch," was all I heard before he slammed his car door, still yelling something or other at my dog and me.

5:49 P.M. Scanner: A subject in a hospital gown was walking away from Pacifica on Mountain Peak Highway. Escaped prisoner – hospital patient from the mental ward? Lock doors!

6:00 P.M. Well, I am wasting away anyway…

6-03 49° Misting.

Grape Italian Soda: Ice, 2 shots of grape syrup, soda water within an inch, top with Half & Half.

8:28 A.M. I just got busted for the second time in my retail history, singing to my bird, in my real voice! A man was standing at my counter for who knows how long and listening! "Old McDonald had a…", "I've Been Workin' on the…" This guy didn't even bother to clear his damn throat, or wiggle, or anything! Brat! God, I was embarrassed!

A busload of parishioners stopped in! Thirty to forty drinks of all shapes and sizes. Whew! Had to get ice and whipped cream from the back storeroom a couple of times. Lots of blended drinks and Italian sodas. I felt as though I was making an attorney's salary! I received a couple of God Blesses. Can't hurt!

I had some lengthy chats with people today. A local we call The Goat Man is in here right now. This will mean enduring that customary hour, while he looks over 102 items and never purchases a single, solitary thing. I should get him to help with inventory when the time comes; he must have all my merchandise memorized by now! All his hundreds of goats have died, leaving only one and he will not buy anymore because he is seventy-five years old, although he really does look sixty-five. He has lived his golden years up Frothing Ham River Road in the hills and is finally ready to do some traveling. Besides being famous for all the horned critters, he is possibly the slowest driver on Mountain Peak Highway. He goes 40 mph and spends his days going up and down our highway, getting honked at, passed up or flipped off. He told me today that he stopped at the bar to have a drink (*Irish Catholic all the way – it was 11:00 A.M.!*), to un-stress from the crazy drivers. One furious driver followed him right into the bar to cuss him out for his snail-speed and told him to crawl back in the shell! Poor guy. He has his own motto, and taught drivers' education for ten years at a high school. He always told his students, "Better to go slow for five minutes than be dead for one hundred years." Point made.

7:34 P.M. Buck called. "You know, Christy, good-looking people like us look good even doing it on the floor." When he calls and begins and ends his conversation with smut-talk, then I know he has been poking it everywhere this week…or at least somewhere…somehow.

8:23 P.M. I closed and went upstairs, and it was flipping winter in my house! I *refuse* to close the windows. Who spread the ugly rumor that it is summer!

I'm sitting here daydreaming, in my layers of four shirts, about the categories of men's looks: Clean cut, biker beer slob, hippie, computer geek, jock, rugged, cowboy, shy types, suit and tie. There can be No. 15's, on the foxy scale, in all of them – but – jerks too.

9:17 P.M. I'm freezing. Must wind down and calm down...

6-04 48° Cloudy.

Lemonade Latte: Ice, a shot of lemon syrup, espresso shots and milk.

8:41 A.M. Some guys are supposedly going to show up and buy at least twenty of my RR ties! Take these sticky-tacky things out of here! They called and asked how many sixteen-footers I had left. Like I was going to go out and crawl around on creosote, fighting off the brown recluse spiders to count these ties? No way! I gave him an estimate and told him how much fun he could have by coming and measuring for himself. I really couldn't leave the store...

11:10 A.M. They are here. They ended up buying eighteen of the black, gooey mothers and drove off with a bent tire on their trailer. Watch out on Mountain Peak Highway! A major hazard is heading your way!

12:50 P.M. Scanner: A black bear was trying to cross Interstate 5!

Buck came by with two more historic photos! One of them was of the Keystone Hot Springs Lodge that dated back to the 1920s. The other picture was of one of the railroad trestles up Frothing Ham River Road, about thirty seconds from my store. That trestle saw a lot of whoring in its day, as it crossed over the red-light cottages! Thank you, Buck! I gave him his share of the RR tie money and loaned him a rental movie for the night. To watch at his own place, of course! Whenever he brought these historic goodies that he knew I adored, there was always a personal note attached. And I quote:

"2 fast, 2 far, 2 soon. Sometimes yes, sometimes no...or maybe. I wish we cud start all over and put this junk aside. Weer good lookin'. We have nice hair and yur cute enuf ta kiss. Weer gonna be honest. That's sensashonal. That's great.

You're a do-er. So am I. Mercy, a guy, he needs to be serviced and ya know what he thinks of ya. That's not me, Christy. Love Buck."

That, my ladies, is a logger's bullshit note. Lovely, ain't it? Anyone wants to try and decipher it for me…

2:12 P.M. Scanner: Car fire, westbound, two miles west of the summit.

3:00 P.M. My *personal* toilet in back was not working! To flush, I had to stick my hand into the *deep* waters of the tank (*incredibly old* toilet), lift the slimy black rubber thing up until the water was gone (seemed like minutes). Then leaped to the sink in the commissary (pants still around ankles cuz I don't dare touch anything!), washed the black shit off my fingers, dried them, got dressed and rushed back up to the front! This took waaaaay too long. So, I inspected with a flashlight and found the damn chain! It was the loop on that greasy-oily-slippery-slimy black thing that had rotted away. I needed all new guts; I was sorry to discover. I turned the water knob to off, with a sigh. What is with repulsive toilets! It was time to fix this and install the new garage door too. Enough procrastinating! The honey-do list was getting as long as my childhood Santa letters.

Rosie the Comedian stopped in to find me in the back hole – literally. She had a couple good ones – on cue, "What would get your man to put the flippin' toilet seat down? A sex change operation. Arh Arh Arh. One more, Christy. Why are men like public toilets? Because all the good ones are engaged, and the only ones left are full of crap!" And she left, laughing herself into a crazed stagger…

New signs for the two doors: Be Back In 2 Minutes. This gave me time to get upstairs and take care of business. I need that fire pole!

9:04 PM. I'm out of it…

6-05 47° Rain.

Cherry Shot: Espresso shots over ice with cherry syrup drizzled on top.

7:43 A.M. Scanner: Someone local fell off a rooftop.

8:29 A.M. One of my regular customers just came in and she vented about this third marriage of hers. Her new had-to-have-him-at-all-costs-dreamboat was treating her like crap! It was her birthday last week. She knew he would forget it, so she bought her own periwinkle luggage, put the bow on the huge box, and wished herself a Happy Birthday. Mrs. Periwinkle Luggage stood there crying, "I took a half-day off work, hoping he would surprise me with a dinner out. Time passed…nothing.

Why had I rushed into this marriage thing again?" A week later she was still pissed off – and she was still sleeping on the couch. Couldn't shut my mouth, "Why isn't he sleeping on the couch? With no pillow and a blanket that is much too short? Happy belated, Suzie."

2:15 P.M. My Catholic Goat Man was back. Today the Pope would be proud - only three of us in the store and all are Catholics. I was starting to like the old lookie-loo, and today he actually laid down some dough on some sweaters I sell. He whispered, "I will only love my animals till *my* dying day. People let you down." This barista could relate!

2:42 P.M. Gosh, the mother and father of the thirty-two-year-old who committed suicide just came in to return the two last flares I had given them. They handed me a three-page letter, thanking me and explaining their son's schizophrenic disease. I had seen their son in here before now seeing his photo. It was a sad, sad story. I about cried reading the letter and told them, "Unfortunately, we all have to go to our own *bottoms*. And we live life in our own way, until we are ready for help. I have ran from depression for years, and apparently he did too, in a different, much more brutal way. Now take good care of you and the rest of your family."

One of No. 7's sheriff buddies just stopped in. He was thrilled taking pictures of trains in our neck-of-the-woods. He wanted to know where the trestle was around here, and I gave him directions up the Frothing Ham River Road. I explained how the train started winding a lot from here on down. "I'm going to head down and get into the NO TRESPASSING section, near the tunnel. What are they gonna do? Call the cops? *I'm* the cops!" Arrogant – like all of them – but unique and fun personalities. I missed those high-energy guys.

3:37 P.M. Today's cheap husband that skipped the birthday and Periwinkle Luggage just came in! Payton Place this afternoon! He needed to vent too. Now I knew where they both stood. She felt ignored – he felt pressured. I felt like selling him some of my glass roses to surprise her. Came

That close! But then he would know that she and I had already talked. I weighed it and skipped it. Although maybe it would have brought them together under fresh sheets for the first time in a week! She returned from the Porty Potty and took his empty hand into hers. Go figure.

BMW Brian came in for 1.52 hours! I could not really tell you one thing he said since it was all so boring. I still didn't offer him the royal seating, behind the counter – on a chair. Almost two hours was too damn long, for God's sake! My ears were finished, and his feet must have hurt like hell on the cement floor! And I wanted to drop "down-below" to get a rental movie. Damnation!

Two burly Harley guys stopped and asked for a beer in my drive thru. "Now… now…boys, how many espressos stands carry booze?"

8:00 P.M. I was thinking of closing. Oops – not over till the fat soprano sings! I started the long process of really getting out of here and my keys were hiding! Where were they? Who stole them? It was pouring out and I really needed to pee…now! The rain was not helping that situation! I grabbed my spare car key and hunted bumper to bumper. No keys. I scoured the parking lot with my flashlight; I was getting soaked and no un-lockers. I did have a spare house key, hidden in the back fucking forty, under a fucking rock, under the red-wood table, and it was fucking dark and raining like a SOB. My sandals and socks were soggy, I was soaked, and I had to climb my six-foot fence like a ten-year-old. I tromped through the wet grass and found that one mystery rock. Got 'em, though they were kind of rusty. I got back over the fence, but Cinderella lost one of her slippers, on the wrong side, in a deep puddle. Then up the stairs and into the house. No keys were in sight, but a toilet was! I peed for ten minutes, got some real shoes on, and started the search again. Well, the keys were sitting right in my commissary, just about a friggin' foot from where they were supposed to be! I'm losing it! I looked up and ask for forgiveness for all the cussing, grabbed the umbrella, retrieved the glass (leather) slipper, and was already coming apart at the seams, and tromped back out to the back forty and replaced the secret keys and rock. Now I positively, without a doubt, needed a fucking plumber.

9:59 P.M. All in a single day in the life of an isolated barista up at **OUTPOST ESPRESSO...**

6-06 49° Sunny but rain ahead.

Raspberry Lime Granita: A cup full of ice in blender, a pack of fake sugar, 2 inches of raspberry daiquiri mix, a splash of lime syrup and 2 inches of Half & Half. Blend.

1:00 P.M. Just back from my weekly jaunt "down-below" to get supplies. I had super-bad-hair-going-on and garlic sandwich breath. And of course, my very first customer was a new guy that wanted to chat for an hour about *mercury*, and how it was making him and heaps of other people real sick these days. He nattered on and on about un-natural illnesses in his body. Yeah, right, and you would be *whose* type? He left me his phone number in case I had any desperate mercury questions in the middle of the night! Maybe he is the mental patient who just escaped from the prison hospital? I made damn sure he didn't escape with my three biscotti's without paying. I could hear the monotone-mumble in the background while I went about the *important* business of killing two big flies, disinfecting the cart (of course, he had to check the ingredients on the bottle), and stifled yawns!

4:08 P.M. Got an email from our Stanford professor, who had spent the last twelve summers here, all by his lonesome. Every year he stayed in the same old camp cabin that used to belong to the whores in the RR days. They were cheap and all had remnants of the crazy days gone by: notches on porch rails, a red lantern in the back cabinet, brass headboards, and old chipped, beveled mirrors. He was looking forward to chatting with me again, this year and maybe I will ask him to read a few more of my poems. The new bird babies in the pipe were getting super loud! When Mama or Papa brought them the beat-up worms, they could really let out a scream now. I could see their little beaks poking out of the hole. They have grown a lot. I will miss them when they abandon their keepers. Do the parents go through a mourning period?

8:40 P.M. I'm bushed. I'm going upstairs to check my mercury level...

6-07 48° Cloudy.

Chocó Caffé Blended: MY ORIGINAL! In blender: A squirt of chocolate syrup, 2 packs of hot chocolate powder, a sprinkle of cinnamon, 2 espresso shots, ice, 2 inches of Half & Half, whipped cream!

8:13 A.M. Rosie had no caffeine in her home and was blaming the two fights this morning with hubby on that. He hadn't given her a thin dime for gas or groceries for over a week. And of course, she had a "tab" here that was starting to look like the national debt! She needed air, a sip of my drug, and really needed to get out-of-the-house. More trouble in River-City?

9:02 A.M. Scanner: A chicken was running in and out of traffic at the intersection of Mountain Peak Highway and Highway 9. Cluck...cluck...

Rosie came in for her second 24-ounce iced mocha. She was getting back to normal now with some of this speed in her system. Her sister and she was talking about getting boob lifts. Both had mega-quad-E's...minimally! Her sister was wondering if they had sales on breast surgery. "We need a 'doc' who would do three boobs and throw the fourth boob in for free. Or maybe he could just give us a bargain per pound."

1:11 P.M. One of the "walking on Mountain Peak Highway" bums just stopped in; this time he was able to hitch a ride with a young gal. Are drivers crazy?! He was totally spaced-out and was pulling $100 bills out of every pocket. I had taken down two license plates so far today. Drugs, anyone?

8:23 P.M. I'm quitting all this excitement for another day...

6-08 48° Cloudy with sprinkles.

> Washington Red Apple Cream Soda: Ice, a shot of apple syrup, a
> splash of cinnamon syrup and a touch of raspberry syrup, soda
> water, top off with Half & Half.

12:07 P.M. Jack and Pete came in. Jack immediately drank his usual *very* hot Americano and Pete had two Almond Joys, since I was out of pastries. Northern Rail had some beautiful and luxurious "people cars!" One just rumbled by and they looked like movie-star-cars. They have seriously outdone Amtrak's design. The "boys" just had to comment on that opinion for 9.5-minutes.

5:40 P.M. I just installed my new garage side door on my barn! It shuts with the pressure of a flippin' pinky! This door has its first ever deadbolt – dating back to 1910 – and its plum beauteous if I do say so myself! I chiseled out the wood for the three hinges; felt like a famous woodcarver – maybe the Statue of David next? And being the close-fisted broad I am, never did buy the hardware. Luckily, I found the two old hinges lying on the garage floor and one was still intact on the old, dilapidated door. I stripped some of the screws, so that set me on another desperate search. The doorknob and deadbolt were the real challenges. The instructions were NOT in English! But all was good and it is locked up, snug-as-a-bug – and without the aid of a man!

WE CAN DO IT!

6:29 PM. Massage anyone…

6-09 49° Partly sunny.

> Hikers Delight: A shot of chocolate and walnut syrups, espresso
> shots, steamed Half & Half.

10:37 A.M. Scanner: A rollover car up Trout Creek Road, abandoned and possibly leaking fuel.

And then the day died off…completely.

1:11 P.M. Three customers, or so, have been in for drinks in the last two hours. They were so colorless I couldn't even remember anything about them. And then the shit hit the fan!

A couple and their two teenagers came in – one frappe, one mocha, a hot tea, and a hot chocolate. I made the two detailed drinks first and the mother headed out to put them in the ice chest. She came barking through the side door, "Who in living hell has drunk all the gin?" I was wondering why their son was trying on my jewelry and the girl of about sixteen was playing with my old solid wooden kiddy blocks. The father headed for the back room and was no help at all. He was aware of how disastrous her wrath could be. "Goddammit, somebody better speak up and speak up soon! William, where the fuck are you?" The stillness was like descriptions of what precedes tornados. Turned out that every time they stopped for something or other on their trip today, the kids hadn't joined their little adventure and instead made trips to the cooler in the trunk. They had a full-fledged, all-out family war, intervention and counseling, bitch session, right here in my foyer!

A customer attempted to come in for drinks but could hear the war from outside the building and turn-tailed. The mom won, the kids were grounded for a year, and the husband was a wimp dishrag the entire time! If I were a bettin' woman, my money would be on the side of him being out of luck too for a year, getting anything akin to affection! God, I was glad I was past the point of raising kids these days.

5:54 P.M. Boring...boring...boring. Time to eat like a glutton...

6-10 55° Sunny and warm.

Cold Chocolate Milk: My original! Ice, mix a shot of chocolate syrup and a pack of hot chocolate powder together in a shot of hot water. Pour cold milk over ice and add warm mixture. Stir.

8:00 A.M. I got up and out early and spread salt (again) over my weeds. It had rained so damn much lately that my weed killer had been a waste! I also sprinkled the wildflower seeds all around where the fatal accident had happened. I made sure the salt was nowhere near. I hope they grow and are colorful. I can still smell the scents now and again. A weird sourness. Sad.

11:32 A.M. I was finally able to have my first tea! The whole world stopped in again. My neighbor, Rosie, came in for her 24-ounce iced mocha. She was full of piss and vinegar as always and funny as hell! A lady pulled up to the drive thru and I judged her to be a bitch, instantly, but silently. Rosie blurted out, "God! She looks like she could bite the butt-off-a-bear!" And she could…and did. She was on-the-rag about something or somebody! Then I found out… she just got fired. We both gave her as much sympathy as we could, but she was not in the mood for a verbal hug – at all! Her husband was going to have an agonizing evening!

I emailed No. 2 Bachelor and accepted his offer to take me to an auction. It had been years since I'd gone to one of these functions – not since No. 5 and I used to try and get sweet deals on antiques. I had known this No. 2 catch, in the State of Washington, for over three years. He was worth millions, dark, fine, forty-six-years-old and single. He said, "It's time for me to release you from your cocoon, up on the hill!" An auction would be fun, busy, and loud. The *perfect* date for the *nervous*.

3:10 P.M. A magnificent No. 20 on the Adonis-scale just sauntered in. I will *never* be giving out that number again – this scale of winsomeness comes along *maybe* every ten years. This married man was so gosh darn physically alluring, I was wide-eyed, I am sure. Then a religious fanatic gal came in. I believe in and love *my* God, don't get me wrong, but puuuuleeeez! She wanted to give me a bottle of the *special* water she had prayed over. I told her that I didn't eat or drink from strangers. She got upset and started treating me like a heathen. Okay, lady, enough! GET LOST! She left in a huff, *with* her piles of propaganda.

6:42 P.M. My daughter called with incredible news! A wonderful man who blew through my life in the past was looking for me! He just emailed her, requesting my contact information. He had lost my telephone number, address, and email handle, but knew how to get a hold of her? I was going to ignore that Red Flag for now... You all know how I feel about the male species. This one was different – or – could turn out to be the very worst.

When we first met, I was in a blend of chaos and mayhem, between Nos. 5 through No. 7. I was not ready for anything resembling sane or rational and he had a girlfriend. During our stint together, he broke it off with this current flame and ultimately met the one and got married. It was his third. We had not conversed for close to three years. He lived in California; however, sometimes his career brought him to the Northwest (an airplane company like our Boeing). He was a fox and surfed like a powerhouse pro too; I didn't even need to describe that body! This one could bite! I Think I advanced into a dreamy fantasy, going from 1-100 in a matter of microseconds. Where is the reality here, Cinderella? He wasn't "into me" enough three years ago, to change his wedding plans. And now he emailed. Was I supposed to be his beckon call? Get a grip, Christy – this is how it works these days. Tiptoe on your very own rules: Keep calm, keep a clear head, keep in your head and not your heart, and keep very low-key. His financial future made me even dream more, since the aircraft industry was flourishing...

BOEING

In 1903, two events launched the history of modern aviation. The Wright brothers made their first flight at Kitty Hawk and William Boeing left Yale for the West Coast! He made his first fortune trading forestlands around Grays Harbor, Washington. He moved to Seattle in 1908 and two years later, attending the first American air meet, when he couldn't hitch a ride in one of the airplanes, he was determined to build his own biplane. His favorite phrase: "Never Say It Can't Be Done!" My sentiments exactly!

7:22 P.M. I'm upstairs in my home now and in a *heartbeat,* when that very *first* shoe hit the tile, I was ripping shit out of every hiding place (from my ex's) to find an old picture of this re-surfaced California cutie-pie.

9:09 P.M. Success! Dummy...

6-11 48° Cloudy.

Strawberry Shortcake Iced: Ice, a shot of strawberry syrup, a splash of vanilla syrup, fill with Half & Half.

8:22 A.M. My first customer was my new friend, a huge Christian biker / semi-truck driver. We became acquainted after I reported him to his company for continually honking as he drove by. I thought it was No. 7, showing off, right after our divorce and trying to get-my-goat. And, the similarity of the big guy – and the truck – was uncanny. His rendition following all this and our actual *first* meeting: "Hi, gal. I am your extra-friendly truck driver with the stuck horn. My company accurately deciphered the complaint – the area, time, and date – and came up with 'me'! After the handcuffs were removed and they discontinued the strip search, they finally were satisfied. And I'm just kidding about the first two. *My* rendition and reasoning bailed *me* out, plus the fact that we had never met. I could have been giving an eighty-year-old couple the toot-toot! Boss, sir, 'I see this little building isolated all alone up on the highway and it's *always* Open-For-Business. I just thought whoever was inside needed *someone* to honk a friendly *hello*.' So, it's nice to finally meet you!" I introduced myself, apologized and we shook hands. He stops in religiously now and we still howl over my *formal harassment complaint.*

9:11 A.M. Ms. Gossips No. 1, No. 2 and Rosie came in again. Another session of butchering the two-legged sex with a kickstand! *That* was Rosie's one-liner for the day! Genuinely funny! "And it explains why men sleep better on their sides – it's *always* at attention!" Then as we were rolling, one of our soon-to-be Charlestown County sheriffs walked up to the drive thru. I shut my nasty mouth and made his latte. The gals bought a 24-ounce iced mocha and a 20-ounce caramel mocha. No tea parties here – we were having a full-bodied espresso/coffee-klatch!

10:52 A.M. Mama and Papa birds are now cleaning up their nest in the pipe. They are taking full beaks of dirty nest material out of the hole and dumping it somewhere. I wonder if they bury it to hide their scent. They are both working furiously. I will be sad to see them go.

3:31 P.M. An old man came in and asked how long I have been here now. "Seven years." He asked if I took care of all this property myself. "Yes, sir." He asked if I tried to stay open in the winter. "Yes, every day, sir." He called me an old-fashioned pioneer woman! That was music to my ears, for some reason. I guess I was proud of myself and the daily challenges that I conquered. I have started to really believe we women *can* do anything we set our minds to! Of course, there was still the toilet...

A couple came through in their truck. Ordered a tall double mocha and an iced peppermint mocha Grande. She was sitting in the middle of the front seat – they were touching! What era did they think they were living in? And on which planet! I hardly ever saw this anymore. Even the automobile manufacturers have given up on romance. Consoles are taking the place of family members! I remember in the '60s, what an opportunity to take care of some of those male favors. Those were the days, when our streets weren't so crowded – and we traveled on roads instead of highways. What the hell would the amount of the ticket be if caught? Have any of you "done it" while rolling? Me too!

5:28 P.M. Today was nuts. Harley Dennis called to see if I had heard from Mr. Terrific, from California. Buck came by to save me from the newest stalker and stayed for two hours!

9:03 P.M. Still downstairs. My new package of cups and dome lids didn't fit properly; they were either dripping or flying through the air. Either way, they were making their messes everywhere. Mister wanted to be petted. Buck wanted sex. Stalkers were stalking. Straights were drugging. We have had three storms waltz through and wash away my *third* application of weed killer – on over ¾ of an acre!

A couple just stopped to order an eight shot 32-ounce breve! They claimed this was *normal* for Seattleites. Well, you *won't* be normal in about thirty minutes, believe me!

9:46 P.M. I glanced over at my computer and my eyes involuntarily closed. They were smarter than this old gal. Enough! Goodnight...

6-12 47° Raining.

> Granola Bar: My original! Shot of each: cranberry, almond and banana syrups, espresso shots, steamed milk.

8:43 A.M. My neighbors, both Gossips, came in for the third day in a row. I could get used to this! Rosie was missing, though. She didn't have that option of leaving the house anytime she got a wild hair. We all agreed we could not live under that roof, with that man, for half a second.

An old man came in to get an espresso and asked if he could tell me three clean parrot jokes, but only if I told him three in return. "Okay. But I only know one *dirty* quip." He instantly forgot about his hygienic witticisms and whispered, "Tell me your off-color one." I laughed and told it: "An old man was sitting on a bus and was staring at a kid with several colors of hair and wearing feathered earrings. The kid blurted out, 'Hey old man, I bet you have never done ANYTHING crazy in your life by the way you are staring at me!' The old man looked at this young man and calmly said, 'Hey ol' boy, when I was in the service, I went to Singapore and fucked a parrot. I thought maybe you were my son.' The kid was floored silent!" The old man left the store slapping his knee and decided to drive down to the senior center with his new jewel. I *love* old folks! They are so easy to please...

11:20 A.M. I emailed Tony Terrific in California last night. We will see his response. Is he still hitched?

This day was getting nutty! Harley Dennis came by *again* for an hour!

My best girlfriend, who is dating my brother, called me bawling her eyes out, because my bro didn't want her to move into his house so soon. I had a lot of experience in this field. *He* was the only mature and sensible one in this duet!

12:33 P.M. Mrs. Periwinkle Luggage came in with a big smile on her face. Her hubby, Mr. Numb-Nuts, was being really nice again and promised to never forget another birthday – then she laughed hard and said, "Till next year."

3:00 P.M. Next...my girlfriend called again, sounding like a record album on the wrong speed. I was flying around like a crazy person and she was droning on in flat-tire speed. No email yet from California. Second red flag, dummy. Maybe he was just sticking all his feelers in the Washington waters, so on his next trip he could cut through the entire preamble. Knowing California, he probably attended a seminar on the subject: Organize Your Booty-Chick-List via the Net!

4:12 P.M. I hadn't had one break to go upstairs to the bathroom all day... not once! Right now, there was only one lady in here. I told her I would be right back. "Can you watch the fort?" She obliged. My girlfriend called one more time! She was a mess. Relationships suck sooooooo bad! BMW Brian had stopped by from the "city" and brought me a bag full of gifts from the road trip down south in his convertible sports car. In between espresso rushes, I accepted gift after gift, up to the little "white box." I apologized for not having time to open it right then. I could see the torture in his eyes. But I had lines of customers – truly. Buck pulled up in the drive thru and handed me a bowl full of his mama's famous macaroni salad. I tried to balance that, the wrapping of gift purchases for my customers, and couldn't find a *sec* to open Brian's souvenir. I introduced those two men and, miserably, Buck drove off in a huff.

I finally got to unknot the bow. GOD, it was a sterling silver and Black Hills gold bracelet. From a customer! I will have to have ten links removed or gain twenty pounds for it to fit. Where is he going with this? I was clueless. Jewelry *before* sex is bizarre...fucking rare in *my* experiences anyway. "Thank you" ... I think. Brian left with his huge, broad, proud smile.

Why does PTSD crave to hook up with more PTSD? I have read that it is like home, our comfort zone in an astonishing way. Nice guys scare us to death. It's extremely uncomfortable although we crave just that. Add OCD into the equation, and plan on the pattern to continue to the ends of the earth, at least our entire lifetime without therapy. Wow. I need help, now.

Right on Buck and Brian's heels, some gals who were camping up the Frothing Ham River Road stopped for their late afternoon mochas. They told me about their experience at the Crag Rock Bar last night. "We saw a ton of cars so we thought it would be a great place to stop for some yummy hot food! Wrong! There was not a single soul in the restaurant; we ventured back to the noisy bar and asked some patrons if there was a restaurant around. 'Naw.' Then we questioned the location of the closest laundromat. 'Holy shit…if we had one of them, we'd have to clean up. No laundromats. No sewers. But we got some great booze!' We moved on and gingerly asked another crowd what or where we could find some dinner. Like we were complete imbeciles, they yelled, 'Olives, cherries, and pickled pigs' feet; youz can see them right there on the back bar, ladies!' And when a man with a two-foot-long beard walked up to us with an invitation to go to his house to dry our wet clothes, we flew out of there like we were gas-powered!" They described the patrons as "Freaks and Inbreeds and Hillbillies." "Yup." Then come to find out, they lived on Capitol Hill in Seattle, the piercing, purple hair, tattoo, gold-toothed capital of freaks! Just a different kind than they were used to!

8:45 P.M. I am closed because my espresso machine broke down. I'll worry about it tomorrow, when I need to remember to be thankful that it waited until dark…

6-13 48° Pouring!

Marshmallow Fantasy: My original! Ice, a shot of marshmallow syrup, espresso shots, Half & Half.

7:36 A.M. I came into the store, turned on my *screwed-up* espresso machine – it takes a while to warm up. Could not wait for the disappointment so I took off for the P.O., hoping my absence would bring forth some sort of a miracle?

8:23 A.M. I'm back. It's fucked! I was expecting it to be Utopian! I knew better than that. Dialing the service department, I heard the dispiriting news, "We can't have a tech there till Wednesday morning." "Wednesday! This is Monday! At $1,500 a year I pay for a maintenance plan – that is an unacceptable time frame! I'll be broke by then! A little cooperation here, please…" "Okay, we will call another service company and see if they can come any sooner to save your life." The response was dripping with sarcasm, but who gave a shit – I didn't have to look at her sneer. So, I gave her my cell number and took off to get weekly supplies.

I ended up going to fifteen stores and got all that I would need for my week, including toilet-fixing crap...for the crapper...more security junk and a new bike!

I was looking for a "no decisions" type of bike. I had to tax the brain all day long and so didn't need to decide on gears when I was just plopping my cheeks on a hard-butt-holder and going for a joy ride! I found a '50's style beach-cruiser with *no* gears and *no* hand brakes. It even came with cute, white-walled tires and was only $99!

The seemingly muscular challenged kid that tried to help me pitch it on top of my Jeep was worthless! Besides scratching my roof rack, I don't think he'd ever seen a bungee cord in his whole miserable life! Were all teen-agers useless these days? I sent him packin'! I started back home, with illegal studded tires, dodging the cops and hoping the bungee-cord-thingy job would hold this new piece of shiny steel.

Forty-five minutes from my destination, the repairman called my cell, "I'm about ten minutes from your place." I lied, "I'm just twenty minutes or so – can ya just hang?" What? Their secretary couldn't make a phone call from the office to let me know that today was the day? Or did the driver take a scenic drive, checking out the cute baristas along the way, and finally remembered to give me a jingle? I was flying! It must have looked cartoonish - red jeep, blue bike – didn't seem to be attached – but seemed to be going to the same destination, on Mountain Peak Highway! Don't leave, repairman! By the time I got home, Mr. Bike was hanging halfway down the side of my Jeep! Fuck. Talk about scratching the damn car! He waited, he fixed - we conquered!

4:20 P.M. Raining and slow, so I attacked my email. My Californian (hopefully future husband—oh stop it, ya dummy!), Tony, replied: Yes, Christy, I'm getting a divorce – I've been out of the house since February. I'd love to come up for a ski vacation, and to see you. J Do you still country-dance? Love, T. My reply: Come on up, any time of year for any reason! But dancing is performed *only* while drinking alcohol and that's *out* for me these days! J Mental Sidebar: But I can think of plenty of things to do to fill the evenings! We had *met* dancing and playing pool in the bar scene. A western, cowboy-style bar. All those fine and dandy drinkin' days and the tight-ass-jeans-men were a thing of the past for me. Buck will shit when he gets a load of this dark-skinned, buff beauty!

Speaking of Mr. Buck, he told me that he just bought a large diamond ring for me. He would like to give it to me now and see me wear it forever. "No thanks." He wanted to be the first to give me an *actual* rock, not just a band. "Rocks are heavy."

10:30 P.M. I remembered to put out Ben the rat's glue pad. I will be thinking of Tony throughout my romantic movie…

6-14 54° Sunny 80%. Flag Day.

Fireside Espresso: My original! A bag of hot chocolate, a bag of Mexican hot chocolate, a shot of vanilla powder, a splash of cinnamon, fill with hot water, stir and top with Half & Half.

9:11 A.M. Buck is no longer in this book! I have had it with his zillion character flaws. I am over-the-top hearing him accuse me of bedding every man in town, available or not; me, the only gal on the hill that *isn't* getting laid! It's been so long now; it's probably grown shut! Good riddance and I'll leave it at that. He is out-numbered now anyway!

11:32 A.M. I just had some druggies in. The men were exceedingly difficult to deal with! The four could barely talk with so much meth in their systems. Ms. Gossip No. 1 came in while they were here, which was *perfect* timing. One of the men ordered a large English toffee latte then came back from his car with his own new 24-ounce cups and lids. He was angry that I already had them made – wanted them in his own paper hot-cups! Who carries a stash of espresso hot cups in their car? Freaks of the day! They also swiped the toilet paper out of the Porta Potty. Dirty rats! I got their plates for the sheriff just in case they wanted to cause some real trouble.

My girlfriend, who was with my bro, called. Samo-samo conversation that we used to have in the old days, back when she was with her ex-husband. But that one was mental. He used to put a padlock on the TV before he left for work! "No relaxing around here, ya lazy old bag, while I'm out breaking my butt!" One night, when the ex-came home from work, she asked him if she could get her hair trimmed. "I can do it! Do you think I'm made of money, slut?" They stood in front of the mirror and he asked her to show him how short. Before she could even get her hand up to her head, he took the scissors and chopped a big chunk off at the ear! Naturally, curly blonde bushy hair was now pointing straight out, exactly his plan. He would have died in his sleep, and not so peacefully, if he had been married to me!

3:10 P.M. I had not seen or heard Ma and Pa birds today. I hoped nothing happened to them! Maybe they had to move them somewhere else when they got too big and chubby for the pipe? I missed them and all the chattering tweet-tweets. Next year...

9:37 P.M. Life is just okay. Closing down the fort...

6-15 47° Sunny.

Royal Fizz: Ice, shot of each: cherry, lemon, and orange syrups, a shot of espresso and fill with Half & Half.

9:04 A.M. It will get warm today. I went to the P.O. this morning and returned to a terrible two-car accident at my place! Two cars totaled and an elderly woman hurt badly. I was sure the men were hurt too. There little dog Snoopy was fine. I ended up flagging for two hours since we had a blind bridge at my east end. Now my lot was full of broken cars, fire trucks, and aid vehicles.

10:00 A.M. Finally got opened. Then a driver with a truck full of insulation decided this was a terrific spot to break down! NOT! I quickly suggested that there is a gas station two miles further. Thank goodness they kept going.

I just pumped air into my new bike tires and will ride tonight. It is not raining. Course, I already got plenty of exercise this morning, running up and down the highway in my tennis shoes to flag.

2:32 P.M. An old guy, who did metal art, came in for a tall double vanilla latte with a splash of cinnamon. He wanted me to carry his wares. On his way out, he handed me a basket of freshly picked cherries. Yum! I think it has been more than five years since I've had some. He used to own a farm in Ellensburg, Washington, and they still let him pick to his heart's content. These bright red balls couldn't have been any fresher and sure didn't taste like the ones from the store.

I picked weeds and swept the parking lot and looked for my pipe baby birdies again. They had flown their coop for sure.

4:44 P.M. Welcome to the cruel world – be careful...

6-16 62° Overcast.

Green Cooler: Ice, a shot of crème de menthe syrup, a splash of lemon syrup, soda water.

8:27 A.M. First on the agenda – clean up the parking lot – all the car parts strewn about from the accident.

I did go bike riding last night and felt like a young, free, little girl again. I didn't realize how much this place reminded me of my childhood stomping grounds: forests, buttercups, fragrances, rocks, moss, wild rhododendrons, huckleberries, salmonberry bushes, birds, slugs, and spit bugs. I grew up on a horse acre surrounded by more acres of woods. So last night I had a blast zooming down some of the hills with my legs sticking straight out to the sides. My head was tilted back, and I closed my eyes for a couple of seconds and took it all in. Why did we allow so many decades to pass without experiencing that cherished childhood cheer? I stopped on the Mollson River Bridge and took in the glorious sight, with the locomotive's bridge as a backdrop.

A neighbor pulled up in front to inform me that another cat was brutally killed last night. Well, we know now it was not BOO. BOO was gone. Butch and I didn't hear a thing, but then again, my movie was blasting, and the damn windows were closed again and covered with plastic for warmth. I am glad I didn't hear the nauseating screams! Even this macho neighbor had the shivers.

1:30 P.M. Ms. Gossip No. 1 came in for her 20-ounce hot caramel mocha. We got on the BOO and mutilated cat's subject. She told me that there were a lot of Vietnam Veterans living in these woods. The state was supposed to gather them up and read them their rights as citizens and help them realize that they didn't have to live in tents. Maybe they *preferred* canvas roofs? I explained to her that it was exactly why I did not want **OUTPOST ESPRESSO** to be the meeting place for her Pacific Crest Trail hikers. You couldn't tell by the way they dressed whether they were bums or hikers, and they consisted of 90% men. She understood.

The new espresso business "down-the-way" seemed to be out of business. *Good!* I had not seen any sign of life there for over a week. *Better!* I saw a For Sale Sign at their home when I was bike riding. *Best!*

5:48 P.M. Two good-looking gents stopped late, tried the doors, and landed in front of the drive thru. They were upset that the gift shop was closed. "You are going to miss a lot of harassing – but all-in good humor." "You guys, there are only three places men can still get away with harassing – espresso shops, restaurants, and bars. You've been cut-off at the pockets!" The taller one said, "We know, we know… you baristas sure earn your tips! So do waitresses and barmaids. We always ask permission to harass, first." Amen! "Hey, you two, come back again sometime, earlier, and I'll let you in, but I will have a contract for you to sign that I give you permission to harass me and you give me permission to kick your butt!" They left howling – yelling, "We'll be back for sure, now!"

9:45 P.M. And now that I had accidentally slammed the window almost through to the other side and practically broke the entire frame, I was closing for good…

6-17 52° Sort of sunny.

S'mores: My original! A shot of chocolate syrup, shot of ginger and toasted marshmallow syrups, steamed Half & Half.

7:38 A.M. One of my cool truckers stopped. He was due for his *free* punch card drink. Then Ms. Gossip No. 1 came in and it was also her turn for a freebie. Another local came by and his card was one drink away from the freebie – and he needed two. I was giving the store away before I even opened! Thank you all for your business, and I was smiling.

My bro's gal called again; they were going to find a relationship counselor. If you ask me, when two people need counseling during the Fireworks Stage, it is a mess from the get-go! Rocket-and-sparklers-fanfare-period should last 90-180 days, minimum, not 14-36. They leaped right over Stage No. 1 - Lust, flew past No. 2 – Analyzing – and jumped right into Stage No. 3 - Crap.

I just had to rig up two mousetraps. First had to figure out how, then get past the fear of popping and smashing one of my fingers to the bone, while transporting them to different destinations in the store.

Nasty things! I bought those mouse glue pads, but we're talking baby mouse size, not big mouse – or rat, for that matter. I caught a rat earlier this year on a big rat glue pad. It was really disgusting! He wandered off about six feet, half dead, and kicked-the-bucket under one of my outdoor fireplaces for sale. It took a while to find him. Sometimes the odor can run ya out! Traps are ready – aim – fire! I just know tomorrow I am going to trip over a bloody mess…

Leeeeeet meeeee catch my breath! The "20" just stopped by again. It's been seven days, but who's counting? This superb, perfect, married "20!" Now you are talkin' a real dessert! I was interrupted by Harley Dennis calling to see if I would like to hurry up and drive seventy miles to lie with him in his new hammock. I'd rather spend the 1.3 minutes just looking at my "20," thank you. Damn, he was movie-star-makings without the make-up!

8:52 P.M. My life might not be exciting, but it isn't ordinary either…

6-18 58° Balmy.

Color of Sunset: Ice, a shot of each: apricot, mango, strawberry syrups, and soda water full to the top with Half & Half.

8:53 A.M. Store and dog and birds are all organized. No snuffed-out, departed mouse yet. I will put the set-up out again tonight. Maybe it's his game – he feasts on the poison and grabs a hiding place, and intends to give off an *aroma* that drives customers back out into the weather?

10:26 A.M. Nothin', nada, nil, zero, zilch, and nary a customer.

11:11 A.M. Both Mr. & Mrs. Periwinkle Luggage came in, to vent. I felt strictly in the middle of these silent wars that we all have experienced. The conversation was not quite as fiery when they were here together. Boiled down to male-female-relationship-communication-fuckups. I see people like these as my *heroes*, my *saviors*, with their shots of pure reality, daily, saving me from ever contemplating a relationship again. I hope this book does not open so many eyes that divorce rate goes beyond epidemic! HA! We are all going to be lonely, old hags and love every minute of it! Her hubby was behaving as the pathetic victim today and she wasn't buyin' it. Neither was I. Until next week... As Our World Turns with Only T*wo* Choices… male or female.

3:51 P.M. Some nice old people were looking for some '70s garb for their granddaughter. She had decided on that décor for her new home. I could not believe *my teenage years were considered an era.* That is freaking rude! I felt O–L–D! **OUTPOST ESPRESSO** is the place to shop for generations! Lots of 1920's, '30's, and '40's antiques, clothes, trinkets, and house wares – to – pink flamingos, the craze of the 1950s…and today. This pink flamingo craze reminded me of relationships – ya either love 'em or they make you stick your finger down your throat!

A man just walked in from New York and said that this store looked like a *party*. Cool. Another man came in from Holland for an Americano. A motor home with New Mexico license plates rolled in for lattes. They left a jalapeño for Mister and wow; did he hate it!

5:00 P.M. My time of the month is coming. I can feel it in my rage toward disrespectful, impatient customers! The matter really is, I need a nice rest on my throne upstairs and ultimately to take another bike ride. Exercise soothes a myriad of ailments - cramps to cellulite!

6:27 P.M. Two motorcycles passed in triple digits! With the deer, cars, bikers, hikers, RVs, and blind curves, they were only plain brainless.

I had a scared, exhausted lady with eight kids stop for an iced 24-ounce triple vanilla latte. She mentioned the motorcyclists that flew by her and came too damn close for comfort. I just called 911, "Eight crotch rockets passed westbound in triple digits." More scared ladies stopped, needed caffeine – bad.

8:28 P.M. Still hangin'…good girl…

6-19 60° Sunny. Father's Day.

Almond Roca Mocha: A shot of chocolate and almond Roca syrups, Espresso shots, steamed milk.

8:40 A.M. Just heard on the news that the weather was going to be spectacular for all the Father's Day celebrations! How fun for all the little kiddies. And I wanted to be the first to wish all the "good" fathers a wonderful, cozy, awesome time with their loved ones…the "real" fathers who were *nurturing* their children and spouses. For the rest of you, including mine, you can *suck my d__k*! The truth regarding me *having a d__k* is equal to the truth regarding some of them having *real love in their hearts*. Did not exist in my life…never did… never would. I have zero patience for *abandonment*!!

Anyhow, back to business – and the very first sign on how this day would go. My first customer got his soy espresso drink and handed me a poppy plant. He was one of my regulars, with a girlfriend, who didn't happen to be with him today. Hmmmmm. Did poppies have some sort of a hidden message? I've read that poppies were cultivated for their instant, brilliantly colored, but short-lived blossoms. May not have been Webster's account on relationships – but it was mine! The beginning was red-hot, middle was fading, and the last meager breath was very shallow. Or – he could have purchased a "poppy" so that the next time he was in with numeral uno, it was guaranteed that the plant would have croaked. "Pretty – thank you! The net says, they are successful in removing warts and restoring failing eyesight and the pods can be used to make opium." Was he trying to get me stoned? He chuckled and left.

12:40 P.M. A DOT worker, who toiled on this highway last year, just stopped by with his little whore. It made me sick just to see him again. He is married, a father, a perverted stepfather, and was coming on to me back then, with, "Can't you bat at least one lousy eyelash at me?" "Not even if I had a cinder in my eye!" Well, looks like he got what he wanted – an incredibly young stripper, and a sleazy one at that. Ms. Gossip No. 1 was in here also and watched them in disbelief, as this female only had to *look* in the direction of an item in my store and he forked over the bucks – repeatedly. I told Ms. Gossip that we had to keep our traps shut right now, as I continued to ring-the-register. Poor guy will go broke with this *latest* affair! His hair had been dyed too damn dark, his shirt was unbuttoned to the navel, and he had on a new big gold chain overlaying his pukey chest. Tom Jones anyone? I charged him full price for everything. Ms. Gossip and I were disgusted as they swaggered out the door, looking adoringly into each other's eyelashes. Snake-of-the-Day with his new toy! Point off guys!

My second reptile was a man about fifty not wearing his shirt this time. He was one of those no-shirt-fake-tan numbers, with a fit body and a chest covered in white hair. He thought he was some sort of a solid gold Adonis. To me he looks like a hollow centerfold wanna-be! These artificial show-offs made me feel queasy. Could they be more insecure? Ms. Gossip was still hanging and said, "What a gas! This place is way more colorful than my hair salon!"

4:05 P.M. Ya gotta give the guy credit for all the different ideas and diversions he came up with! Harley Dennis just called to see if I would close and jet on down for some prime rib, salmon, Beer-Up-The-Butt-Chicken (true entry on the menu), and corn on the cob. "No, Dennis, as always." But yum! I never heard of this bird recipe, but sure sounds like a Saratogan Specialty! Perfect name for a restaurant, in "these-thar-hills"!

4:18 P.M. Scanner: A Porsche, Lamborghini, and Maserati, all at high speed. Catch me if you can! An old logger was in for an espresso and kinda hangin' out. Then I found out he was kind a' waitin' for Buck to show up. I refused to call him. They could both take their cigars and chats to the other end of town, thank you.

4:35 P.M. Scanner: Brush fire, one mile west of the ski lodge. Possibly a lightning strike.

I was almost out of supplies - sort of forgotten it was Father's Day. I had blanked it! The "Duty Day" was over. Tomorrow some *fathers* would be returning to their jobs, secretaries, and mistresses. Family time had been fulfilled...

7:24 P.M. Doors were locked, only the drive thru was open, and I could relax for a sec. The Forest Service cop just stopped for a chocolate smoothie. I guess the forest fire was out by the time the troops arrived earlier today.

9:27 P.M. Ta ta...

6-20 60° 100% sun.

Hawaii Special: Ice, a shot of pineapple and vanilla syrups, soda water to the top, splash of orange juice and grenadine syrup.

4:58 P.M. I went to see a darling cockatoo for sale that I had called on yesterday. She was malnourished but beautiful to me and friendly. I was shocked when she snuggled into my neck. $500 later...on a hand-shake-payment-plan, I returned home. Ice was melting in my Jeep, customers hot and thirsty, and No. 7 calling! He wanted to get together. Fuck that! Not in the mood to even talk to you – I was busy thinking about my new friend with wings!

Buck (I know I said he was "out of the book" and you didn't believe me) came by to pick up Mama's salad bowl. He was only here for a few minutes but helped me give instructions to some customers on the best way to get to Rushing Falls.

Tonight, I hope to ride my bike, and then watch a movie. Tomorrow I hope to go to the dump, mow, and watch a movie. Buck and the old slut of his were sexually hitched again. Maybe they never really *weren't*.

8:56 P.M. Mowed instead…maybe I am bored. More likely, lonely…

6-21 64° Sunny.

> Iced Tea: My original! Pour 2 inches of hot water over 2 tea bags, swirl it around for 30 seconds. Separately fill a cup with ice and cold water leaving enough room for your tea mixture. Add sugar if desired.

7:57 A.M. The loggers returned. I could hear lots of crackling, then trees banging to the ground. I kept thinking it was a customer's car door slamming shut. There went another huge tree. If I were outside I could, feel the ground shake.

11:52 A.M. A Native American, 6'5" and *huge,* maybe 350 lbs., stopped by for a newspaper. I was getting ready for action. Would a bullet even *penetrate* this guy? "I don't sell newspapers." But he still hung and was not the most pleasant person on the planet. Did not drink espresso or coffee for that matter, mumbling complaints, banging into displays. He finally left, but not until some other customers walked in, thank God! He virtually made five of me! I wanted to hug my customers who basically escorted this grizzly out. I called our gas station and they got him too and he was his same, disagreeable, unpleasant self. They took down his New Mexico plates and called it in. Was he ready for a rumble?

4:44 P.M. Finally, I went to the dump. I was almost in tears (*yes, me*) from the smell-from-hell in this load. I felt like I had just switched careers to waste management – definitely *not* a barista today! With our rains and heat, the whole load became *maximum* biohazard! Bugs were flying in and out of all the sacks and, of course, I did not remember my Girl Scout motto, *"Be Prepared with A Pitchfork".*

8:11 P.M. It was time for this chick to head for the coop…

6-22 56° Raining.

Mediterranean Espresso: Shot of chocolate and anisette syrups, espresso shots, 2 inches of hot water, whipped cream.

8:40 A.M. A hell-of-a-frickin' day. No business so I decided to re-arrange my whole espresso cart. This required grunting through beefy, bulky carts and cabinets, re-doing plumbing, wiring, new carpet, and cleaning those spaces that had never been seen by the human eye. I needed a lot more room in my cubicle. It was too claustrophobic for *umpteen* hours a day! Buck came to help. He helped me roll the mighty espresso cart and I re-hung Quaker's cage to a more feathered-friendly spot. Of course, like most men, Buck klutzes around breaking, smashing, dropping, and acting clueless in the *oopsie* department. I swear they *act* stupid on purpose, forcing us to *nag*, just so they can *pout*! I needed a strong gal friend!

5:36 P.M. Well, my espresso area is remodeled, organized, and clean. It is huge and almost has a living-room feel to it. Maybe I will get a comfortable chair so the Privileged Princes could visit and sit with me.

7:20 P.M. I had a very "desperate for caffeine" couple in my drive thru. Each got quad 32-ounce mochas. One dark and one white. The order came to $10 and they gave me $15 for just being open! I *peppered* their lids with extra chocolate-covered espresso beans.

Buck came by again. Wanted to snuggle. Swore we would be together one day – forever. He said, "Weel be here for a long time, Christy. We're gonna need each other." How did he sneak in the back door again? God knows…

9:01 P.M. Closed. And up the steep stairs…alone…

6-23 58° Sunny.

Mexican Shooter: Espresso shots with cream, cinnamon and chocolate powders sprinkled on top.

7:53 A.M. It was so nice to walk into my newly decorated, enlarged espresso area! It was lovely. I could even hold out both arms and twirl! I am spoiled already!

What is this? Grizzly week? I had another *giant* man in! It was an African American this time. I asked him if this was professional football week. He asked why and I told him that he was the second huge guy in here this week. "I work for the laborer's union." He was genuinely nice. He continued like I just opened the floodgate, "I had to go to work as a young tad to help feed the family. My dad split-the-scene *way* early." He had real sadness in his eyes. He ordered a strawberry and peach smoothie and bought some gifts for his family. Then he introduced himself and held out a *monstrous* hand! I *had* to shake it! He could have flipped me right over the counter in a split second! This had been some scary week, indeed!

10:50 A.M. Buck stopped in to visit again. "I just wanted to play with Butch for a while." Now he is trying to get to me through my birds *and* watchdog!

A Middle Eastern guy came through and I recognized him from four years ago. I remembered he brought in some of his porcelain merchandise for me to sell. Had a girlie on his arm and if my memory served me correctly, he was married! This time with his arms still full, but with a new chickie-poo, for God's sake! "We'd like some espressos," in that new-lover toothy-grin. He also had six grown children. So, let's see…he was married, had two girlfriends, so who knew how many kids were involved now. Claimed it was the Italian/Middle Eastern heritage that required all this entertainment. I would stake my life on the fact that none of the bunch was aware of the others. Point off the men's column! "Sir, would you be okay if your wife had a young stud or two in her apron pocket?" His eyes became as big as saucers, he gasped, made the sign of the cross, and screamed, "She would never do such a thing – she is Christian, for the love of God!" Wow.

8:57 P.M. I just got back from my ride. Even wheeled through the new, beautiful homes in the millionaire neighborhood on Groovy Street. Lots of Microsoft lumber going into these grandiose *cabins.*

9:33 P.M. Angel was finally ready to get on my arm and play. Warmed my soul…

6-24 62° Sunny but overcast.

Popsicle: Ice, a shot of amaretto syrup, orange juice within an inch of the top, top with Half & Half.

7:20 A.M. There is a classic car show on the east side of the summit this weekend. Lots of beauties driving by.

11:41 A.M. Well, Philip arrived from Stanford University, where he is a professor in the English and Writing Department. He'll be staying up the Frothing Ham River Road at "The Camp" again this summer. It was good to see him again. Today, his challenge was deciding between two different dilapidated cabins for his three-month adventure. One was almost in the river, while the other sat a few yards from white water. He chose the one that any day could become a houseboat.

My regular hiking gay gals came in. They had been coming here for three years now. Overly sweet lesbians, and full of interesting topics and novel recommendations. They were two of my kindest regulars! They loved stopping here just to see the birds.

9:05 P.M. Unbelievable. Mr. Middle Eastern Stallion stopped and gave me 25 lbs. of Starbucks espresso beans! And I had been so nasty to him. Sorry…sort of. I guess I will put 1/8 of a point back on the men's column.

Clint 15 came by to preen. Yes, he looked like Mr. Boater, Mr. Golfer, and Mr. Pro-Player, all rolled into one. "On one hand I want to settle down, Christy, but on the other hand I still want to do a lot of naughty things that I can't get away with if I'm tied down." That statement could be engraved on too many dicks in America! He added, "Unfortunately, I don't have the money to jet-set around with these women, like some of the other guys out there. Get turned down sometimes and I really believe it's only the *bucks* that keep me from scoring!" Ego much?

9:59 P.M. Still struggling to get the mortgage money up. Tomorrow is another day, another dollar…with only five more twenty-four hours to go…

6-25 62° Overcast.

Orange Cream Blender: Cup of ice in blender, cup of orange juice, cup of Half & Half, blend.

10:14 A.M. An old guy came in and bumped into Freddy's cage and things fell over and went flying. Well, so did the birds, since they were all startled. Mister fell off his perch, Angel flew out of her cage, and Quaker was hopping around in circles. Got them all back to sanity, including the elderly gent. It was partially my fault for having loaded the top of Freddy's cage with more gifts for sale!

3:48 P.M. Philip (Stanford) came in and asked if he could park his SUV here while he walked to town. He did it last year also. Absolutely anytime! I sure loved his hats. He had a collection of old and new chapeaus, for warding off the sunlight; apparently his skin was super sensitive, from past California abuse. One day I caught him walking by with his shirt OFF! That was unusual for Philip as he came across so strait-laced and shy! He was tall, stately, extremely worldly and intelligent, yet incredibly quiet. Still waters run deep. Looked good for his age. Those damn Californians and their fit bodies!

8:22 P.M. Angel has come alive. She already will lie on my lap and tuck her head into my arm. She snuggles and closes her eyes. Strange compared to Mister the Brat! He would rather wrestle with a towel in my hand and try to rip the shit out of it.

9:13 P.M. Buck stopped by with apples and bananas for the birds. Nice of him.

10:00 P.M. Goodnight everyone…

6-26 62° Overcast.

Summer Cocktail: Ice, shot of rum syrup (or real), a shot of raspberry syrup, and fill with soda water.

7:00 A.M. A couple in their motor home from Wisconsin was shocked that our espresso costs $4 for two Americanos. "Welcome to Seattle, the Espresso Capital of the World, ya mid-westerners! Do not even *think* of ordering "down-below" in the big city, though, you might just faint at *their* prices, if you can even get in the doors! I can't get away with highway-robbery up here."

Just about had another wreck out front! A semi just took years of life off his brakes and the same rubber off his tires. The black remnants went for yards.

10:11 A.M. I also had to piss off another motor-home owner. They were setting up camp for the day, totally blocking my store! Idiots! He yelled at me, "We will *never* stop here again!" "Exactly my point…thanks!" More rubber…

3:12 P.M. This was Buck's third visit. He got a glimpse of the new fashionable No. 12 that I had cut out of a magazine today and taped to my desk. Poor baby! Poor Buck! Buck needed a shower bad! He smelled of wood sap and sweat. He cannot walk in here again without one and I told him so.

5:00 P.M. The fat, fart stalker stopped and told me that he would come during the week to chat when I was not so busy. I told him that I didn't like to chat for long and my boyfriend would be very upset if he came by. "Boyfriend?" "Yep. I expect a ring any day now and he is huge and muscular." I lied through my teeth, although Buck promised that ring and gooey kiss in front of this stalker. He was not convinced. "What does your boyfriend do?" I'd use Buck today… tomorrow I'd try Philip on for size. "He is a logger and owns a dump truck, third generation guy up here and doesn't mess around." The stalker left in a huff, finally. It took a lie instead of just a frown to get rid of the old dreamer.

7:49 P.M. Another motor home in the parking lot – this time it died. I racked my brain and sold them some antifreeze for $10 and sent them down two more miles to the gas station. Let my *competition* have overnight guests.

9:13 P.M. Three more days to licking the stamp for my mortgage payment… and I just ran out of ice…

6-27 56° Raining.

Tart Spritz: Ice, a shot of raspberry and lemon syrups, and fill with tonic.

6:59 A.M. I had to leave for supplies. I was afraid I would need to be up here for ten days in a row, with the holiday coming.

2:15 P.M. Scanner: Car was off the highway at mile 46. Seemed to be a non-injury.

Harley Dennis came by just now and filled me in on his party lifestyle this past weekend in the city, west side. His friend Joseph hit his girlfriend in the eye, so-and-so got a DUI, and Dennis got sex. Then so-and-so passed out on alcohol for the second time in one night. Nice.

While I was shopping, I bought plenty of the one fix that will not go rancid – chocolate therapy for my ten days of captivity. Women's favorite department, in the department stores - Frangos! A little anecdote for those who may not be familiar with their history:

FRANGO

Few candies melt-in-your-mouth like a Frango. Their origins date back to 1918, according to their trademark documents and Frangos were first introduced in the sophisticated Tea Room at Frederick & Nelson's, a new department store at Sixth Avenue and Pine Street, in downtown Seattle – a building now occupied by Nordstrom's flagship store. Originally it was only available in maple and orange. Folklore has it that the 'Fr' was from Fredericks and the 'ango' was most likely coined from the tango dance craze. Another version is that Frango was an acronym for Frederick And Nelson

Goodness. Marshall Fields and Fredericks had been wrangling over who's-on-first for centuries.

6:10 P.M. I had Miss Snooty come in for *coffee*. I told her that I had espresso and could make her an Americano. She rolled her eyes and accepted the option, but without a happy face! Didn't she watch 20/20? You *never* roll your eyes at the person *fixing* your *food!*

6:24 P.M. Her attitude just sent me upstairs to my home sweet home. Goodnight, world...

6-28 56° Overcast.

Italian Latte: A shot of each: Amaretto and real Galliano, espresso shots, steamed whole milk.

9:43 A.M. My older upholstery guy came in this time in an open jean vest. Yes, he was in his fifties or early sixties and was very fit. Washboard stomach, for cryin' out loud! Knew it and showed it.

1:11 P.M. I just realized Buck has re-disappeared. Must have found a new cookie for his jar.

The loggers stopped by for their Italian sodas and my own creation of an espresso granita. They were hooked. I could *see* the trees falling now – Timmmberrrrrr, crackle, snap, and *bang!*

2:11 P.M. Scanner: Male subject walking along Mountain Peak Highway, at milepost 46. He seemed to need aid.

A seasonal guy, who owns a house in Moosehead Town, came to stay at his getaway cabin and saw smoldering embers where his old shed once stood. His neighbor, the shed-poacher, torched the building (déjà vu?), but not before stealing some of the new wood for re-building his own deck. This owner was flipping mad but did not pull his gun, this time. The law will handle it if the law ever gets its ass back up here.

Apparently, there was a bum living at our baseball field park, who entertained himself for over an hour in the female restroom at our gas station. Even attempted to rob an old-timer's place overlooking the station. That old-timer was someone you really, *really* did not want to rob, unless you wanted your nuts chopped off! The vagabonds and drifters come out when it is warm.

2:40 P.M. Scanner: Car fire at milepost 55. *Finally*…our sheriff has returned as I recognized the voice on the scanner. It was about damn time! The end of *mob-rule*!

Oh my God! Our fire chief just had a heart attack *at* the car fire scene! That is the *second* volunteer that had one on an aid call just this year! Massive adrenalin! He is going to live, and the aid car is rushing him to the hospital. Forget the car fire, you are on your damn own, you guys!

Boomerang City opened. The huge firecracker joint on the Reservation in Marysville, Washington. The Biggest and Best in the Northwest! People came there from miles, even on the first day. Loads of explosives, bombs, and illegal powder gadgets. We used to go to those places growing up in the '60s and '70s, but times changed and almost every city outlawed fireworks – period.

9:24 P.M. Bushed and cannot wait to just be upstairs and wrap myself in *sloth*…

6-29 64° Sunny after all.

Split Cappuccino: First steamed milk, then foamed milk, then espresso shots.

10:10 P.M. I just got home from shopping all damn day. Eat your hearts out.

10:28 P.M. Okay…Buck raced by. What is up his nose? Sometimes I wonder why I even *breathe* in his direction…

6-30 68° Muggy.

Limeade: Ice, a shot of lime syrup, a shot of lemon syrup, a shot of soda water.

7:35 A.M. Some bikers stopped and one of them had been to the Iraq war zone, twice. Thank you, soldier!

An old couple came in. They met forty-eight years ago in eastern Washington and came back to see their old neighborhood. They lived in Arizona now. They were sad, "Nothing was left in our old town that we recognized – or that even looked familiar."

Another couple stopped who were passing through on their way to Alaska, via auto.

2:15 P.M. Philip came in from his *camp* on the river. I am poisoning him with an unhealthy latte and a coffeecake muffin. He is not supposed to eat that crap, but I am not his mother. I hinted at my concern and he flashed a genuine smile.

My daughter called from Alaska and informed me that she found the man for me (again?). She is going to try and find out more about him. The rational for this match: "He is a nice-looking guy walking down the street with his parrot on his shoulder and a Pomeranian, pulling them both along on the sidewalk."

Mr. Gorgeous 20 (forget the Alaskan, darling daughter) came in today. They were finished commuting by here, *but* he took a punch card, since his kids did ski-school up on our pass. I may get to see this attractive male specimen all seasons.

9:51 P.M. The last headlights I could handle; some Canadians stopped for an espresso with raw sugar, a Coke, and bottled water.

10:17 P.M. It is late. I made my mortgage…

JULY

Sunset colors settle over waterfalls, while
the tea leaves dry on the string

7-01 54° Overcast.

Iced Kahlua Eggnog: Ice, shot of Kahlua syrup and eggnog syrup (or real eggnog), espresso shots over cold milk.

8:44 A.M. I believe I know why Buck has vanished like a fart in the wind! The laminated picture of the sexy swain perched above my computer pissed him off – to the marrow! Jealous – cheating – ass! He would like *his* image to be my *screensaver.* Dream On, Dude.

9:05 AM. Scanner: A guy was holding a gun to his female passenger's head. Two cars were staying with it and keeping 911 notified of their whereabouts. We also had another guy wielding a gun. A sheriff was chasing him on foot. "Shoot him in the balls!" This was right on Mountain Peak Highway – not sure how far away. Maybe I should be a little intelligent here and lock my doors! Psycho-maniacs have snaked out of their black holes *this* weekend!

A group of chicks that worked at Starbucks just came in and they were *on a roll*! They were having a blast critiquing and trying to frustrate the hell-out-ta-me! Customers did that to them all day long – so turn-about-fair-play. They were lovin' it, "Let's spice up our morning drive making other baristas crazy!" They all wanted an Irish Cream fix because the giant, the leader, the bucks-up Starbucks discontinued this popular flavor. Go figure? Turned out they were a blast. We swapped stories – mine were the most astonishing – this *isolated* barista in the sticks!

Bobby the Braggart rambled in. He *always* strolled, trying to imitate a slow, suggestive saunter. He is sixty-three, no one would guess, so he did have a little something to bluster about. He slurped his drink loudly, grabbed some calories, and looked around for butter. "Sorry." I *barely* mumbled something about possibly running out of these coffeecake muffins over the weekend and in *exactly* one hour he showed up with three flats of them! He went back up a point, but there were shrouded motives, I am sure. Damn, I should have told him I was completely out of pink yarn – and low on Tampax!

12:55 P.M. Philip came in to fax some papers. He was right in the throes of a bank loan on his new construction – a huge vacation home on Lake Havasu. He *forced* me to accept $1 per page. I could charge *usury* rates, with these little grey machines being so scarce in "these-thar-hills".

7:33 P.M. Doors were locked. Drive thru was open. It's the Fourth of July weekend! Mellow day, mellow moods and most of the drinks were Italian sodas. Such ease! A *physical* break for this barista and super profit margins…

7-02 54° Rain.

Super Chocolate Cherry Shooter: Three shots of espresso, a nice splash of cherry syrup and a squirt of chocolate syrup, stir.

10:03 A.M. Busy morning! Just got to my *own* tea 'n crumpets, finally. The birds were perky in this cool weather. Customers were excited to be out of the house and on their way to holiday *expectations*.

12:10 P.M. My mom, of all people, thought I'd get a kick out of this 1950's "Women's Rules to Live By" article:

THE GUIDE

Show your husband, with *absolute sincerity,* that you *live* for his comfort and contentment. Have his dinner *ready,* hot and delicious and filling when he walks in the door. (*Who in the hell knows what time that will be? Did he stop for a beer? Will he be late again? No cell phones back then, but he probably would not have used it anyway…)* Do *not* ask him his whereabouts and/or with whom. Fifteen minutes before he arrives, put on a pretty dress, check your makeup, and comb your hair. (*Righto! He has been coveting, or worse, with that petite secretary all damn day.*) Be happy and cheerful. Lead him to his favorite chair and remove his shoes. The house should be immaculate. Tell the children to be on their best behavior. (*Good fuckin' luck with that one!*) Keep in mind he has had a long, stressful, hard day at work. Listen to the chronicle of his day. Provide a warm fireplace, a drink, and a backrub. Never, ever, refuse his advancements. Remember, he is the Master of His Castle. A good wife always knows her place. And most importantly, BEHAVE! (*That word could seriously give me the strength to massacre!*)

No wonder that's when the divorce rate started to rise and some of the ladies took to balling the milkman!

6:30 P.M. I did take some breaks to serve espressos during my rant.

7:45 P.M. I will go and contemplate my freedom …

7-03 58° Overcast.

The Logger: My original! 32-ounce cup, 4 shots of espresso, 2 shots of chocolate syrup, steamed whole milk, and plenty of whipped cream.

7:49 A.M. Some of my customers and neighbors have given me a new name. Bird Lady Spinster. Cool. Could not be closer to the truth.

I just had a local couple in who were temporarily living in a neighbor's tree-fort. I guess they considered that better than their car. What car? They were on foot! No wonder CPS has already taken the kids. They always seemed to find the cash for drugs and several $3.25 drinks. I wondered if that structure was zoned for living quarters. Not.

2:00 P.M. Buck is still missing. There is a newbie in town, a slutty gal who lived here a few years ago. She's baaaaaack… I'm sure he's real biiiiiziiii these days. She is twenty-three years old and free as a bird – CPS has her kids too.

Mr. Mercury Poison, who eternally overstays his welcome, was here again! I do not think he can pronounce that simple two-syllable word *Good-Bye!* Today, he parked his elbows, his fists propped up his jaw, and talked and talked and talked for an entire hour, I believe. Of course, I had to slap him off my counter to serve guests every now and then. He spent $10. *He* should be charged "Counseling Rates!"

3:45 P.M. No. 1 Bachelor in Seattle stopped in to say "hi." He wanted the 1950's wife description emailed to him. He said he had to insert it on his construction website. He did not ask me for dinner again. He won't.

Philip came in for his usual – a double latte. Besides being a writing professor, he is a published author and pretty darn interesting. I picked his brain every chance I got. He was also strait-laced, so I loved telling him that I just heard that the particular cabin he rented every summer was *the* one used by the three "Ladies of the Night" who serviced The Fortress – way back when. He was aware of this! I may have him pegged wrong in a good way.

I just had a car with two hearing-impaired adults. They wrote down their order – two 20 oz. lattes. I handed them a doggy treat for their furry buddy in the window, with the tongue hanging out. What puzzled me: their radio was blasting country music! For the dog? I have been told that they can feel the music.

Finally Missing in Action (and plenty of it I'm sure), Buck materialized. He *innocently* handed me a love note and wanted to schmooze. Hadn't seen his idiotic face or heard his asinine voice for over a week.

4:22 P.M. Scanner: Two-car injury collision at Crag Rock Café, blocking Mountain Peak Highway.

4:49 P.M. Scanner: A forty-five-year-old woman walked into our fire station with chest pain.

5:27 P.M. A guy just spilled his untouched 32-ounce Italian soda – outside. He hoped I saw the mishap, cuz he wanted me to *donate* another one. "Okay." Then, "If you'll tell me where the hose is, I'll clean up my mess." I chuckled, "Hose? You have got to be kidding. We don't have such a thing up here!" "No way!" "Way!" I watched him scratching his head and walking around the building in search of a plumbing bib.

A guy was telling me that he and his wife were up here for the weekend and hoped to "make-a-kid." "There are lots of dirt roads, trails, and waterfalls, where you can slip out of the ole jeans and…" T.M.I on both sides of this conversation! I'm losin' it…

I haven't eaten or taken a pee or sat down for six hours!

9:28 P.M. I do not care about anything right now but sleep…

7-04 64° Sunny. Fourth of July!
- Let those American flags fly!

> **Big Bang: Four shots of espresso, four sugar packets, and tons of whipped cream!**

7:00 A.M. It is going to be a hot July 4th! I had to open up all the doors early to try and drop the temperature a little for my cubicle and birds. Pretty soon I will close up tight and try to trap this nice cool fresh air. I have heard the whole town is racing for *their* spot to watch the softball game between Saratogan and High Valley. Rivals to the max! The band plays off and, on all day, and the people's butts are firmly planted there until the fireworks show. On a scale of 1-10, our light display is a ten! Hazard insurance should be sold to protect against their neighbor's pop-bottle-rockets and beer sprays. All the family, friends, and enemies will gather together in the grandstand and eat and act merry. Lots of gossip tomorrow! Who swapped with whom? Who stripped naked? Who landed face-first on the dance floor? Who handed the first punch?

Some customers came in *not* wanting to pay the extra fifty cents for a cup of ice, lid, straw, and napkins. Tough shit! "Consider it the shipping and handling charge."

10:42 A.M. A man and lady walked in and *he* informed *her* that *she* was paying, "Cough up the cash lady – that's what ya get for mouthin' off!" The hair on the back of my neck was at attention… Here came that *uncontrollable* blurt, "Did she mouth off for the hell of it or in response to something you said?" He stared at me for a minute, then smiled and finally, "I *may* have started it – how did you know?" Reality: He paid for the drinks and the three bracelets she picked out.

A little girl kept asking grandpa if he would buy her *two* toys. He said, "No and don't ask again!" Sound familiar? She asked again and again. I could not help but pipe up, "Well, my kids would have lost their chance to get even *one*!" This elder was surprised. "I can't believe you would be on the side of losing a sale for the sake of discipline." The child wanted to spit on me!

2:05 P.M. Clint 15 came by, exposing a sunburned chest and red eyes to match. He was hung-over and looked plain crummy. To boot, he did not have a fun weekend. "Is it really worth all the trouble?" Downtrodden, "Sometimes… I just keep playin' the odds."

9:31 P.M. Fireworks will detonate any minute – animals will be fleeing everywhere. I put Butch's sensitive ears and tail boo-boo upstairs before the blasts begin. He has some sort of skin condition or growth near his backside. Vet tomorrow morning.

10:17 P.M. I think I am just going to try to mellow-out and play like been-there-done-that and ignore the sky-sparklers…

7-05 58° Sunny.

Kiwi Smoothie: My original! A cup of ice in a blender, a pack of fake sugar, 2 inches of kiwi daiquiri mix, 2 inches of Half & Half, whipped cream.

8:30 A.M. The vet could not take Butch till late afternoon. Good time to drop him 'n shop. First, I hoped his malady wasn't serious – secondly, not expensive.

10:36 A.M. Dennis was here on his Harley to sip and snivel about his absolute best buddy. He nailed Suzy-Q; the gal Dennis had coveted for the last six months. Early on, she enticed Dennis to come and visit her in San Diego. The weekend was pricey. Unfortunately, it was also scrumptious and steamy. He was hooked! She wasn't. Dave-The-Bud was offered the same experience, with her picking up the tab for *that* pleasurable trip. "Neither Dave nor Suzy-Q had the frickin' *decency* to mention their three-month affair. The whole time I've been making a weekly goof out of myself over the telephone wires to her – and – pouring my *guts* out to Dave-The-Bastard!" A point off both columns! Lower than a snake, he slithered out the door and wound back up on his bike.

Jack, my old guy, came in, finally! He is living in his RV on a Native American reservation while his young wife is blissfully sprawled out in their new paid-for home. He has not even filed for divorce. This man broke-his-butt for fifty years and now he lives in a home-on-four-wheels and pumps out his holding-tank. I must deduct another point off the women's side – she tossed him out a month or so after he satisfied the mortgage.

5:10 P.M. It is slow and so I am leaving.

9:37 P.M. And what an evening! Butch had a hot spot in his backside and must wear a cone on his head for an indefinite period. This Husky dog is having no part of this *unreasonableness* and he politely and promptly removed it before we even left the parking lot. He is now the proud owner of a white plastic cone, secured by a beautiful *silver* necklace – of duct-tape. Bugger! Means I will probably have to shave him to get it off.

I mounted more killer-rat-pads, hoping to glue "Ben" to the floor, once and for all!

10:20 P.M. Gobs of heavy shit to unload. Later…

7-06 57° Raining.

> **Iced Apple Cider: My original! Two packs of powdered apple cider in a cup with 2 inches of very hot water, stir, fill separate cup with ice and water leaving enough room for hot mixture.**

10:57 A.M. A guy my age, closer to fifty (*wash your mouth out, Christy!*) came in and remembered this place from many moons ago. "I am overwhelmed with the changes to this particular building, and the entire locale, actually. I have fond memories of this place: homemade ice cream, mixed with the scent of gas at those not-so-regulated pumps, bonfires, barbeques, children squealing with glee, and river-wet clothes hanging to dry from every tree." He left, licking the foam off his cappuccino, like he was mentally re-visiting those ice cream cone days, and mumbling something about it being *hell* to have to grow up.

Cone-head Butch had taken to trying to beat up the fence. The cyclone was winning that match. He was searching for any avenue to remove his unwanted ornament.

4:30 P.M. A couple of men, a five-piece family and a few teenagers, stopped in here, all for their first time. And thank God, there were some males to scream at, "Sir, can you come and kill this brown recluse! (*Two in a week!*) Like now! Hurry up!!! Oh…Please. I just read about these the other night…and!!! Snap it up!!! Please." He looked at this fanatical female and his eyes reflected zero patience. "First of all, those spiders don't live on *this* side of the mountains." "Well, he hitch-hiked then, and I actually know a guy who was sick for six months after being bitten by one of these ON THIS SIDE!" He continued, "And secondly, I'll never understand how women can take boiling hot wax, pour it onto their upper thigh, rip the hair out by the roots, and still be afraid of a lil ol' spider." He would be incredibly wise indeed *not* to consider turning his back on all the women in this room right about now… In the end, we had one proud man who got to say his piece, one slaughtered recluse, and one happy barista. He came through after all!

7:06 P.M. My cubicle is getting claustrophobic…

7-07 60° Sunny.

Steamer: Fill cup with steamed milk and add flavor if desired.

9:00 A.M. Cone-head figured out that feeding time meant spray butt with medicine and checking the duct-tape for security. He is enveloped in his own personal torture-chamber, if he dares to move a muscle, as it yanks out one hair at a time. He glared at me and would not touch a bite till I left the room! He was developing a nice little grudge.

2:15 P.M. Nothin' going on! Might as well do some calisthenics smack-dab in the middle of my aisles. Or maybe I should purchase that fire pole after all and start dancing. Good exercise but one of my customers just may be the sheriff…I could see the headlines now: "Barista busted for lattes and lap dances; don't rush, guys, she's a displaced mountain woman and fully dressed!"

A sawdust-covered logger above my RR tracks stomped in. "Got beer?" "Nope." The cranky geezer settled for a Sprite but was pissed. "Drink on the job much? With heavy power equipment?" He stalked back into the brush like a long-in-the-tooth Daniel Boone. *He* won't be back…

4:21 P.M. Professor Philip came in. "My Refuse Service Sign now means you, buster!" He had some minor medical conditions he was trying to reverse and had been knockin' back a few too many muffins a week. Today I embellished the ungodly nutritional facts I read off the labels the other day: Serving Size One – Calories 2,850 – Calories from Fat, just about rivals that – Trans Fat is 50g – Total Fat 99% - whereas Vitamins are *possibly* .2 – and any Dietary Fiber is nonexistent! He grimaced! Then, like any junkie, "Can I have just *one* more?"

2:12 A.M. Sleep, ya fool…

7-08 58° Raining.

7:46 A.M. A new baroque journal. First entry: I was up until after 2:00 AM, unfortunately solo!

11:38 A.M. I headed out to the yard to give Butch some needed attention. He has had it! Poor boy can't scratch, sniff or lick anything.

Buck has disappeared as requested.

The professor came in again. Philip was tall and slim with prematurely white, thick hair. Up here, his uniform was a brimmed white straw hat, pressed crisp tee-shirt, pressed Calvin's, wide belt with one of those Black-Hills gold buckles, and laundered running shoes – diametrically opposed to being *The Suit* every other day of his life. He looked quite sharp and elegant even in his vacation garb. Today he was sad. *His* beaver family at The Fortress was missing. Passing each day, sitting on his covered cabin porch, he wrote, read and even *more*, missed watching them flirt and slap their tails at one another. Why couldn't I talk myself into a nice dinner with this kind and gentle man?

5:00 P.M. A masculine female trucker was complaining about my $2 Americano. Couldn't figure out if I were supposed to say Sir or Ma'am, so I just ignored the salutation, "Cheapest drink *you'll* find in *this* neck of the woods, or any other for that matter! Why don't you roll 'em on down to Seattle where the baristas will *all* charge you double that, with a completely clear conscience!" So…she changed her mind. "Okay, got your drift – make it a 20-ounce cup, with three shots of espresso; fill the cup half full of Half & Half and up to the top with hot water." "Sorry, but your drink just became a breve in *my* book, and that will be $4," just for being such a pain in my derriere! Another restraining order?

9:48 P.M. I'm done and pray I don't dream about court houses…

7-09 58° High clouds.

> Quad Iced Mocha: Ice, mix together 4 shots of espresso and a shot of chocolate syrup, and add cold milk to ice leaving enough room for the shots.

5:12 A.M. My watchdog was snarling at the window. Apparently, some poor sucker slept in his non-running Volvo in my parking lot last night. Some noisy buddies were there to pick him up at o-dark-hundred! They yelled up to the window that they would return for the car in a few hours. If it were not a *decent* car, it would be towed by 10:00 A.M. On the plus side, hoped Buck would drive by – this overnight decoy would certainly ruffle a few feathers. Too bad it was parked so far away from my personal home door, missed out on the full impact!

7:45 A.M. A couple just came through the drive thru. They were making out so profusely you would think they just heard it is the Second Coming of Christ! I practically had to pry their lips apart to get paid. I forgot what that felt like!

3:00 P.M. BMW Brian did show up! He had not found a "Better Barista" after all. I asked if he had found a new gal but…no. He handed me a beautiful, beaded bracelet, costing $49. He (accidentally?) left the price tag on. All in humor, I told him to let me know when he was ready to get married. I could see panic on his face. God, it wouldn't be *appropriate* to break the family record! Not *one* of his many brothers had ever been married either. I could just picture it, "Hey, mom and, meet Christy. I get to be her eighth!"

A car-less freak came in. It was apparent that too many drugs over too many years had destroyed too many brain cells. This man had lost his car, his family and friends, his self-respect too. I could tell. He couldn't make up his mind so he decided on zip. And I was sure he didn't have two coins to rub together. The brain was fried. He walked slowly down into Treetops Loop…probably debating how he could talk his fellow druggies into a rolled favor…

7:00 P.M. A couple of young baristas came in and we spent ten minutes hee-hawing…discussing some of the *bonkers* customers we got and agreed that *fellow* baristas were the ultimate pain-in-the-ass customers of all! "Do you have any white chocolate powder?" Nope. "Do you have vanilla bean syrup?" Nope. "God, you are so lucky, isolated up here. You don't have to serve a zillion different item. In the city, if we don't have something special, they just head to the other corner and move their future business – permanently!"

9:37 P.M. My sister called me from California and together, on portable phones, we locked all the doors, brought in the signs, cleaned the machine and giggled over nothing.

10:21 P.M. Thanks, sis…

7-10 57° Overcast.

> **Milky Way Latte: A shot of white chocolate and caramel syrups, espresso shots, steamed milk.**

9:00 A.M. I was surprised how many parents let their children load up on real lattes. Real caffeine. I even have a *threatening* sign in my store: Keep An Eye On Your Children Or They Will Be Given a Free Espresso – *And* – a Free Kitten!

4:00 P.M. Today was so busy it required Depends. Thank God BMW Brian stopped by on his way back down the mountain. He smiled when he saw the bracelet on my wrist; "I was thinking I would find it on your Jewelry-For-Sale rounder." Lucky me – it could have easily been… He relieved *me* so I could relieve *myself*, upstairs. "Just tell the customers I finally got a chance to change out of my wet undies and take a pee!" He wailed, "I think not!" When I came back, I pleaded for one more favor. He slipped down to our gas station for a few bags of ice for this barista.

9:55 P.M. I am closing, sweethearts…

7-11 62° Partly sunny.

White Coconut Iced: A shot of white chocolate syrup, shot of coconut syrup, mix in with espresso shots, and pour over milk in ice.

8:45 A.M. Flew down to the bank and returned to three customers waiting – and pacing outside of their cars! UGH! Pressure was on as usual, with ice melting away in my Jeep. Same shit - different day. Shouldn't complain, but damn! I still had to unlock, lights on, rev up my cart, and wash up. Of course, they were long gone when some scary guys stopped looking for pocketknives. I did not even glance up. "Don't carry that kind of shit here!" They luckily left, didn't bother to look for themselves. I called down to the next public stop, the gas station, to give them a heads-up. They phoned back to thank me. The guys *did* stop in, harassed the Asian owner, and hung around, not buying a thing. And they noticed no rear license plate. I emailed the sheriff.

8:24 P.M. The thunderclouds were a rolling in. As the skies were, I was in the throes of that opaque uneasy mental state…like when you were waiting for someone or something and you couldn't quite bring the *"what"* into focus. Like trying to scratch that illusive itch. If I would be quite guileless, its *"handle"* would probably be *"loneliness!"*

I emailed my most recent contact, BMW Brian, and asked him why he was hanging around and constantly giving me gifts. He emailed back: "I just see things I think you'll like." What kind of inefficient answer was that? It wasn't. No wonder he'd never been married. Reply: "Dig a little deeper, Brian Baby, and see if you can spit something out…" I was just sitting, mulling. Okay, Christy, it doesn't take a psychologist to solve this riddle – you are in need of a real, honest-to-goodness hug.

9:00 P.M. And right now,…

7-12 60° Misty.

Christy's Back Slide: 2 oz. strong black espresso, 1 oz. B-52 syrup, 1/3 oz. lemon juice. Fill with whip cream.

9:01 A.M. A gal came in for a triple espresso granita, "Hopefully this will grow hair on my chest!" Okay, I bit... She continued, "My mom and my best friend both told me I have to toughen up. My boss and a couple other guys in my life walk all over me." "Listen up, girlfriend. If outsiders care, remember *they* have glasses on – blinders embrace *your* cheeks." She is young, she'll learn...

10:37 A.M. Scanner: Seventy-year-old man had fallen on a local trail and was injured.

A whole truck full of loggers from across the road thundered through the door! God, they were a rowdy bunch. Buck was here and decided to show off for the crew. He knew them all slightly – worked with each at some time or other. He started flappin' his flabby lips for the audience, "I have this Blistering Barista on my line and just might consider reeling her in...if she's lucky." At the risk of putting him in an extremely bad light, I must tell you, that was a direct quote! The guys weren't impressed. They knew he had been trying to reel *me* in, then have me stuffed and mounted on his mantel so I would be "out of circulation!" And that was a direct quote from the last one to leave. Men! For eons we'd been told that only women did the show- 'n-tell bit. Bullshit! They all stuffed their mouths with massive calories as I accommodated all their drink choices, racking up a genuinely nice bill!

1:11 P.M. A very married man came in who was not afraid to say so for a change. Dapper and wearing a bright gold ring. I liked him already. "Chocolate, chocolate, chocolate mocha, please." "I think I've got the picture, sir." And then of course the conversation headed to the "M" subject. His take, "Twice a week we go out to dinner; I go on Wednesday, she goes on Friday. We always hold hands when we strolled the malls; if I let go, she shops. Just last week I asked my wife where she wanted to go for our anniversary dinner. She said to make it somewhere we hadn't been in a long time, so I mentioned the kitchen. She didn't hit me, but it explains why I have to go out to get my own espressos." He was funny, quick, and happy at home. It was a treat to see!

3:33 P.M. Today I had an airhead, a fellow brunette. What do ya know, they do exist, dammit! She had no clue what town she was in, had never heard the word "barista," but the best one, "Do you like all these birds?" "No, lady, I keep them around to service me!" She started to ask... She left.

Had a couple in for a triple, three-flavor, Half & Half, whip cream and eleven lumps of sugar, Americano. "Ever read 'Sugar Blues'?" Right over *their* heads too. Maybe it was just in my seventh year that I had gotten to be such a hard ass! It was notorious – *The 7-Year Retail Burnout*. It was probably not much different from that 7-Year Itch, but I didn't have any more *scratches* left!

I know why BOO was booted out as early as he was! His whole camp was *leveled* today. He was lucky to escape with life and limb. Seems like just a little while ago the huge trees were going down like bowling pins. I wondered if he hopped a freight train, for one last peek. Ex-Con thought this *logging* unearthed the cat murderer, I heard through rumor.

8:51 P.M. If it wasn't so depressing, I'd keep track of my hours around here – but I do believe this is my 90th, just *this* week? More cars...

9:20 P.M. Closed for damn sure now and playing plumber. I was trying to change the water filter in the espresso cart. Leaked the very first round today. CRAP! Doing it by Braille. It was like a spaghetti factory under there – I could not turn my lights back on as they were all attached to the flashers and neon *OPEN* signs. This binary code eventually worked. Good girl.

9:45 P.M. Pretzels and hot chocolate for dinner tonight. Bad girl...

7-13 61° Overcast.

Why Bother: **Two shots of decaf espresso with non-fat milk. No sugar!**

9:05 A.M. Harley Dennis called last night. He has been dating a new gal for three weeks now. On one hand, he still loves the San Diego beauty – on the other he isn't that crazy about this one but will poke her every chance he gets – and with a third hand he's flirting with me, "She's not as sexy, cute, and fun as you are, darlin'!" You know if men had ten hands and a few extra dicks, they'd use every damn one of these appendages daily. They could become incredible jugglers – of women that is! Point off! I wish I could tell this woman to dump him like a wet, smelly rag.

An old lady walked in and immediately, "That sure is a damn loud bird." This is the second old person swearing over my loud birds this week. Maybe they both just got their new hearing aids and haven't had them adjusted yet.

Second customer was a guy my age with dreadlocks. He was simply happy traveling along in search of every *true* hippie community in the USA. He was rambling about this band and that, the radio talk show hosts here and there. Never heard of *any* of them. Bye, bye gypsy.

3:33 P.M. One of our regular bums on our highway came in for a *free* candy bar. "Where's *that* sign?" I spit. He moaned and tried again, "But…the gas station up here gave me a *free* cup of coffee!" "Then I'd go bandage-my-butt to that non-profit building!" Got to thinking…what if he was *really* Jesus in disguise and looking for a fish, or something, to multiply – and I was being a selfish broad! I was smiling by now and tossed him a banana, "This is much more nutritious!" If someone, somehow, cut a foot off his matted mane he would be decent looking, except for that checkerboard smile. "Now don't rush back!" We high-fived as he went out the door…

6:56 P.M. Andrew called. I told him about my new technique for staying young looking, "I take my trusty-little-vibrator, put it on low speed, and slowly and softly run it over my face! I swear to God, it's refreshing and revitalizes my skin." After he quit snorting, he told me a great story about his seventy-eight-year-old mom in Omaha, "She happened to read that vibrators might help with arthritis, so she bought one. When I was visiting about a month later, I noticed a friggin' dildo on the kitchen counter! I asked her what the hell is this all about? She explained…then I explained! She almost died! Her dishwasher repairman had been there the same morning and had to move the damn thing out of the way, twice! Then she hung her head and said she would never leave the house again!"

8:19 P.M. Obviously, more phone calls than sales today. Signing off...

7-14 64° Sunny.

Sparkling Espresso: Ice, espresso shots, soda water.

8:00 A.M. I caught a rat on the glue pad overnight, but he escaped again with his life. He left his calling card – two turds and loads of hair. Back to the drawing board.

I rushed down to the P.O. and I locked my keys in my Jeep - *with* the engine running! Now what was I just saying about a brunette airhead? I felt like a fool. The local Slim-Jim expert said, "Yaw know the whole town will hear about this by evening." "Yup". $60 later...

Home now to impatient locals for their, "Caffeine – Caffeine!"

3:43 P.M. Scanner: An unbalanced patient was arriving at the Saratogan Fire Station from the County Sheriff.

I was anxious for the sheriff's story; was it a local, man or woman, one of my customers...

Two of the Tip-Top Seattle Bachelors on my list called. "How are you doing – when are we going to dinner – been too busy to stop by, etc." "I'm fine – I'm too busy for dinner – and DO stop by." Just sniffin' around. I think there were three of them right now... God, I should start a new business, "Mountain-Matchmaking." A heck of a lot rolled through here...

4:00 P.M. Served 9-10 drinks in the last hour or so. Smoothies, iced mochas, pop, and some espresso diehards. Would people leave gooey, wet, dirty straws on *their* counters at home? Germy sticks, straws, grimy soiled napkins, gum, old balls of fluff, and pennies from their filthy pockets - *on* my wee counter space! I have tried a trashcan, in clear sight, but all it seemed to attract were shoes that inadvertently used it for the game of kick-the-can. It is *never* in their line of vision!

6:11 P.M. A man walked in, "These birds must be as much work as a husband." I screamed, "MUCH less!" He was cute, and he apologized for the male species and ordered his espresso shots. "Do you know anything about these particular birds' intelligence levels?" "Sure do! Between three to five-year-old children." Immediately, "Then, they *are* just like husbands!" I *adored* this man!

9:20 P.M. A fucked-up day...really. Goodbye to *this* one...

7-15 62° Overcast.

> **Chocolate Kick: Ice, a shot of chocolate syrup mixed with espresso shots, pour over ice and fill with Half & Half.**

8:47 A.M. My bro and girlfriend broke up. Whatever...in tomorrow's phone call, they will be "whipped creaming" each other again.

I am sooooooooo mad at BMW Brian right now. I may never speak to the barbarian. His reply to my sharing my new bird email: "I can't help but think of the laptop upgrades you need, how that money would/could have been better spent." Didn't he know that right at this particular *moment* I was in the throes of proud parenthood? This was a direct insult to my new *child,* for God sakes! That agnostic, demented dweeb.

1:00 P.M. Denny, my neighbor, returned from Alaska. Long story short, "I sold my home of thirty-seven years and basically sold my whole *life* in a garage sale. It's been quite a horrific few weeks, almost *more* unbearable than when my wife dumped-me-in-the-trash-can a few years ago." I think I already deducted *that* point before.

Supposedly, the tree-fort-drug-dwellers were booted on down the highway – or ran for cover? The male *tenant* did not show up for his required court appearance to get his ankle bracelet installed.

3:55 P.M. Speaking of criminals…Ex-Con hired a secretary, and he doesn't even work! A secretary for what? Blow jobs, that's fucking what! His neglected wife was just in. Rosie *looked* sad, but her lips were sealed…for now…

I had a mom in today allowing her daughter to touch anything and everything. Finished and bored now, the brat headed for the "big room," my gift shop. "Oh, no you don't. And mom, she can't be in there without you." The mom glared and snapped back, "She is ten years old and she isn't going to do any harm! Apparently, lady, you haven't had any kids of your own!" Oh boy, she was askin' for it now, "Listen up, sister, I'm a grandma and my two kids and my one grandson don't touch!" She shut her fat mouth and went to collect the little monster that was kicking and screaming her head off. Point made? Doubt it…

4:44 P.M. Rosie came in for her *second* huge, iced mocha. Ex-Con was pulling some real nasty shit – she never got out of the house twice in one day – and he never gave her this much cash. The home front must be a warzone. She was heading down to her sister's place and grunted, "We're gonna drink every fucking last drop of beer in Tillamuk tonight. When the hops are gone, we're gonna switch to any other hooch available."

5:12 P.M. Scanner: A vehicle over the embankment at Trout Creek Bridge. Injury.

9:30 P.M. Ex-Con was out prowling around with a flashlight, looking for the cat murderer, I guessed. He was sporting the beam and a nail gun.

10:00 P.M. Cannot hear another story today…

7-16 58° Rain.

Cheater: Decaf espresso shots, steamed milk, topped with six choco-late-covered espresso beans!

10:06 A.M. Scanner: Injury accident at milepost 50. A car rolled down an embankment.

10:31 A.M. Last night was sheer hell! With my schedule, I cannot get the *minimum* of seven undisturbed hours in the prone position *needed* for sanity. My comatose state was invaded two or three times! For sure, once was at 3:33 A.M. and again at 5:00 A.M. The cat murderer was making his/her/its rounds again. Those almost human like, grueling screams. Ex-Con was out scouting, as usual, minus a weapon. I take that back! I strolled through the parking lot and peered towards Ex Con's dump of a house. There, crucified to a nearby tree *was* the cat murderer, Mr. Raccoon sporting numerous nails. Inhumane? Brutal? That is my neighbor.

Rotten egg, Ex-Con just freaked out *on* his latest new "secretary." This office (?) worker came screaming into the store scared as hell; she was practically airborne! She said Rosie told her if she ever had a *situation* to come here. "He's going to kill me and if he finds me here, he for sure will!" I was trying to re-group. "Do I dial 911 *now*?" She left and ran down the highway to the next nearest phone. I emailed our cop and called his cell phone.

The sheriff paid me a visit. He received my email and frantic call. He will pay this gangster a surprise visit!

7:00 P.M. Some drab customers made for an anemic day. Absolutely *nothing* to toot about.

10:09 P.M. Praying for a silent night's sleep…

7-17 58° Total sun.

Peanut Butter Mocha Iced: A shot of chocolate and peanut butter syrups; espresso shots mixed into syrups. Pour over ice and cold milk.

9:00 A.M On the dot. Mr. Argentinean dinner date, someday, and No. 1 catch in Seattle came in, finally. He is such a fabulous contractor; his expertise was requested from here to Cabo San Lucas.

Two elderly couples stopped. One of the ladies asked, "What kind of coffee do you have?" She meant sizes, but I didn't know that, so I started reciting my usual lifeless list, "Lattes, mochas, cappuccinos..." She interrupted me with, "Oh God! I *forgot* I was in Seattle! I need whatever is closest to a normal gas station coffee, like we get in other states." Americano it is.

I had not even gotten to unlock the east side door and a local needed an extension cord. "Listen, sweetheart, you'll have to wait until I get this joint opened up completely, before I can head to the barn, swat at all the spider webs, and then try to untangle the snarled cables. But I will...just for you!"

11:58 A.M. A lady came in just to see this building. The Bowers were the owners and she lived in the back in 1961. Her husband owned one of the big logging outfits up here in Saratogan and this was their temporary dwelling, until they eventually settled in Treetops Loop. They partied with the best of 'em "down-the-line." She knew the sons, the fathers, and the grandfathers. I asked, "Did you know Buck and his dad?" "Yes. I believe Buck was just a tyke, but the dad and Big Sam were somethin' else! I worked at the Saratogan Hotel, the Lumberman's Chalet, Train Blow Tavern, and Bowers, and they were a very visible part of my day. Those men were the town fixtures and their feuding partner, the Olsen family, were notorious! The men up here were crazy – married or unmarried, it didn't matter. Cheating, drinking, fighting, abusing on weekends." In my opinion, "This town is still pretty much stuck in the 1800s!" "God help us," and she was on her way again.

4:37 P.M. The surprise visit happened already! The sheriff found Ex-Con had illegally resided in Denny's house while he was in Alaska, holding his own garage sale, selling off what was left of Denny's possessions here in Saratogan! Maybe it was *also* time for Denny to chat with the sheriff. If we all got together, we could bring Ex-Con *down*. Which reminded me, Rosie wasn't back from taking the cork out of every bottle in Tillamuk...

5:05 P.M. Scanner: Foot injury.

Mr. Cowboy, a fifty-something-year-old, easily a No. 15 scale kind of guy, came in again. He was Paul Newman-impressive. He had a ranch in Wenatchee and soon would be sliding into a comfy Boeing retirement. A full-time cattle farmer was his dream. Waiting patiently for his flavored latte, I saw him grab one of my cards. Ding-Dong and the doors keep opening. Why did the whole fucking world have to come in at this very minute? Damn! Was he going to contact me? Did he have a ring on? No – but was he married? Was he false? Probably not! My brain was jumping in supersonic speed! Watch it, Christy...

6:54 P.M. An overweight mother with her overweight daughter came in. Damn, forgot to lock the west door! The little brat kept me open for twenty more minutes, touching everything within her reach, with chubby, sticky-candy fingers. She was trying to decide exactly which beads she wanted for a little project. "Spoiled'" didn't even begin to cover this one! Finally Mama begged for the ninth time, "Honey, this lady wants to close, so pleeeeeez choose." At the nineteenth minute I got pissed, "I'm closing and closing now, goodbyyyyyeeeee." Her daughter grabbed a handful of those colorful glass balls and threw them across the floor. Mama tried to bend down and pick them up but couldn't. She grabbed four new ones and paid.

11:30 P.M. This is no bullshit. I finished cleaning my espresso equipment and as I was taking a milk jug back to the commissary, something of *decent* size and black was crawling across the carpet. I flipped on the light, naively expecting a sick mouse. Wrong! It was a fucking bat! He must have flown in through my drive thru window. I took a canning jar off my $2 sale table and a CD to use as a lid. Got him! Oh...geeeeze, he was screeching! I was almost sick! I ran outside holding this contraption away from my body as far as my arms would stretch and flung the whole damn works in the air. He and I both ran off, luckily in opposite directions. I will worry about all the broken glass tomorrow.

12:02 A.M. What a bitchin' long, insane barista day...

7-18 68° Sunny.

> Blueberry Spritzer: A shot of blueberry syrup, fill halfway with ginger ale and top with soda water.

8:55 A.M. Hot morning. State troopers were out in full force.

2:22 P.M. Speaking of police. A customer just walked in, "I just got nabbed by one of our new undercover state troopers. He gave me a sobriety test in front of God and everyone – in broad daylight!" I added, "Bummer, but to top that one, about three years ago, I was driving west on Mountain Peak Highway, in Alpine, and stopped at a signal. I was over the slowpokes, so when the light turned green, I sped around Dawdling-Donna, right in the middle of the damn intersection. She called 911.

As I was relaxing in a hair salon in Tillamuk, with twelve-inch spiral perm rods anchored to my head, in walked a cop. "Who owns the black Camaro out front?" I raised my hand like a preschooler. He wanted my ID and my registration because, allegedly, I passed illegally. My face must have looked like it was covered in cabernet! I know my head looked like a voodoo-doll! "Don't make me go outside!" He obliged and took my keys. Paperwork was all in order. He returned, gave me a huge, long, loud lecture, right there in the middle of the crowded beauty shop, and wrote up the warning." Hair is now straight and long…

4:40 P.M. Sure enough, Mr. Gorgeous Cowboy emailed me! Oh my! I responded with a short note: "Are you married?"

Rosie finally returned home to her madhouse and mad husband. Another neighbor in for his late-day decaf said he heard some powerful yelling next door to me. Besides her hubby Ex-Con, BOO, bats, and long nights of animal screams, this place was starting to creep me.

10:19 P.M. Just got back from all the supply stores.

10:30 P.M. I am pooped…

7-19 64° Hot day!

Sugar-Free Root Beer Float: Ice, 2 shots of sugar-free root beer syrup, soda within an inch of top, and finish with Half & Half.

8:15 A.M. Shit! Mr. Cowboy *was* married! I emailed back: "I'd let you come howling at my doorstep if you weren't married!" Boy, if his wife ever penetrated his computer, the grounds for a divorce were just a printer away. He sent me a picture of himself and I am trying to download it now. Customers can just hold their britches! I am extremely busy! I had better smarten up right this minute – married is married. A point off the male column, you ever-lovin' cowboy player, you...

10:45 A.M. It is downloaded. I peeked at the picture and it was a beautiful, expansive photo of him climbing up a steep, mountainous hill on horseback. There was a beautiful river below. Now he was a combo of Paul, the Marlboro Man, and Tim McGraw! I am in trouble here... Harley Dennis just passed me in the train and honked! He called, "Can I get an espresso-on-the-fly? This is my most scenic trip so far – it's so grand and clear out." Now I could hear him honking down at the crossing. Fun.

12:00 – 5:00 P.M. I am on overload. It is not the responsibility of the land and home and store and animals. Its men. Or should I say "man!" Everything seemed suspended; in my head there was an awkward silence, where peace, happiness, and expectations of life used to reside. Enough! I picked up a broom and attacked the walkways.

6:15 P.M. Cowboy emailed two more times! He wasn't "getting" it, so I asked him to not stop here anymore. Get a grip, girl – you don't even know this person! Smack!

6:34 P.M. Closing. Enough of this captivating, compelling consumption...

7-20 68° Sunny.

Icy Lemon Espresso: In blender combine: 2 cups cold espresso, one pint lemon sherbet, and a shot of grenadine syrup. Makes four cups.

9:02 A.M. Drug out of bed late. Didn't care. I sprayed weeds again. Didn't care. I served some espresso and couldn't care less. Damn that splendiferous cowboy! Damn ME! He emailed again and in short: "I would never be unfaithful to my wife; just like to bring ya some pizza from "down-below" and if anything, ever happens between my wife and I, you can expect a trailer to show up, and you'll be the first thing I load!" Flirt much?!

11:14 A.M. I had to get out of this place. I wanted to hop the Amtrak. I felt like I was on a roller coaster and it was going backwards. I was being a horse's-hard-on and at least I knew it. Car ride.

6:00 P.M. Came back to customers and my third or fourth bare chest for the season. Tanned, muscled, and perfect chest hair. I cleared my throat and tried to clear the head.

Dead Evening – Joke Time. Five Ways to Know If You Drink Too Much Espresso: 1. Your only source of nutrition comes from Sweet & Low. 2. You attend AA meetings just for the free coffee. 3. You have virtually built miniature cities out of little plastic stir-sticks. 4. Starbucks owns the mortgage on your house. 5. Your birthday is a National Holiday in Brazil! Har har…

8:21 P.M. Some guys stopped for directions to the *old* Keystone Hot Springs and ordered Milky Way lattes. I explained for the thousandth time, they were closed indefinitely – and would re-open if/when the new owner had the money for all the required legal repairs. It closed two years ago; he had owned it for one.

Amtrak whizzed by – it was loaded with tourists.

9:21 P.M. Still in the 90s. My customers were beat from the heat. Me too…

7-21 78° Sunny.

Plantation Frost Espresso: In blender combine 1 cup cold espresso, 3 tbs. sugar, one cut-up banana, and a pint vanilla ice cream. Makes 3 cups.

7:59 A.M. Today is "D" Day – Diary Is Half Done! Publishers, look out, here we come...

ANOTHER SEATTLE GIANT

Amazon – the American electronic company based in Seattle, Washington. Jeff Bezos founded Amazon in 1994. He figured the largest bookstore might sell upwards to 200,000 titles. With that in mind, an Internet bookstore could sell many times that! Seattle had done it again.

8:28 A.M. Scanner: Brush fire at milepost 64.

I am sending Gumby, Pokey, and the coffin back to Brian. He made it clear that he needed them back. Cannot find any more on the net for his bedroom. W E I R D O!

1:55 P.M. Scanner: Driver was threatening other passenger with a golf club.

3:22 P.M. 97 degrees. I'm melting. I've served three hot chocolates today in this heat. Figure that out...

9:21 P.M. I'm hot and done in and bored...and lonely...

9:30 P.M. And obsessing...

7-22 64° Rain.

Irish Summer: Put 1.5 tsp. sugar in bottom of cup, a shot of Irish whiskey next, add two shots of espresso, hot water within 1 inch of top, stir together, top with whipped cream.

9:00 A.M. Cowboy emailed: "I'll see you around five. I'll be the one driving by with a reeeeeal looooooong honk!" I'd have divorced his ass or maimed his body or downright killed him slowly if I were his wife. I couldn't be the first flirtation…could I?

A super car accident at the Frothing Ham River road turnoff, just over the bridge, 150 feet from me. A young gal took out the barrier and crashed down into the creek! Her car was mangled and there was a lot of blood coming from her head. I ran an eighth of a mile, both east and west, and set out flares. This scanner has been going off all day. Crashes everywhere. A little rain, lots of tourists, and add *Friday* to the list. Whew!

5:20 P.M. Cowboy just drove by and *laid* on his horn. He didn't stop…A cute redheaded gal came in. She was also a bird lady. First, she tasted her espresso granita, then cried, "I married the man of my dreams, fifteen years ago. We have two beautiful kids and he just filed for divorce. I didn't have a goddamn clue that anything was wrong. All he would ever say is, 'he doesn't see me in his future anymore.' Right up to attorney-time, he took me to bed three times a week and he won't try counseling!" Okay, gents, another point off your column. No… two!

8:49 P.M. Cowboy emailed again. Now he was asking questions about my children – best way to any women's heart! He was no dummy, I'll give him that! On the other hand, was he just making sure I had no rug-rats to get in his way? This guy was a neon red flag!

9:09 P.M. And the game continues…

7-23 62° Sunny.

Espresso Buttered Rum: Mix together a shot of rum, 2 tsp. maple syrup, slice of butter, sprinkle of nutmeg, espresso shots, mix and enjoy!

11:52 A.M. I thought it was about time to take inventory: Cowboy was ranching, Dennis was driving a choo-choo, Buck was fucking around, Clint 15 was tanning on his river lot, Brian was worrying about something, Jack was in his RV, Seattle No. 1 Bachelor was busy or most likely in Mexico with his senoritas, BOO was hiding, No. 7 had neglected to call for days, No. 5 was coming next weekend to visit my son, Boone from Stonewall was keeping his distance, Philip was a daily joy and still brought me DVDs, Tony in California had lost the luster, my brother was bouncing around on a pogo-stick with his galfriend, our sheriff had disappeared again, Ex-Con would rather abuse his wife than track the cat killer, Butch was a cone-head and Freddy and Mister were always squawky but still couldn't give me a proper hug with those wings. That was the run-down on the males that weave in and out of my life these days. Quite an abstract smear of pigment...

5:47 P.M. I began to wonder...could a married man be perfect...for now. That special, rare, naughty, delicious, loving we all craved. I had heard stories about how the *other woman* got showered with lavish gifts, *almost* perfect behavior, an abundance of attention, and got to enjoy the *other side* of the man – the one who wore clean clothes, fresh underwear, and cologne. You got the romantic side of the man – not that dirty laundry, flu bugs, remote-control junky, cranky, boring side. You weren't smothered – this affair *couldn't* be on a daily basis. You got plenty of time off – because you wouldn't be included in holidays, special family events, school plays, dinners with the boss, neighborhood functions, major surgeries or relative get-togethers and didn't plan on having children because the "player" was having babies with his wife. Also, better buy yourself a down comforter, because there would be *no* memories to keep you warm when he slid you into deep-freeze, as he sauntered off with a hotter chick, to satisfy his dual personality and confused ego. The other shoe *must* drop – and *we* become "the old stinky sneaker." That is what *makes Players* tick.

6:16 P.M. Still monopolizing that brain, ain't it, gal...

7-24 64° Sunny.

> Daiquiri: Blend together a shot of lime juice, 4 tsp. sugar, 1.5 cups
> ice, two shots of rum. Have a shot of espresso ready to wake you up!

8:11 A.M. Another scorcher.

The highway bum was back again with a bunch of twenties in his pockets. He was either starving to death or he had hundreds. Had to be drug money – a pusher or a runner. I gave him a two-day-old pastry and waved bye-bye, all in the same motion. His hair was cut short now and he was looking a little better and you could even see some features, like blue eyes and nice skin. I just realized he was about 6'3" and with the shorter flashback hair! He may have been the freak in my truck the night I had to draw my gun and my son came out of nowhere to rescue me! Hmmm…

4:26 P.M. I was serving like crazy and running out of change. I was just heading to my purse and tip jar, when lo and behold a car full of five ladies paid for their drinks with all silver! They were a Godsend!

7:57 P.M. A man in his camper needed water. Thinking it would help if he purchased something before asking for a favor, he ordered a white caramel iced mocha then *begged* for a hose. "You can *beg* all night, Mister…no hoses up here in this country. Sorreeee." A couple of buckets later and the grateful gent exited.

8:31 P.M. I am closing now and I'm begging for peace and quiet, mainly in my head…

7-25 67° Sunny.

> Frappe Chiller: Crushed ice, one shot of your choice: brandy, crème
> de menthe, crème de cocoa, fruit liquor or sloe gin. Straw.

7:34 A.M. This takes the cake! I was relaxing upstairs late last night, doing laundry, having a snack, and a freakin' BAT flies over my head! IN MY DAMN

HOUSE! I screamed, bolted for the bathroom, and slammed the door. What in the heck was I going to do? Butch had spotted the black shadow now; I could hear him thrashing around the living room! Maybe I would just make up a bed in the bathtub and let my killer-dog handle it. Oops, forgot. He was Sir Cone-Head! I opened the door and called him in. Somehow, I got the duct tape and plastic shield off his head. God, I hoped he would kill this thing! I snuck out and saw the bat perched up on top of my curtains, just staring down at us. At 11:14 P.M. I finally had to go to bed. I closed the door and stuffed clothes into every possible crack of light! I arose to a cold carcass. Good Butch!

10:17 A.M. The perverted Middle Eastern came in, this time by himself. He was "over" all the different nationalities and sluts and was looking for an, "American girlfriend now." This old, fat slimebucket had better stay the hell away from here! I do not need his free Starbuck's beans!

2:59 P.M. Some old hippies came in who had not been in Saratogan since 1973. They said, "This town was *hopping* back then, from bed to bed and railroad car to railroad car." "Indeed. And it hasn't changed much."

4:04 P.M. Cowboy emailed three times today. His wife left for a week again. Maybe her schedule, working with *only* men, 75% of her time, week after week, was getting to Home-Alone-Handsome-Cowboy.

7:00 P.M. I did not bike ride after all. So, I will do thousands of sit-ups instead. Too rushed and the birds were being too cute. Be honest, Christy! You would rather wait for a *breath* from Cowboy on email, than get a *breath* of fresh air. Caught me!

I now think Ben the rat has left us. If I were getting all my hair yanked out by the roots, I would find a better habitat too! There are no more tunnel holes in the bird's cedar chips and no more trails of garbage.

9:04 P.M. Poor Ben. He's gone. And so am I…

7-26 64° Sunny.

Iced Toddy Caffé: Mix together 1/2 tsp. sugar, 2 whole cloves, cinnamon stick, lemon slice, and a shot of one of these: whiskey, bourbon, brandy, gin, Irish whiskey, rum, scotch or vodka, a shot of espresso all over ice.

8:56 A.M. A guy came in…and… "Watch that first step!" I hollered. He was in some other world, singing "Skip-To-Ma-Lou-Ma-Darlin," and *bam*, he was down! He was laughing so hard he couldn't get up.

11:55 A.M. My espresso machine was just repaired again, by my (militia) service guy. We will probably both end up in the same compound someday if this country does not wise up! We started a conversation about gays since he had been in the music industry and, believe me, they had slang names for us heterosexuals too! One of the names they called *us* was "breeders." I learned something new and fun every time he came here.

3:00 P.M. Philip came by and met mom and sis, niece and nephew. Sis was visiting from California too, so they chatted about the overcrowding and prices of homes that challenged your wildest imagination. His parents met in Totem, Washington. Fitting – both Totem and Saratogan are nearly ghost towns – with prismatic scenery to die for…and vivid ghosts.

Cowboy emailed twice already.

7:36 P.M. Phone call. A couple of nights ago, my son was going to fly up for a visit. That is no longer happening, since his girlfriend backed out and will not join him on the treasured flight. He is destroyed. Coming north, solo, isn't appealing to him so he is staying south to try and mend the relationship. Kids!

10:59 P.M. Going to bed as usual with a prayer for my offspring…

7-27 68° A.M. Sunny as hell.

Iced Black Russian Caffé: Ice, pour over with a shot of vodka, a shot of coffee syrup, and a shot of espresso.

10:00 A.M. Had eight toned bikers from Canada stop. All were cops and firemen and buff. Courteous and clean. They bought every piece of beef jerky I had and eight *different* kinds of drinks.

Clint 15 called to see what I had been up to and to tell me that his ex-wife stopped by his place and tried out his new hot tub. T.M.I. She was engaged to someone else but now said she missed him. Have fun, fool.

Fools…Cowboy emailed again. I *forced* myself to email him back explaining how rotten I felt about this communication – we should cool it. I should cool it!

4:00 P.M. Iced drinks galore, gifts, snacks, all day long. Business was booming!

Here was a strange coincidence for today. In all my seven years, I never had someone ask to borrow my electricity – wanted to use my one outside outlet. This was such a luxury; *nobody* up on this hill even had one! She had eye-spied that little metal box. It was for her kid who wanted to plug in his hand-held computer game. Anything to keep bored kids…out…

Then, an elderly couple stopped and asked if they could plug their cell phone outside. It was dead. "Sure – have at it!"

9:47 P.M. No shopping spree tonight…

7-28 70° Sunny.

Sober Time: A triple shot of espresso with maple and cream.

7:46 A.M. Today, the railroad gangs were working on the tracks right above my store. They gave commands on some sort of a loudspeaker system. It sounded like they are sitting right in my lap. My neighbor, Denny, three doors down called, "It sounds like this bellowing is coming from my couch!"

Cowboy emailed. He was replying to an old email, pretending he had not read my Dear John yet. His name has been changed to Crafty! The new name he had given me is Christy-Sue. Was that fucking flirting or what? And fucking adorable! Damn him, he was so particularly good at this. He is putting his west-side house on the market to become a full-time rancher. I emailed back: "Now that you are selling the house that is so convenient to work – and – your acreage, if you were not married, you could park that belt-buckle right here. I'm smack-dab in the middle of both!"

Now I am flirting. Ugh!

10:02 A.M. Philip was here with a local gal. They wanted to pick my brain. "There are about fifteen towns 'down-the-line' and we want to know which one you feel is the evilest." Without a second thought, "Snow Peak Mine takes the cake, then came Crag Rock! You can just about *feel* the iniquity!"

I think a famous golfer and his family just stopped for blended drinks. They lived on the 9th hole in Washington and the 9th hole in Palm Springs and he just *looked* famous. I didn't ask – hate to act like a groupie.

4:41 P.M. The Crafty-Cowboy responded to Christy-Sue, but *not* to the belt-buckle offer: "Just an update, honey, I love smooching, smoke two cigars a week, a beer here and there, and I want to come by for an espresso tomorrow, and again on Sunday. I want to call you for the traffic report on my return from the ranch." Shit on toast, he was playing me like a fiddle.

5:13 P.M. I *am* getting on my bike to clear my stupid head!

7:45 P.M. I opened just the drive thru again. Might as well, I have to sit here and do some computer work anyway. And sure enough, No. 7 emailed and still wanted dinner. In his dreams! I deleted without response.

10:08 P.M. Still here! I should have called the book, **'THE BARISTA OWNER'S DIARY'**. Employees would have sued over these *hours*, *conditions*, and the *pay* around here!

10:59 P.M. Getting the tushy upstairs like a normal human being...

7-29 70° Sun.

> Alexander Espresso: Ice, a shot of brandy or gin, a shot of crème de cocoa and cream.

7:45 A.M. Cowboy emailed: "I hear you loud 'n clear. You don't want the toe of my boot over your threshold, so what are you going to charge me if I just drive *by* the Toll Booth? Don't be nervous, I know when to eat 'n run." Backatcha: "You can't afford my fees! They entail an awfully expensive Divorce Attorney!" I got to thinking – what if the fool wasn't even *married*, like Grant and Bergman in the movie, *Indiscreet*, where he just pretended, keeping *all* women at arm's length! I'm going to Google him today! This was too exhausting! Was he for real – was he married – did he own all this real estate he's bragging about? Type, type, type…

10:24 A.M. "Keep it up, girl, one foot in front of the other!" Baristas were expected to be unstoppable, accommodating, high-energy, friendly, cooperative sweeties, with a flashy, toothy grin, at the drop of a stir-stick.

4:59 P.M. Cowboy should be here in two hours and eleven minutes and… But who's counting!

Iced chai's, granitas, smoothies, Italian sodas, iced espresso drinks, all day long. I gift-wrapped presents for two separate weddings.

Cowboy was here. He looked a tad bit older than I remembered but still resided in that fabulous rodeo body! He asked me to dinner! "Did you get permission from the little woman?" Sheepishly, "She's out of town." Big Point off! "Let's give her a call then." He brightened, "Sure. I'll just tell her I'm having dinner with someone who just breezed into town." Second Point off! Be gone!

Soon after – the phone rang, "Christy Sue, is there an auto parts store in the area?" Fuck, we don't even have condoms! Why would our isolated area have car-innards kickin' around! He was helping a couple that broke down nine miles up the highway. Just then a man ran in, "Where do I get groceries?" "Hell, if I know, and I'm serious, Mister. There isn't a food market within twenty-five miles! How do you think I stay so thin?" The frown turned to laughter at this point. "But…we are in a camper! Will we have to eat bugs and squirrels and shit, like in the movies?" "Yep!" He busted up. "Seriously now, where can I get some matches then?" I sent him off to the local gas station, but not before forcing some espressos on all of them.

7:00 P.M. Cowboy rang again. "The couple has a tow truck coming, and I just want you to know what a good and honorable Eagle Scout I can be!" Why was I participating in this game? It was quicksand! Why was I running a brush through my hair and checking my lip color, listening, emailing, and answering telephones? Tell him, Christy. Tell him no more visits, calling, online correspondence, no dinner, no temptations, no nothin'! This could be the gosh damn inspiration for a Western Gold Album!

8:33 P.M. A cute couple came up to the drive thru and desperately needed espresso beans for their overnight stay at a cabin. We compared Starbuck's prices down in the city for just "the beans" and came to the conclusion that I could sell them a 12-ounce cup, full to the brim, for $5. Fair. Especially since that "Perverted Middle Eastern guy" loaded me up.

I just sent *the* goodbye email to Cowboy. He will not get it now until Monday. But I will be seeing him again this Sunday. I'm going to doll-up and try to *knock him dead* on this last visit. It's only fair, since he's trying to kill *me*.

10:36 P.M. It was *him*, on the phone. Still on the road to the ranch. "Have you ever been in a bubble bath full of stars, Christy Sue?" "Sure, all the time," trying to appear worldly. "Hold on cuz I'm gonna blow a couple your way!" I was only half listening, I was focused on how hard this shit was on a lonely, single, overworked gal in the hills, staring up at my own meteor burst, all by myself. I was counting down – only 2.5 days until he knew he was axed. I would miss the bastard…

10:41 P.M. I've hardly the strength to plump the pillows…

7-30 64° Sunny.

Orange Blossom: Ice, 1 tsp. of sugar, 2 shots of orange juice, fill with soda water.

8:01 A.M. It is so funny when customers place an order that ends in a question mark. Of what are you unsure, sir? Are you asking *me* what *your* tongue likes? It always goes something like this: *Maybe I should have a latte? What do you think of a chocolate smoothie? Perhaps an Italian soda?* I don't question it – I just turn the question mark into a period by barreling through the mixings before they think I should change *their* mind.

Mr. Mercury-Poison came with his ten-year-old daughter. Fatherly *won't* work either, bud.

6:06 P.M. Two young gals pulled up in their bikinis. The driver asked, "Do you make a good mocha?" "Nope. I'm only passing the time pushing nasty brown sludge." I knew it! They were baristas from "down-below!" She ordered up. The passenger asked me if I could make her an iced caramel macchiato. Testing, one two! They thought just because they found me in Hicks-Ville they could throw me a curve with that one. "Sure, as hell can! How would you like that? medium?

Or rare?" I finally got a laugh out of the brunette, as she requested a caramel and vanilla with soy. The blond was still trying to digest my last comment. You could almost picture the T-bone floating around in the air, where the brain should be! "Knew you were baristas the minute you started flipping me too much shit." They giggled.

7:37 P.M. A middle-aged couple in a shiny yellow Jeep just stripped to the derma out on my west side parking lot! And as casually as you please, they took off swimsuits and threw on some "underwear-less" clothes. They could have at least stepped inside the opening of the chapel. When they came in for iced Americanos, whipped cream, and four equals, I couldn't help, "Hey, thanks for the striptease show!"

10:02 P.M. It is bedtime…

7-31 70° Sun.

Pink Lady Soda: Ice, a shot of lemon syrup, a shot of grenadine, soda water to top.

8:15 AM. Two overnighters from Treetops Loop beat me to the door! My Pet Peeve – nothing like *immediate* pressure. "Espressoooo!" Sometimes I felt like just chewing-the-fat with them for a while like I was waiting for the damn barista too.

I just had a young neighbor gal come in to tell me about Buck cattin' around down at her girlfriend's house in High Valley. He was drunk and being obnoxious, threatening to take liberties with her, right then and there. "I love a challenge, little girl," said Buck, with that half grin that didn't really belong to his real emotions any longer. God, he can be a stupid abusive asshole! And I went there?

12:39 P.M. Scanner: Motorcycle down two miles west of the summit.

5:09 P.M. Another hyperventilating Starbucks barista. They *never* know what they want. This one had been here for twelve minutes; I was suspended in flight between the window and the machine. "You gals at Starbucks are going to have to start meditating over the menu during your work-breaks and establish your druthers!" She apologized for her indecisiveness…but still couldn't decide. Finally, "A 16-ounce iced Banana Split One-Shot Latte with whipped cream." While I was steaming the milk, she continued, "Men are filthy, abrasive, pushy pigs! Starbucks had to quit making nametags for their employees and had to start hiring more men – just because of all the harassments! I've been a manager for seven years and we have started calling our espresso shop Sexbucks instead of Starbucks!" Amen!

5:47 P.M. Scanner: Vehicle injury accident at milepost 61. Vehicle rolled down the embankment and over a cliff 300-400 feet! Patient was conscious.

6:00 P.M. There was a dead mouse or rat or some other foreign creature in my gift shop. I can smell it. I sprayed perfume and lit candles in various spots till I had time to hunt. Better I find this stiff-as-a-board furry corpus delicti before some customer's kid does. "Mommy, can you buy me this Ben.... pleeeeeeze?"

Two young guys ordered cappuccinos and were arguing over whether the gal at the bar in Lake Charlestown last night was the same hottie barista they saw earlier in the day. They had a buddy who was "addicted" to baristas. He traveled to hundreds of espresso booths and worked on all the cute ones until he got a date with them. "He must be broke!"

8:27 P.M. Oh God, this was the busiest day that I remembered in a year! I must have single-handedly mixed 250 drinks today, plus gifts.

Cowboy came by on his way home. Just before he pulled out, he left a little piece of himself – a branded chunk of wood with his ranch insignia. He left me in tears. He just plain moves me. I would ride off into the sunset with *this* one. I have only known this man *in-person* for twenty measly minutes and my life shuts down.

I am sitting here thinking – my son is in the middle of a messy relationship and his life in general sucks, period. Buck is gross, period. Cowboy is a rotten husband, period. And the rest of my groupies up here can just fuck themselves. I'm feeling very sorry for myself right now. Slap!

9:14 P.M. Closing. Bye, y'all. Bye, Cowboy...

AUGUST

As the branches break during the icy night, beans are harvested under hot sun

---

8-01 63° Raining.

Tom Collins Fizz: Ice, a full shot of lemon syrup, a shot of grenadine, soda water.

8:23 A.M. Hello, August. Hello, Smell! The gift store reeked of death. Ben the Rat! I grabbed Butch, slammed on his leash, and we played Dick Tracy and his pal through the store. Sure enough, he led me to the exact corner. So did the flies, swooping around like buzzards. Some customers from California walked in and heard me scream as I spotted Ben. The husband did not pay for a thing that day! He dislodged Ben from the wall, even with the maggots crawling *out* of openings! This man about lost his lunch. I have now 409'd, perfumed, and bleached Ben's death bed, and most everything in sight!

2:53 P.M. Cowboy sent me two emails: "You asked so here it is. My wife is a fabulous 5'10", blonde long hair, and a *great* body!"

Reply: "Okay Cowboy, bring her in! Let's see if she's okay with our dinner date, smooching, star bubble baths, emailing each other all day long. Oh, and let's not forget the gifts. *If* she is okay with all of this, then by God, let's *go-at-it* and dinner is on me!"

6:11 P.M. Well, Cowboy didn't respond to my last email and probably won't. Now to contact his wife. Hmmmmmmmmm, tempting…

7:08 P.M. Going on a bike ride, hoping to get hit by a tractor…

8-02 50° A.M. Sunny.

The Rose: Ice, a shot of apple syrup, shot of lemon or lime syrup, shot of grenadine, soda water to top.

12:30 P.M. One of my guys across the street came for the loggers' orders. I told him that I would deliver to all of them if I could, but the verbal molestation would be unbearable!

3:37 P.M. A whole van of hikers stopped. Tons of drinks!

A big guy came in off his motorcycle asking, "Where can I get food around here?" I told him to go down to the gas station or liquor store. He said the liquor store was closed. What's new… "Well then, that leaves the gas station, dude. Oh, I forgot to mention the tavern and their deep-fried chicken and jo-jos." His eyes lit up. "Now you're talkin'!" He then wanted to know what time I opened. "Around 9:00 A.M." He happened to be camping up the Barklett River Road. *Now* I understood all these questions. I thought he was only passing through or planning on pitching himself right here.

8:40 P.M. And email-less…

8-03 68° Sunny.

Cognac Kaffé Smash: Beat 6 eggs and a grated peel of lemon until fluffy. Add a cup sugar and beat until thick. Stir in espresso shots (and a shot of brandy) slowly. Serve in chilled glasses.

8:06 A.M. While heading to the P.O. I noticed something wrong with my Jeep. I was going to head down the highway to Lou Sampson's for a checkup but saw hordes of cars heading up my way. I did an immediate U-turn. Couldn't miss work and a possible $2 a head! Thank God I came right back because Angel was helping herself to my cash till! Money was chewed up and strewn all over my cubicle! She also decided to horse-kick all the change around too. My money-grubbing cockatoo. Typical Angel behavior! Typical *female*!

2:45 P.M. Three customers today, I left after all, to have my Jeep fixed. 'Bout time, too, it just turned over a scary 200,000 on the odometer! I was five miles west of here and had a rear tire blowout! Buuuuck! I limped-it along to the first wide shoulder and parked. I discovered to my delight that I had a spare with air in it, a jack, and a lug wrench! In between ducking for cover from cars, buses, and trucks (the flat of course was on the highway side), I started my chores. I got the cute, miniature wheel cover off, and simply jacked the car up. Now, to those nasty lug-nuts. Ladies, this is where we get stumped! Who *says* a woman can do this? Driver's Ed…BE FUCKED! I called the same tow company that just unlocked my Jeep a couple of weeks ago at the P.O. and yes, another $60 to loosen a few silver bolts!

7:21 PM. Email-less… Bushed…

8-04 70° Sunny.

Apricot Orange Hot Tea: Combine 2 cups apricot nectar, 1 cup orange juice, 1 cup water, 1 tbs. sugar, 1 tsp. cinnamon, 4 lemon slices, 12 whole cloves, 2 tsp. instant tea. Bring to boil, steep 5 minutes and serve.

8:48 A.M. I locked Angel in last night to protect my money.

Had a rush of ladies this morning. A bunch of 24-ounce iced lattes and earring sales.

3:15 P.M. I have had three separate parties in from New York today. One couple was on a rented Harley and having a ball. The second set was clueless on espresso, so I had to explain everything. Frappe…what? Machia…who? Latte or cappuccino? Finally, "Do you have coffee?" but they were just kidding. The third set of three were rude, East Coast mentality and two of them tossed their chewing gum right on the floor next to my cart! Of course, I told them what they could do with that gum – and they did, even if it was to put it in the trashcan – and not quite where I had suggested. What the hell do the sidewalks look like in the Big Apple? Polka-dots?

9:30 P.M. Roadside Over-Night? I could dig it, I suppose. A man broke down here tonight in a beautiful convertible '70s Cadillac and I was already upstairs. His headlights quit working. I put my gun in my back pocket and brought him my cordless flashlight. I safely handed it out through the locked gate, hoping he would have the light required to fix the problem and get outta here. He called his wife to tell her he was staying right here! Here? I offered my chapel for cover, but he wanted to sleep in his precious Caddie. He was carrying a canoe so that could be his bed. Now I was outside the gate, searching like mad in my store for fuses. Then I really lost my mind and unlocked my car gate, so he could camp on my back forty. I gave him two bottles of water, a cookie, blanket, and pillow. I figured I would have a yard guard, in case Ex-Con went cat killer hunting.

10:31 P.M. Food and shower. Goodnight, Mister...whoever you are...

8-05 68° Sun.
-North-Westerners are not sick of this samo-samo weather report – at all!

Iced Tea Sparkle: Combine 6 tea bags, 3 cups boiling water. Boil for 4 minutes. Let cool then add in a lemon-lime carbonated beverage.

8:21 A.M. Butch woke me at 5:56 A.M. I was surprised he hadn't barked and tried to attack Mr. Cadillac earlier. You are slipping, watchdog! He left soon after and forgot to lock the gate but left the blanket and pillow and an envelope with a twenty-dollar bill. His note said: My faith in kind people who offer help and assistance has been renewed. Signed and printed stationary of an Attorney at Law.

11:47 A.M. A friend of mine who considered buying the old Lumberman's Restaurant down the way a couple of years ago emailed: "You are to be commended on your bravery, or insanity, for even going near that place, Christy, to check out the trashed apartment for the new investor. I have been there. You can smell rot from the front walkway!" Reply: "It was nothing compared to my Ben, maggots and flies. He had gone through numerous poisons and tortures."

His reply: "Lumberman's stunk when it was open for business as a successful restaurant and the resident rats were extremely lively. One of the cooks was ordered to fire up the steam table every day and pour vanilla in the water to cover up the dead smells!

No toots from Cowboy today, but No. 1 Bachelor from Groovy Street came in and chatted. He wants to buy another quarter of a mountain up here.

9:59 P.M. I am off duty…

8-06 60° Sunny.

Sugar-Free Pink Moo Iced Latte: A shot of sugar-free raspberry syrup, espresso shots, poured over ice and milk.

8:43 A.M. More emails from Rick regarding the Lumberman's and this town: "The best thing for catching rats at the 'Willard' (his name for the worn-down restaurant) is a garbage can and a couple of Mary Lynn's dinner rolls. You can snag 3 or 4 at once! Once they get a whiff, these rodents just can't restrain themselves – then one bite and they keel over! No wonder tourism fell off…"

You know, I just thought of something. This town does not have a cemetery! Where went all the bodies?

1:34 P.M. Baristas and bartenders are twins. Everyone lets it all hang out in our presence. I could be mute and still be the recipient of much complaining, truth-telling, and scandals. Starbucks misses out on sooooo much; they are too busy to care and with all the bodies before them, no one vents. Course their image would be trashed. People also don't vent at Nordstrom either.

1:36 P.M. Thurston, a local, is having a huge deck party tonight. They no longer *compete* to the bashes of thirty years ago. People remember the old parties as being the *fun ones*. Age does that. Fights, wife swapping, nudity, drunks, missing persons, missing teeth, and sorrowful souls the following days. I'm *not* going because Buck *does*.

2:01 P.M. Scanner: Hiker injured on the Pacific Crest Trail. Ankle distress.

A blind man came in with his dad. This chap was so interesting and asked lots of questions about the birds. He wanted to know what kind and color. I fully described Mister and Angel and let it drop. "What about the other ones?" he said. I felt like a dodo! He probably knew the count better than I did! So, I described each one of them for him. He loved Freddy the best; he is the only bird that customers can touch – a cute old cockatiel that *must* have his head scratched! Somehow this man knew!

5:32 P.M. Scanner: Police were in pursuit of a bandito on Mountain Peak Highway, but still 40 miles "down-the-line" from me. I wouldn't lock up quite yet.

7:04 P.M. A new record! I had a seven-car line-up in my drive thru! They all happened to be camping together, I will admit. Cars were now lined up practically into the highway.

8:36 P.M. I'm going to go call my kids, sibs, and mom...

8-07 64° Sunny and will boil.

Purple Cow Smoothie: A cup of ice in blender, add in 2 inches of Half & Half, cup of grape juice and a cup of vanilla ice cream.

7:49 A.M. Three of my fly fishermen are heading back down to my secret fishing hole again. They are determined to outwit those slimy swimmers! They ordered smoothies this time.

11:42 A.M. A couple stopped yesterday evening to get an espresso and asked if there was a motel nearby. "Yes, on 'down-the-line,' either in two-minutes – or the next opportunity for a pillow is another forty-five!" They chose Saratogan – they were horny! I could sense this urgency and they were not the type to be sneaking up logging roads. I sent them to our finest motel on the river. I warned them about *expectations*, but, it *may* be AAA Approved. They were back today to talk about their experience. "We decided to spend the evening at your local pub – I think it's called the Train Blow Tavern. They practically *forced* us to get *wasted*! Got any aspirin, or hair-of-the-dog, to add to our espresso?"

This reminded me of some of my camping gals at the beginning of the summer. These females related their experience at our local tavern. "We were bombarded by *crazies* and a few were coming on way too strong. Every single person in the room was drunk, toothless and the breath to match. My friend about lost it a couple of times and gave some of these *ogres* a taste of her cowboy boot. As soon as we whipped the ass off the locals in pool, we were invited across the RR tracks to someone's party. No way José."

3:44 P.M. Life was sure rough for some... My adjacent next-door neighbor and her guy just landed at our airport in their private plane, hopped on their bikes and peddled here to their snazzy cabin.

3:52 P.M. Scanner: Driver of vehicle appears to be twelve years old.

4:10 P.M. Scanner: Possible vehicle fire at milepost 63.

7:43 P.M. I miss the black brim of his hat...

8-08 67° Sun.

Buttermilk Float: Blend 3 cups buttermilk, one pint lemon sherbet, sprinkle cinnamon and sugar.

7:39 A.M. Today started off with loads of pathetic-picky-people! Do you have honey? NO. Powdered chocolate? NO. Ice cream? NO. Yogurt-based smoothies? NO. Drip? NOT. Calorie-less anything? IMPOSSIBLE!

I believe a few of my groupies have dropped off for good. If men do not *eventually* get a piece-of-tail, which seems like their *only* goal in life, they split the scene.

12:40 P.M. I just had three Russian men order lattes. One of them asked if I had china cups for their hot drinks. Excuse me? "Well, Starbucks (here we go again...) gives us that option, even has saucers, on request!" "Is that so...Well,

I'm not here hosting a tea party, sir. You are in "these-thar- hills." Sorry, but you can take your designer paper cups out to the only sit-down option. Have a comfy seat out in my park, appreciate the scenery and the rushing waters of the Rockfish River, and watch the fly fishermen cast their lines, right before your eyes. Does Starbucks offer that?"

4:39 P.M. "Water is a dollar, and this isn't an auction house, lady." She and her husband stopped here after hiking and she wanted a few bottled waters but did not have enough cash. "Oh well..." Then her husband ordered a strawberry/banana smoothie! I did not get it...thought they were broke? But I *did* get the reason why her shirt was filthy, and grass-stains covered *the backside*. Must have been one of those Adam and Eve moments, up on the trail. Just for the hell of it, I asked her if she *fell* on her hike. Her face turned the color of a succulent persimmon, but her husband was laughing so hard he dropped his drink. So, I didn't discount their waters, but I did replace his smoothie! "I prefer Zout to Spray 'n Wash." Now he completely lost it! For my sarcasm I was rewarded with pinching my finger on my cart's refrigerator rack...dammit!

A lady from Canada just came through, raving over my clean Porta Potty. Thanked me for putting the hockey puck in the urinal. I hated to disappoint this clueless woman, "I didn't do it!" I did tell her that the Porta Potty guy took care of all that.

7:52 P.M. Frozen pizza...

8-09 56° Sun.

> **Summer Cocoa: Mix 2 packs of hot chocolate powder, a shot of vanilla syrup, decaf shot of espresso and a splash of toasted marshmallow syrup.**

7:21 A.M.

I had one of those sighing guys in this morning. He ordered an Americano and slumped against my counter. I hardly participated, trying to keep this short

– and - sweet, plus his huge fifth wheel was parked blocking the view to my store. He had women problems. Two longer, hot breaths. This could take a full hour. So, "My boyfriend will be in any minute and we are having breakfast together – sort of a little romantic get-together." That only reminded him what a horrible life he had now. Finally, he got the message and kind of oozed back to his vehicle.

My Willard restaurant describer Rick emailed: "Well Christy, if you had just taken Ben the Rat for a swim, he could have gone down stream to Saratogan to visit one of his relatives. They used to stuff their little, dead furry bodies in the foundation cracks of the Willard, to scare off the other rats. Like that even works…"

1:00 P.M. Scanner: A hay fire at the summit. I think I will go water my plants…

7:12 P.M. An irritating gal walked in with another lady. She walked up to my counter and *yelled*, "Oh…can I pleeeeze have a *freeeee* chocolate-covered espresso bean?" I just pointed to a huge sign, practically covering the front of the container that reads: 10-Cents Each. "Now I'm upset, I don't have any money on me." I was finally coerced into a response, "I'm not a big chain like Baskin and Robbins and I don't give out *tasties*, lady." The friend paid for her bean.

7:34 P.M. Some tuna and a heating pad…

8-10 58° Cloudy.

Hot Buttered Milk: Combine one quart milk, 1/3 cup brown sugar, 4 tbs. butter, sprinkle of nutmeg. Heat in saucepan just until butter melts. Serve with whipped cream.

8:09 A.M. Boy, it sure is difficult to get a logger to laugh. They've heard 'em all, up in "these-thar-hills"! I am proud to say, today this barista mastered the feat; we've heard 'em all too – and more. One of those hefty tree-men from across the highway came by *car* fetching his friend Matt's espresso drink. Normally they hiked across the railroad tracks, up and over the bank, down the hill, over the highway, and across my parking lot. But someone was in a hurry for his caffeine! Matt even scribbled instructions, probably written with a dull carpenter's pencil, and although detailed, it was illegible. Luckily, I knew this boss's preference for a sugar-free caramel nonfat latte, or we would both have been lost. Matt, the owner of this logging company, normally sported around in a nifty truck, petting his Labrador. He had to load trees today. I could not help it, "What are Matt's soft hands going to have to say about being on the chain-gang today – aren't they are only meant to hold a *briefcase* now?" The guy let out a roar like the big brut he was.

4:11 P.M. More "Willard" memoirs from Rick via online mail: "The day I first walked through the Willard with the inspector, we should have taken photos of the 'ski-jump rat-trap.' There were teeth marks, at cooking level, on all the beams. Besides that, every one of the downspouts in that building were directed right into the crawl space. I wonder if the water is still in the waterfall. Do not go near there since I did dump a shit load of 'bug dope' in the water to kill everything in sight. It was alive. The drain from the A/C was dripping onto the clean dish rack. The walk-in cooler drain, supposedly plumbed into the septic tank, did a U-turn right back into the bottom of the refrigeration. The walls were so out of plumb, it took a minimum of three drinks to bring them back into focus!" I now wonder, why did No. 3 Bachelor buy this inopportune, ghastly structure?

9:16 P.M. No bike rides. *I'm* afraid of trolls…

8-11 56° Cloudy.

Cranberry Mist: Mix one pint of pineapple juice and 16-ounces of cranberry juice. Pour over ice and garnish with a slice of lemon.

8:09 A.M. New Sign: Inquire Within Regarding a Saratogan Women's Gossip Group. Once a week we could meet here for espressos and trash the loco - locals. All that laughing would be extremely healthy! And you can't have too many friends.

11:07 A.M. Ms. Gossip No. 2 stopped here frantic; she was categorically certain she would be going to hell! Thank God there were no other customers this time! "I just called a pastor a fucker! My disabled daughter got sent away from a school fieldtrip over one goddamn, measly, miniscule, missing, MOM signature on some goddamn consent form. My poor daughter was in tears. She can't understand something like this! So, I got right on the phone and screamed 'fucker' several times at this Man-of-God." To cement her case of hell and damnation, she told me another story, connected with the very same church – her most embarrassing moment, prior to today! "You know my house, Christy. My A-frame is beautiful for up here in this neck-of-the-woods and I get so tired of people stopping their cars to take it all in – staring in my windows! One day I'd finally had it with gawkers, and it was about 4:00 P.M. I ran out onto my porch like some dizzied lunatic and flashed my boobs. Turns out, it was this same pastor as today, but this time his wife was in the passenger seat. They had come to pay a friendly visit and couldn't give me any notice cuz our phone service was turned off. Been awhile since we paid that bill, I guess!" Just another interesting half an hour in the Life of a Barista.

2:00 P.M. Two couples stopped with their campers. The first joyous treat was a man ordering a 16-ounce latte. I charged him $3 plus tax, although he only wanted a single shot. He stared at it for a mere twenty-one seconds, and then asked why I charged him the same for a single as a double. This guy was royally pissed! His face was turning red and his friend was telling him to calm down. He was in his sixties and acting like a two-year-old. "My sign says *all* 16-ounce drinks are $3 and when you only want a single shot, we must fill the cup with milk, or flavors, which are even *more* expensive than the espresso." He looked at the other non-supportive passengers, but still thought for another 43-seconds.

3:49 P.M. Then a couple in a home-on-wheels was visiting from Canada. They owned a pawn shop up there and she was appalled that my Native American goods were from Mexico and China. She thought I should have local stuff. Bitch City or what today! "Listen up; I couldn't even get $3 out of the last guy for a damn drink, let alone $75 from you for a dream catcher!" Her husband, looking for a diversion and probably was used to his wife taking on the world, reached over my counter and grabbed one of my chocolate-covered espresso beans! His fingers touched a bunch of them. (Where's my flyswatter!) I charged them for the whole lot, either touched or snatched! And then I disinfected my bean spoon, right in front of them ole - big - eyes. They weren't sure what just went on...

6:ish P.M. I did not even know what damn time it was anymore – or what day. I went out to trim up my drive thru plants and received the usual dozen honks. It doesn't take much to entertain the people around here! I would have flipped them off if I hadn't had my man-sized gloves crammed into my scissor handles.

7:30 P.M. To all baristas, everywhere, with flower boxes...may our perverts, inside and out, be magically transformed into caring gents...if just for a day...

8-12 58° Sunny. Not again.

Strawberry Spree: Put 2 tbs. of grenadine syrup in 4 glasses. Beat together one pint of strawberry ice cream, 2 cups whole milk. Pour over grenadine in glasses and top with fresh strawberries.

7:50 A.M. Getting old is only fun for children. The aging process has been screaming so loud lately, that I have taken to applying my make-up with an 8X mirror. I can no longer see those evil chin strays with the 5X, even *with* glasses on! But I will tell you one thing, this magnification business is highly overrated. These mirrors increase, multiply, and even *glorify* wrinkles! Damn!

2:00 P.M. I feel like I'm growing old on White-Trash-Mountain. Lately I've been getting new local customers, from High Valley and Crag Rock, but it is hard to tell them all apart since they all have filthy clothes, dirty boots, shitty cars, and that daily hangover complexion. Antennas are still being installed on cars in the city, aren't they?

A lady ordered an espresso granita. "Do you want whip?" She asked, "Is it in a can?" "Yes, it is, lady. I didn't get up an hour early to prepare a stiff batch just for you." "Well, I like Starbucks because they make their own and have this nifty cylinder thing that squirts out the real stuff." "What? Do you really think

I give a damn if you want the 'real' white fluff or not? I do not have a grandma out back, churning away, and I doubt Starbucks does either. Maybe they have the cheap-ass can *hidden* inside of their nifty cylinder!"

8:42 P.M. Rick emailed again: "Saratogan is a ghost-ridden oil dump, full of hippies. And what a disgrace with its A+ potential, location, and scenery."

9:10 P.M. Get me out of here…

8-13 58° Sunny.

Espresso Punch: Combine 3 cups Americano, 2 cups apple juice, 1 cup apricot brandy, a tsp. ground ginger. Heat slowly just to simmering. Remove from heat. Stir in 16 ounces ginger ale. Ladle into mugs.

9:16 A.M. Thank God for fresh days. One of my fishermen came in for his triple mocha, dangling a 25-pound steelhead! "Get that stinkin', drippin' fish out of here!" He waited for his drink on the *outside* of my window, the drive thru. Congrats…but men are *blank*!

10:22 A.M. The cops are having their annual weekender up Frothing Ham road at the camp. The ghosts would have to behave during the troops visit. Philip looked forward to all of them visiting his summer bailiwick and will pork down each morsel of homemade food. Course the target practice hour is not his cup of tea.

12:03 P.M. A true militia stepped in to buy the largest latte this barista could serve up. I had my bear spray handy and closely listened to him ramble on for twenty minutes about coyotes, eagles, bears, cabins, his business, tractors, boats and a description of his various tattoos along his arms and neck. I wondered if those guys are as wild in the sack as they were out in the woods. Christy!

12:41 P.M. Scanner: A forty-year-old male with amputated fingers from his pickup's tailgate at the campground.

2:40 P.M. Help me! A man stopped with six teenage boys. Their irresponsible vehicle had broken down and it would be at least an hour before Mr. Tow arrived. They were horsing around, jumping onto my landscape rocks and I debated whether I should send them onto the highway to sweep! I was thankful I did not have to offer them my back forty for the night.

4:00 P.M. Forest fires were the current news items. Hundreds of homes in Washington's eastern side had burned. Resort towns had a price to pay because of hot sun and desert life.

4:16 P.M. No. 1 Bachelor pulled in. He panted through my door, "Could I borrow some jumper cables?" With his contractor heavy machinery comin' out of his ears, his doesn't have cables? Of course, I put my life and customers on hold and took a stroll with this catch out to my garage, as Butch went nuts for new meat. He scored on some rump roast as I scored and found the man's needed cables. "Thanks sweetie," rolled past those No. 1 Bachelor's lips! God, my mind and ears could be so weak at times. Those are only words and either words or actions seem to never pan out…

6:33 P.M. I got a huge tip from some guys in my drive thru who witnessed me losing it on a family in a van. The van load pulled up, their side door flew open, while eager kids, trash and dogs fell out. They sprinted towards my doors. I yelled, "My store is CLOSED!" "But we need the bathroooooooooooom." My voice went up an octave as I screamed and pointed towards the Porta Potties. All ten raced for the solo unit. The fellows at the window gave me one weak smile and told me keep the $7.50 change and they beat it outta here!

7:55 P.M. Drive thru window was also retiring from the herds of today… zero Cowboy…

8-14 64° Hot.

Black-bottom Cooler: Squirt chocolate syrup into 4 chilled glasses. Blend 1-quart vanilla ice cream, 1.5 cups whole milk and 2 shots of espresso. Pour into glasses.

7:22 A.M. I had to write fast today – I was slammed! Serving along with a screaming brat, a possible new fence sign lease, phone calls, birds and worries of running out of milk.

8:10 A.M. BMW Brian emailed to tell me how much he missed talking with me and of course he shared info about his miserable corporate life. If I were in that lifestyle, I would have clubbed someone by now.

10:44 A.M. Gossip No. 1, who had recently called her pastor the 'F' word, came in much calmer today except for the ranting about hubby-this-and-hubby-that.

12:50 P.M. It had become a Kotex/Depends afternoon. There wasn't a spare *sec* to escape to the bathroom. I guess baristas could connect themselves to their cart drains via *catheter* hosing. And when are women free from the "curse".

I finally had to leave with a store full of people, possibly pocketing everything in sight. I hid my tip jar and flew through the gate, two doors, nineteen stairs, undressing along the way, inserting that female contraption while wishing I was a genie. I tore back into the store to see the line had grown for *anything* iced. Now for my cramps...

2:11 P.M. Mr. Hunk Wyatt came in to show some skin. God, he's gorgeous! He ordered wood stain from Australia for the Microsoft cabin on Groovy street, no local brands were satisfactory. The millionaires that were beginning to saturate our area would soon find out that they won't have any secrets up here either. *Any* gossip is considered the *highest* perk up in these lands! We would all know everything about them through our locally hired laborers. Hunk Wyatt had now caused me to lose track of my count on bare-chested men. To delicately describe his chest could be put into one word...perfect.

3:46 P.M. Biscotti for lunch, I consumed it. Starved to that spinning feeling, I could not watch another piece of food being rung up on the register without downing *something*.

In walked a father who was willing to pay for a few 32-ounce cups just for their puking kids in the car. They knew that more was on the way before they got safely home. I was going to have a nervous breakdown. Sickly germs put me into insanity. I washed my hands and disinfected everything and prayed the air cleared.

4:40 P.M. Two scraggly guys entered, "We need ice for a sprain." "Well, you'll have to go two more miles to the gas station. No ice here!" I figured they really needed it for their Rum and Cokes.

5:05 P.M. I am losing my direction. Blended espressos, blended coffee drinks, granitas, smoothies, frapps, frothy things, whipped whatevers, blended, iced... People were as confused as I had become. All those names for just one *thingy*.

6:33 P.M. Ms. eBay Bitch had struck again. Now it is through PayPal. The entire war had been over a simple $4.00 item!

Well, I'll be darned...the historic *whore/cop camp* was far more elaborate than imagined. Philip came in and told me more details. It consisted of properties on two forks of the river with twelve cabins and a cook house! He and the cops had a very fancy breakfast together inside of that old building this morning. A perfect movie back drop!

I am weary of the insipid heat. It is so hot in here that my chocolate covered espresso beans had become rubber marbles. I had to spoon each one up very gently to present them in their finest state for the customer.

8:04 P.M. It always gives me a little tickle when *non*-paying customers stop to use my property for various conveniences when I am in sight. Oh, how polite they become and so incredibly careful. *Thank yous* dripping from their lips, almost bowing to the barista. Never unloading their vans full of trash into my receptacles and wouldn't dream of letting their dogs' shit in my planters. I needed to present myself outside more often.

8:51 P.M. I called Rosie. I needed to know if she was still breathing. "I have the stomach flu and the bastard is pissed I caught the bug." I told her to serve him up some barf soufflé.

9:00 P.M. I am over men this instant...

8-15 64° Sunny.

Cardamom Espresso: Place 2 crushed cardamom seeds in each single (demitasse) espresso cups. Fill cups with espresso shots.

7:50 A.M. Buck just drove by. Tried to be sneaky about it but I had been walking along my parking lot. Busted. I believe he has a new girlfriend about twenty-three years old. That is child *age* for him.

All was vacuumed. Birds were bathed. While I cleaned, I found some of Ben's stashed snacks. Now for dusting...

8:43 A.M. Mrs. Periwinkle Luggage came in. She still wanted hubby to build himself *his* doghouse outside...anywhere! They should just call it quits and end the misery. People who know me and my past sometimes ask, "Do you regret your life?" I suppose a tad of the first half but why on earth fret about the first half during the second half. Let go and live and embrace forgiveness on both sides.

I decided I'm leavin' by 4:30 P.M. Needed supplies and I will deal with *impatients* "down below" for a change.

10:10 A.M. A tattoo artist strolled in and was covered with designs from head to toe. I do not believe there was a minuscule of pink skin tone visible. I always wondered what these people looked like when they were eighty. Ghastly. They will come up with a tattoo lift by then, I'm sure.

2:58 P.M. Overheated, picky, demanding, unhappy, mismatched, booze breathed and down-right screwy people in today. A couple asked my opinion regards to sitting in the hot springs with naked people. "Don't even go there sweethearts, unless you would like to take a precious throned seat back here on my stool for a piece of my mind!" Disease, smell and bodily secretions, meant only for nature, were all I could picture. She disagreed, "Actually they are meant for sitting in, while in your natural state, as you get circulated out!" Whatever the fuck that meant...

A group from the east coast ordered. They were snooty snobs, were in the area to spread *so-and-so's* ashes into the Puget Sound. T.M.I. Second one in six months at **OUTPOST ESPRESSO**.

I destroyed Ms. eBay Bitch's 100% feedback on her account. She asked for it.

6:00 P.M. Never left for errands. I could not have left with all the sweaty customers that pulled in and it was too hot to shut the doors. I will need to bike every bit of the twelve miles tonight since it was another Bad Mood Monday.

7:40 P.M. Gone biking…

8-16 Don't know temp and don't care. Partly sunny.

Chocolate Fuzz: Mix a shot of chocolate syrup, 2 tbs. milk, fill ¾ with soda water, stir. Then add 2 scoops vanilla ice cream. Top off with soda water.

10:00 A.M. I bolted down to Costco early this morning and right in front of me in line was a good looking, perfectly capable guy. He would not unload his cart for the checker. He grinned at her and asked if he was behaving like a bad brat. She handled it too well. I almost took over. When I finally reached her, she shared, "You wouldn't believe how many people a day do that. Super selfish!" What a joy he must be around the house. Amen to my knowledge of creeps.

3:51 P.M. Feels like 9:51 P.M. I have got to finish chores. Put supplies into their hideout upstairs and in the commissary.

10:12 P.M. I cannot move another muscle. I have climbed 798 stairs. Bedtime…

8-17 59° Misting.

Quick Turkish Coffee: Six 1/3 cup servings. Measure 3 tbs. instant coffee into pan. Stir in 2 cups boiling water. Serve in tiny (demitasse) cups with dabs of whipped cream.

7:45 A.M. Very cool and nice day. I've heard that the leaves on the east side of the pass are already turning color - straight to brown. Icicle Town's Fall Festival will be a bust with the leaves' void of color, or no foliage at all. Our waterless summer…

I considered installing the plow; it began to feel we may get a *real* winter this time around.

11:40 A.M. Both Ms. Gossips came in with *no* gossip. How dare they do such a thing, while I drummed up their concoctions. Their lips seemed sealed for some strange reason.

A few loggers walked in and that group of mountain folks shared with each other about where to steal their firewood for winter. Up this gravel road, down that lane, over that trail, past 'ol Roger's, as if I were on Mars. I went back to the computer, while the Gossips had found their subject of interest. What happened to our trashing of men? No fun today…

5:51 P.M. Four local chaps walked by with their fishin' poles made of sticks, heading to hit my fishing hole, without licenses. Yesterday they had a 15-inch hanging from the ol' twig.

7:39 P.M. I am running away for yarn and pizza…

8-18 62° Sunny.

Warm Summer Nights: In saucepan, combine 46 ounces tomato juice, 1 can condensed consommé, 1 tsp. grated onion, 1 tsp. horseradish, dash of pepper, 1 tsp. Worcestershire sauce. Stud lemon slices with cloves, add to juice and heat just until boiling. Serve immediately.

9:08 A.M. Perfect weather when not over 80 degrees. Angel escaped her cage this morning. Chewed more desk, supplies and only kicked the money around this time. I installed more chicken wire work around her area.

11:45 A.M. The railroad track workers are making too much noise today. Yellin', hammerin' and squealin'. The loggers and railroad men were having a ball annoying each other.

3:11 P.M. I got down to ¼ bag of ice and sure enough a family from Idaho with their four grown sons, wanted 24-ounce iced drinks. I scrimped and nursed, practically counting cubes, while using double product that costs me far more. That was the choice.

Then a lady scampered in wanting a cup full of strictly ice. Ice only? With my short supply I had to charge her a dollar. This shit is presently my frozen black gold.

4:59 P.M. Two *cubes* left. Please only hot drinks people.

6:04 P.M. The two cubes had melted away. I will now melt away myself…

8-19 60° Sunny.

Rocky Road Latte: A shot of chocolate syrup, shot of toasted marshmallow and almond syrup, espresso shots, steamed milk.

8:13 A.M. First things first. A road-worn red Harley pulled up. The guy took off his helmet, let the matted hair fall, gave it a shake, and stepped off his bike.

He walked the ten feet to my fence and urinated on my barking dog's head, right in front of me, traffic, and God! I stepped out and asked him what the hell he was doing. He grunted with an obvious English accent, "Nothing. Got it covered!" The fucking bucko! I am emailing the sheriff with his license plate right now!

I turned down a dinner date for tonight from the Mr. Mercury-Poison…again. Who knows just *what* is flowing through this guy's veins? All I know is he is sick all the damn time! I am starting to feel a little unsettled; I may have already been infected.

10:12 A.M. I had to move the chocolate-covered espresso beans, napkins, straws, and drink stirrers out of the reach of grabby customers! They almost stretched and grew right before my eyes, reaching up and over my plastic wall-surround to grab for any item that suited their fancy now.

Trucker Bitch next door arrives September 3rd. I don't want to even *see* the whites of those squinty, beady balls, or a hair on that numb skull. But I would like to pull it out by the roots.

1:32 P.M. Two big guys in campers came in needing pancake mix. Pancake mix in Saratogan? Pancake mix at an Espresso & Gift Shoppe? "If the gas station has any," I sent them in that direction, "Better check the expiration date and make sure it didn't previously belong to the original Betty Crocker!"

2:34 P.M. Scanner: Someone was run over by their vehicle and had a fracture. It happened while huckleberry picking up one of our near logging roads.

9:31 P.M. The Porta Potty guy was a new driver tonight and arrived late to clean up those begrimed boxes. "Are you having a 'shitty' Friday night?" I yelled across the parking lot.

10:00 P.M. Off for forty-four winks…

8-20 58° Sunny.

Pecan Mocha: A shot of chocolate syrup, shot of pecan syrup, espresso shots, steamed milk.

8:30 A.M. I refused to be the middleman! Another war was brewing in Rockfish River Estates (Groovy Street). Millionaires vs. millionaires. They were calling me for names and phone numbers. No way. I told "B" that I would call "A" and tell "A" that "B" wanted to chat in a bad way. It had something to do with clearing land down to the river for a nice beach. A no-no with the county. An hour or so later, "A" came in, ready to fight "B," who was ready to sue the world. *For once*, it was not *my* fight.

9:43 A.M. The sheriff showed up, "There is nothing I can do about the *public canine urinater*," and he couldn't stop laughing, picturing my dog getting whizzed-upon. "But he lies with me on the couch at night, and that *head* is in my lap!" I wailed. Then I told him about the latest neurotic war going on up the street between "A" and "B." Naturally, he already was aware.

1:58 P.M. Scanner: An eighty-two-year-old man possibly having a heart attack in a vehicle, parked at a local's house for assistance.

4:44 P.M. No. 5 called. We were racking our brains trying to come up with some favorable reasons for dating. We both thought dating sucked. You went out with a total stranger, who by our age had slept with approximately 250 people. Their exes were ensconced in their lives: their kids were embroiled in the same shit we were all doing at their ages, from the teens to the thirties. This stranger then arrived in your life with several bills, nasty bad habits, and miserable memories. Why date? To get laid for the 251st time and do it all again and again and… Abstaining was becoming extremely appealing to both of us.

9:34 P.M. Another day…another dollar…alone…

8-21 61° Sunny.

Butter Toffee Crunch: My original! Lightly blend a cup of ice, a shot of chocolate syrup, shot of butter toffee syrup, two inches of Half & Half and a shot of espresso.

8:01 A.M. Smoothies first thing, plus math. The lady was trying to exchange all the coin at the bottom of her duffle-bag purse – for paper – and she couldn't count for shit. I was too busy. We ended up tossing all the silver-circles into the register and trusting each other.

11:20 A.M. A guy pulling a boat lost control and continued right through my front planter, ripping the surrounding logs right off! He came to a dead halt, just three feet from my drive-thru window. I was stunned. My inside customers were hysterical. The driver was distraught. I had to grab screws, nails, and tools for the repair. He didn't even buy a drink. I should have contacted his insurance company.

2:59 P.M. One of our married Microsoft cabin owners came in and invited me to his place for pork chops tonight. His wife and family were not up with him this weekend, so I wouldn't go. Point off!

8:22 P.M. Almost dark. Just had an SUV full of Canadians stop. "We will have to pay the balance with Canadian funds." "Not on your life. I have an adding machine, but my bookkeeper is on vacation and she is the one who figures out exchange rates!"

8:42 P.M. I was spent. Could not take this bondage-lock-up much longer.

9:08 P.M. Mr. Microsoft brought me dinner on a *real* plate and told me that I was not getting out of it that easy. Yikes! "Christy, could you please return the plate tonight?" Now that almost required another Point Off! If I do not show up, he can pick it up tomorrow. Plan on tomorrow then, Pops. He did not dare have the little woman find her plate at my house.

9:43 P.M. No more…

8-22 58° Tad of clouds.

Strawberry/Banana Granita: My original! A cup of ice in blender, a pack of fake sugar, 1.5 inches of strawberry daiquiri mix, an inch of banana daiquiri mix, two inches of Half & Half, blend.

8:43 A.M. I could not move. I felt as though my body was frozen in time. C-o-w-b-o-y j-u-s-t w-a-l-k-e-d i-n ! I saw the truck, then that cowboy hat, and a beautiful body stepping out with those long legs. Jeans, boots, and buckle bigger than his waist and those blue eyes – more resplendent than a lagoon in Tahiti! "I waited miles and miles to have espresso here, Christy Sue." Was he having a brain fart? Was he drunk? I was stunned; this guy had balls. Can you imagine me getting a No Contact Order now? That would be nasty. Wouldn't his wife just dig it? I forced myself to make it quick, snappy and happy. Wait until he gets home for *this* doozie email! Fucker! I needed a cool washcloth for my brow…a tranquilizer…a Bayer…a tissue for my tear… Goddamn him!

A gal was now throwing up in my parking lot and her friend wanted me to wet her rag for the clean-up. At my cart sink! Get you and your germs and your rag outta here, FAST! I fixed her up a nice, wet paper towel pad.

12:42 P.M. I ran upstairs for that two-minute-put-the-signs-out and the birds and I porked-out on pea pods and teriyaki chicken.

1:42 P.M. Philip came in and saved the day by giving me some new DVDs to watch.

Well, with Cowboy reappearing, every other guy has been placed on the back-burner in my eyes, my head, my heart, my psyche…once again. I literally *tingled* when he walked in. Hundreds of men a day, for years and years, and nary a prickle. So, I knew I would not send the searing email quite yet, choosing to be a complete nincompoop, for another minute or two…

8:43 P.M. Was just about to pull the plug when a guy with an eight-week-old St. Bernard puppy stopped for a mocha. I would stay open all night long to play with that darling, stuffed animal! Worth every minute of overtime to me!

9:20 P.M. *Now* for sweet dreams…

8-23 58° Overcast.

Sugar-Free Vanilla Italian Soda: Ice, a shot of sugar-free vanilla syrup, soda water within an inch of top, and topped with Half & Half.

11:32 A.M. The loggers from across the way bid on another big job, just a mile down the highway. I hoped they get it. I liked these guys. They are clean, for loggers.

My copper gossipers stopped again. But almost immediately, the Microsoft dinner-plate guy came in to fetch his porcelain before his better-half missed it. I gave them that *hush* look, and they left shortly…cuz he didn't! Missed out on more local gossip from the old locals.

7:48 P.M. Cowboy has not emailed, which *slightly* surprised me, but he will by Friday or Saturday. Stopping was his first *careful* step, until his desires overwhelm him. I even had horses galloping in my head last night again. On one hand I wish he would stay away; on the other hand, I ice-skate around with asking him to go upstairs…for life…

8-24 57° Sunny.

Alaska Mint Latte: A shot of chocolate syrup, a shot of crème de menthe, espresso shots, and steamed Half & Half.

8:10 A.M. Fall is nearing. People seem to think we have a heck of a snowy winter coming this year. Farmer's Almanac is not too worried either way. I sure hope so!

2:47 P.M. Well, I was history! Cowboy emailed and I did not respond. I needed a cold shower. Maybe his wife had MS and he was looking for her nursing home and the next love-of-his-life? Dream on, sister…

I'm goin' out back to burn. A bonfire can always cure a ton of gloominess.

5:58 P.M. I'm closing to go sulk, make some parmesan popcorn, and watch a DVD…

8-25 56° Sunny.

Iced Macadamia Nut: Ice, a shot of macadamia nut syrup, espresso shots, steamed whole milk.

7:43 AM. Cowboy emailed. I emailed. It has begun again. Now he tells me that when he plans to move to his ranch, full-time in three years, his wife will not be joining him; it is not her cup of tasty tea. I would oil his gates any day. I would wait the three years, being a perfect angel, if I knew I would wind up *there*.

3:50 P.M. Terrific! It calls for a celebration! Ms. eBay Bitch who demanded a refund didn't get the proof to eBay's PayPal in a timely fashion, so I won that one.

Another SUV just hit my front planter right at my drive-thru again! I have been in business here for seven years and it has never been hit! Now two crashes in a week! Karma? Theirs or mine?

Cowboy emailed: "Why don't you have a 'partner,' Christy Sue?" Reply: " With your vast engineering skills, I'm curious as to what you mean by 'partner.' It is a very broad word. And who says I don't? Clarify, please."

7:38 P.M. An exit…

8-26 60° Sunny.

Espresso Crème: Two shots of espresso, a cinnamon stick and topped with whipped cream.

7:29 A.M. The whole town of Saratogan is gearing up for the hordes of people, classic cars, rain-rain-go-away. I would love to see the cars, but I am gearing up for crowds myself.

1:21 P.M. Scanner: Car fire at milepost 53.

1:41 P.M. Scanner: A bovine jumped the fence and was running around on Mountain Peak Highway!

1:49 P.M. Scanner: Someone was having an allergic reaction to a bee sting. Patient waits at our fire station.

2:32 P.M. Scanner: The allergic bee reaction was a thirty-five-year-old female having difficulty breathing.

Cowboy and I were getting deep. Communication was a deep subject. He wrote something like: "Wanting to spend tons of time together, *but still have separate lives,* enjoying each other's company."

4:00 P.M. More emails. So far, Cowboy and I have covered the subjects of sex, religion, when is dinner, when and where the foot massages will be conducted, and what color polish I would like on my toenails. Holy shit!

A young couple came in and the wife was desperate for a bathroom; *anything* other than the Porta Potty. "Sorry, that is all we've got around here." "But I need a nice bathroom, I'm on my period!" T.M.I. "That IS a bathroom!"

7:00 P.M. Cowboy emailed: "I will do my best to locate Wet & Wild red polish. I just like the name! (Oh…God!)

8:00 P.M. I think I will go upstairs and pray…

8-27 61° Sunny.

Milk & Honey: Stir 2 tbs. of honey in warm milk, sprinkle with nutmeg or cinnamon.

8:00 A.M. I must back up to last night. I left on my bike and enjoyed the warm ride, smelling the ripe blackberries along the way. I slowly rode through the campground where campfires overpowered the scent of *their* Porta Potties. I still did not see any fish in the rivers.

I was just about to head for home on the 6-mile ride and the damn pedal fell off my bike! It felt just like running out of gas, forty miles from a station, and it was getting darker and darker out. Trying to screw the idiotic thing on and a good-looking guy (a local I found out later) stopped to help. My gun was out of my fanny-pack and in my back pocket. He could not fix it either and offered me a ride home in his truck. "No thanks." I started heading home. Now it was pitch black and I was surrounded by woods, blocking out in my mind any troll ideas. I made it to the town of Saratogan – with only two more miles to go and here came Buck in his truck! To the rescue! Popped my bike in the bed of his truck, as though light as a feather and gave me a ride home. We arrived at the railroad crossing and were blocked by three different trains over the next twenty-eight minutes. So, while we chatted, he fixed my pedal. Left-turn threads, dummy! Just then Buck reached into his glove box and handed me a one-carat diamond solitaire ring! All in a fucking half hour! What could I say? Life as a barista will have an interesting two weeks ahead. I could marry Buck, have Cowboy paint my toenails for the wedding, and talk over my outfit and flower arrangements at dinner with No. 7.

10:13 A.M. Scanner: A dog bite, involving a fourteen-year-old boy at the car show.

12:52 P.M. Scanner: An illegal burn investigation on the highway.

Mr. Mercury Poison was here, and it cost me at least an hour. He was talking away, telling me that we definitely had a connection, and I flashed my carat. I told him a local gave it to me, just last night! This guy was bugging me.

7:10 P.M. I am over customers…

8-28 62° Sunny.

Orange Blush: Ice, orange juice, a splash of grenadine syrup and topped with whipped cream.

8:43 A.M. I am dolled up for Cowboy. Actually, in long jeans today, a little extra mascara, and cute top. They feel so much better than shorts, especially when Angel is perched on my lap with her sharp talons.

Pleasant customers so far today.

10:46 A.M. Mr. Microsoft dinner-plate stopped in for his one-on-one goodbye for the week. Why is he coming in *here* to say goodbye?

Mrs. Periwinkle Luggage stopped on her way to her Annual Women's Week up at the Skagit.

Mr. Mercury Poison came in again. Oh God, he was *really* becoming a pest. He left, saying he was suddenly having a seizure from my fluorescent lights!

3:18 P.M. A guy came in for milk. "Twelve ounces?" I asked. He said that he needed just a little for his girlfriend who was doubled over with indigestion. "That will be $2 for twelve ounces." Too much. "Well, half that size is $1," dunce-cake. Then he wanted FREE coffee, like they served at the rest areas. "You are at the wrong location, sir; I don't serve *free* anything, and Americanos are $2. So, no matter how long you stare at this situation, you'd be better off ordering the half cup of milk for a buck." He settled for that, and then complimented my shirt.

4:48 P.M. Philip was walking to town and Cowboy would be here within the hour. I've primped and prayed that Philip didn't show up and interrupt our reunion. I was not falling – I'd *fallen* in love with a married man! I won't go do anything stupid, though. If I did, then I might as well burn this book up and throw away all the strength and power I'd struggled for, so desperately, over the past few years. They would appoint me *President* of the Female-Fucked-Up-Society.

8:28 P.M. I'm leaving and I'm not mentioning you-know-who…

8-29 56° Rain.

Summertime Fling (appropriate?): Mix together one can (6 oz.) of frozen concentrated pineapple/orange juice, 1 cup water, 12 ounces apricot nectar, 28 ounces lemon/lime flavored soda. Pour over ice.

4:30 A.M. I jumped out of bed and headed down to Wooly's, and the rest of my stops. The video store was one of them; I had to get the movie that showed the man painting toenail polish on his gal's toes. Supposed to be very sexy! Fuck me tonight when I get screwed up emotionally. Cowboy emailed four times, giving me all his phone numbers in case I had an "emergency foot-rub need."

5:00 P.M. I have had maybe twelve people in since 11:00 A.M.

Andrew called to see if I knew whether dinosaurs went to heaven. His store must have been even deader than mine! I told him that all animals went to heaven. He said, "So, why are we working our asses off to be good and all that, just to meet up with a shit load of dinosaurs in heaven?" "Yes, Andrew. I'm sorry business is so slow, Andrew. Why don't ya take a drive up here and help me clean up puke, dog turds, beat off the druggies, and fight with complete strangers?" Suddenly, he was *in love* with his card shop business…

No more goofing off. eBay needs two hours of my time.

7:31 P.M. A lady walked up to my window with a lit cigarette and all the smoke swirled in here. I dealt with her through an inch of open window and explained that her smoke would harm my birds. She was almost chipping her teeth she was gritting them so hard in anger. "My birds have rights too, lady! Plus, the shit makes me sick, but it's *killing* you!"

8:15 P.M. Cowboy called with Christy Sue this and Christy Sue that…

8:50 P.M. God help this barista…

8-30 52° Overcast.

West Coast Icy: Mix together, one can (6 oz.) frozen concentrate of strawberry/lemon punch, 3 cups water, 24 ounces orange flavored soda. Over ice.

9:24 A.M. Cowboy was emailing like crazy. He sent three more photos of himself up at the ranch.

Braggart Bobby stopped to give me a copied old photo of Mountain Peak Summit from 1928. Priceless! I gave him his free 24-ounce sugar-free white chocolate smoothie in return. No tip.

7:38 P.M. I returned from a bike ride. The campground smelled of sewer. I saw an owl and we stared at each other for a long time. While riding, Ex-Con pulled up in his sports car. He told me that a van of Mexicans was at my store asking for me. Then offered to give me a lift home! No F'ing way! "I will go check on them and see what they want." Ex-Con a fucking Good Samaritan? I thought not. Apparently, they had dropped off some tea samples for me to try in my store. Weird.

10:00 P.M. The nail painting movie sucked…or was I not in the mood…

8-31 56° Sunny actually.

Double Raspberry Frost: Stir a cup of raspberry syrup in 2 cups of water, then stir in 2 frozen cans of concentrate lemonade and 28 ounces of raspberry-flavored soda. Float lemon slices.

9:00 A.M. Cowboy emailed this morning. He was going to call last night but was worried I would be in the middle of my toenail movie.

Philip was starving for news and substance, so he headed "down-below" where a little cognizance and communiqué is possible. Cowboy would be calling at noon. Scanner was quiet.

Okay, I just axed Cowboy for the second serious time. I was obsessing and not even enjoying my life! Screw you, my precious and the horse I never rode.

9:19 P.M. Sulk, steak, medium rare…

SEPTEMBER

The birds and beans, where both struggle
for shade and twilight

9-01 58° Sunny.

Double Free: Two shots of decaf espresso topped with foamed Half
& Half.

8:00 A.M. Cowboy did not email like a good boy. But looking back on yesterday's reply, the pig said, "When you change your pretty mind, let me know."

3:50 P.M. Boone from Stonewall stopped by. What gave him the idea I wanted him to visit? He may be "hot'" but was also *slightly* aware of that fact. After calling him a slut for months for *using* the gal "down-below" and another youngie just a few months ago – and telling him he was trash, a pig, a jerk, and no different than the rest of the "down-the-line" guys up here – he still stopped in? Maybe we should visit the same *shrink* and get a discount!

8:10 P.M. I just got back in from mowing my whole acre-plus – three-plus hours. My mower is in for hibernation. Fall and winter hits very early up here. Had a little gas remaining in the tank so I put it in my Jeep.

Philip stopped with four DVDs for my long holiday weekend. What a doll he is.

9:59 P.M. No rest or foul-play for this barista…

9-02 52° Cloudy.

Cuban Hot: Use a shot of rum and crème de cacao syrups. Add hot
water within an inch and top off with two shots of espresso.

8:43 A.M. Fucking Cowboy emailed! He has got bigger balls than our globe! I wasn't going to respond but couldn't help it – just a few lines: "64% of women cheat. 70% of men cheat. Only 4% of married men leave their wives for their lovers. Fuck those odds! Get divorced, Cowboy, and look me up and *only* if I'm not otherwise spoken for... Don't want anything about you or from you or with you, till then!"

I was developing the uncanny knack to sniff out baristas. Two just drove up and I asked them right off. "Yep, sure are." They worked for Starbucks in the same area that No. 7 used to frequent with the rest of the sheriffs. They did not know him. Ha ha...

Remember the local Hunk Wyatt who always lost his dogs? He popped in to get my advice. His wife of less than a year moved out three months ago (I can relate!). She now had her own place but still wanted to have dinner soon, on their almost First Year Anniversary. He asked, "What's up with this?" Well, I informed him, "She wants to have her own place, her own space, her own time, her own money (from you, dude). You decide! Do you want to play this game?" Did you really want advice, or did you come to tell me this so that I would know you were all alone, abandoned, and available after 9:00 P.M.?

5:19 P.M. Cowboy drove by wailing on his horn. So, what, Christy...let it go. Don't call the cops for harassment quite yet...

7:21 P.M. Doors are locked. Window barely open. I am seriously depressed...

9-03 52° Cloudy/Overcast.

Quick to Go: Two shots of espresso with one shot of hot water.

1:01 P.M. My mom and her best gal-pal paid a visit. They referred to their group of friends as The Bellevue Bitches since they all have lived in the richie area and have known each other for thirty-five years! They both gave me permission to converse with Cowboy, since his wife chose to never be home. As they walked out the door, they yelled, "Converse!"

Ms. Gossip No. 1 came in and heard it all! Just saw the carat rock from Buck. This info will rage through town like an out-of-control forest fire! I gave it about 43-minutes. Buck drove up to the window as if his ears were on fire too. Handed me a note that of course was full of shit, as always.

Then a part-time cabin owner came in and had the gall to ask if I would let her daughters set up a lemonade stand here. Go back to *your* city and do it! I *sell* lemonade! Everyone wants a piece for nothing…

3:50 P.M. Boone from Stonewall stopped by again and we talked outside for a while. I guess Buck just recently tried to get a date with the same gal Boone was *using* last year. The carat will be in the return mail. I missed Cowboy, even chatting with *this* handsome thing next to me.

7:44 P.M. I am mentally whipped…

9-04 52° Cloudy.

Iced Dream Nut: Ice, mix together two shots of espresso, a shot of Tamarindo syrup and hazelnut Syrup, soda water within an inch and top with Half & Half.

7:58 A.M. Yesterday, Ms. Gossip No. 1's husband told her to, "shut up" in *public*. They were in our local restaurant – and this was in front of other locals! Mister, this will cost you $4,000, one way or another. Baaaad move! Both Ms. Gossips came in together today, but we were rudely interrupted by customers, so we couldn't get down 'n dirty. I was dying to hear if there was any bloodshed at that restaurant! I told them that my diamond was signed, sealed, and delivered to the P.O. Also, mentioned my barriers breaking down with Cowboy issues. No comment, since they were both married. Ah well… Told mom I wouldn't let him lay a finger on me. Too bad, because this book could get real juicy! But this book is trying to be about strength – not stupidity!

10:08 A.M. Two *snooties* came in. I can pick up the scent of a *bitch* a mile away. When the *first* gal was pissed that I was 8.2 seconds late in helping her – with *total* undivided fucking attention – I knew I just snagged a ripe one. She huffed about the cup size, snapped cuz I was not allowing her to put her grubby hands on my Half & Half container. Finally, the price of Americanos. So, I added another 25 cents and internally justified it as a "Bitch Fee!" The second flippin' female was *really* pissed now, because it took too long to satisfy No. 1. She was charged a 75-cent fee.

11:23 A.M. Holidays! Today feels like Saturday and tomorrow will feel like Sunday. The rest of the week will feel plain weird.

9:05 PM. I have been on the phone with No. 7 and he's demanding dinner. My choice – any place, any time, any menu. We'll see…

9-05 46° Sunny. Labor Day.

Fall Cooler: Ice, a shot of apple syrup, shot of anisette syrup, soda water and a splash of grenadine syrup.

9:24 A.M. Scanner: Medic call on Mollson Creek Road for an accidental ingestion. It was a one-and-a-half-year-old little guy who took/was given way too much allergy medication.

11:47 A.M. The solid stream had begun. Traffic can back up from here to Pacifica, some fifty miles! Goody!

A wife was apologizing to her husband for being caught walking through my gift shop and leaving his sight. He looked at me kindly, then told her that it was all okay by him. "Take your time, honey." I realized his polite *show* was for my eyes only. When they walked out, got into their car, and he revved the engine, I knew he was the abusive type. He has got *that* one down pat, the impatient imbecile. I am again reminded quite often why I'm not married! You guys just lost another point!

3:33 P.M. Buck drove by and waved. Crap ugh. Cowboy, where are you?

Philip came in and, on his way, down here, he buried a black cat that was killed on the highway. He had an extra special spot in his heart for black cats – *his* was named "Mr. Midnight."

8:28 P.M. Cowboy stopped! He was still under the impression that he was not allowed to even *breathe* my way. Okay...let me get this straight? I told you to stay the hell away from me until there was no more spousie! So, what the hell are you doing here? So, I let him in my locked doors to chat. He even pulled part of his shirt down to show me the tattoo on his gorgeous chest. A point off both of our columns, for him partially stripping and me for ogling! He was even demanding dinner out soon! He actually told me that he couldn't help himself and wouldn't stop this nonsense until I got a restraining order. He knew about those. This guy was chasing hard! Well, just dinner, maybe. My girlfriend called later and said, "Now don't show up at the restaurant with that huge purse of yours full of guns and stuff." I already had the outfit picked out. Another point off the women's column only. Bite me! This *wasn't* the Prince! This *wasn't* the Pauper! *This was the Player!* This guy didn't just have baggage – he had Super Expensive Luggage! A wife.

9:00 P.M. Is there a shrink in the house...?

9-06 52° Sunny.

Deception Pass Soda: MY ORIGINAL! Ice, a shot of orange and apple syrups, soda water and topped with Half & Half, whipped cream.

8:55 A.M. The Russian guys made their first trip to pick up some of my railroad ties. They will be coming for a second load. $$$!

Cowboy and I are going to dinner tonight. Mexican food in Tillamuk. Our own cars. I am scared! A date with a married man! Just not my style. What the hell is wrong with me?

11:08 A.M. Two German ladies drove up. They were telling me about the parakeet they used to own. He would drink beer then start dialing the rotary phone and begin jabbering. True story, they swore.

12:44 P.M. Scanner: Seizure at the school. Must be my neighbor's daughter – again.

Dinner was confirmed for 7:00 P.M. I won't need to eat; I have enough butterflies in my stomach to feed us both for a week! Feeling giddy and it feels good.

The Russians were back. If the driver checked out my ass one more time, I would club him with the creosote log!

4:33 P.M. I will change my shirt, brush my hair, blush my cheeks, and put on my old shit-kicker-boots. So…Cowboy's double, short Americanos with no lid have weakened me to this? Shall I burn the book now and get back to a counselor? Men & Relationships make me think of Wine & Guns! Oprah, Dr. Phil, and Dr. Laura would have some answers and suggestions. The first two would kick my butt. The latter would bust my chops but good!

9:09 P.M. I'm back. Chalk it up to a new experience. I had plenty of time to mull it all over on my drive home. The immediate depression that set in caused me to stop and buy some new CDs, almost shoes, no chocolate. But I thought of wine – a lot! Even walked the liquor store parking lot from one end to the other. That was close! Luckily, my cowboy boots were killing me.

A fucking married man! Dinner was quiet and empty as hell. I almost didn't get out of my car when I arrived. What did a woman talk about with married guy, after the time it took to drink a cup of coffee? There was no past, present, and for sure no future to discuss. Small talk? I did not have time for that shit! I refuse to be the third shoe for anyone, and I believe this whole damn time I'd been in love with his damn cowboy hat. He was bare headed at dinner and he looked pathetic to me. The meal was a dreadful-doomed-date from the start! You know, it would be hideous to survive with a married man. I didn't! I would rather have stayed home with my bicycle and my ever-faithful canine. Plus, I spent one-quarter of the dinner in the bathroom, dying. Losing my stomach.

My nerve. My ego. My serenity.

11:00 P.M. Tonight, was certainly an eye-opener…

9-07 48° Sunny.

Skinny and Wet: Non-fat milk, steamed, and espresso shots.

8:44 A.M. Us single gals have nothing in common at *all* with married men. Their lives are "we" and our lives are "me." Let us look at this dinner as an investigation. I am still leaving the point off the women's column – since I did go! I hit the keyboard and composed the email from hell. I was honest and told him I had a terrible, boring time and it may have not been much better for him. We were like mutes! I said my utmost temptation would be to blow the whistle to his wife and if he did not stay away, I would do just that. AND I WILL!

10:10 A.M. I needed a break – day off – any place but here – the further the better – goodbye regular life!

7:00 P.M. I just got home. I left the minute I served one latte – I just could not face the espresso machine…or humans.

I was singing and smiling down the highway, enjoying the break. Depression lifted much faster these days now that I was straight and more honest with myself.

Buck just stopped to say "Hi" and I could not let him even help me unload.

8:00 P.M. I'm home and being good, and getting damn good at it – dammit…

9-08 54° Sunny.

Cuban Hit: Over ice pour in a shot of rum, shot of lime syrup and fill with Cola.

8:25 A.M. Holy Mother, what a day! Stapled about 200 feet of Christmas lights, teetering at the top of an extension ladder. Up down – up down… Painted a gallon of polyurethane everywhere that looked weathered. Rode my bike for twelve miles and swept the 350 feet of parking lot. I think my extra, angry (Cowboy) energy is about used up. Time to think of others…and other things…

And sometimes we think we all have it so tough. A man who has a month to live almost fell into my arms here today, inside my espresso area. My only seating was outside, so I helped him to a chair. He asked his friend and me to show him my various plaster cowboy statues. Why that subject again? So, the friend and I grabbed a few and carried them outside for him to admire from his chair. He bought four of them! He was on his last legs and he was shopping! What spirit – what spunk! I loved it! You're not dead until you're dead and nobody better get in the way!

3:35 P.M. I've served a few granitas today and plenty of chai teas to some people from Wisconsin. Mochas too. A variety day.

The rain was supposed to come tonight. Clouds were here. Cowboy flew by and honked his bloody horn on his way down the hill, towing his boat. He had better leave me alone or I'll ask his wife if she has any influence over the situation. Yep! No problem on my end doing just that! If he even *thinks* of stopping here on Sunday, he is a bigger ignoramus than I thought – and will be a very sorry boy.

I had a "Joe" call me today to tell me that he would not be coming tomorrow for espresso. Joe-who-are-you? I was rude and told him I wouldn't have noticed if he did or didn't come. He sounded upset but I didn't need another barista *groupie* right now. *Weirdo's* for short.

4:00 P.M. Buck hung out here for an hour today. He kept mentioning how nice it would be to be held. "THEN GO FIND A *HOLDER*! Eighteen to eighty for all I care but GET AWAY FROM ME!"

8:47 P.M. I'm going upstairs to eat and throw in a movie. Back to being a *serious* barista tomorrow. I haven't behaved much like one the last two days. Well, maybe more like a month…

9:37 P.M. Over and out…

9-09 50° Pouring.

Good Morning: A shot of anisette syrup, espresso shots and foamed milk.

8:51 A.M. No. 1 Bachelor from Seattle stopped in. He was pissed that his ski cabin was not finished. I will *never* be ready for that friendly Argentinean dinner with him now, especially after Cowboy.

Three sets of customers and $60 between them. Awesome! Pays to be back at work – in earnest!

No. 1 Bachelor checked his house again and was back to order an Americano with soy this time.

12:48 PM. I just had a bizarre one in! He stayed and stayed. I got my mini bat out and banged my beans bin, had my finger on my panic button, and opened the secret door to my gun. He kept on calling me "kid." He *was* "on" something, but alas no incident, except wasting my time. Whacko!

I should keep a diary sign-in book for all these newcomers to our industry. One lady asked, "What is it with this espresso thing here in Seattle?" I told her that we were the Espresso Capital of the USA and she had better enjoy every caffeine hit. I offered her my special succulent treat – a dark chocolate-covered espresso bean. I had to explain that you first let the deep, dark, rich chocolate melt in your mouth. Then experience biting into the bean itself. Forgot to tell her that the bits and pieces settle in between your two front teeth, so she left looking like she just dove into the pepper shaker.

4:09 P.M. A guy pulled up to the drive thru and asked, "Are you still pumping?" Pumping? Pumping what? Gas? Chocolate? Breast milk? "Yes, I am, sir." He ordered an Americano with cream.

You know, it would be nice to get old and blind and not even see the fuzzy mold growing on my blueberry muffins for sale. I'm done with this brand of muffins. If they can't last for thirty-three years on the shelf, like Twinkies, then forget 'em!

I sat there wondering how some of those locals drove around all day in their sports cars, buying beer, smoking cigarettes, and never went to work. Welfare fraud? Drugs? Prostitution? Internet porn? It was disgusting, whatever it was. Many of *us* broke our backs to pay for *their* checks in the mail.

6:22 P.M. I have a 100% record now for recognizing other baristas here. "Do you have powdered white chocolate?" she asked, playing with the hair "flip." She practically came through the door boobs first! I asked her if she was a barista. "YES!" She screamed in that fucking ditz voice, highest pitch possible. "How in the hell did you know?" I smiled, "Just thought so…no powder… and what would you care for?" I gave her the customary 7.5-minutes to make this monumental decision and went back at my computer. I knew the 'Sister-Barista-Drill' and figured I may as well get something done! She finally *sighed out* her drink order through pearly white teeth.

7:02 P.M. See ya tomorrow morning…

9-10 53° Rain.

Scenic Fresh: Ice, a shot of crème de cacao and orange syrup, shot of almond syrup, soda water.

10:08 A.M. It was Ms. Gossip No. 2's birthday today so I comp'd a giant mocha and gave her a little candle for the bathtub.

Mrs. Periwinkle Luggage stopped. Her husband's sixteen-year-old son was acting up again. "I'm just frantic over that damn kid of his and I *need* a mocha. Kids and husbands are gonna kill me – why did I sign up for this again?" She was stuck and stuck good. Her husband felt the same way.

12:32 P.M. Scanner: A tree fell and was blocking Mountain Peak Highway, westbound at milepost 48.

I leased a sign space on my fence. This one would advertise some overnight rentals.

My fall bow-hunter, who will attempt to kill Bambi, came by. He thought he was just thirsty; he didn't know he was going to get a tongue lashing too! "Just checking things out, looking at tracks, getting my bearings. I'll swing by in a couple of days and show off my 'kill.'" With that I went at him.

"I wonder if baristas lose any lung capacity from breathing all the exhausts in our drive thru's." Especially those old trucks with gabby guys. If they appeared to want to gab for a while, I asked them to turn off their engine, "I'm slowly suffocating in my cubicle," sir.

6:00 P.M. Tonight, I will attempt to clean my house. Has it really been a month and a half…?

9-11 50° Raining.

Troops Special: Four shots of espresso, any flavor your heart desires, and steamed Half & Half, topped with all the goodies you deserve!

7:59 A.M. I guess there was a rockslide on I-80. It killed some people, and it was closed. We were the only highway available to eastern Washington today, bringing constant traffic my way!

3:05 P.M. Some cute "chicks" swung in. Definitely baristas. They were challenging me. Uncertain what would be the very best decision. Not wanting to waste a penny or a calorie. My famous question again, "Are you gals Starbucks's baristas?" Shoulders and hair thrown back, giggle, then in unison, "Why, yes (giggle again), and how did yuuuuuuu knowwwwwww?" "You are a *pain-in-my-aaaaaass*, that's how (my short-lived giggle)!" They ordered the reputable macchiato and could not believe I knew how to make one (I'm guessing sillies). They raved, "its sooooooo tasty!" Thank you, girlfriends.

A gal just came in with her baby. She sat the poopy diaper-filled kid on my serving counter and he immediately smeared a gooey cracker over everything in sight. The still-dry cracker crumbs in the other hand were now covering my supplies, including my cookies for sale! The smell almost made me sick. You know that mixture of poop, Ritz chunks, and stale apple juice spit-up. How did we women survive…sometimes with two and three of these little squirts at once?

6:11 P.M. So, will Cowboy honk or stop? That is the ten-cent question…

7:50 P.M. Scanner: A rollover ten miles up the Barklett River Road.

7:58 P.M. Scanner: Rollover up on the Barklett was DOA.

8:09 P.M. I'm pullin' the plugs. Enough fun and games…

9-12 47° Partly sunny.

Southern Winds: Ice, a shot of peach syrup, shot of mint syrup, Half & Half, whipped cream.

8:18 A.M. Happy birthday to No. 5. He is forty years old! We met when he was just a babe of twenty-three and I was twenty-nine. Seems like a lifetime ago…

An eighty-year-old couple came in. They got married four years ago, after dating during the *daylight* for only three weeks. Darling people. She said, "I'm so unbelievably happy, my only goal today is to keep him alive!" God, that was refreshing! They both threw their first mates out with the bathwater and both had second spouses die. He retired from the sheriff's department years ago, after being shot. The shooter committed suicide, just two blocks from the incident. He never could go back to the career.

8:38 P.M. Today was indescribable. I spent ten hours, between serving customers, dressed like a filthy pig in pink fluff and silver duct tape, as a result of putting insulation into the ceiling of this store! Up and down two different sizes of ladders. Face and hair being entwined in all sorts of spiders and webs.

Balancing on pinnacles of furniture. It may be close to a half a century since this area has been seen, much less touched.

My head looked like a ball of cotton candy. That was basically yoga for ten straight hours! And I only broke two items in the entire store! I have blisters on blisters from my staple gun and they are wrapped with that champion silver tape. A job well done. It sure as hell better make a damn huge difference in the drafts this winter – like NO drafts! Women Rule! I am going upstairs to scrub and never think back!

10:00 P.M. End of a darn good day – and ready for some damn good dreams…

9-13 47° Sunny.

Shelled Purple: A shot of almond and grape syrups, espresso shots and steamed milk.

9:43 A.M. Cold morning. I was haggard and sore and in no condition to tackle installing the plow yet. Or fixing the blasted toilet in back.

5:13 P.M. My regular customer, Ms. Rachel Welch 5-Carat, pulled up in her fiancé's Corvette. I had heard she *earned* it big time, being with this dandy. She always looks totally Hollywood and never seems to be aware of it. Neat gal.

8:06 P.M. Tomorrow is another day…

9-14 48° Clear.

No Whip Mocha: A shot of chocolate syrup, espresso shots, steamed milk and NO whip.

8:55 A.M. In the very first three seconds, in huffed, an insane, ignoble bitch. She was trying to return some backless earrings she claimed were sold to her backless, who knows how many months ago. And no display card or receipt. They were drug out piecemeal from the bottom of her messy purse. "I'm sorry, every pair I sell has backs on them – or they couldn't adhere to the cute cards." Back out to her car and she brought me some plastic yellowed, old, ear-waxy backs and tried to continue with the return. "I'm sorry, those aren't mine." Now she flipped, "You are so inconsiderate! No wonder you are single! You are plain rude!" Okay, lady, you had better fucking duck for cover, "I am NOT Nordstrom's. I can't afford to support scams like they do! Now take your filthy, germy shit and leave, or I will dial 911!" The climate changed. "Excuse me, I will keep my mouth shut but I would like to look at more jewelry." "I don't play that game either, with you making your own exchange. Now please leave." As this *lady* slammed the door, hitting her skinny butt, she flipped me off a good one through the window! Unbelievable experience! She said her son was a state trooper and sure as hell, I will check that out. She inadvertently dropped his name. Bitch from hell, with an old fart of a boyfriend waiting in the car; I would too!

Two Pacific Crest Trail hikers came in for smoothies. They were buddies even though one was a computer geek from Silicon Valley and the other a carpenter from the Netherlands. Nice guys from vastly different walks of life. The trail takes approximately five months to complete.

3:11 P.M. I called Buck. I wanted to give his mom some French truffles I got in recently and I picked *him* up a new CD on my last trip to Wooly's. Pay back. He stopped in for a chat and his free mocha.

8:46 P.M. Upstairs alone as usual and I will watch the news.

P.S. Headline Topic: Two baristas robbed at gunpoint "down-below." The newscaster was gabbing away about how the robber got away with hundreds of dollars. Geez, thanks dude, for sharing with the world about how much money *they* could expect to lift off espresso stands.

9:03 P.M. Attention Robbers: **OUTPOST ESPRESSO** is *isolated*, so we *never* have that kind of cash…

9-15 48° Sunny with clouds.

Caffeinated Chai: A cup chai tea, cup whole milk, but leave room for one shot of espresso and whipped cream.

8:40 A.M. Ran into the Bitch Trucker at the post office. I pretended I didn't notice the mongrel and her boy-toy.

7:48 P.M. I wonder if any man will even make it through one chapter of this book. They may pick it up for the history and railroad information, but I don't think they can take the heat! There will there be too much male truth, causing way too much damage to their precious pride! They in turn have caused our Cinderella Complexes. We were in a submissive state waaaaaaay too long. Went from our wicked step-mothers – to them. Men might have been able to keep this concept alive for even more centuries, but along came Ms. Independent Barbie and Women's Lib. Men immediately regrouped and now they impregnate us, watch our boobs fall, and our feet grow right out of those sexy five-inch spikes.

Then they run off with the Barbies after all, trading us forty-year-olds in for two-twenties, with magnificent breasts, fake eyelashes, and tiny high heels. Case closed…men suck. Still.

9:31 P.M. Store closed…

9-16 52° Sprinkles.

Sweetheart: Apple cider with a shot of passion fruit syrup.

11:09 A.M. An SUV full of baristas stopped and didn't leave a tip. SHAME ON YOU! Otherwise, a slow, boring Friday and now it's raining.

A thirty-year-old gal came in. She remembered this place twenty-seven years ago (she was only three years old for God sakes) when her grandmother would drive by and tell her it was a magical, mystical place. I told her that I had *always* felt this spot was right out of a storybook and that is why I bought it.

She beamed and thanked me for keeping her dream alive. "I actually do dream about this cute building a lot." I knew what she meant. I told her, "I would love to find the house I've dreamt about many times. It has three stories, is empty but is all white and old-fashioned throughout."

5:00 P.M. Whatever that all means…

9-17 52° Overcast.

Vietnamese Espresso Style: Espresso shots, add ice and fill up with sweetened condensed milk.

8:41 AM. The divorce is still on target – colliding with celebrating their first anniversary tomorrow! Yes, Hunk Wyatt was here first thing, sounding like a broken record. He was lookin' snazzy, like an ad for Patagonia with his chiseled face, olive skin, and just the right clothing. If I were into men right now, which I'm not, he could kinda cause a little heavy breathing. He laid down $50 for one of my flamingo stained-glass pieces to hang in his empty house here in town. "My wife took everything else. I mean, I'm surprised there's still paint on the walls." As I was on my trusty ladder again hauling down his piece, he was checking out my rear. "No wonder you are getting a divorce!" That is all I had to say and if the truth were known, I check his out every time he leaves my store.

2:50 P.M. Philip saved my sanity and dropped off a couple of good Western DVDs. I was about ready to ask him "to take the ribbons from my hair."

8:03 P.M. And I'm hittin' the lights...

9-18 48° Sunny.

The Coffee Latte: A shot of coffee and vanilla syrups, espresso shots and steamed milk.

8:22 A.M. Buck came by for a minute, just in the drive thru. He had a logging job today.

9:54 A.M. Scanner: Called in by me! My VIP neighbor was burning brush while we were right in the throes of a statewide burn-ban. Who in the bloody hell did these richies, with the numerous vacation homes around the world, think they were anyway! We all had brush, get over yourself! The fire truck was on site extinguishing, with those embarrassing lights flashing! No bank account was going to get them out of doo-doo this time.

4:05 P.M. Scanner: Smoke seen in the area on Mountain Peak Highway at Crag Rock.

6:49 P.M. What a day! I couldn't sit once, even peed on the run. A good poop was completely out of the question. Business was grand! I served up hundreds of vanilla lattes and smoothies. Nobody complained about the Porta Potties. Everyone was tippin' and trippin'! Great moods! I could finally breathe. Apparently, the traffic going back down to the city was backed up to Crag Rock! No broken-down cars yet. No traffic accidents all weekend, except for an awfully close call when a camper simply and silently rose from its truck and sailed down the highway alone... No Cowboy honks. Great.

7:31 P.M. "Tha-tha-tha-that's all folks," for this old gal...

9-19 50° Overcast.

> **Orange Blossom: Mix 1 cup Americano and 1 cup hot chocolate.**
> **Place an orange slice in 2 mugs, then pour the espresso mixture over**
> **slices. Top with whipped cream and cinnamon.**

7:48 A.M. I went to the bank and grabbed myself an extremely healthy fast-food breakfast and opened by 10:00 A.M. Tasty to the tongue but the arteries weren't too pleased.

The earring lady's state trooper son called me and apologized for his mother's behavior. I was not the first person she'd tried to buffalo, and he was mortified that she was dropping his name all over the countryside. It gets him in trouble with his sergeant.

2:00 P.M. I have had a lot of wedding attendees stop here on their way home from Icicle Town. Some of these singles, traveling together in vans and cars, were visibly uncomfortable with each other. The girls were politely ordering singles instead of doubles, absolutely no whip as if I asked them if they would like a shot of arsenic.

6:44 P.M. Scanner: Vehicle accident involving a motorcycle. Injuries. Only a few miles west of me so I lit a flare and waved traffic as best I could.

7:39 P.M. Okay…I deserve a bike ride and mellow evening…

9:00 P.M. Back and just heading upstairs when a local filled me in on the motorcycle accident. We did have a local casualty in this evening's wreck. The Harley that was hit head-on by a van, belonged to the man that ran and maintained our tiny airport. He was also one of our fire commissioners! The driver of the van was being charged with vehicular homicide.

9:30 P.M. Now, I slowly drag upstairs for a little television to take my mind off this event…

9-20 52° Partly sunny.

Another Viennese: Melt a cup chocolate in a saucepan, stir in 4 tbs. light cream, stir in slowly 2.5 cups Americano, beat until frothy. Pour mixture in 4 mugs and douse with whipped cream and sprinkles of sugar.

9:03 A.M. I just had a couple in from Florida. The husband has only had black coffee his whole life. I talked him into a butter rum Americano with cream! He loved it. Leave it to Seattle baristas to assist in expanding a guy's horizons and waistline.

2:33 P.M. Buck's love letters started again: With winter comin', weel need each other for warmth! No Buck, I know better now. That's what "down-the-line" is for. And these letters were re-runs. Or should I say, dittos, carbon copies, replays, recycled or handed-down, "down- the-line" for generations? A private investigator could trace these empty promises, numerous/simultaneous promises, back to Buck's Great-Grandfather, Big Sam. Luckily, women began seeing through the lies, the mistresses, and started breaking out of their own cocoons back in the '60's. So many women in this 21st century, including myself, still fall for Buck's type of innocence, declaration of love that was unknowingly being declared, simultaneously, "down-the-line." I'm telling ya, it was that shy, innocent act he had down pat, from watching the pros around him for all of those decades. Handicapped by his lack of style and poor living conditions, Buck had found a way to adhere to this day and age and its women, with or without class. I fell for it and I understood it! I would never, ever, ever marry again, without hiring a private investigator to tail my man's tail…

4:56 P.M. Closing before 5:00 P.M.? I may get fired…

9-21 50° Sun.

The Bob: A shot of chocolate syrup, shot of banana syrup, espresso shots, steamed milk, and whipped cream.

8:44 A.M. I'm taking today off! I mean the *whole* day off!

4:07 P.M. I did errands. I bought supplies. I ate and I ate, and I ate… Just as I got back home, the birds welcomed me with screeches like I had been missing a month. And cars parked immediately. I was not planning to even open today, but then the Russians came by for more railroad ties and the cash paid for my whole day, plus all the gorging! Buck came out of the woodwork just as I was saying goodbye to the loaded rig. He must have a *homing device* on my damn car! Instead of sharing this dough, I gave him a candle and other edible goodies from my shopping spree. Now the money is mine.

I went for a ride to check out Groovy Street's recent erections. No. 1 Bachelor's pad was almost sexy and it's not even finished! Unpainted cement walls and windows that crank open, allowing the outdoors in.

The river meandered along behind and around the structure. The biggest whirlpool tub, I'd ever seen. Loads of small black tiles decorated the masculine master bathroom from floor to ceiling and wrapped down into the "pool." Easy clean up after a wild romp and/or water fight. The five-foot-wide, floor-to-ceiling stone fireplace was recessed into the cement wall, making quite a spectacular statement. The kitchen/great room was accessorized in stainless steel. The entire house had the same huge rollout windows. An awfully expensive bivouac just for weekend get- a-ways! A steam room was located downstairs, with an outside entry.

Thus, the order of things: a swim in the river, a nippy run to the steam room, a dash upstairs for a leap into the whirlpool, and the bed was just a few yards across the same stone floor. The Argentinean dinner was looking more enticing by the minute.

I continued the twelve-mile bike ride and stopped to take in the fall leaves and the vibrant colors. Out of nowhere, a *serious mountain man,* on his horse, *appeared* along my road. I was startled and stuttered a limp, "Hello," but he just stared back with coal black eyes – zero emotion! I tried again, looking for an escape hatch, a tool, a something! "Beautiful horse." Still no response from this strange, bearded, large man. I bolted around him and luckily, he bolted too - in the opposite direction. I patted my pocketed gun.

8:20 P.M. I was so freaked that when I returned home, I jumped back into my car and went "down-below" again, to investigate security systems and buy more eyelash yarn.

As I drove back home tonight, I noticed that someone had placed a very pretty, gothic style cross where our local commissioner recently died (gotten killed!). I had heard his leg was severed and he died instantly from the impact. A small blessing…

10:15 P.M. Signing off…

9-22 46° Sunny. Beginning of autumn.

Strawberry/Licorice Latte: A shot of strawberry and licorice syrups, espresso shots, steamed milk.

7:49 A.M. Three Pacific Crest Trail hikers were waiting for a ride back up to the trailhead, to continue the last leg of their journey. One came in for a hot mocha and was freshly shaven, which was so rare. He explained to me that when they started at the Mexican border, they stuck a hand and a foot under the dividing fence so they could claim they were *in* Mexico. Then they continued through bandito land, where there were several warning signs posted to alert the hikers of the illegal aliens that may cross their paths and could be armed and dangerous. Several hikers had their campsites searched by the U.S. Border Patrol, since they had heat sensors that alerted them of any warm body in the area. The PCT hikers were an inconvenience for the border patrol. *I would* start north of L.A!

5:11 P.M. Two cars just raced through my drive thru, stopped, then took off again.

7:31 P.M. And going home (upstairs)...

9-23 47° 100% sun.

Spumoni Latte: 1/2 shot of cinnamon, crème de cacao, orange and almond syrups, espresso shots, steamed milk, and whipped cream.

8:34 A.M. I sure have been having fun and juicy dreams lately. If only my life was so damn exciting. Not that every barista couldn't live them out if she chose to. We are the sexy female bartenders of the century, so living in sin is only a snap of the fingers away. But why give the jerks such a fantastic opportunity?

A retired bartender gal came in. She ordered a 20-ounce mocha and told me stories of working seventeen years in the same bar in Idaho. (Speaking of inbreeds!) She said she married a FEW of her customers and referred to her job as the "Adult Daycare." She also saw her share of *Hollywood* come through her doors as she struggled with OCD her whole life too! She ended up having a partial lobotomy (seriously!) and it only took away her short-term memory, for her sanity. (God, I begged my whole life for one of those.) How have we women survived our many businesses and multiple hubbies? I wonder just how many movie stars she bedded under those stars, since she was a red-headed beauty.

6:44 P.M. Philip is possibly leaving for Stanford tonight. It is sad to see him go. He left me with four DVDs for the winter. Thank you, Philip. This time I got his mailing address out of him. Course, I cannot read his writing, don't know anything about his love life and still no clue on his birth date.

7:04 P.M. Goodbye, friend…

9-24 37° Sunny.

Spicy Licorice Latte: A shot of licorice, orange and cinnamon syrups, espresso shots, and steamed milk.

9:21 A.M. Some local cabin owners came in to drop off their brochures and they were all excited over their first nightly scheduled rental. Two Pacific Crest Trail hikers walked in for lattes and talked for quite a while about their six-month venture so far. "We're almost to Canada," they said, "And we've sacrificed jobs, relationships, apartments, and San Francisco for this hike. We know reality is near and we will no longer be able to afford our previous lifestyle. We are returning home to no roof over our heads, but ya only live once!"

7:59 P.M. And today is coming to an end. It will be a Philip movie tonight…

9-25 38° Sunny.

Espresso Silk: A shot of chocolate and anisette syrups, espresso shots, steamed milk, and whipped cream.

8:47 A.M. Mrs. Periwinkle Luggage stopped by to vent about husbands and kids and how hubby left the discipline to her, since he had no balls or the strength to lift his behind off the sofa. He patted his son on the back of the head for bad behavior and left the caning to her, on *her* time. Heard 'em all, honey.

5:00 P.M. Nothing else exciting to report today. Can days be called blanks, voids, nothings…?

9-26 49° Sun.

Lemon Americano Fizz: A shot of lemon syrup, espresso shots, fill with ice and soda water.

2:33 P.M. Buck climbed the ladder eighteen feet up to install some chicken wire in one of my eaves. The birds perched on this ledge and their poop never missed heads! It was called Bombs Away and Beauty Damage! Buck went a step further and washed my signs, without me even asking him for the favor! Catch me before I hit the floor! The bird droppings had been piling up for months and were creating a colorful mountain. I gave the male column a point for such excellent behavior!

6:47 P.M. I had a real strange guy stop. No shirt and nipple rings galore. It was repellent! He wanted to work on his car right next to my building and asked for a hose. Long story short, I told him he needed to leave *now*, or I would call a guy to escort him. He was furious and at that exact moment, Buck pulled up, tailed him, and wrote down his plate number. Maybe Buck was not *supposed* to be my significant other – maybe he's my male guardian angel? Seems to stumble in here in some of the most opportune times…

7:19 P.M. Later alligator…

9-27 46° Pitch dark and stars are out!

Maple Latte: A shot of maple syrup, espresso shots, and steamed milk.

9:45 A.M. Buck stopped with more time for my honey-dos. The back room toilet? Not. Too clumsy for that old cast iron piping.

4:10 P.M. Cowboy just went by and honked (tack strips anyone?). I would enjoy running into him and his wife one day. "Well, hello. Marshall Thompson blah blah blah. How is your tattoo doing?" I could, would, should do this!

I just got a drive thru customer! YES, a customer! Drinks and gifts. Now the electricity is paid for a few days!

I walked my grounds and did some weeding. Emptied my *park* trashcan, which was only a once-a-year chore. I found $2 in the bag! Someone's way of tipping? The leaves were gold and it was windy, so my park was carpeted in a bonanza of tawny blond. The river was a glorious sight with the rocks rising to touch the fall-colored trees lining its edges.

4:50 P.M. Well, a guy just dropped off fifty English tea bags for me to try. "No problem, thanks."

I wondered where my perverted Russians were. I wanted them to get the last of these railroad ties out of here!

An apple and pear salesman just stopped to give me four *samples* of fruits-slices. "No, thank you."

7:12 P.M. Almost dark. Buck drove up. Why? He'd been in the hills chopping wood and wanted me to feel how sweaty his shirt had become. "Yes, Buck, it is soaked, and that might turn guys on but not us women." Unless it was during wild, passionate sex, the kind that left your body limp as his dick! I guess my mind went naughty for seven seconds.

Blame it on Cowboy's honk.

Philip emailed me with a sweet, "Thank you, Christy, for the compliment." I had mentioned to him that I thought he looked stylish and dignified. Philip was *special*.

8:00 P.M. I'm going to sleep well tonight. Hope you do too, friend…

9-28 38° Sunny.

Orange Amaretto Breve: A shot of orange and amaretto syrups, espresso shots, and steamed Half & Half.

8:20 A.M. My espresso machine repairman stopped, with no notice, to do an unscheduled maintenance job. It is not like this is a real handy location, and just down the street from his last service repair. I believe the only other machine like this is eighty miles away. That was sweet and I can cross that chore off my list.

I was so bored I went online to see if we had any local sex offenders. There was only one! Amazing.

Trickle…trickle…another slow day. I should set up a cot and sleep between the door chimes. The sheriff came by. Both counties were now keeping their eyes peeled on Ex-Con. He would slip up eventually. I mentioned the sole sex offender showing online and he told me *that* one was long gone. But there were a *few Level 1* offenders around here. I figured as much…

4:15 P.M. The dark clouds were rolling in. Buck did his sneaky drive by to see who could be flirting with me at this hour. Being "friends only" will never work either. And just days into our comfortable relationship, an inch becomes ten feet in the matter of minutes!

Andrew called, to tell me that I was able to get high-speed computer service up here now. He was the second person to tell me that today. They were all full of bunk. I called the company he mentioned and they howled when I mentioned Saratogan!

7:07 P.M. It is still damn well dead. I did install a blind today. Several naughty words flowed from my lips while I struggled with hooks and cords and slats, teetering on top of shelving.

7:10 P.M. It's lonely, high in the mountains, secluded from the world…

9-29 52° Raining.

Elves Pleasure: A shot of Irish cream syrup, shot of cinnamon syrup, a splash of crème de menthe syrup, soda water, and topped with Half & Half.

8:46 A.M. Hunk Wyatt came in and he had his muscle shirt on. Hubba-hubba! But he was still a *local* and I mustn't forget it. He just finished staining the Microsoft cabin with that state-of-the-art oil from Australia. A sweet job to get locally! Drank a cup of espresso and wandered through my store looking for more décor items for his empty house.

12:31 P.M. Another good-looking local, who lives by carnivorous rules for getting women, "down-the-line." He pulled up in the drive thru in one of those new sporty Mercedes and wanted to chat; it was pouring, and I was getting wet, but he and the inside of his car were getting soaked. His cigarette smoke was swirling inside my shop! He was enraged over the end of his steamy love affair with his married nanny, who lived next door to him down in Stonewall. She now felt (after several months of wild sex and according to him…quad orgasms) that she should bow out and concentrate on her marriage and two small children. Although this local was quite upset with her change of plans, he was browned-off hearing rumors that she was banging a few other locals lately. What do men think with…oh yeah, I forgot. This gal must be from another state! This was a fucking small town and she had just fucked herself! A point removed from both columns!

3:44 P.M. Then biker Boone from Stonewall pulled up drinking an open beer while driving. I guess I wasn't *alone* feeling sorry for myself as light dwindled. It was fun talking and listening to someone else's anguish on the "R" word. Arm's length was the key.

4:44 P.M. Closing early. No sense in twiddling-my-thumbs in public…

9-30 52° Overcast.

Chocolate & Rum Mocha: A shot of chocolate syrup, a shot of rum (you decide 'REAL' or syrup), espresso shots, and steamed Half & Half.

8:38 AM. Rivers were seriously swelling! It reminded me of our usual November flooding, always in time to spoil Thanksgiving. When our peaks get dusted and warm rains arrive – there you have it.

I was getting some customers, thru. The birds were all cleaned and fed. I was unsure of what day it was until I was forced to look at yesterday's receipts. Welcome to the season of doldrums.

2:12 P.M. Buck just came by and warned me that he was logging within sight of me for a few days. He was watching the comings and goings. Spying for short.

Cowboy just honked. Fucker.

Lots of old folks came in: "Watch your step down…watch out for that bump…the birds bite…here, I'll help you." My store was a hazard. Then add hot drinks, shaky hands, and poor eyesight to the list.

A gal who was a code enforcement officer from a foreign county came in. She had been at a huge meeting in Icicle Town, where a lot of counties went to be trained by Homeland Security, etc. They were being conditioned to not only do their building code enforcement, but to keep their eyes peeled for meth labs, chop shops, pipe bomb-making plants, and a mess of other criminal activities. Hmmmmmm, Saratogan?

4:40 P.M. A ninety-six-year-old man came in. He yelled to the rest of his party, "You all need to come back into this gift shop or you haven't lived!" His wife died a year ago at the spry age of eighty-nine. "We definitely made it past the honeymoon! It was what you guys call 'togetherness' today. And it was every day!" Before I croak, I would sure like to know the answers as to how you accomplish that. Maybe *she* always cooked, and *he* did the dishes. Or she stripped the bed, and he washed the sheets. He washed the car and she vacuumed it out. Maybe the children's goodnight stories were her deal, and he said the prayers with them. Or he drove and she pumped his gas. He probably raised the flag at dawn, and she folded it at dusk. Or he asked her *gently* to make love to him and she did with a *smile*.

5:55 P.M. We all know how to do it…we just refuse to…

OCTOBER

The Indian sun hides behind mountain peaks,
as we unwind with music and brew

10-01 47° Overcast.

Eggnog Ireland: A shot of Irish cream syrup, shot of vanilla syrup,
steamed eggnog sprinkled with nutmeg.

7:59 A.M. A ski report? Maybe soon? Our snow level was supposed to come down to the 4,500-foot elevation today. Rad! I will ask the first person who's been over the pass if we got dusted. My customers know more than the media! Well, forget those plans…the first customer who staggered through the door could hardly walk and talk in tandem, and it looked like it will be days before he can handle *anything* approaching aplomb! A cloud of *old* alcohol wafted through the room. "Sweetie, let's hop-to-it and start pourin' two cups of coffee, and make it quick and throw me a big smile and a coupla kind words cuz I'm hurtin'!" Then he opted to *refuse* my Americano – wanted drip and *only* drip. I couldn't help it, "Same frickin' thing, ya big hangover-hardship, and I'm not your *sweetie*, thank the lucky stars!" Awkward silence as he left, both of us were swearing under our breaths…

2:00 P.M. Lots of *draggy* people ordering *quad* mochas on this rainy day. Did *everyone* get *wrecked* last night?

No white on the hills was the word from some customers. Then two dirt bikers came in and claimed the hills were dusted! Who's on First…

6:12 P.M. Scanner: A "domestic" in progress, just west of Trout Creek

Bridge. Brown Cutlass with big burly man forcing female back into car. Our sheriff was on duty today and he was handling it. If I were that huge barrel-of-a-man, I would turn into a meek-little-mouse over the next few minutes!

Buck came by in his usual *pant-pant* mode, begging for some sexual attention. No, bub…but an *on-call* someone to rub *my* feet and back was a nice thought.

6:56 P.M. Autumn Fest was a happening event in Icicle Town this weekend, so tomorrow should be busy with folks heading home. I think I will go make myself a delicious meal, slop on my shabby sweats and watch a good long movie. *Desperate* for a man? Not *quite* yet!

7:22 P.M. Closing up to all you lads and lasses…

10-02 43° Overcast.

Marshmallow Licorice Iced: A shot of marshmallow and black licorice syrups, espresso shots, steamed Half & Half, and whipped cream.

7:49 A.M. I could see the mountain peaks. Today there was a *touch* of white! People were already talking about skiing and were even buying up the few cabins left for sale around here. This increase of supply and demand over the last couple of years was hiking up our prices!

10:11 A.M. Hunk Wyatt came in for a visit. His divorce was well on its way now and he was selling his house in Saratogan. He will use that money to get his new home built, right across from the million-dollar Microsoft cabin. He wanted to be a part of *Groovy Street*. I felt as though I was on Bourbon Street! Just needed some booze and dancing girls to go along with my store décor, which was getting wackier and whacky equals Kitsch.

I was sitting here in the lull, pondering Groovy Street. There were four extremely hot *bachelors* living there now, or would be soon, as their builders finished the final construction projects. And this was a *noticeably short* street consisting of Mr. Hunk Wyatt, No. 1 Bachelor of Seattle, a state trooper, and another new one I hadn't even met yet. Lot No. 5 was a very-married-Microsoft employee. No. 6 was owned by a semi-married couple. Two more sales to go and there you have it...

1:59 P.M. I just dialed 911. Some punks from Canada came whizzing through my drive thru at 50 mph! A customer stood in here in utter awe. When I confronted the driver, he smarted off, emptied his trash onto my parking lot, honked, and sped off. "Jeep, medium blue, 2001-2002, speeding." Jerks!

4:00 P.M. An array of customers today: rough and tough, old and nice, young and sarcastic, rude and impatient. A lady shook her head at me in the drive thru. "I'm just finishing up with another order and I'll be with ya in a sec!" Thirty seconds, tops, the bitch sped off. Give me a fucking break!

5:56 P.M. My doors were locked, and a couple begged to come in. I relented. They paid for two drinks with a fifty-dollar bill! That could almost be considered a possible hold up, but they just wanted to hang around and reminisce about the good ole days, thirty years ago, when he used to stop here for homemade blackberry ice cream.

A *string* of vintage cars passed by, slowly, in this rain. Their cars were more precious than their passengers – must have been a show in eastern Washington.

6:42 P.M. Rainy and dark, giving our woods a more ominous, brooding feel – turning our trees from green to black. I will hang for a little while longer and play with my birds...

10-03 46° Partly sunny.

Blackjack: A shot of dark chocolate and white chocolate syrups, pour espresso shots on top and top with whipped cream.

8:41 A.M. My first customers were from La Jolla, California, and had never had an Americano or chocolate-covered espresso bean. What? And California constantly bragged that they were the first, on the cutting edge, of everything! HA! We chatted about La Jolla as they enjoyed their experience.

12:12 P.M. Mr. Hunk Wyatt came in looking very handsome as usual. He was checking to see if I possibly had a box for his gift. I could see he was now drumming up excuses to come in here to visit. He bought a juice for a buck just to be courteous. Figures…my hair was on its third day, twisty/twirly atop my head. My own special dreadlocks AGAIN! Oh well, he's a bad boy. A bad-boy-toy to die for.

It has been a nippy day. Upstairs will be colder than hell-frozen-solid! I'll have to turn on my heater and close every door except the room I'm in for TV time. Then at bedtime, turn that off and take a flying leap into a stiff, freezing cold bed. I tug on as many covers as I own, kick my feet like I'm learning to dog paddle, hug both body pillows (my men) and finally feel my natural heat fill the bed.

4:38 P.M. I'm going to run errands.

10:01 P.M. Got home. The drive was breathtaking. You would not believe the spectrum of vibrant fall colors clashing against the backdrop of fresh brilliant snow on Mt. Crag Rock.

10:22 P.M. Crawling to bed…

10-04 34° Clear.

Caramel Cream Steamer: A shot of real caramel, steamed Half & Half, whipped cream with caramel swirls on top.

8:28 A.M. Buck did one of his special spy-drives again late last night. Lights off, sneaking down the logging road, to see if anything special was going on around here. I've decided he's not only a bad *liar*, he's just plain *stupid*! He was on-the-rag again, maybe even the sauce, wrapped up in his own personal shit. He knew Hunk Wyatt was in yesterday and when he found me gone last night, he had us pictured in a bubbling Jacuzzi somewhere, soused on champagne and peeled grapes, making mad passionate love in sixty-two different positions – again – all night long! He gives me more credit than I deserve – I'm getting too old for an all-nighter! I told him to get lost and take out his stupid insecurities on some other barista "down-the-line."

9:03 A.M. The perverted Middle Eastern came in today with one of his other whores. He brought me more unwanted Starbucks beans with his typical wink. What a rat. Whining once again about how he needed these whores. I informed him that I remembered his drill quite well: The little woman (wife) equals same hair, same skin, same no-makeup, same recipes for dinner, for thirty-five years. He thought he *deserved* these diversions! What a pig! Hopefully wifey was fucking the mailman on a regular basis.

10:44 A.M. Buck called again to bitch about Hunk Wyatt. He actually called *me* a bullshitter and said that I might as well get Wyatt to do my chores around here. I told him, "I would have *no* problem getting a multitude of other guys to help me with just about anything! So…Kiss My Sweet Rosy Ass!"

2:55 P.M. Jesus himself just came in! He sure would pass for Him anyway. He was tan, fit, 6'4", and had exceptionally long blonde hair. Immediately, something intangibly spiritual came across. The only giveaway was the Scottish cap perched on top of that flaxen head. He was deeply into what I call *The Psychic-Soothsayer Level,* so I will turn him onto our local Ms. Claire Voyant. They will appreciate each other's hypothetical powers and beliefs. He was remarkably interesting, though, in his unique, quiet way. He moved to Crag Rock from Montana (probably got tired of the cowboys shooting at the *otherworldly* one) and today was his fiftieth birthday. He finally left with just a (boring) Lipton tea.

I called Ms. Claire Voyant, but she already knew about Mr. Mystic from Crag Rock. He was going to be this month's main speaker at her ladies *Paranormal Psychic Powwow* (my words not hers). At least now I knew he was semi-legit and really *did* live around here.

The sheriff drove by with a toot – always comforting.

4:00 P.M. I told Ms. Gossip No. 1 what Buck called me today. She said, "He calls you names and claims that you are letting every man on the planet with a zipper in the front jump into in your hammock, because that's exactly what he's doing!" Thank you, Ms. Gossip! This woman was married and had to ask her husband for every red cent!

"So, they want to control us, do they? No problem!" she said. She tells him that she is going grocery shopping, "I need $200, darling, sweetie pie, lover-lips." He hands her the dough. "I stick half in my bra and buy a frickin' $100 worth of food with the rest, and the pinch-fist-at-home knows nothin'! Men don't have a clu what food cost these days. All they heard on the news was 'we are in an inflation!'" So, she has squirreled away $5,000 a year that way. A point off each: he for being clueless and she for lying.

5:12 P.M. I re-routed some plumbing pipes this afternoon, snaking them through the gift section, dodging the large furniture items. No more land mines to pitch a customer right to the floor! A little PVC and that disgusting purple plastic pipe glue from the barn, and 2-hours later the *bump* was history.

6:18 P.M. Chicks Rule…

10-05 42° Overcast.

Banana Cream Breve: A shot of banana syrup, espresso shots, foamed Half & Half, and whipped cream.

9:16 A.M. Hunk Wyatt stopped by to vent some emotional anger – divorce proceedings, arguing with both lawyers. He called her a cunt. He called the other lawyer a prick. *That is* okay…but his description of his wife made my teeth itch! I would *never, ever* date a guy that used that term! Almost a *guaranteed* abuser in my book! I was getting a clearer picture of this guy by the day. The alcoholic, temperamental, barhopping kind of guy that loved to fistfight, with looks to die for. Yes, he would be fun for just about a four-hour stretch.

Trees were crashing to the ground across from me again with such a thud! Made two customers jump a mile. I'm cleaning up their spilled mess.

1:00 P.M. I talked to Andrew today. He was home extremely sick with a kidney stone – again. "Someday I will share the last one with you and bring my microscope!" That was plain revolting! Men were such babies! I know, I know, these hurt, but did *we* keep *our* placentas in a velvet bag for future viewings? He said the stone looks like one of those spiky Viking balls. "I thought I was gonna die. Mine was almost the size of a BB, but it felt like a watermelon, traveling down through my, uh, private."

2:30 P.M. I'm outta here...

10-06 47° Overcast.

Toffee Banana Nut Grand: Pour quickly: banana, hazelnut, caramel, and coffee syrups, espresso shots, and steamed Half & Half.

11:20 A.M. Yesterday was slow – today is *dead*! First customer graced my doors, and it was almost noon! I drove east yesterday to see the leaves and they were grand! Vibrant reds, sunny yellows, and ginger oranges. The fall foliage could put most rainbows to shame.

2:58 P.M. A hot shot from Icicle Town stopped for a hot chocolate but was bummed I had zero marshmallows. "Sorry dude, would you like some marshmallow syrup added?" He took it.

Andrew called and was still tossin' pain pills down like popcorn. He was swallowing his way to giving birth to the *stone*. This stubborn little rock was refusing to exit his body. I asked him if he would like me to plan a shower for the birth. He was not amused.

4:07 P.M. Joe in the black truck stopped. He sure was a sticky kind of guy. The kind you couldn't shake, no matter what carat ring you were wearing. He got a triple Americano and it cooled down as he hung around - overtime.

5:03 P.M. Adios…

10-07 49° Raining.

Egged Monkey: A shot of banana syrup, espresso shots, and steamed eggnog.

8:41 A.M. Baristas in certain areas know the patterns of people's lives first-hand. We see and learn a lot from our claustrophobic existence. We see the big bills; we see the smaller ones as the days of the month roll by. We are asked for credit in the lean times. We watch the daily movements of these people and listen to them vent. They share their frustrations – it's a trust thing. Our jobs *could* become dangerous since we also see the dark sides of people. I try to stay neutral and passive. Passive? Me?

2:02 P.M. Mr. Periwinkle Luggage came in. He needed to vent about life once more. Marriage and teenagers were pushing him over the edge too. He said they were sabotaging him, and he felt like he was on "Survivor." And this was in *his* home, where he allowed *them* to take up residence! No thanks…

Some potential customers pulled into my drive thru area, stopped, got out, and took off with their dog! I flung my window open and told them that they needed to move their vehicle. The guy said, as he lit his cigar, "We are going to get an espresso later." I repeated, "Move your damn car first! I'm not waiting until your dog shits and you finish that butt," but I toned it down a little. He jumped in and moved it to the east, parking it sideways, completely blocking the entrance to Treetops Loop. They proceeded to let their dog do his thing on private property, then they drove off. Couldn't they bring a baggie – or kick "it" into the woods? People wonder why baristas get burned out!

6:00 P.M. I talked to Andrew again. The kidney stone was still very comfy just where it was and apparently was not planning an exit any time soon. He was practically despondent!

I sold quite a few blended and *iced* drinks on this wet- 'n-cold, fall day. My customers must really have the ole car heater cranked up to want ice.

7:35 P.M. Still down here. Buck drove up to the window. "I miss talking with ya." The other day was *talking*? He has been working "down-below" and is getting laid. So now *he* wanted to grill *me* about what *I'd* been up to. "Fucking the entire male population of this entire town! What would you rather me say? Buying new batteries for my female toy?" *Not-on-your-life!*

8:05 P.M. Lights are out. No more espresso…

10-08 48° Overcast.

Sun Worshiper: A shot of coconut syrup, shot of lime syrup, and steamed whole milk. Whipped cream.

8:51 A.M. Quick update. I'm already in a pissed off mood! It was dead out. A lady parked in my drive thru and wanted to use my phone. No Parking signs were everywhere and about four No Public Phone signs were on the front of this building.

I had to break up a car full of guys teasing the hell out of my dog.

Angel, my cockatoo, wouldn't stay out of the bubble wrap. *She* needs to learn how to vacuum.

A drug dealing neighbor's daughter came in to bum a free chocolate-covered espresso bean. Then I had to hand my phone over to a complete stranger to give 911 more descriptions of the fire she spotted on the pass. Her nose was beet-red with a nasty cold. Help me!

10:16 A.M. Scanner: Smoke detected at approximately two miles west of the summit, above the power lines. According to the scanner, it may be coming from the Keystone Hot Springs area again.

11:14 A.M. No. 1 Bachelor of Seattle stopped in. I told him that I took the tour of one of the most unique and masculine cabins ever built up here – *his* on Groovy Street. I left out the word "sexy" but told him I loved it! "Remember, Christy, you promised to have dinner at an Argentinean restaurant." "I know. I know. Eventually and I will let you know when," was my stammered response. What I *didn't* say but was thinking – I'd fall in love waaaaay too fast, so forget it! He is going to have me over when he gets all his new furniture set up in the *cabin.* Is the bed ordered?

1:27 P.M. Today is beginning to look up. Some normal groups through the doors. Here came another clean-cut kid, a Pacific Crest Trail hiker in for a chai tea. He was from Indiana and his partner quit the trail about 1,100 miles ago. I was curious how many towns they visited along their five-month journey. "About twenty-six. Most of them are small like Saratogan and don't have grocery stores *either.* But the residents are super friendly. I visit a small town or tiny village approximately once a week, for a total of five months."

5:45 P.M. Doors locked and of course a shit load of walk-ups. They were all being bitchy about my gift shop being closed. If these people could guarantee this barista's safety and some extra rings on the cash register, I might oblige!

Buck drove up and started fanning himself with a thick wad of fifty-dollar bills. He asked if I would like to borrow some for my mortgage payment. "Screw you!" That's NOT his offer! It's a bribe! That one *totaled* a $500 sex session. "And by the way, Buck-i-poo, my payment is sent – early! Now take your dirty ass and filthy truck out of here."

I just had to make two separate flavored smoothies. It took all my self-control to finish these while the customer was staring down my throat, watching my every move, as if *that* would control the outcome. I felt shitty today.

6:00 P.M. I stepped outside to pull my signs and turn off the neon's. There stood a regular-looking male customer, but unknown to me. Why I felt inclined to invite him in out of the rain was beyond me. My doors had been locked for the last two hours! Barely inside, he suddenly became Mr. Protective when another car pulled in. A few more sets pulled up and he became Mr. Personal Bodyguard. Next, he wanted to walk with me outside to help me close. Dude, I do this every frickin' night by myself! He got the hint. I am really off today! That was just plain stupid of me!

Then that absolute *fucker*, Cowboy, drove by honking, honking, honking! Our song – seven honks in sequence. I wanted a glass of wine, but this month marked another year dry.

7:11 P.M. No cryin' in my beer tonight…

10-09 42° Partly sunny.

Knockout Latte: A shot of real rum and real Irish cream, one espresso shot and steamed whole milk.

8:39 A.M. Yes, I now know why I felt bad-humored and crotchety yesterday.

There is a real art to preparing the "throne" for puking at 3:30 A.M. I didn't throw up but was prepped. I simply cannot sit on a dirty floor and hang my head into a filthy toilet. So, the floor was padded with towels, the rim was covered with paper, and a scented candle was shedding a soft light, just in case. This morning I have had to run upstairs, customers or not, at least eight times for some *amazing* restroom attacks. Excuse me, but who else can I say this to…I keep looking at the calendar, wishing this were *not* a Sunday! I want to close! I want to nap. I want my mommy. I don't dare eat or drink a flippin' drop of *anything*! This is going to be one of those *try-to-make-it-through-one-hour-at-atime* days. Ugh…I just remembered that October Fest in Icicle Town is over today. All the humans on the face of the earth will be getting out of their cages (motel rooms) and will be heading home. Down my highway. Good luck! I may or may not be here.

12:00 Noon. No. 1 Bachelor of Seattle popped in again. He spent another night in his sexy ski hut. I have got the same sweater on that I wore two days ago when he was here. Oh well, I wasn't interested anyway…or was I?

My stomach has settled down now and it really *had* to. I'm slammed.

Ms. eBay Bitch struck again! She arranged to have another one of her friends buy one of my high-quality items and then trashed it with negative feedback. An attorney's letter will be sent tomorrow. *Get A Life Ya Old Battle-Ax!*

1:01 P.M. Scanner: Possible auto fire.

4:04 P.M. Fill the espresso bins, Christy. Get more milk, Christy. Stay focused, Christy. I felt like an ill robot. Now I was down to ¼ of an hour-at-a-time. I was really tempted to call Buck tonight and charge *him* a few hundred bucks to come over and rub *my* feet.

Some crazy shit just came in. A guy tattooed from head to toe, around 6'3", apparently from New Zealand. He ordered a latte. The other guy with him was dressed to an Al Capone tee! They came in separately but left together and stood outside. Each lit three cigarettes. Casing the joint? What the hell? Get out of here! I shoot first 'n ask stuff later! I'll email the sheriff their plate.

I just had one of those "save the trees" couples, ordering soy lattes. They brought in their own cups and they were upset over the fact that I still had to steam their drinks in a paper cup. "I can't stick *my* drink-wand in *your* been-who-knows-where cups. Health Department, ya know!" They were still frowning, so I told them, "Just go take a walk through the gift shop while I make these, and it won't hurt so badly!"

6:51 P.M. And I quit. Good job, Christy!! Now go upstairs and clean the bathroom again…

10-10 50° Wet.

Brown Sugar Shot: Four tsp. of brown sugar, add 2 inches of hot water and espresso shots. Top with whipped cream.

9:05 A.M. "Costa Rica was the place to invest in right now," according to several Canadian customers. Apparently, this was the *hot* retirement area.

I drove to the bank and it was closed. A holiday called Columbus Day. Duh! Forgot all about it.

Jack and Pete came in. Pete recently bought himself a brand-new travel trailer to live in. He was beaming over these new digs with pushouts. Now they both can live in the same trailer-trash-mobile-home-park and pay their fifty dollars a month for the security guard to zip around in his golf cart and make sure married Susie is not over seeing single Fred again while her husband Samuel is walking the dog. I pray I don't end up there.

4:21 P.M. I had a couple of Italians in from Chicago. They order cappuccinos. One of them planned to retire in Italy. They said they envied me way up here in all this beauty, where it seemed like decisions were few and slow…

5:50 P.M. My only decision now was when to take my queasy-self upstairs to bed…

10-11 47° Sunny.

Brown Mocha: Fill cup halfway with brown sugar, a shot of chocolate syrup, espresso shots, and steamed milk.

9:33 A.M. A bit chilly this morning but I warmed up by grabbing the shovel, rake, and broom and went out to clean up a few ratty spots in the yard.

There was one engine on the train, chugging up the hill, painted yellow and orange. It was beautiful against the backdrop of the pumpkin-colored leaves of the same hue.

No. 5 was calling, badgering me about a loan we had, some fifteen years ago. Give me a break! "You need a girlfriend!"

3:38 P.M. Today was a circa 1919 day. Two ladies came in for lattes and gift shopping – mother and daughter. They were both natives of Redmond, Washington, near my old stomping grounds. The mother was born there in 1919. Then my neighbor from Alaska came through the drive up window and we began talking about this new bird flu epidemic. He was sipping on his sugar-free hazelnut Americano, telling me some of the stories he remembered. The day his father fled with the family from New York to Maine to avoid the flu of 1919. Dillingham, Alaska, turned their entire hospital into an orphanage that year. So interesting – I loved getting history lessons from customers. I love coincidences…

5:00 P.M. The Diary of a Barista…

10-12 47° Overcast.

Coffee Cake Latte: A shot of buttered rum syrup, a dash of cinnamon and French vanilla syrups, espresso shots and steamed milk.

9:35 A.M. I opened late. Customers can bite me! I was in dreamland for a change, waking up with that mouth-hanging-wide-open-corpse-look.

A Mountain Peak Lodge employee just drove all the way down from the pass to my espresso window for her boyfriend's quad Americano, with a splash of hazelnut syrup and an inch of milk on top. His words to the gal friend, "There ain't no better espresso *hit* than at Christy's **OUTPOST ESPRESSO**!" He worked in the ski repair shop and they were now gearing up for the season.

11:47 A.M. Scanner: Smoke investigation at the summit, Mountain Peak Highway westbound. Our fire truck went screaming by. Saw them just return, call cancelled; it was just a false fog alarm.

My Rachel Welch 5-Carat customer came by for her chai tea and invited me to her clothing sale party in Sunbird tonight. Afterwards, these single gals all go out for drinks and she said she knows the fun places. She wanted me to come and meet some guys from that area. O-baby! Me? Go out with a bunch of female thirty-somethings that look like a zillion bucks and are dressed fit to kill in their $350 outfits? No thanks. I don't drink, don't go to bars, and would prefer staying away from another Cowboy adventure.

2:05 P.M. Ms. Claire Voyant came in panicking about not getting her firewood order delivered and could I please arrange for Buck to sell her some. He was still trying to cram $1,000 down my back pocket by saying that it would be a "no-strings-attached-loan." Buck needed to understand, and believe me, he had been told, that my seventy-plus hours a week were now paying all of my bills…just fine these days. I did call, though, and Ms. C.V. shall have her wood today.

An older couple in their seventies came in for *one* latte. She was a bit snobbish, but he was cute and had a big grin on his face watching me feed Mister some pistachios. He wanted some for himself. Mrs. Snooty interrupted and said, "Those nuts are a luxury for the holidays and much too expensive to be feeding to birds and humans, just so casually, like this!" You know me tooooo well… With that, I *immediately* poured some pistachios into a little cup and handed them to her sweet man for the drive home. I could just see it now… She will be driving, and he will be tossed in the backseat, so he won't make a mess on *her* floor! Point off the lady's side. Lighten up! They were a perfect example of that slogan: A woman marries a man expecting, hoping, he will change. A man marries a woman hoping like hell she *won't* change. The opposite happens!

6:17 P.M. Would be humorous if it weren't so true…

10-13 52° Overcast and rain.

Peanut Butter Rum Mocha: A shot of peanut butter and buttered rum syrups, a shot of chocolate syrup, espresso shots, and steamed milk.

4:10 A.M. I left the house. I ran errands. Wasn't totally out of supplies but couldn't sleep anyway.

11:39 A.M. Returned feeling like it must be closing time by now. This is going to be another looooong day!

12:33 P.M. A man just saw my store, slammed on the brakes, and came in screaming about living here, above the old Bower's Restaurant that stood on the west corner of my property, some sixty-plus years ago. He was nearly breathless he was so excited. In 1952, he was a junior in Saratogan High School and his parents ran the restaurant. He went to school with Buck's dad, Big Sam! He claimed that "He was the craziest guy in the school and the only smoker on the football team." The following year, Saratogan won State! I told him that the Big Sam's generations were still here and still nuts. They were quite a force and ran this town for many years. On my wall, I had an old photo of the Bower's Restaurant and parking lot where he pointed out his 1937 Ford. This man standing before me went on to become a *well-known* Seattle radio D.J., until his retirement in 1975.

3:47 P.M. Buck just stopped by to ask me if I would like to *casually cuddle*. I *casually* said NO. You would think one of us would get bored of the repetition. He's a patient soul, I'll give him that...

5:03 P.M. The sheriff, heading eastbound for home, stopped at the drive thru for a cappuccino and a chat. That is, it for today. I am beyond a chiropractor...

10-14 44° Semi-sun.

Fruit Cream Soda: Ice, a shot of strawberry syrup, apple and pineapple syrups, fill with soda water, top with Half & Half.

8:35 A.M. Angel was screaming and preening because she just saw an eagle circling in the sky above my RR tracks. I noticed there was a huge eagle's nest in one of the four trees the loggers spared. Cool.

The manager of Mountain Peak Ski Resort just stopped for his mocha. He was psyched this season. They were starting to look for beds and rentals. The season was approaching quickly and looked promising as hell.

10:23 A.M. A guy walked in, asked for the bathroom, even with *all* my signs *and* the Porta Potty truck right out front and pumping, loudly. "You couldn't miss this if you were half-blind and had lost your sense of smell!" I told him. He said, "I think I'll head on down and search out a *real* bathroom, and NO I don't want an espresso – have to go too bad as it is!" Course, he would have had to wait for the pumper to finish!

11:31 A.M. Scanner: Smoke in the area at milepost 59.

A second couple stopped and mentioned smoke too, so I called our fire station. I was sure I would have other worried eyes stop. Fire was great for business!

12:08 P.M. Oh, my good golly – there *is* a GOD - there *is* justice!!! Gossip is a-buzzin'! The sheriff and the code enforcement officer just swept through Treetops Loop and busted all kinds of building code violations. Ex-Con next door has been evicted from his aunt's illegal cabin! Health hazards, no permits, possible drug business. The authorities had received a multitude of complaints. Boot 'em *all* out! Slowly but surely, these creeps will be *squeezed* like a stinkbug.

4:10 P.M. Four hours later, Buck brought me a present. It was a heavily used stationary bike. I thanked him for the great bike and made him a large white chocolate mocha. We were yackin' away when a big truck pulled up to the window. Oh God, it cannot be! Yes. It is definitely a cowboy hat. Then I lost it! He had more nerve than surgery without anesthesia! What the hell? He acted as if there was nothing unusual about him being here. Cowboy glared at Buck – Buck practically growled at Cowboy. He was calling me "darlin" and invited me to come to Ritzville tomorrow for a party. Didn't I just tell this person to fuck off and die? Didn't I just threaten to send all our past emails to his wife?

Was his marriage that much of a sham? Unbelievable! Buck was just standing there, tongue-tied. Angry red slowly crept up his neck and covered his twisted face. He didn't like one solitary little thread in this guy's hat! This willful, stubborn, abstinent, determined cheater was seriously not going to give up – till I give-it-up! He looked fabulous...

5:51 P.M. Christyyyyyy – knock it off…

10-15 47° Overcast.

Holiday Pumpkin: Heat in saucepan 1 heaping tbs. canned pumpkin, 2 tbs. vanilla syrup, 1 tsp. ginger spice syrup, and 1 cup milk. Heat gently then blend on HIGH for 20 seconds until foamy. Top with nutmeg.

7:49 A.M. I was not even open all the way, no heat, half the lights on, still in a heavy coat, when a couple stopped to buy a southwest blanket. She wanted a latte. I was in the back, climbing a ladder to the top of an armoire, grabbing the throw and more people were up front hollering for their barista. Help! I had been lollygagging this morning – the highway looked bare to *me*!

11:09 A.M. Scanner: A brush fire a half-mile from the summit. Maybe a *real* fire this time?

I was still busy as hell. Big day! Lots of drinks. People just throwing ingredients my way and I concocted the ratios. I loved this! But I had cramps…bad. I had to get upstairs for a two-minute session of deep breathing.

3:49 P.M. Buck dropped off a big plate of meatloaf and spuds. My care package. His mama was a great cook, purely homemade. She was a lifesaver. I had been on junk food for days. I ate the whole damn thing and enjoyed every single morsel.

4:23 P.M. No. 5 called. He had a blind date tonight. I did not know how this made me feel. But I *did* know she had better be nice to him! Or else…

Movie night for me. With a lower back heating pad attached to me like a second skin. Ahhhhhhh… But at least I still had periods at my age. When they quit, I am afraid that everything in my system will go straight to hell and I will be shoved smack-dab in the middle of the big "M." Technically, I'd read it's called Climacteric, or Change of Life. Occurs when the ovaries have stopped producing estrogen, throwing the body into changes like hot flashes, increased depression, anxiety, irritability, mood swings, vaginal dryness, and urgency of urination. What was God thinking? I had always wondered, who dreamt up the word MENOPAUSE, because to me it said – taking a "pause" from "men!" If that was the case, I was smack dab in the middle of the damn thing right now!

7:41 P.M. Sweet dreams…

10-16 48° Raining.

Espresso Supreme: In saucepan combine 2 cups cream, a cup sugar, 4 dark chocolate candy bars (broken in pieces). Cook over low heat until smooth. Stir in a cup espresso. Beat with wire whisk until foamy, top with whipped cream.

8:43 A.M. Buck lost sleep over Cowboy last night and was here first thing this morning with insults. "The guy is just plain ugly, has bad manners, and that hat looks stupid!" I couldn't hold my tongue, even if I had tweezers. "Don't even *try* it Buck! You *digested* this Cowboy Charm-Boy with your eyes and you know damn well he's a stud!"

2:00 P.M. No. 5 called to let me know that his parents had been in a car accident! His mom may have a broken collarbone. They were the *very last people* in the world to deserve this! And they were on their way to church!

3:52 P.M. A male customer came in looking for his two female companions. Figured at least one of the two was a bona fide shop-o-holic, so this was the natural place he should be searching. "They are not in *here*, wearing out *my* cash register!" We walked the property and found them peacefully sitting in my chapel that sits along the edges of the river reading from the Bible. "WHAT? My friends?" He was dumbfounded. "Sir, you definitely don't know your *women* as well as you think you do!" He was still scratching his head as he walked slowly back to his van. Men certainly have a lot to learn…

5:55 P.M. Buck came by again. Cowboy hasn't. It's Sunday evening and I'm over it…

10-17 54° Partly cloudy, rain at times.

An Unusual Mocha Latte: Microwave 1 cup water and 2 tbs. ground espresso for 1 min. Let cool for 1 min. Pour through coffee filter and discard grounds. Stir with 2 cups milk and freeze mixture in ice trays. Blend frozen cubes with a 14 oz. can of chocolate

> sweetened condensed milk, 1-pint softened coffee ice cream. Top
> with cinnamon.

10:21 A.M. And not *one* sale. I was tempted to *take-to-the-road*, but I won't
until 5:00 P.M. What a treat to come in to work this morning and have time to
dust and vacuum the entire store. Feels nice. Good girl!

Cowboy honked by last night, just about 12-minutes after I closed – not that
anyone was paying attention. I missed him. I washed my hair yesterday for
nothing. My thinking *seems* warped.

11:53 A.M. Scanner: Another cow on an off-ramp on Mountain Peak Highway.
Was there a farm convention somewhere?

A lady walked in with her sister who was visiting from New York. "Oh my
God! Look at this *world* in here! Is this *your* world?" "Yes, it is. Fun isn't it?"
They shopped to their hearts' content and bought lots of treasures. Her sis
ordered a *second* Americano. A first *ever* for me!

1:00 P.M. Lots of male testosterone ran in and out of here today. After all, it
was the hunting season. These guys were super grungy gorillas, but fun and
polite. Buck stopped for his white mocha. This time he was mute.

Brent from Stonewall came by to pour his heart out; he was crying-in-his-
beer again over his married nanny that dumped him – gone back home to
hubby-kins. He described how he got her off with their new $140 vibrator.
$140? Did it come with a lifetime guarantee for multiple 'O's? He had been
spending lots of money on lingerie, expensive wines, CDs, and fucking away in
his dump truck. Classy. Remember the WD-40? Apparently, she grasped her
conscience and went home.

1:55 P.M. Then to cap this bitch session off, my regular lesbian couple walked
in while this Brent continued his disgusting talk. He said, "Did you know that
dicks cost $30K an inch? And did you know that the hookers in Las Vegas –
babes – not your sleazy whores, cost $300 an hour?" "Hookers are hookers,
Brent!" He wanted to change the subject and get back to *his* stuff. How much
his wife took him for in the divorce – how much money he just spent on the

cheating nanny. He said, "I did the math the other day and I realized all the shitty blow jobs I ever got from these two costs me $6,000 each!" Okay Brent, it was time for you to leave. Male *and* female customers treat this place more like a bar more than an espresso shop some days. Well… Italian bartenders are called baristas!

4:50 P.M. Running my errands tonight will feel like going to Sunday school, after *that* visit…

10-18 52° Sunny.

Chai Warm Punch: Mix a cup chai tea, 1 cup cranberry/raspberry juice, 1 tsp. orange juice. Heat and serve with a cinnamon stick.

10:00 A.M. A spectacular day – business hauntingly slow – yin/yang! Every year I forget just how sluggish fall can be. And spring. Get over it, Christy. I put all my new supplies away and was completely stocked up, waiting for the *rush*. Eggnog was on the market now and customers would rejoice!

11:53 A.M. Jack and Pete came in. It was always an education. Buck stood there in disbelief, "I can't believe you guys are *talking* like this!" Jack slid right in on that, "Hell, Christy is our counselor and with twenty marriages between the three of us, we *ought* to have something interesting to talk about!" Today's subject was the Philippians. Pete served his Navy stint down there, jumping from planes *and* from the various whorehouses, rooftop to rooftop. Then at the ripe old age of twenty-two and back in the good ol' USA, he got a job selling insurance, door to door. There was a favorite lady he liked to visit. Every visit cost him 44 cents. He would sell her a little insurance and have sex. Following the "appointment," he would fill out the sale in the books, but *he* would have to cough up the money. He eventually couldn't afford this routine – neither could she – so they had one more exalted goodbye screw! He was an old fart now, but he had some magnetism-to-his-manhood in the old days and had lots of carnal memories to keep him warm.

3:39 P.M. Business was a bust today. A few neighbors ordering and running out just as fast as they entered; all with places to go, things to do, and people to meet. I was invited and each time, to the barbeques and such, I could not accept. I began to wonder why in the world I had "trapped" myself up here at **OUTPOST ESPRESSO**, high on this mountain. "*Schizzed out*" came to mind.

4:24 P.M. Boone from Stonewall called me and reminded me that his birthday was on Saturday. Was he hinting for a present? If I don't ignore this completely, a card was all I would do. Remember exactly one year ago, I took him to dinner for his birthday. I ate while he scoped out every female in the entire restaurant. Then he drove to his place expecting to jump my bones. That was the time my boots never came off. And neither did anything else! That night was the beginning of my growth, I believe!

My nose is growing…Cowboy.

5:54 P.M. There are no bells ringing anymore and definitely No-Round-Two for this damsel…

10-19 56° Rain.

Ippuku Matcha Frappe: Mix 6 oz. milk, 5 tsp. matcha latte powder. Blend mixture with 1.5 cups of ice.

8:23 A.M. Buck showed up first thing. He was beginning to irritate me. He just would not get it. I did not want him back. F-R-I-E-N-D. Look it up in the dictionary!

11:47 A.M. Cowboy and I were emailing again. Never had I been in a situation as this, falling in love with a married man. I kept those thoughts to myself. He didn't have a clue – just thought we were having some laughs and enjoying each other's company. I would *never* get between the sheets with him, until there was a divorce. I will bet he *never* makes a move in that direction, for *monetary* reasons. Why was he horsing around like this and tempting a restraining order? Best I just settle for the Friday and Sunday espresso visits. I just looked it up – my insurance policy did not cover *heartbreak and misery*. This book is all about honesty and strength, so I must admit I started emailing again. But he made me do it! With his surprise visit! (God, Christy, this sounds just like a childhood whine and its bullshit! Where are those smarts you were just bragging about a moment ago? One point off the women's column!)

2:30 P.M. I had to leave today to get a loan. I call it: My-Annual-Slow-Business-Time-of-Year-Tune-Up-Loan. I drove through all the fall colors in the valley and it gave me some peace and perspective. The beauty seemed to cleanse me. I arrived home to a broken-down truck in my parking lot. The owner was sort of a sleazy guy and it was pouring down rain. This was one time I just *couldn't* stay up and help.

8:00 P.M. On my way home I noticed all the baristas I passed were still open. It was after 8:00 P.M., so they must need more slow-season-skins too. I *refused* to feel too bad about the small, temporary loan.

9:33 P.M. Not tonight…

10-20 48° Overcast.

Vegan/Vegetarian Chai Latte: Fill teapot with water. Add 1 tsp. ginger, 1/3 cup turbinado and bring to boil. Reduce heat to warm. In tea press, place 1 heaping tbs. loose-leaf green tea, a tsp. cloves, tsp. cardamom, tsp. cinnamon, tsp. powdered sweetened carob, tsp. nutmeg. Fill with teapot water and steep for 10 minutes, then press tea. Meanwhile, using a milk frothier, heat non-dairy vanilla flavored creamer, pour desired amount into frothier, and froth. Pour creamer, then tea into mug.

8:49 A.M. No. 7 called and wanted dinner this weekend. I might as well go, even if it's only just to remind myself that I'm still female. It's been a long, long time since I've been in a restaurant – much less with a male…single that was. I could also get off the Cowboy-Kick for an evening. He emailed again: "If you and I ever get to the motel in Ritzville, I promise to curl your toes!" Now I was curious. I emailed back, asking him how he would attempt this feat.

A family from Oklahoma and a couple of guys from Michigan stopped. Espresso was new to all of them. Each person requested something unique, just randomly picking off the menu. They wanted to see the difference. I ended up making five drink varieties and the families passed their cups around to each other, giving tastes, for ten minutes! I *love* educating on espresso – knowing that mine really is the very Best-In-The-Northwest! ☺

2:04 P.M. Buck called and I told him I would be going out to dinner with No. 7, so please do not stop if you see his truck. He thanked me for the warning and rushed right down, offering me another tarnished paper clip holding ten, one-hundred-dollar bills, just to watch a movie together. Oh God!

2:46 P.M. Scanner: A semi-trailer rig had crashed and was hanging over the embankment up at the summit at milepost 64. Our sheriff was already there. It was a forty-five-year-old and he was trapped inside the cab and unconscious. The truck was very unstable and dangling. Sirens of all kinds sped past me. Airlift headed to the airport, for the patient hand-off.

3:05 P.M. No. 7 called *again* and was looking forward to dinner and I agreed. This was highly unusual – now I am suspicious…of *both* our motives! Time for some introspection…

4:01 P.M. Scanner: The driver of the semi had been extracted. A possible passenger ejection during the accident.

5:53 P.M. Three more troopers passed by. I was still open. Some ambulance-chasing customers grabbed their espressos; they all tossed too much money on the counter and blasted out of here to follow the sirens.

6:44 PM. A trucking company employee stopped for a pick-me-up and said the driver was solo. Whew.

7:04 P.M. Curtains closed…

10-21 46° Sunny.

> Rainforest Shake: Mix 3 tsp. brown sugar into one shot of espresso. Let cool. Blend separately a shot of espresso, 2/3 cup vanilla frozen yogurt, a cup coconut cream, 3 tsp. brown sugar and 2 tbs. crunchy peanut butter. Blend until smooth and stir in 2 chopped Brazil nuts. Top with a tsp. shredded coconut.

11:43 A.M. Slow Friday. I have had only two cars and no walk-ins.

12:24 P.M. No. 2 Bachelor of Seattle called and wanted to have lunch, as he was finally able to clear his calendar – a tad. Too *busy* for my taste! I never did make it to that auction planned. I had backed out once again. Even with his compelling, marvelous, magnificent millions and his graceful, good looks! My grandmother always told me, "Beware of good-looking men!" And *this* one met the criteria!

1:55 P.M. Now No. 7 wants dinner on Monday instead of the weekend. What? A better offer came along. I'm over this! Remember…Christy, you could not stand being married to the dictator/sheriff! I have been of two minds over this whole situation. Clear as a bell now!

2:36 P.M. I just had my first Eggnog sale of the season. This year the prices went up quite a bit on this creamy seasonal treat, so I had to increase the rate a little. Customers will pay no problem, the addicts.

I felt alone *and* lonely today. A chemical, hormonal imbalance of some sort? I have tried salt, sugar and chocolate today, but still felt like crud. I watched all the Seattle people head out east for a romantic getaway in Icicle Town. That sure didn't *help* matters. If I would be honest with myself, I'd have to admit that Cowboy, No. 2 Bachelor of Seattle, and now being practically jilted by an ex who I didn't want anyway, had all gotten to me. It was time for some serious meditation or an AA meeting – or both…

Mr. Mystic came in again. He stayed for an hour describing one of his healing machines, however he *did* spend $30. It certainly extended my patience for the sixty-minute, *far-out* dissertation.

Plenty of iced drinks today. The clouds had *vanished!* There was an unusual lemony glow in the sky and people in the Northwest *worship* the sun.

It just dawned on me how long it has been. Ms. eBay Bitch *must* have received my attorney's warning letter today. I hoped it scared the shit out of her and ruined her month! No…YEAR!

4:08 P.M. I just had two bicyclists, husband and wife, stop for hot apple ciders. Their trek started in Washington, D.C., and they had been on the road for fifty-three days. They were caught in the middle of a huge snow blizzard between two small towns in Montana. Being seasoned bikers and campers, "We had the equipment to hunker down and ride it out. But it snowed and blew like hell for two l–o–n–g days!" From here they were heading south to San Diego for some sun and R&R and then would follow the southern route back to D.C. A five-month ride was their intention. They were looking for a campground or RV park for a couple of nights. "We don't have RV parks, even though some of our neighborhoods could qualify. And the campgrounds are closed now. Sorry." They could probably pitch their tent in our city park, but they wouldn't get much sleep; it almost sat smack-dab on top of the RR tracks. I'd also be afraid that some of our trolls would hop right on into their tepee, looking for warmth. I forgot to tell them to pick the Train Blow Tavern for their evening meal and old-fashioned amusement.

6:37 P.M. With all that is going on in my subconscious, my appetite is history…

10-22 45° Sun.

Chocolate Chai Nog: Combine 4 oz. chai tea, 4 oz. eggnog and heat. Top with whipped cream, powdered chocolate, powdered sugar, and raw sugar sprinkles.

7:44 A.M. Our tow truck driver stepped in for his raspberry white mocha, describing the semi accident up at the pass. "It was a *woman* driving the rig and rollin' *way* too fast. She flipped it and took out ten feet of *double* cement barriers. She was in a coma and needed life support immediately. They had to cut a hole in the roof of the cab to get to her."

A group of people came in to talk "birds" for at least a half an hour. Customers were calling them all by their names now. And Angel, Freddy, and Mister all responded gaily to this *personal* attention.

No. 7 is full of shit! I am *not* going to be his Monday night call girl! I am a Friday or Saturday night dinner date, bastard! So, screw you! And I told him so…

Today is Boone's birthday. He will probably come in with that pleading-dinner-date-look on his face, just like last year. Been there, done that!

I called Buck on his cell, since I made a white mocha for a gal and she forgot to take it. His favorite was here if he wanted it…haven't heard back. Probably in between some raunchy ole sheets somewhere "down-below." Okay…I gave it fifteen minutes. It is in the trash.

10:00 A.M. My bud Andrew called, and the kidney stone had vanished without a trace. He was ecstatic! His New York live-in returned to Seattle. Sure… now that he did not need nurturing! I was not sure I was going like this broad. What kind of an East Coast broad was he tangled up with? He is now calling me his "Secret Phone Pal." He still wants to see my rump off this mountain for a friendly sushi dinner.

Cowboy was in Georgia with his wife. They were attending a family member's wedding. Too bad he did not just vanish completely – without a trace. Would be much healthier for me. But then again, who is responsible for our own mental health?

Mr. Mystic came in again today! He had never been to Icicle Town and stopped by on his way. I *tried* to get this blonde Jesus passed off to Ms. Claire Voyant for good, but *she* doesn't make espresso.

No. 1 Bachelor came in to buy his dog the usual giant bag of beef jerky. Then he bought his goddaughter one of those huge goofy snakes I made last winter. They are cute and colorful.

11:58 A.M. My usually shirtless, classy customer, crowned with the thickest white hair ever, came in to order his mocha. A burly guy then barreled through the door with a suspicious long leather case in hand. I locked eyes with my regular, Michael, and silently pleaded for him to *stay* a few minutes. I could tell he *got-it!* He gave a discernible nod.

This stranger was hanging back with his drink order and I jokingly asked if he had knives in that satchel. He answered, "Yes, cooking knives." I asked him for a business card. None. I assumed he was waiting to be alone with me, so I told him to leave. He got huffy, and then Michael chimed in. He pretended to be interested in a possible purchase, "But let's take our business outside." I watched through the window as Michael rejected the sale and I watched the stranger's car leave. Michael returned. "Christy, you aren't safe here." No kidding!

Buck drove up and told me a man just drove off the highway and crashed. Wanted to know if I had heard anything…just as the scanner went off!

4:38 P.M. Scanner: A car crash on Mountain Peak Highway at milepost 43 near Trout Creek Tunnel. Car was ten feet down the embankment. Male subject was conscious, walking, with only minor injuries. Our sheriff was just about to the scene. Maybe it was the Knife Stranger.

Ms. eBay Bitch emailed me. It read: "Looks like your negative feedback is expanding. If you'd sell *quality* merchandise, this wouldn't happen, and you wouldn't be jeopardizing eBay's foundation. Have a nice day." Her name has just been changed to *Fucking Ugly eBay Bitch* and she's tempting me to print her real name with address!

6:06 P.M. A guy pulled up to my drive thru and immediately honked. It wasn't a little friendly toot either; he was *lying* on the steering wheel! Didn't read the sign: Please Wait 15 *Seconds* Before Honking! The lady I was serving inside was even more pissed than I was. She considered heading right out there to give him a piece of her mind! It was pretty, funny. What we baristas put up with! A *legal* drug and its addicts.

Another customer asked, "Why does the syrup sink to the bottom in Italian sodas?" "Baristas aren't scientists, sir, but my best guess would be that the sugar content is so horrific that it far outweighs the liquid. Now…how many may I serve you?"

The sheriff stopped by with his version of the semi accident: "The first thing I had to do was chain the cab to the trailer. The only thing holding that dangling cab was the fifth wheel mechanism. I climbed onto the cab, trying not to look down and opened the upper door. I realized I couldn't get this gal out unless I jumped down onto her, and somehow hoisted her out. I waited for aid. Then, yesterday I had to shoot an injured deer on the highway. Animals and kids really get to me! That was worse!" He and I quietly rejoiced about Ex-Con's eviction, just as we saw him drive past the store. Perfect timing. A sheriff's car parked right in front!

7:25 P.M. One of our ski patrol fellows, a cabin owner in Treetops Loop, walked up to my window. It was dark but I recognized him, so I opened it up. He needed two mochas; his "ski-bunny" was in the car. These two drinks were for the peppermint schnapps he planned to pour on top, just as they lowered themselves into his hot tub. He left with one last little tidbit; he heard it was going to snow at the pass this week.

8:15 P.M. I will fall asleep urging the clouds to comply...

10-23 49° Overcast.

Cappuccino Mocha Frappe: Combine in blender: 4 scoops of frozen chocolate yogurt, a cup espresso, 3 pumps of chocolate syrup, blend until smooth.

8:39 A.M. A very *ugly* train was passing carrying lots of scrap metal, chemicals, old auto bodies, and plenty of graffiti. Not a pretty sight in the middle of our beautiful forest.

I have had lots of macho guys in he-man trucks this morning. Deer hunters have been empty-handed this year, but they still throw the ole caveman testosterone around. Having to kill a deer rips the sheriff's heart out, while these jockstraps love doing it on purpose. If these swaggering studs were killing for food and their families were starving to death, I would *reconsider* wanting to shoot *them*! I do not like hunting season one damn bit.

10:10 A.M. No. 3 Bachelor came in. He is the one who became the proud new owner of Lumberman's Restaurant down the road. Bachelors, around here anyway, were all the same – male cookie cutters. This one had been in a few times with his main squeeze. They weren't joined at the hip today. I asked how it was going and he immediately piped up, "Oh fine...I only see her a couple of times a week." She had been fucking-with-no-future now for ten years. I gave him my *disgusted* look, "So, you two just scratch each other's backs when needed?" He chuckled. I pressed, "Does she know that there's no future?" He finally came out with, "I *think* so, but I guess she's always hopeful. I haven't *actually* come right out and told her I'm not committed in any way!" Then he chuckled some more, and I frosted. He had just illustrated your typical bullstud in the corral. The rich, bold bachelors, who banged their way through ten years of your life, and sure…. took you on a trip or two, refreshing your hope every four to five months, while they refreshed their you-know-what, twice a week. He ate your food, pissed on your toilet seat, and soiled your sheets, all the while knowing full well, he was never going to surrender a ring! What the hell were we doing? A point off the male column for toying with a woman's soul, and thinking it was humorous! He could cram his chuckles! And a point off the woman's side, for buying into the ballsy bullshit – it is now the 21st century, for Pete's sake!

12:05 P.M. Mr. Hunk Wyatt came in. I was still fuming. "Really bad timing, sir!" He wanted to buy a large terracotta sun for just the right spot in his new home. Grabbed a soda and wanted to complain some more about his estranged

"C___," oops, and he raised her description a notch to "Fuck Bitch." He knew full well what I thought of that other word and he was not to use it in my presence! He had also decided that he was going to start hanging out at the country bar in Pacifica. My old hangout! Dance lessons in a meat-market chock full of fake cow pokes/cow gals. Maybe I will pop in one night when he is there, and then again, maybe not. I would probably run into No. 6 and I didn't need a reminder of that spineless wife-beater!

5:41 P.M. I have about had it.

6:02 P.M. Up came a drive thru. They wanted eight drinks. Movie money!

No. 7 called, and he had the stomach flu. *Sure,* he did…*whatever* Divine Intervention gave me an out for dinner tonight, I was grateful. I had forgotten to call and cancel! And even *that* was good news to my psyche – it meant I was not *obsessing* over this bum!

7:16 P.M. Turning the phone off…

10-24 50° Sunny.

Harvest Canadian Campfire Coffee: Use course ground coffee. Use equal parts coffee grounds and water (2 tbs. coffee grounds per cup). Add an extra cup of water and a couple extra spoons of coffee "for the pot," whatever that means. Set pot on hot coals, not flame, and bring to slow boil. When boiling, remove from heat, steep for 5 minutes, add a bit of cold water to settle grounds, and serve.

8:50 A.M. A man stepped in for a white chocolate/vanilla mocha and tried to sell me on a new type of job, making loads of money in my spare time. All I would have to do was drive around to new construction sites, making sure their permits were in order. It paid $40 per house. He claimed I could make $1,000 for no more than half a day's work. "First of all, you homeless wonder, I don't have any time. Second of all, why are you driving a truck that looks like it's not going to make it to the next gas station?" After he closed his mouth, he was outta there in 1.5 seconds flat! A full-on scammer with an earring!

Cowboy's email: "Cold shower? Whew! I can think of a couple of things to do with an ice cube or two. You name the day!" He was home from Georgia and the wedding on his wife's side of the family. Didn't hit the reply button, needed to think.

12:52 P.M. My daughter called to tell me the Anchorage Press had a new section called "Sexiest Barista of the Month." No wonder men chased us!

I cleaned out all my aviaries today. Dust from hell!

2:45 P.M. I had to leave a bit early today because one of my Jeep tires looked like it was tempting a flat.

7:00 P.M. I'm baaaaaak. Had to leave for new tabs for the Jeep, grabbed some *staples* like chocolate, milk, chocolate, Half & Half, chocolate, and TP and hit Lou Sampson's for the tire repair. It was *not* my imagination. I passed Buck on his way up the hill and the next thing I knew, he was in the chair next to me in Lou Sampson's! He must have thought I left work early for my hot date, so he did a U-turn at Snow Peak Mine. I was polite, as Dr. Laura would insist since we were in public.

8:06 P.M. It was good to be home. I was starting to feel like a good little Catholic girl these days with all this clean livin' and *all work* and *no play*. My great-grandfather in heaven would be so proud. Boy, was he *staunch*!

Cowboy emailed while I was gone, and he was fucking asking me to do the ice cube/whipping cream thing with him! He was "bachin'-it" for the week and, "It sure would be fun." Do I owe it to the book? Any excuse... My reply: "By the way, I'd consider when you are not living like a bachelor, handsome, but more like a divorcee! I am a good Catholic girl!" Just stay the hell home, Christy.

8:41 P.M. Stay the hell home...Stay the hell home...

10-25 40° Sunny.

Special Espresso Granita: In bowl mix 2 cups espresso, a cup sugar, 1 tsp. cinnamon, a tsp. allspice, a tsp. ginger, a tsp. clover. Put in freezer until frozen. Serve with whipped cream.

9:00 A.M. Temperature was almost in the thirties! My son was supposed to come up for a first visit from his dad's in California, second try, but now there was a warrant out for his arrest. He missed his court date. Kids for Sale!

My sister called bitching about their four days of dreary weather in Santa Barbara and she wondered how I could live like this! She said, "My brand new, thousands of dollars later, remodeled backyard is even lifeless! And the brand-new solar lights don't even *fucking* come on!" She could always get me laughing.

2:49 P.M. I have had a half dozen customers. Stop your pumpkin carving and get up here for a visit! Another mortgage payment is due again soon! How do these months fly by so fast? Oh God, I am getting old – I can remember my mom saying this…

I just had a couple in from the Freak Show. A tad early for Halloween? His shirt bared his chest almost to his navel and he had more gold on than Mr. T.! She was wearing nothing more than what we'd all consider plain ole lingerie, and an entire tube of bright red lipstick. She was teetering along on five-inch stilettos. They must have forgotten their clothes in Icicle Town…I mean… I hope they did! They couldn't possibly walk around like this daily. He ordered an Americano with nine sugars and two inches of Half & Half. She bought one of my gaudy vases, while she called me every sweetie name in the book. Wow.

5:19 P.M. Things worked out! I have tried to get the heck out of here for the last hour, for the 2.5-hour drive to the airport. My son was coming this time after all.

Andrew called and wanted me to play a shopper-spy at his retail store near the airport. He cannot trust his employees lately. The till didn't seem to reflect the inventory. His *numbers* had dropped like crazy. "I can't possibly get down to South Seattle before the plane lands…sorry, old friend."

In the last twenty minutes my daughter called from Alaska and needed to talk about *life*, my son called from California to say he was on his way to his airport, Mr. Hunk Wyatt stopped to run in and lay down a hundred dollars on a piece of art, No. 5 called to tell me that his semi trucking company just had a fatal accident and it could have easily been him, No. 7 called from his truck just to talk, and I was supposed to be ¼ of the way to the airport by now! Cowboy called three times this afternoon and wanted to get together anywhere, anytime, any day, for any reason. Mr. Hunk Wyatt wanted me to go to the cowboy bar this weekend. "I have to do some two-steppin' with ya some *other* time, dude. And the good news is, maybe you'll even have the hang of it by then…"

8:00 P.M. Couldn't wait to get my arms around my big boy! That is, if he would bend down far enough so I could grab his neck instead of his waist…

10-26 42° Wet.

Espresso Liqueur Mousse Smoothie: Blend cup of ice, a cup maple syrup, a shot of espresso, a cup of coffee liqueur, 1/8 cup cognac, and 1 cup of Half & Half. Garnish with whip.

7:34 A.M. My sonny-boy is here, and it is already fun to have a warm body around!

A lady I had not seen before came in. She had run out of gas in my parking lot and I called our town hosts to come and help her. She had worked at a store in Icicle Town for twenty-four years and stood here spilling her guts out. Her life's story, about catching her boyfriend of twelve years with her next-door neighbor lady. She said, "We used to fuck-like-monkeys, but with menopause and stuff, I was not in the mood as often. So, he found himself a fill-in-fuck-monkey." She couldn't seem to walk out the door until *all* the facts were shared with me - *and* - our male town host while he waited to taxi her to the gas station.

12:36 P.M. Some meth-heads came in and tried to pay for two lattes with a hundred-dollar bill. I told them no way! So, they called another local drug-head in Treetops Loop and he immediately came down with a twenty. I cannot even *put into words* how much I hate these maggots, these scumbags! Wish I had some syrupy rat-poison for their drinks!

4:00 P.M. What a mess! DOT painted new lines on our wet highway yesterday and they smeared everywhere. I had a river of white pigmentation flowing across my parking lot and right into our river! It looked like another drunken Saratogan road job, like in the old days. It is only taxpayer's money…

5:02 P.M. Hunk Wyatt's stepfather came in, "Wyatt says that you are going to teach him how to country dance." "Really? Sorry, but I have to *drink* to *dance* and I ain't got no more tolerance for that *magic* liquid-confidence." He left. Let us get honest! If I even *felt* those big strong arms around my waist…and looked up at those sea-green eyes and Roman sculptured features…and had to watch that perfect frame movin' and groovin' to the beat…I'd be a goner… No dice!

5:55 P.M. Upstairs to make dinner for TWO! You haven't heard me say that in a coon's age…

10-27 31° Sunny.

Espresso Yogurt Blend: Blend a cup of ice, a shot of espresso, 1 cup Half & Half, a cup vanilla yogurt, 1 pack of fake sugar.

7:45 A.M. Cold as a witch's tit! I thought that description would be appropriate this freezing Halloween weekend! My Californian son keeps going back and forth to our thermometer in disbelief. I quickly scanned him this morning as he came out of the bedroom: he is wearing his thermals beneath his new tee shirt, poking out from under a sweatshirt, covered by a smaller leather jacket, below his down ski coat. He is half frozen!

10:58 A.M. My kid and I are going to run away for the day.

10:15 P.M. Hi, we're back. We drove east to Squillene Falls, south to the new Narrows Bridge at Gig Harbor, hit some thrift shops, then west to pork-out at the world-famous Poulsbo Bakery, and north again to meet up with family for dinner at my brother's house in Kingston. After dessert and hugs, it was back east for a fun ferry ride. My Jeep hummed through this gigantic circle, close to 230 miles.

11:15 PM. A wonderful day off – but Home *Sweet* Home...

10-28 42° Rain.

Bourbon Mocha: A shot of chocolate syrup, a shot of bourbon, splash of hazelnut and vanilla syrups, espresso shots, steamed whole milk.

8:52 A.M. Ready for reality again. *That is* when you *knew* it had been an enjoyable, packed to the gills, day off! It felt like I was gone a week instead of twelve hours.

Cowboy's email said something about a party near his ranch this weekend, but he was not sure he'd go, "Because I may get in trouble." Now *that* comment right there just excluded *me*, my friend! Those *six little words* transcribed *and* described all I ever needed to know! So, Fuck You for Good! No more emails or phone calls would be coming from this end that was for sure! These half a dozen words told me you WERE a player, ARE a player, and ALWAYS WILL a player! I was not special after all...just a new notch on your turquoise buckle. I am now hugging myself.

11:18 A.M. A man came in who stayed here at Bower's Camp back in 1947. He was only a one-year-old. There used to be a dump in the old Bower's Camp, and it was a constant food supply for wild animals. The story goes, his parents took a little stroll to gather firewood and returned to find a bear inside their tent – with the baby! They watched helplessly as it almost stepped on his little head. They were paralyzed with fear. A minute later, the huge wooly thing just turned around and walked back into the trees! This baby was now a fifty-eight-year-old who lived with his wife down in High Valley.

Another nice cowboy-looking seventy-year-old, new customer to me, chimed in. He overheard the conversation and said he camped here with the bears too. He said the reason they were fairly tame was because their bellies were always full. He had gone to school here in Saratogan until the sixth grade. Lots of loggers and truckers in his family tree. His father used to chase the bears off and play with the cubs. I loved getting more history about my **OUTPOST ESPRESSO**.

4:40 P.M. Buck came up to see my son. He brought some of his mama's tasty macaroni salad. We inhaled every morsel like a group of starving predators. Oh…homemade! Those two stepped out to have one of those…*ahem*… "man-to-man-talks." Buck returned to talk for an hour about another barista "down-the-line" that wouldn't quit bothering him when he stopped there – three times a day. I whipped out the dental floss and sewed my mouth shut after flossing boringly. He had a reprieve from Christy's wrath for the moment. He was being nice to my son!

7:32 P.M. It feels like snow outside…

10-29 43° Rain.

> Fall Traditional Campfire Coffee: Bring 2 quarts of water to a boil over campfire. Take from fire and add 2 handfuls of finely ground coffee. Steep for 4 minutes. Add a few spoonsful of cold water to settle grounds and serve. Adjust as desired.

9:21 A.M. Pomeranian Bear's parents came in. Mom looked great! She had healed nicely after last year's accident. They left here with mochas in hand. Bear was not with them this trip.

Mr. Hunk Wyatt came in and somehow squeezed himself behind my cart to do some emailing on my laptop. In my personal space? Oh well, he is here now. At that *exact* moment, Buck pulled up and about shit. He sped off – imagination reeling. Wyatt was barely a foot from me now. Damn, he got better looking the closer you got! That is not normal!

11:37 A.M. A tall, clean-cut, nice looking cowboy came in. A *senior* cowboy. Idle chat, chat, chat…then he mentioned my mom who he had met last night! My ears just woke up! He immediately started bragging about all his business involvements, property he owned, etc. Then the other shoe dropped when he asked for her phone number. "Does this espresso shop look like senior$%#@ over espresso.com?" I display business cards on my counter for professions I try and promote. I might as well be invisible now – he just found hers. I may not live through this one! Email: "Dear Mother, a Rocky somebody-or-other came in today and he found your card and…"

3:58 P.M. My mom responded. She had received my email. And his – already! Returned mine only: "No worries, daughter. When I met him, just last night, the manager of the private club spoke right up, 'Stay the hell away from Rocky, as far away as possible!' That took care of that!" Wow – did not take him long to drive the hundred miles roundtrip to interrogate me and brag!

5:39 P.M. It was time to close. Funny day, funny people…

10-30 44° Overcast.

Granita Di Limón: Blend together a cup of ice, 2 oz. Real Lemon juice, 2 inches of Half & Half, 2 packs of fake sugar. Serve with lemon wedge.

8:20 A.M. A couple came in and was extremely flattered that I recognized them from *days* ago. The clue? A *single* 20-ounce sugar-free caramel decaf mocha. A rare order – a why bother – no kick!

Buck picked up my son as planned. He is going to give him some work – he knows the kid is *broke-to-the-bone*! They are going to go nab some huge logs up by my RR tracks. I can watch them from my cubicle.

Several sets of repeats strolled in. "We're back! Haven't set eyes on *you* for a while! Long time no see!" I positively *cannot* get the ole' brain-computer to pull them up. Sometimes it was merely the difference between seeing them in drive thru and then on foot.

1:43 P.M. One of the slowest *Sundays* in months.

4:24 P.M. With Daylight Savings Time no longer in effect, it was already dark as coal! Finally – my lights, twinkling against the murky black, brought the cars in by the droves.

I have had several local yuppie cabin owners come in and buy home décor. That is so splendid when business is slow like this. eBay seemed to have dropped off the face of the earth again, too.

This place feels like a tomb. With the change of time now, I must lock up early for safety. I do not like it one darn bit! Tell me again, why do we have Daylight Savings Time? Somebody said it has something to do with farmers and cows. Another thought it was kids and school buses. What is the dang truth?

6:00 P.M. Cowboy called from Soap Lake. He must have not found a new cowgirl. He wanted to know how late I would stay open "for him." "Eat shit and I told you, I haven't put a hitchin' post in the drive thru yet!"

6:01 P.M. Food time for our little family of "two" …

10-31 43° Pouring.
-Almost "Cold as a Witch's Tit,"
so Happy Halloween!

Java Fudge Latte: A shot of chocolate, 3 tbs. corn syrup, dash of salt, 2 espresso shots, a shot of vanilla syrup, splash of toasted walnut syrup, steamed Half & Half.

9:00 A.M. Self-inflicted torment, as I headed to the dump early this morning in a hammering monsoon! You used to be intelligent, Christy, and do this horrid job before it rained.

On my way home, via the P.O., I had to veer around a big, white, *glistening* lump of snow! Had the Snow Gods arrived?

Some regulars, originally from Australia, stopped for lattes. They had delightful "down-under" accents. They confirmed that eastern Washington had four inches of new snow! Mountain Peak Summit a wonderland! Way to go! Why didn't I wake up to plow trucks rumbling and clattering along the highway?

12:49 P.M. Buck drove up for his usual white chocolate mocha – a full load of wood turning his truck into a low-rider. More liquid cash for the ladies...

Then my cute English couple came in; they had been worried about my social life. *That* was the conversation at their dinner table last night and again for breakfast.

3:33 P.M. No. 7 called, filled me in with the usual bullshit, "Let's have dinner. I almost died in my semi on Friday. I hate living with my brother. I have a toothache." "You need to slap your sheriff's badge back on, so you have more to worry about than just *you!*"

4:34 P.M. Doors were locked to keep out the Halloween boogie-monsters. I started to see cars with snow on their roofs. Cowboy was noticeably absent from my espresso shop *and* my computer. I guess his motto is: If they don't "*Play in Person*" then I won't "*Play in Cyber!*"

8:25 P.M. I removed my witch's hat and considered eating the leftover holiday candy. My son is with his friends for some fun and mischief.

11:12 P.M. Enough! Nite-nite, sleep tight, and don't let the goblins bite...

NOVEMBER

Pumpkin and spice join, as cinnamons and nutmeg sprinkle foam

---

11-01 38° Pouring rain.

Café Vanilla Nut Mocha: A shot of chocolate, a shot of vanilla and almond syrups, splash of hazelnut syrup, espresso shots, and steamed whole milk.

8:13 A.M. Whistler Resort in Canada was opening this weekend – earliest in thirty-eight years! Mountain Peak Ski Resort was getting snow accumulation. Maybe it was *our* year. *My* year! Got a little *skinny* last year in the snow/cash register drought. Now we will all plump up and get real fat and sassy!

Philip called me about a "Behavioral" article in the Times. I was instantly paranoid – self-esteem in the toilet – he thought I needed major counseling! Turned out to be a super article concerning the relationship between birds and their mates and compared to those of humans. The alleged facts were that cockatiels had only a 10% divorce rate. What Philip didn't know, or ever would if I could help it, was that my odds had been 100% every twenty minutes! Then more about cockatiels' personalities and disposition, being so closely related to the human psyche. Bird lovers already knew this.

Mr. Hunk Wyatt came in, to bitch (Oh God…) about "Sugar Britches," his name for *her* today. Luckily, a new customer blasted through the door and I was saved from more of this ongoing modus operandi. "Wyatt-Bitchy-Britches – want some cheese to go with that whine?" "Shudddup, Christy!"

12:00 P.M. A very cold, dark, and gloomy day. Made for a perfect sledding and snowmobiling weekend. I will take 'em any way I can get 'em! Bodies were what I needed! I hoped this wasn't just a huge *tease* dump of snow, followed by that inevitable Thanksgiving flood consuming the entire state.

Jack and his ex-wife stopped in and I couldn't help but overhear the "honeys" and the

"sweethearts." I may have to stick my finger down my throat. What the fuck? This bitch was shoulder-to-shoulder with him for a few years, then promptly took him for anything visible, practically right down to his shorts. There must be another pocket that still had some loose change hanging around. The gullibility of life and love continues to baffle me…

A logging truck full of Mexican workers came by for mochas. They asked, "What's egg…?" They were asking about my new holiday eggnog – a new word for them and a new taste. Half of them wore it proudly on their upper lip from the *same* tasty cup.

Ms. Gossip No. 1 offered, "God, Christy, you look blank today! What is missing? Lipstick – that is the culprit!" She *never* missed a damn thing!

2:57 P.M. Scanner: Injury car accident on Mountain Peak Highway at milepost 62. Snow and slush on highway. One person rushed to the hospital.

Mrs. Periwinkle Luggage came in the drive-thru, shaking and worried to death about the drive she had to make over the *snowy pass*. A *first* in the season for *all* of us. She felt she *deserved* a mocha – wished it could be *stronger*.

3:03 P.M. Buck and my son crawled out of the woods like afflicted animals. Buck had been injured. A huge treetop fell on his arm. My son yelled from across the highway, "We are heading home so you can see just how bad it is, mom!" There are a few logger rules that you always abide by – he broke two of them. He didn't wear his hardhat and he didn't cut out his get-a-way trail before sawing on the tree. Breaking half of one simple rule is what kills our loggers. And we've lost many up in "these-thar-hills". I patched him up and gave them each a butter rum latte.

6:30 P.M. Buck for dinner? Okaaaaaaay…

11-02 41° Calling it sunny - that may be pushin' it.

Whipped Cappuccino: Fill cup half full of foamed whole milk, espresso shots and fill rest with whipped cream, stir.

8:16 A.M. The ski report today said it was 31° with eleven inches of new snow. Snowburg and Mount Pearl were opening this weekend. This was my first day in snow boots; I retrieved last year's unscratched, unblemished pair that appears to be just unwrapped from tissue paper. If the weather cooperates, these will be worn for the next five months…straight!

A couple came in who's birthdays were only a day apart. They were heading out for a two-night get-a-way in a dreamy cabin in Icicle Town, the world-famous German romantic town. It is simply perfect for what they had in mind. He saw my cockatiel and yelled, "Hey, an old girlfriend of mine had one of these!" Without a brain in his head, he continued describing the bird's name, what year, and where it all took place. The references to his past, as if it were the best part of his existence to date, were a major mistake. His gal friend drummed her fingers and stared at my cement floor. Dude, remember where you are heading and why. Miss B was getting pissed-as-hell, hearing about Miss A and her fucking bird. One more tweet-tweet and it's all over! You just took a gum-eraser to the first BJ!

11:15 A.M. Buck came by. He handed me a full-on love letter, written on a paper bowl. That was not an easy feat – but it's going to be even *more* difficult fitting it into my shredder.

Ms. Gossip No. 1 came in while he was here. Buck, who knew she constantly trashed him, handled it pretty darn well. They were each being *Miss Manners* polite. I couldn't be bothered, so I got back to business, trying to fill orders for a finicky lady at the window. She ordered three unheard of drinks. Then she *needed* cup sleeves, napkins, more straws, dropped her chocolate-covered espresso beans, needed new ones, and and and… I was running around like a crazy person – it took at least eight trips back and forth to the window. She promptly *laid* on the horn like she just suffered a massive heart attack and was in dire pain. "Yes, Your Highness, what can I do for you now?" She needed

Kleenex. I believe the "F" word slipped out, but who cared at this point. I had other customers at the counter, who understood the situation and were in stitches. Buck and Ms. Gossip No. 1 were still being courteous...

9:01 P.M. A big storm was supposed to come in tomorrow. I needed to get a darn generator! My son is visiting with a new gal he has already met up here. Where is myyyy other half?

9:31 P.M. I guess it's just me and some vinegar & salt potato chips and a good movie...

11-03 38° Rain.

Café Brulot Latte: My original! A shot of orange and lemon syrups, 3 sugars, sprinkle of cloves and cinnamon, shot of cognac, espresso shots, steamed whole milk.

7:59 A.M. The big storm will hit today. Probably while I am in transit, taking my son back to the airport.

8:30 A.M. Back to the day...a couple came in and ordered a Snickers mocha and an eggnog latte. He asked, "Are you the only store up here besides the gas station?" "We are the only two stores you can count on being open." His wife kind of shivered. "We went into the gas station and the guy working the little counter had two front teeth missing and picked his nose before taking our money." "Welcome to Saratogan, where the guys are fortunate to have *any* teeth left! Most have been knocked out by other men, animals, trees or only plain ole neglect." The wife shivered again.

12:00 Noon. Buck was now demanding that I get four studded tires on my Jeep. I explained that I needed a generator and could not afford another $480 at this moment. I could only do one big purchase a month – if I were lucky! I'm practically stranded anyway if we get the winter, we are all praying for. So, *what* if I had to stay home even *more* when the roads got bad. I was still *relatively* sane... He said that he was handing me the money on Monday and I could pay him back later – or *hold* him for an hour. I would drive on wheel-rims before I'd cuddle or take *his* dough!

It was snowing bloody hard up at the pass. Reporters from Seattle's Channel 5 stopped and informed me that Mountain Peak Ski Resort was opening Wednesday! Yeah Team! Their photographer came in for a mocha. I think every local within three miles scurried in here, like mice to Swiss. I could just hear the town crier now: A Television Truck Is in Front of Christy's Store! What did she do now?

The entire mountain, and most businesses, suffered last year in our drought. Then reality set in. This just might be the beginning of the busiest season we have ever had on this hill – snow, skiers, shoppers, snowboarders, and more espresso than I had sold in the last two years, combined! Yahoo!!!!

5:55 P.M. Buck was explaining why I should take *half* the tire money. I started laughing and could just picture the two rims in the front and two new studded beauties in the back.

Goodbye, men, I must leave for the airport.

12:12 A.M. Sweet dreams, son. Hurry back. I miss you already… I am heading up to try and find my bed – amidst all your mess…

11-04 38° Raining.

Turkish Delight: A shot of toasted walnut syrup, a tsp. crème of tartar, splash of orange syrup, espresso shots, steamed Half & Half.

9:16 A.M. Had to sleep in. Last night's drive home from the airport was gnarly! Two hours later, 40 mph on Mountain Peak Highway, lightening striking around me, and I somehow made it. Bleary-eyed from squinting through the windshield, I could not even *think* of sleep. I cleaned my filthy sty until 1:00 A.M. Teenagers! Men! They were born sight and hearing impaired!

Buck was here first thing this morning. He got spoiled hanging around here so much with my son, his laborer in tow. How quickly "we" became a habit – a habit that must be broken – fast! He handed me another psycho note: "Weer an Empire. Love is honest. Love duznt abuse. Weer Indipendint. We stand Alone. Love iznt selfish."

Buck, "we" aren't a "we!" Buck, back off! Buck, for the 1,113th time!

11:34 A.M. I had some more snowboarders in. They returned from their hike up the mountain ridge for their few runs down. "Several times, we left the major trail and made our own in the backwoods, where it falls right back down onto the highway. Then we hitched back to the resort and did it again and again." They were my son's age, and I was worried about these guys. "It's a big gamble way back there in no-man's land. If you get hurt, you're on your own, and who's to be the wiser? Plus, all of those tree-wells!" Blank stares.

Mountain Peak Ski Resort had twenty-five inches today. They needed thirty-three inches to open. More storms coming! Way – To – Go!

What do ya know...Cowboy rang. Wanted to know if the pass was closed, although he mentioned just getting off the traffic cam up there. Bullshitter! Why in the hell was I still talking to the cheating bastard? Cuz... He would be by later on his way to his "spread." Or, maybe only as far as Soap Lake, to take another swing at the party-girl. Was I going to keep doing this shit to myself?

4:55 P.M. He called again, "Hi there, Missy. Save me a couple of shots of espresso, will ya? I'll be by in an hour or so." Sure, Cowboy, but my doors will be bolted.

5:40 P.M. It is now or never, little girl. Can't anyone around here take a firm stand? I decided to stand the Cowboy-Husband up! He was expected any minute. It was pitch dark outside, no customers, so I closed down all of my signs. Just as I got back inside, I saw his truck pull in. I made it to the back of the gift shop in a crablike crouch. I wanted to roll on the ground laughing – until I realized if I really let go, I would be rolling on the rug, bawling. He was slowly driving back and forth in the parking lot. This married man needed an education on the word NO. You can go fondle your Soap Lake lassie now and stop including me on your list of quick stops!

8:21 P.M. TV, thinking, and just *maybe* some sleep...

11-05 34° Raining.

Buttered Hazelnut Breve: My original! A shot of buttered rum and hazelnut syrups, dash of salt, espresso shots, steamed Half & Half.

7:51 A.M. Fuck. Both of my Porta Potty huts were knocked over last night by some rotten ass (es). My dog didn't bark, which meant they laid them down very softly – but how? How many guys would this take? It was not a lightweight job by any means. Revenge – it is such a sweet word... I was surveying the damage when my darling couple that took the honeymoon before the wedding pulled up. We three got them upright. Then we tried to envision the damage there *could* have been if these huts weren't sucked dry just yesterday. The airborne damage would have polluted one square block! I had been considering getting some night vision cameras installed. Confirmed! But first I would invest in a paint-ball gun to pummel the maniacs – if there *was* a next time. Glow-in-the-dark-bad-boys. Yes!

Buck came by and I asked him to screw them onto the 4 x 4 fence posts. Yadda Yadda Yadda– "I'd like to screw something..." "Ya, Buck – here's the screw *gun* – now hit it!"

Report: Twenty-seven inches of snow at the pass. Last year broke all records for *no* snow. This year already broke records for early openings. Next weekend would be my first "rush" in a long, long time. I always got the jitters right before a busy weekend began!

2:52 P.M. Mr. and Mrs. Periwinkle Luggage stopped. They were both ranting again about the rotten teen at home. I expected her periwinkle attire as before, but she had added to her collection – a shocking purple and midnight blue patent-leather backpack, with chartreuse cording, for God sakes. The birds squawked. So *that is* why she was here – she wasn't thirsty at all! She twirled around a couple of times like a model on the catwalk, took her drink, and was gone.

People from all the cities "down-below" took a drive, just to *see* the snow. "It's no mirage, folks!" Sledding and snow hiking going on too. Festive start this year – made for great moods.

Jack and Pete popped in for a mere forty-five minutes on a weekend! Too long! Waaaaay too long! They listened to the sheriff grilling me for facts on the Porta Potty *abuse*. They wide-eyed me when the sheriff informed me that I could not shoot people with paint balls. "Why not?" I whined. "They contain salt." Well, rats!

4:55 P.M. I am locked. Dusk comes early as hell these days.

Buck dropped off his anniversary rose today. He forgot about my tires and my safety. He was now offering $1,000 for a thirty-minute session. He *actually* said, "I can't believe you! You are making a big mistake. All that money!" Too bad, cuz that would re-roof my garage. Whores must have real deep treaded tires and snazzy roofs that don't leak…

I sent a 'Fuck Off' email to Cowboy: "Please stop this shit right now. Do not contact me anymore or I am going to forward all our emails to your wife. And do not you worry that *big head* of yours, I'll be sweet as pie when I ask her to get you the hell off me!" Exact words. I was beginning to hate him – because I was so *crazy* about him! *Starts at a glance and ends in the truth.*

Lots of steamed milk flowed today! The most interesting drink was a chai eggnog. The most interesting customer's name was Kezia. I only had one couple in who were clueless about espresso. They were visiting from Pennsylvania. Never had one before and loved it.

A guy just backed into my fence and punctured two holes through one of my leased signboards. He wanted to pay me $30 but I did not have the heart to take it since my board will eventually be covered with someone's professional sign. He bought $9.92 worth of lattes. "Hey, thanks. And thanks for being honest about the collision."

I think I will maybe look up No. 2 on the net, just for shits and giggles. Heck, if you don't live life on the edge, you're taking up too much room!

6:56 P.M. Closed. Done. Finished…

11-06 32° Light rain.

Irish Breve: 1.5 shots of Irish cream liqueur, a shot of vanilla and white chocolate syrups, espresso shots, steamed Half & Half.

8:27 A.M. As I came downstairs into the yard this morning, I noticed a hint of white in the dog's run. No, it was not a strange form of mold - it was snow! It was just a blush – but it had tried last night. I had to sweep off my walkways – would salt later. Nobody was gonna fall on my dime! Porta Potties still upright.

Then, as I was vacuuming the store, I found bits of mice poison lying about. I was flying around the store like a crazy woman checking my rat-glue-pads. Found Ben! Reincarnated? Nope. Unfortunately, he was still alive! He was staring at his savior. Oh God! Shit, shit, shit! I grabbed some newspaper and picked up a bitsy corner of the glue pad and ran this wiggling rat out to the trashcan. A few moments later guilt overwhelmed me. I started thinking of my own destiny…how would I like to be put, half alive, into a disgusting dumpster? Butts, garbage, used diapers, repulsive female products, and stale everything plus, a slow, torturous death! NO! I must shorten Ben's life! I personally have never handled the physical suffering thing very well. Death, okay…but make it damn quick! I had to make this a fast euthanasia – with the least number of nightmares tonight.

I read somewhere that drowning is the best way to go, so I filled a bucket of water from my espresso cart and headed back out in the rain and dug Ben out of the trash. He was craning a left eyeball at me! Fucking shit! I dipped Ben and the pad into the bucket; he struggled to keep his head above the water line.

I held him down, glancing every ten seconds or so to see if it was *over*. Twice at least, I inadvertently came forth with those horrified, heartfelt, comic-book noises, "AIEEEEE!" and "EEEARGH!" Oh, God! I was *counseling* myself, out loud, *in* the parking lot, *in* the pouring rain. The paddy wagon will be here any minute, I am sure of it!

No wonder rats *flourished* in sewer drains in New York for so long - it took a good 1.36 minutes to kill the little sucker! I laid him to rest back inside the trashcan. I needed a drink! When I signed up for this barista career, I didn't quite expect it to involve mayhem, asphyxiation, and *death*. More glue pads were on my shopping list... Back to business!

Squillene Pass had another rockslide, and the interstate was closed again! This situation threw scads of business my way – on a silver platter. This time no one was killed in the crash so I could be grateful – out loud! I should be slammed this weekend. Breaking News: All traffic headed to eastern Washington should consider alternate routes – like Mountain Peak Highway! God...I love TV!

1:59 P.M. Ms. Gossip No. 2 was at the drive-thru with her mouth just a'goin.' "I am SO totally pissed off at my husband that I want a divorce, now! Oh, yeah... German chocolate cake mocha, please. He ignores me half-the-time and can't get enuf' of the rest. I am starting to feel like a pin-cushion!" I told her that I planned to be alone for life; I couldn't live with nonchalance physically, mentally or sexually. So, it was settled! She had a good one: "We spend all this time and energy trying to impress them with cleaning, cooking, make-up, keeping the kids out of their way, and buying new lingerie. They do nothing to try and impress us but fart in bed and ignore nose hairs!" True, my dear...so true. I told her that both my mother and I had these dream men walk into our lives recently, both cowboys. Mine was married and hers came with a huge, yellow, CAUTION sign on his chest – placed there by a reliable source. We've both decided: "Applicants Need Not Apply!"

Occasionally I thought about our grandmothers, and even some of our mothers. They gave up their names for their husbands, took off their veils, went into the home, and were practically never heard from again... Gave me the creeps!

I needed this next visitor like a finger splinter. Wow just hang around **OUTPOST ESPRESSO** and you'll get an education you don't particularly need! A fellow came in that I grew up with, from grade school through high school. He was from one of the infamous, rich Italian families of Bellevue. He was getting divorced after 18 years of bliss and was really *ripped-up* over it. He was *so* sad, that within 7-1/2 minutes he came out with, "*We* could be a match-made-in-heaven! I love it up here in the sticks! I could move in and help you run your business!" I was completely flabbergasted, but did manage to sarcastically stumble out with, "My dream come true, how special!" I don't even *know* what to say anymore! If I lived to be 102, I would never understand men…

Our highway was crammed with cars. Thousands who didn't bother listening to the news had been turned back on the other pass! I was quickly running out of supplies. A gal walked in, "Do you take debit cards?" "Yes." "Can you do it if I don't have the card with me, but know all the numbers?" "Nope, it's against the law." "Starbucks always, always does it for me." "Really? Well, that'll be a new item for the history books after they read this!"

A little boy came in with his dad. Dad needed a caffeine hit – son needed a candy bar. Dad got his; the little boy was out of luck. So, he diverted his attention to a sign he doesn't understand. It read: 'Husband For Sale.' "Daddy, what *is* a husband?" His frowning daddy said, "I'm mommy's husband." The boy still looks puzzled. I offered, "A daddy is a husband." Ohhhhh. Now this little tyke thought the sign was *really* funny and showed it to his dad. Dad's furrow deepened and now *he* was acting like *he* didn't understand it either. No humor in this adult!

Cowboy called to ask why he was stuck in bumper to bumper near Icicle Town. The jerk… He thought *traffic* was irritating…wait until he got home and digested the threatening email. A picture would instantly flash through his mind - his wife sitting in a beautiful leather- 'n-glass attorney's office.

7:47 P.M. Cowboy zipped in. He didn't even need espresso but got out of the ugly traffic line to see me. Cowboy, with hat atop the handsome head, looked straight out of a Western GQ. Only a fucker to me but to the rest of the world, he was one handsome dude (tall, tan, rugged, with bright blue eyes and a brilliant white smile). I was short and rude. The mercy killing went quick. I closed and he left. Then I re-opened the drive-thru because the cars were at a standstill! Great diversion for my mental state! People *poured* in for espresso, begging for "spirits!" Everyone's nerves were fried. Only drive thru now.

An older couple stopped in a Porsche and I unlocked and let them step inside. They were from Australia and admired my birds. We chatted over hot chocolates as they told me about the hundreds of cockatoos that were everywhere down-under and were considered pests. Peanut farmers shot them on sight trying to save their crops. Even the rose breasted. I couldn't imagine shooting an 'Angel', but then again, I never thought I could drown a 'Ben' either.

9:40 P.M. Properly calmed down now and hoping for a serene night's sleep… G'day mates…

11-07 34° Rain.

Jig Dessert Latte: 2 shots of whiskey, a 4-second sugar pour, splash of vanilla and coconut syrups, espresso shots, steamed Half & Half.

6:02 A.M. I was *open* before the birds were even *up* today. All this unexpected business this time of year was like a Christmas present. That goes for *all* the businesses up here. The pass on I-80 was still closed.

Mountain Peak Ski Resort had forty inches! Skiing opens in 48 hours! 26,000 more cars a day while this rockslide lasts.

Cowboy has read the email by now and is gone! Mixed feelings. Get-A-Grip!

MOUNTAIN PEAK SKI RESORT HISTORY
Sixty-five years ago, Lonny Kimble and Thom Stevenson took a Ford V-8 engine, some wheels and rope, and they created their passion, Mountain Peak Ski Resort. It started as a humble ski lift; it is now one of our Northwest's prime resorts, offering 10 lifts, over 1,125 acres of skiing terrain, 37 groomed runs and 3-day lodging. It is in the Cascade Range. Temperatures

are usually in the 20's. Elevation is 5,061' with a ski peak as high as 6,845' and 1,800 vertical feet on three sides, of two different mountain ranges. Mountain Peak is operated under a permit granted by the USDA Forest Service.

11:54 A.M: Scanner: DOT was requesting that semi-trucks chain-up. Cars with studs would be allowed to continue.

12:04 P.M. A lady stopped for her, "First eggnog latte of the season," and smiled all the way back to the car.

The Senior Cowboy Rocky stopped again to coax more information out of me about my mother. She is NOT going to go out with you! She has been warned. You are a stunning devil for your age! The last warning thrown mom's way, and from his next-door neighbor, "You can't even *invent* how bad he is!" God, who had he killed? What disease did he have? How many unsuspecting gals had he swindled?

2:30 P.M. I ended up leaving – I didn't have a *crumb* of *anything* left!

9:48 P.M. I am back from the hellacious drive. With this abnormal traffic, I was not able to get to Pacifica, where the prices and selection were much better. I also did not have the time to drop off more unwanted clothes at BOO's new home, The Mission. He would recognize this Jeep and it would be neat if he would approach me. *Still* never met him or even seen him from afar. Maybe next trip.

That daffy BMW Brian, of all people, emailed me. I am not responding! He is a negative wimp.

10:42 P.M. I am pooped after schlepping at least 700 pounds of supplies...

11-08 33° Light rain.

Island Palms: 2 tbs. brown sugar, splash of each of these: cinnamon, pineapple, mango and kiwi syrups, espresso shots, steamed milk.

7:46 A.M. Today was much quieter. Squillene Pass has re-opened, rats. How in the world did they get the boulders to vanish that quickly? The only highway crews that I have ever seen in my whole life were yellow-vested men, leaning on the side of the road with a coffee cup in one hand and carrying a fluorescent orange stick in the other. Which chain gang did they import? Oh well, so far it's only one lane each way. Common remaining masses of mineral and ore will start bowling again hopefully.

Forty-one inches of crystal white frostbite awaits the anxious skiers – the resort opens in *exactly* 24 hours! Employees were popping in, excited about their new jobs. Even a janitorial job up there was something to be cherished. The guys in the blue uniforms got a free season pass too. Swab a few urinals and hit the slopes!

Harley Dennis just toot-tooted from his eastbound train.

Ms. Gossip No. 2 came by and I was expecting to be the witness on the divorce papers. Instead, she is going to ask her alter ego for a wedding ring. They had been married ten years and her hand was still bare. He had been shrugging in disrespect for at least nine of these years anyway. Here they were, right in the middle of World War "D" and he tried to slip through the crack in the back door with a his personal brand new pair of $800 skis! And she was one of my customers who tanked up on a Java "Tab". Point off the male column! Almost two! He only opened the wallet and let the moths loose on self-indulgence. *My* opinion, "When he leaves the house, nail those damn skis crisscross fashion up on the peak of your house. Tell him you read in Country Living Magazine that it's the very newest 'Cabin Décor.'"

12:10 P.M. Mrs. Periwinkle Luggage stopped so I could meet her mom. They bought single mochas and some road food. Her mom didn't dress in the renowned bluish/lavender, but she looked like she just dove headfirst into a huge lemon meringue pie! Her white hair was the meringue – every other square inch was the shocking lemon filler. I was dying to see their homes!

4:20 P.M. It is slow. At least Buck visited. I gave him a free white mocha since I would need him real soon to get my generator started. That very first *rope-pull* of the season was always such an arm mutilator.

I had worn parts of the same outfit for four days and maybe shampooed that long ago. I just don't care and it was so darn cold in the mornings. My house was whatever the temperature was outside at 6:00 A.M.! I could French braid the hair on my legs.

7:00 P.M. Will this skiing business really happen tomorrow? It's like being five years old again and trying to sleep on Christmas Eve…

11-09 35° Overcast.

Instant Cappuccino: Mix 1 cup powdered milk, 1 cup powdered chocolate, 2/3 cup instant espresso powder, 1 cup sugar, a tsp. cinnamon and nutmeg. When serving, use 1 heaping tbs. of this powdered mix to each cup of hot water.

7:32 A.M. Cars with skiers, snowboards, skis and poles were racing each other up to the mountain. Unbelievably, no wrecks yet! Mountain Peak Ski Resort had forty-two inches of beautiful, soft, fluffy snow. SKIING IS OPEN! Red-Letter-Day! First time this early in thirty-eight years! I should make up a banner quick: My Potent Caffeine Will Guarantee First Position On The Highway!

Sounded like Hunk Wyatt's court case tied his hands a little tighter than he had hoped for. Not only was he dealing with a divorce with "Sugar Bitch," but now he had gotten himself a DUI! His stepdad came in and filled me in. What a loser! They sure don't fiddle around with DUI's in this state! Not a fun program.

8:00 A.M. – 4:00 P.M. A blur. It is like saying; "I made fun-hundred espressos today and took 5,760 breaths in that same period of time." Who cares? All I know is a girl can go eight hours and not pee a drop – if she doesn't have the chance!

4:01 P.M. My first drive thru was some worn-out skiers and they *needed* 20-ounce mochas. Turtlenecks were back in fashion. So was exhaustion. "The first time up each year is so debilitating." We laughed, they asked for a punch card, and each person gave me a $2 tip. We were back in business! *God*, this is fun!

6:10 P.M. More skiers stopped but nothing compared to weekends. Come-ooooon Friday…

11-10 42° Rain.

Iranian Latte: A shot of walnut syrup, a shot of pomegranate and lemon syrups, espresso shots, steamed Half & Half.

8:00 A.M. A tad bit of rain at the ski resort. But no worries, unless the weatherman was daydreaming again, we were supposed to get a fresh foot of flakes before the weekend.

10:42 A.M. Scanner: A driver of a vehicle experiencing chest pain on Mountain Peak Highway.

Our medics were rendezvousing with the hospital medics. This *was* an emergency! They usually met them halfway to speed up the process.

Buck came by all spiffed-up. He offered to put some pressure on my aching lower back if I would walk on his for a minute. Now *that* was a fair trade. We adjusted each other's backs. I owed him for favors anyway and gave him that promised haircut. That crusty ole logger left here actually looking rather presentable.

Another local guy stopped, after taking a brisk ski session and leased one of my sign spaces. He wanted the #3 sign *location* for his banner that was already punctured with holes. Great!

No. 7 called and may visit on Sunday. I will be too slammed on that day, so I'll cancel later. He learned how to work these machines damn well, in that split second between the marriage license and the divorce decree.

1:05 P.M. I slipped out and drove "down-below." I hadn't heard the 4:30 A.M. scanner call, but as I rolled down the highway, I noticed someone, or something repainted the middle of the highway in a couple of places. Sure enough, through the grapevine gossip at the P.O., this was pretty darn 24-carat, confirmed two accidents. The first was a head-on that involved one of our local youths. She grabbed an angel's wing this time only had a broken foot and facial lacerations. The driver of the other vehicle, a truck, had to be airlifted. An older female driver with chest pains caused the second artwork. In her panic, the car went head-over-teakettle. No info yet…

3:13 P.M. My distant cousin from Roslyn, Washington just called! She is seventy-five years old and a pistol! She gave me more names of relations to look up around here. Lost kinfolk… These were the tough miners in the family, who lived like rats down shafts most of their lives. "Christy, the Hollywood cast and crew of Northern Exposure were offerin' huge rewards to anyone successful in getting me to move to Siberia! I coulda cared less about their flippin' filmin'. When I needed to go ta town, I went, no matter what camera was rollin', the bastards."

5:25 P.M. I'm done, finished and bushed…

11-11 35° Overcast. Veterans Day.

Blended Cheese Parfait Latte: Mix in blender: 1 cup ice, 2 ounces cream cheese, 4-second sugar pour, 2 inches Half & Half, splash of blueberry, raspberry, and lemon Syrups, 2 espresso shots and blend. Whip.

9:00 A.M. A slim chance of getting snow tonight. My plow truck was parked in its winter space, ready to scrape and shove, lift, haul, and dump. Hundreds of cars were passing to get some skiing in. Hurry back, you all, for a fix!

The mother of our recent head-on victim came by for her 24-ounce iced cherry mocha. She told me that her daughter's airbag saved her. The guy in the truck was at fault. Ma was still shaking!

A car full of ladies pulled up, right smack dab in the middle of the drive thru. They were just sitting there *not* honking. This was very foreign indeed, so I stuck my head out and asked what they needed. One of them needed to use the bathroom, one couldn't find her hairbrush, and they were switching drivers. Why do people love to park in drive thrus to handle their personal needs? You would think they were in a grand, glamorous hotel valet entrance in Vegas! They were older gals, on their first trip to our casino in a year and a half, cutting-up and cackling like jackals. I decided not to ruin their day. Normally, I would turn on the bitch-mouth-switch and tell them to haul their fannies outta here and make room for paying customers!

One of my yearly skiers came in for his cappuccino. He was a commercial developer and worked all over the West, from the mountains to Puget Sound, to the Arizona desert. He was telling me how Washington wasn't even recognizable these days. He equipped his rig with the three necessities: skis, golf clubs, and a change of clothes in case he passed a winery to tour. Was this state becoming California or what?

1:11 P.M. Scanner: Medic response at Mountain Peak Ski Resort. A forty-year-old male with a head injury. He was still on the hill and delirious.

1:20 P.M. Scanner: Shoulder injury at Mountain Peak aid room.

Car accidents and skiing injuries. Welcome to Winter Wonderland at the Resort!

2:07 P.M. Buck stopped in to visit. I *threw* his espresso at him and ran upstairs to pee while he guarded the fort! I forget that seeing the inside of a toilet in broad daylight, a rare opportunity, was a seasonal luxury.

No. 7 called *just* to see if I was busy. Fuck yes – *you* must *not* be! I slammed the phone down.

2:22 P.M. Scanner: A fourteen-year-old male with a fractured jaw and facial injuries up at the resort. The third aid call and it was only two o'clock in the afternoon.

I just sold $100 worth of flamingo *crap* to a couple that was playing a prank on their neighbor. "Oh, and don't forget the bright green plastic slime frog!"

Local Newsflash: Mr. Hunk Wyatt was behind bars. His DUI caught up with him and he also may have manhandled a gal at our local bar. Would you say it just may possibly, perchance, conceivably be time for him to take the cure? Bad, bad boy – incredible toy.

The Manning Mountain view from my cubicle looked like a big vanilla sundae smothered in freshly blended whipping cream. All the cars driving down had white roofs. Keep it up, one flake in front of the other…

5:20 P.M. Scanner: Two semis were sideways and blocking both right lanes up at the pass.

I was feeling broken down and starved. I had my nervous "new season" stomachache earlier and had not eaten much. I will pork tonight.

5:34 P.M. My first broken down car for the winter. Two young Seattle boys with pierced ears and numerous tattoos were so polite, I even gave some free espresso and kindness. This response from me when you were blocking my store was a rare phenomenon indeed! The engine was the least of their worries – they were missing out on their passion - snowboarding.

7:54 P.M. I am closed and too dog-tired to tuck these guys in. I gave them some water and brownies and headed upstairs as they layered clothing and worried about freezing to death, waiting for their tow.

8:55 P.M. Today was *hell* busy - and I am thankful for it…

11-12 37° Some rain.

French Toast Breakfast Latte: A shot of each: cinnamon, nutmeg, and butter rum syrups, espresso shots, steamed whole milk.

7:45 A.M. I think I was risking frostbite to open this early – and not one customer in thirty minutes. So why do I put myself through this torture? Because I am a greedy rascal... I've got to remember, early in the morning, the skiers are far too eager to get on the hill before the parking lots fill. These are actually "winter stats" but it's been two years since a snow-memory mattered.

8:55 A.M. My first paying customer. Come on, you sheep, follow suit! There was an SUV parked about 150 feet from the Porta Potty. The wife jumped out of the car and ran through the rain to relieve herself in the "plastic hut." The husband did not even drive their warm and cozy car any closer to pick her up. Hell no – let her run back through another 150-feet of rain. I should deduct a point off for that one, guys. I see this all the time! Why are people (couples) so impolite to *each other*? Friends wouldn't do that. Enemies wouldn't let you get away with it! I'm NEVER getting married!

My daughter called to ask if I would consider going out with her ex-neighbor, that is, if he asked... I told her that I was not interested and was not dating these days anyway. Then she was laughing hysterically and finally fesses up, "Mom, he is the guy who had the sex swing hanging from a beam in his house." "A what?!?!?" Forget it... I didn't even want to know what the hell that was! Date him? I don't even want his twisted perverted hands touching my doorknobs!

11:39 A.M. Scanner: A hip dislocation at the resort. OOCH!

A man came in and bought a 20-ounce triple Americano, got to chatting, and inadvertently left without it. No sense in keeping this on the back burner, though. At 65 mph, he will be much too far away when he absently reaches for the cup holder. Upset? Most likely!

11:55 A.M. Buck popped in to talk bullshit and handed me a love note, written on a piece of corrugated brown cardboard this time, about 3" x 3". It looked like he wrote it with a dirt-clod – couldn't read it, chucked it.

1:27 P.M. Scanner: CPR in progress in the middle parking lot at Mountain Peak Ski Resort. Cardiac arrest.

It was a twenty-one-year-old male who may have recently had some heart surgery. Luckily, our volunteer ambulance was already on the scene, attending to the hip injury. Drugs for the hip – let us tend to the heart! Two more "real" medics were hurrying from "down-below." They had a unit from the east side of the mountains coming too. Twenty minutes later, the medics arrived to the DOA. How totally tragic! Our sheriff was on his way now.

1:48 P.M. Scanner: A fourteen-year-old male with a possible concussion. He was unconscious for just a little while and now conscious and speaking. More medics heading east. WHEW, what a day! Helmets, anyone?

2:00 P.M. Scanner: Twenty-seven-year-old female with a humerus bone fracture. They may call an airlift. A fucked day in paradise!

3:52 P.M. Harley Dennis called to talk about his Naval Reserve weekend and driving his choo-choo train. Andrew called to wish me another busy day and lots of sales.

Otherwise, I will just sit here tonight, unsocial as usual in this non-cherished reclusive state. I cannot seem to learn how to filter out men's bullshit.

Today was one of those "off" days. I dropped glassware, which splinters from here to eternity, my cart's refrigerator was unorganized, and liquids were oozing out every damn time I opened the door. I forgot drink orders, like some ditzy waitress in a crummy restaurant where they were lucky to have convinced her to even *work* in the armpit, and I combined a couple cash register rings. Wouldn't it be sweet if the automatic 'coup de grace' for a shitty day was a backrub! Dream on…

4:55 P.M. A family stopped in close to dark and one of them let out the worst fart. Stunk up the whole place and then a diesel pulled up in the drive thru, finished off our suffocation! Stink in stereo! Everyone ran – I couldn't. Candles are lit!

Denny next door called for the scanner news of the day. After I updated him with all *that* info and a rendition of my day, he made a major decision: "I'm selling my boob-tube, Christy. You are much more exciting and interesting than any television channel!"

It was a horrific day at the pass. The medics, ambulances, and sheriff were probably into very tiring overtime.

9:00 P.M. Shit, I forgot. I didn't even have any fun junk food to pork-out on tonight. Popcorn would have to do. Except I wanted shrimp and pigskin twists, for some reason.

10:03 PM. ZZZZZZ...

11-13 33° Raining.

Canadian Custard Latte: A shot of real maple syrup, a shot of French vanilla syrup, shot of pasteurized beaten egg, espresso shots, steamed milk.

7:58 A.M. It must be snowing a ton at the summit. Skiers were doing their usual 80 mph on a gusty Mountain Peak Highway. No wonder they didn't stop here – they didn't even *see* me! Also, a lot of traffic would be heading home on this highway following the three-day weekend.

8:26 A.M. Scanner: Head injury at Mountain Peak aid room. A forty-seven-year-old female.

Rosie walked up to visit! Her daughter came in and it was so good to see her. I gave her a hot chocolate and mom her favorite, a 24-ounce iced mocha with whip. I also gave her daughter a fish-shaped bead to add to her collection. Any eight-year-old who can hang onto four tiny beads and not lose them deserves another one, every visit!

Semi truckers hate me, and I hate them! I don't need or want their business here. They take up my whole parking lot, block my store, and then they go postal on me when I don't want to chat for an hour. All that for a couple of bucks? No thanks. Plus, three of my exes are truckers, so screw 'em all!

4:47 P.M. Everyone seems to know about my Porta Potties and will trudge in sleet and snow for relief – and won't walk a few steps in the weather to get drinks. What's up with that? Idea for a new sign: To-Sit- 'n-Shit-Get-The-Key-From-The-Friendly-Barista-After-You-Order. Helluva idea!

NO males today except for Buck, and he did not count. Nice talk, Christy! I need to devise a serious neck massage machine that has fingers that squeeze. I don't care if its battery, plug-in or candle powered!

A couple just drove up for drinks. They had two boys in the back seat, and they ordered hot chocolate drinks for them and a breve for dad. I made the drinks, and then Dippy-Dad said that the boys wanted *cold* chocolate milk. Then the wife decided she wanted a latte. I wanted to chuck the hot chocolates into their front seats but refrained. I made the wife's latte. She did not want yellow *fake sugars*, she wanted pink. "I don't have pink, lady, it's yellow or real or raw." Then they decided they needed chips. They asked what color I had. *Now* they are askin' for it! I recited every single one of the damn colors…and clearly. Suddenly, they couldn't live without green, which was Sour Cream & Onion. "I don't have green – didn't mention it." They wanted me to recite all the colors again. No way, José. "I have *most* colors." They wanted a blue one and a red one. Keep in mind; these were *adults* playing this mind game! I grabbed the blue (Ranch Doritos) and the red (Cheese Doritos). They took the yellow sugar, the latte, the breve, the red chips, the blue chips, and their cold milks without the fucking whipped cream. "You had your chance!" I took their money and tried to smile as I gnashed out a thank you.

5:13 P.M. I'm done in. I will give it until 6:00 P.M. A phone call to someone should make the time go, or a nice customer or two. What am I gonna do tonight? Sometimes it is tempting to have Buck over, keeping all clothes on and just snuggle. The problem is, clothes *don't* stay on, so you're *not* going there, girl. Speak of the devil. Buck just pulled up and handed me a big bowl of his mama's homemade spaghetti. Thanks.

5:49 P.M. Can I please close now…?

11-14 33° Clear!

Caramel Beads: My original! A shot of sugar and corn syrup, dash of salt, a shot of chocolate syrup, splash of French vanilla syrup, Espresso shots, steamed Half & Half.

8:03 A.M My brother called to invite me to Thanksgiving, but I work all holidays now. It is a blast and customers are so thankful the whole retail world is not all sealed up like a mummy case. The stories are usually pretty emotional too – some great laughs, some sad cries.

One year a lady came in for an espresso while her family stayed in the van. I *hurriedly* served my other customer because she was bawling, "We had Thanksgiving in Icicle Town! I planned and saved for four months and the kids ended up with the stomach flu. I was so hoping for a Thomas Kincaid storybook holiday." She cried and cried over her latte, while the stranger and I listened and shifted, uncomfortably. Just as abruptly, she dried off, smoothed her dress, and left. My male customer roared, "I'm NEVER getting married!" "My sentiments exactly – and I bet on that seven times an hour…"

1:17 P.M. Scanner: Aid response to a sixty-five-year-old local with liver problems. They were taking him "down-below" to the hospital, an hour away.

2:00 P.M. Slow today and my mind wandered. The Misgivings of Marriage: What is it, this elusive miracle we figure the Union of Marriage will bring to our lives? This portrait we create in our minds. My portrait? His portrait? Let us look deep into this for a moment, especially for those of us who have had multiple trials and errors.

First: The White Picket Fence Theory.

Frankly, it should only take one marriage to figure out that brute strength is needed to dig the postholes. Then, who gets the job of hammering the 1,552 nails into the picket boards? And finally, do we paint the pickets white before or after constructing? If we were to paint the fence white, does that mean the windowpanes, moldings, gutters, dogs, and cars must be white too? Does this hubby-to-be even give a damn what color our fence is? We go off to the hardware store together, hand in hand, not realizing that there are seventy-four different whites. This is the precise moment we experience our first argument. The fence does not get finished and we end up with a weed-patch border instead. Our weeds overflow into the neighbor's yard and mingle with theirs because they are in the same predicament. Mutual décor decisions are no more than wistful delusions. Should we have erected our fence before marriage, when the bloom was fresh, or is the fence the beginning to our end? The spouses who stay together must have agreed to disagree overall, on this enclosure thing – or most everything, for that matter. Because I do see couples remaining coupled, through numerous World Wars. Maybe these couples never had portraits in the first place – my personal plague – my expectations. I did this seven times. Maybe some of you can relate…maybe some of you have the answer. I know I don't.

SYNOPSIS:

No. 1. He and I were thrashing around in his pickup, slapping each other and yelling obscenities, when he popped the question. What? I thought he hated me. But I decided he must have only been frustrated with the fact that he loved me too much. I screamed yes and experienced exhilarating dysfunction.

No. 2. I contacted my high school sweetie after my first failure. He flew out to visit for five days of togetherness. Sexual bliss and, yes, we still had our magic! He popped the question and in fourteen days we stepped into exhilarating dysfunction.

No. 3. Motorcycle rides wound through sand and palm trees, along ocean shores. Hot summer nights that *felt* perfect. With ninety days of perfection under our belts, we trusted our exhilarating dysfunction.

No. 4. Wine and no roses. Pills and still no roses. Sixty days of heaven and hell and he popped the question. Within twenty-four hours we stumbled into exhilarating dysfunction.

No. 5. He had the youth, and I had the knowledge. I will *make* this one right since I have control. The blind leading the ultra-sightless. Ninety days of fireworks and he was exhilarated beyond his wildest dreams. He popped the question and I *unknowingly* guided us into another case of exhilarating dysfunction.

No. 6. By coincidence, I whispered the *perfect* words into his ear. He bent over the edge of the bed and reached for a piece of paper. He had written these exact words down, many months earlier. I was *his* perfect portrait. He popped the question during heightened sex. Of course, I accepted! I was now validated! Finding a minute between our extreme physical abuses, we married and began our bumpy road along bloody attacks. These highs and lows became our very own exhilarating dysfunction.

No. 7. He embraced me against his gold badge. The badge of my savior. He was a cop, and my portrait was one of a brave and caring protector. The portrait I craved! A king at last, with a gold crown on his chest. He WOULD build my fence! I just knew it! He promised white of all shades and we ran off in a hurry before even glancing at the pallets. He dug only three postholes and they filled up with rain. I no longer believed in exhilarating dysfunction.

I did this for a living? This whole game has become a wrestling match - a point-keeping scorecard. We are all so easily exhausted by the slightest inconvenience. Why are we all in such a hurry? Hurrying to climb the ladder of fame, get involved in relationships, have sex, get married, have kids, and hurry, hurry, hurry... And then (statistics) 65% of us get the hell out. Let's see if the *two* of us can build a white picket fence *together*. Let's see if we can *agree to disagree* on the color, the height and the particular vine that will adorn our boundary marker – and still remain dedicated to *us*. It could be our first measurement of reality. Not the fog of exhilarating dysfunction.

PTSD causes some of us to run constantly from the fears of abandonment, more abuse, ourselves, the voices in our heads but "something" draws us back to this dysfunctional comfort. Top it off with OCD, where there is not a single human being that can withstand our expectations of perfection and our requirement that they will fulfill our lives 100%. Save us from everything.

Years of therapy give us hope but we rarely have the patience for the baby steps it demands, and we roll back down that mountain into the same overgrown ditch every time. Faith in our beliefs and our animals are sometimes our ticket to freedom from these chains. Hug yourselves...I just did.

4:41 P.M. Back to business. A couple came in and laid down $200 for gifts! *Sterling!* I had only had a dozen or so people in all day and I wanted to go for a drive. Maybe later...

5:00 P.M. No one ever accused me of not being able to decide – nineteen minutes later I was in my jeep and halfway down the mountain! Damn, I forgot my bank deposit. Hell with it! I drove straight to an AA meeting and in my mood it seemed befitting. Next stop was BOO's. I dropped off some unwanted shoes and clothes and took a quick tour through The Mission. The residents looked remarkably like lots of the folks at my AA meeting, except for all the tiny two-minute tour – seeing so many people this down-and-out, here in our beautiful, flourishing America. I got all my supplies and raced home, under a full moon with Mars shining just beneath.

10:11 P.M. It is now in the 20s outside. Goodnight. This emotional day, analyzing my marriages and yours and our portraits, has marooned me, fully drained…

11-15 31° Overcast.

Fruit Tart Latte: A shot of vanilla, a shot of real apple jelly, splash of strawberry syrup, espresso shots, steamed milk.

11:28 AM. I have only had four people. Two snowboarders, Ms. Gossip No. 2 for her free drink on a filled punch card, and Buck for his *usual* freebie.

11:30 A.M. Scanner: Car fire at our tow truck driver's home! One mile west of me and burning within ten feet of his house. I will get the scoop from Ms. Gossip No. 2 tomorrow.

Mr. Alaskan Sex Swing leapt from his trapeze and emailed: "I am back up north in the tempest and I do not know how soon I can visit your daughter. I want to give her the blow-by-blow of our meeting, but she is 35 miles away now. I miss her neighborly cute, little face and happy-go-lucky way. Nice to visit with you, Cathy. Let us do it again sometime – maybe up here? "Okay everyone, don't get nervous – I typed the below response, but I decided it was best not to hit Send: "First, loser, my name is Christy, and we didn't have a blow-by-blow. And don't hold your breath for a visit from me; you need all the oxygen you can get for your kinky exercises. I can just see it in the Anchorage News: 'Man Cascades to His Death from Some Sort Of Contraption!'

1:00 P.M. It is Generator Day. I couldn't keep ignoring this baffling task. Out to the barn, dragged this 157-lb. generator to the back forty, tipped it over, and drained all the old fuel, put new in and shined it up like a new toy. I was poised to solve this choke "thingy." How hard could it be? Ok…on & off switch – yank the chain. "BUUUUUUUUCK!"

Got a few stragglers. They were all incredibly happy skiers – lots of runs – no crowds.

Hunk Wyatt's stepdad came in confirming, "Hunk *is* in jail." I guess he had quite the stack of paperwork in his file; not one, but two DUI's on his *official* record. "He's not a drunk," his stepdad said for the umpteenth time. "Uh huh… For those of us who have lived through The Program, I'm sorry to strongly disagree. If alcohol is fucking you in the ass and threatening every aspect of your life, like bankruptcy, marriage, and your freedom…then you are a drunk." A guy at AA last night described the lifestyle of a drunkard as a life in a *spider hole*. Exactly!

Mrs. Periwinkle Luggage came in and we somehow got on the subject about cheating. Surprise, surprise! She had a girlfriend caught in a married man's labyrinth. He wouldn't leave his wife for financial reasons (Cowboy), and he had other mistresses besides her (Cowboy). It was rumored she wasn't even his first choice in the trio that pleasured him. Devastation, for four long years! "Where does he get his stamina?" I squawked. A point off both columns.

6:04 P.M. A skier walked in who remembered this place when it was a gas station. I told him that No. 1 husband and I lived here twenty-five years ago. He saw my ring. "Are you engaged to number two?" "Hmmmmm…what was that one's name…ummmmm…let's see…that was such a long, long time ago… Give me a minute." This guy's eyes were getting as big as last night's moon.

6:51 P.M. And so, it goes. Later…

11-16 35° Misty.

Cherry French Breve: 1/2 shot of cherry and French vanilla syrups, a splash of coconut, espresso shots, steamed Half & Half.

8:05 A.M. An uneventful day so far; one customer and its 10:02 A.M. I sure am glad that I am not one of those 4:30 A.M. baristas! I'd be curled up under the desk by now, coppin' some zzz's. My sleep is more important than some half-asleep trucker pulling through, expecting *me* to wake *him* up.

My first buyers were raspberry latte and raspberry mocha buyers. And gifts. "Love you – mean it!"

Buck came in professing his undying love. His phone rang. He flailed around with logging suspenders and pulled it out of a buttoned pocket. He casually glanced at it and popped it back in. Neither of us mentioned it. It rang again and he was uncomfortable now. He yanked it out and said, "Hello, hello, hello?" He slammed it shut and mumbled something about reception, that it was just his boss, both times, and maybe he will try him back in a minute. I innocently asked, "Do we get better reception calling out than accepting incoming calls?" He looked at the floor, knowing full well where I was going with this and that he had been caught...bullshitting again! Maybe the rest of his baristas "down-the-line" had BB's for brains, but not this one. Some gal made these two calls and we both knew it! He slunk out the door...

1:09 P.M. Ms. Gossip No. 2 came by and sure enough, she had the full report on the scanner fire. It ended up *not* being a car fire at the tow guy's house after all. It was *her* car with steam rising. She was not forthcoming with what the hell *her* auto was doing in *his* driveway in the first place. Scuttlebutt about married Gossip No. 2? Now *that* would be a reverse! I will dig *deep* for this clarification...

I am going to an early birthday dinner at mom's tonight. Maybe steak? Even if we *did* have frozen beef up here, it would be a purplish-green-freezer-burned lump at the gas station. I would not *look* at it, much less touch it. Everything in their white box is disguised in ice – frozen and refrozen an unknown number of times. The rats were not the *only* ones who had *personal names* up here – the antique food did too! I cannot wait for the homemade treat!

A train with six engines just passed by. Ca-Chug, Ca-Chug. That was the maximum number of engines I had seen on that particular run – four was normal. Hi, Dennis!

3:03 P.M. Scanner: A local domestic happened in a secured sight where a twenty-two-year-old woman had glass cuts on her hands. Our medics arrived and were frantically waiting for the sheriff to get his butt up here. It takes forever for one to arrive. We are on our own up here – "This Is *Your* Life."

3:32 P.M. A heavily bearded, scraggly, runny-nosed creep slowly circled my whole parking lot, twice, then entered Treetops Loop. He thinks the coast-is-clear. Dream-on, deadwood - you just got famous! Your plate has been emailed to our sheriff, along with car type and color. I'm "Quick-Draw-McGraw." Those fucking druggies are not going to get away with anything if I can help it!

3:43 P.M. Scanner: A hand injury. Did the sheriff do his thing and bust some heads, or was this just *another* domestic? Isolated mountain living is so cultural – so nurturing – so enriching! NOT!

3:45 P.M. It is the night before I was born, some forty-ahem years ago. I *deserve* to blast-out of this pigeonhole…

11-17 31° Sunny.

Baked Breakfast Latte: My original! A shot of pasteurized beaten egg, 1 tbs. brown sugar, a shot of vanilla and pecan syrups, splash of real maple syrup, espresso shots, steamed half & Half.

6:00 A.M. Happy Birthday to Me!!!! Hope this is a *new* day with non-masculine experiences. Last night men drove me crazy! I went to dinner at moms. I was not even out-of-the-area when a male pickup truck driver who was torchin' up and lost control of the wheel ran me off the highway in Tillamuk. Then, Brent from Stonewall caught me out in front of my favorite pizza joint, "Just stockin' up on some delicious discs for the next week or so." "Forget it!" he said, "Come home with me for a great dinner. Just you and me and my skimpy chef apron." "Right-O!" He did not elabarate – his little daughter was in the back seat. He desperately needs to have another session with the married nanny. "Calm down, horn-dog!" and I was off…

Then, I passed Buck and he about careened-off-the-cliff, wondering where I was going at *this* early hour. Tomorrow I will just shyly smile during the grilling. He will set an alarm to fall out of his bunk by 8:00 A.M. for *this* answer...

This morning, bright and early, a couple of tourists came in. The first "mouth" was ill advised. "Why don't you have a name tag on so I can tease you by name – and where is your cute little green Starbucks apron?" I spit, "You will know my name *if* and *when* I want you to – and secondly, this ain't one of the big 'S' corporation locations. I am the owner, and now *I'll* consider waiting on *you*." I laughed and then he risked a guffaw too... What is with the apron lingo lately? As they left, I snorted, "My kids and husbands are gone and so are my aprons!" His friend piped up, "Any man who expects a woman to wear one should be shot." Now, *he's* talking in my language! Come on back!

8:29 A.M. Right on schedule! Buck flushed in. "Too much exertion this early? Or ya got something on your mind?" "Ya, Chris, where ya goin' yestadee so early? Ya never leave mid-day. Whatcha need? Can I help?" He could only do this soft-shoe for so long... "What's his damn name? Hope *The-Nasty* was worth it, cuz I'm over ya!" Silence and only that cunning smile I promised. He about broke the hinges, slamming the door *this* time.

I was waiting to see which, if any, of my exes, male friends, and wannna be's would remember it was my birthday. My brother was my first call. "Thanks, honey!"

Business was good – soy lattes, lots of mochas, some hot chocolates and lots of considered lacking-pizzazz to most, Americanos. This was way cool!

10:57 A.M. Scanner: Twenty-four-year-old male with an ankle fracture. He was still on the ski slope and being transported down.

A guy just in for an Americano with buckets of sugar and a half-gallon of cream added. He claimed there were not any bare spots on the slopes.

1:30 P.M. And then business hit the proverbial brick-wall! I am going to give myself a BD present and take a ride to the eastside of the summit. Bye-Bye-4-Awhile.

8:00 P.M. The drive was mesmerizing with the brilliant sun against the glowing snow. Dark green trees, dipped in white, dotted the hillsides. I drove slowly through the fifty-mile trip to Icicle Town. First compulsory stop – the Candy Shoppe – for *my* almond clusters and English toffee.

I decided to drive to Ellensburg, where Hunk Wyatt had taken up residence in their jail. I called and visiting hours were from 6:30-8:30 P.M. I had never visited *anyone* in jail. Parked, walked gingerly in, pushed the big black button, and just stared at all the green steel. A voice boomed out of nowhere, asking me my business. "To visit a prisoner." "What is his full name?" I responded and stood nervously inside that gloomy, steel waiting area and it felt like a solid month before I got a reply. Finally, "You don't have an appointment. All the *spots* are filled up tonight." It seemed like the guards *enjoyed* this. For sure, they didn't give-a-shit! "How do we set up for visits?" "By mail." Fuck! "I tried, Wyatt!" I was going to continue on east of Ellensburg to see No. 5's new house, but the fog was thick and intimidating. I went to Sunbird and shopped a little before heading home.

9:30 P.M. Home and running for the answering machine. My kids, mom, gal friends, No. 5, followed by No. 7, but no groupies had all called for my fortieth-*ahem*-birthday.

11:00 P.M. End of a nice day…

11-18 28° Partly sunny.

Santa Fe Latte: A shot of powdered sugar, dash of nutmeg and salt, a shot of real maple syrup, espresso shots, steamed whole milk.

9:19 A.M. Brent from Stonewall came in still hoping for the apron service. He has given up on nanny, since she is still in wife/hubby mode. He asked me to go to Lake Roosevelt with him, just for a day ride. He said, "I know you'd be fun." Did he mean on the fender or under the shade of a tree? He's a *sack* kind of guy, so that's where he was going. He got a two-dollar mocha and I sat and listened to him wail about his just-out-of-reach ex-lay. It drove him crazy that she wouldn't trade her security package, husband and house, for more boy-toy. Point off both sides! Even though it tickled me to see this scenario in reverse…

Some Russians came in. "What can I get you guys?" One of them asked for a latte. The rest chimed in, "The same." I asked if they wanted sugar or flavor added. One said caramel, another said sugar, and the last guy said a caramel macchiato. I asked what size: 12, 16 or 20 ounces? One said 16 and the rest chimed in, "The same." Maybe I shouldn't have asked so many questions and just made them all the same. They would have accepted it just fine and never known the diff. I learn as I go…*seven years later*!

I was hoping for a busy weekend with I-80 still down to only two lanes. They planned on a thirty to forty-mile backup on Thanksgiving weekend. Oh God!

11:41 A.M. Scanner: A male had a fractured clavicle at the resort.

12:00 Noon. Today gifts were selling like mad and tons of espressos. 'Tis the season.

Andrew called and said that he was jealous that I had guys like Brent in to talk dirty to me. Was every man in this state a horn-dog and sex-starved? "Nothing to be jealous of, my friend – you can have them all if ya wanna – switch sides!" I could picture his grimace.

1:47 P.M. Mr. and Mrs. Periwinkle Luggage came in with *the* teenager. They surprisingly were all in good spirits. What is up?

Well, it *is* getting close to *THANKS*giving.

What a stressful evening! Nos. 5 and 7 called too many times. No. 3's wife called freaking out about my ex's drinking. My sister called frantic over her child's nosebleed, "Where do you put the cold rag?" Hell, if I knew, with four thirsty customers staring at me. "We just laid our kids down on their backs and told them to pinch their noses. And went about our business."

My son called, too, during all this commotion – from a bus. He had been kicked out of his dad's house. "Where do I go, mom?" Hell, if I know. I'm 1,200 miles away and you wouldn't listen anyway. He headed for his girlfriend's pad. What did I do? Fly him up? I'll deal with it all tomorrow.

4:00 P.M. I then got an email from a groupie, thanking me for his and his niece's lattes the other day, "And I just have to tell you that you are a beautiful woman." Not a fucking clue who was on that other end of the message. So that is what movie stars go through? *Strangers* worming out of woodwork. I am turning the world off.

A regular walked up to my drive thru and asked for two decaf lattes. She had her one-year-old out in the 28° air, hatless. And I never even saw her pregnant.

5:10 P.M. Shut down…shut down…

11-19 32° Sunny.

French Kick: My original! Three shots of espresso, a shot of pasteurized beaten egg, a shot of Irish cream liqueur, splash of French vanilla and cinnamon syrups, steamed Half & Half in a 20-ounce cup.

8:31 AM. One of our DOT rockslide workers, from two years ago, came in with his significant other. He said he loved birds and he had the balls to squeeze behind my desk, after I told him NO. I said to his gal friend, "People get shot for less than coming back into *my* area!" She told him to get out, but he ignored both of us and walked directly over to play with Mister. Mister the macaw behaved, but Angel lost it and bit the crap out of his finger. Idiot! Blood 'n guts everywhere! Next time I will shoot the intruder! He does not love feathers anymore!

First sale of the day was an espresso granita. Blended drinks first thing was a pain in my patootie. I opened at 7:30 A.M. since the loud, busy traffic woke me up early. I am hoping that is a sign for success today. With an espresso booth every ¼ mile these days, it's a wonder we can make a living at all. In the "city" you can get espresso about every eleven steps! I'm lucky though; being the only one for miles and the last stop for *anything*, before the summit.

10:50 A.M. Denny came by and ordered his usual hazelnut Americano. We got on the subject about foods and we both agreed that vegetables suck and taste downright awful. He recalled a man he knew in Alaska that swore he hated veggies more than anyone, ever, and had not eaten any for eight years! I could easily go that long. I will take fruit any day! Does a raspberry mocha count as fruit and satisfy our daily vitamin intake?

Both Ms. Gossips came in. It felt suspicious when they stormed in here together and snuck off to the back of my gift shop. Were they planting a spy bug? Oh, how they hated to miss a thing!

2:02 P.M. Scanner: A fourteen-year-old male with lower back pain from a snowboard wipeout.

2:17 P.M. Buck came in with the wrong kind of smirk on his face. He got laid last night. Eat shit and die! And I sent him packin'...

5:16 P.M. Well, it is hot chocolate hour for me. The doors are locked. A slow and disheartening day indeed – it's Saturday for gosh sakes. Oh well. Over and out...

11-20 30° Sunny.

Cheap Shot: A full shot of espresso but stopping your extraction a bit early.

8:00 - 10:17 A.M. One customer for two hours and seventeen friggin' minutes! We needed snow – not sun! Snow Gods, where art thou? Where are the human beings? Damn anyhow.

No. 7 called last night before 8:00 P.M., while he was watching COPS and complained about every little thing each TV cop was doing wrong during their "bust." He then said, "You will have a big day tomorrow, so get a good night's sleep." That comment was a hint, ladies: "Do not call me later." Oh, I got it. He called me in that last boring half hour before he and his brother hit the clubs. 8:00 P.M. was such a pre-bar time to call; the cologne was still drying, the iron was cooling down, and the glass of wine hadn't twisted the tongue yet. B.S.'ers! All of 'em! Dinner was mentioned but I stayed quiet.

12:10 P.M. Scanner: Twenty-four-year-old male with an open elbow fracture. They were requesting a medic. We are due for a car accident. It has been a while.

12:35 P.M. Scanner: A twenty-one-year-old female with intense lower back pain radiating into her pelvic area. She was alert but in extreme pain.

I am blending and steaming today.

1:42 P.M. Scanner: Twenty-one-year-old male with a left shoulder dislocation and *another* humerus fracture. He needed an airlift. They could not fly due to weather.

A couple came in who had also rescued a cockatoo. It was left in its cage 99% of the time and only fed sunflower seeds. This poor bird had not only plucked all its feathers out, but it had also started chewing through its own chest wall. Half of the bird's wings were chewed completely off. I could *easily* decapitate those first owners without blinking an eye.

3:51 P.M. Scanner: A thirty-eight-year-old male with an angulated wrist fracture at the resort. They administered pain medication.

A cute young couple came in who were avid snowboarders. They heard my scanner going and wanted to know all the gory details of the day; they both had had broken necks to show for their sportsmanship. She wore a brace for three months and he wore a drilled-in-halo for over a year. They were snowboarding again today...without helmets.

4:20 P.M. I just became a raging bitch! Some nitwit couple stopped their car in my drive thru and proceeded to lock their keys in it! I was unglued! My drive thru was blocked on a busy Sunday evening! She started to get sassy and then her punk boyfriend piped up. And that was it! I was fucking mad and about to give their fucking Honda a shove with my plow. I told them to get out of my store and wait outside and freeze to death, for all I cared, while I called our tow company. Lucky for all of us, he was on his way to a tow anyway and would be here in two minutes.

Mr. Periwinkle Luggage stopped and saw the fire in my eyes. He ordered his mocha and decided to do his bitching on his next trip through.

The tow guy left with a free white chocolate raspberry mocha. Two guys pulled up for a white chocolate mocha and a hazelnut latte. They were perfectly polite gentlemen the whole time with plenty of "pleases" and "thank yous". Then they peeled off, throwing gravel and screaming, "You're HOT!"

6:48 P.M. Today is over. And cannot be soon enough...

11-21 30° Sunny.

Grapes in Grappon Smoothie: In blender mix: a cup grapes and grape juice, 2 inches of Half & Half. Blend and top with whip.

9:30 A.M. I trucked to the bank and got some ice from "down-below" in the dense fog.

10:48 A.M. A virile 6'3" trucker came in. He said, "Surprise me." If he didn't have those looks along with a wedding ring and politeness, I would have been rude. I hated when they said that. *This was beyond* service. Aprons came to mind again.

Andrew called to inform me of the new sexual arousal nose inhaler for women. Legal ecstasy up the nose? Now women could start behaving more like men. Rapes will quadruple!

6:35 P.M. I forgot to eat today...

11-22 29° Clear.

Crème Caramel Latte: A shot of real caramel, a shot of French vanilla, espresso shots, and steamed milk.

8:10 A.M. One of my proofreaders for **A Barista's Life∗Love∗Laughter** just called and informed me that she was in love with Buck. Women quit being idiots! Buck just happened to be an angel for just about eighteen days straight and suddenly I am supposed to believe he had experienced some sort of *rebirth*? Yes, his cardboard letters, favors, money, and muscle were all sweet as hell, but we must remember that I was *one of five or six or maybe even seven* at any given time! Where did all his hard-earned money disappear to? And can you imagine all the energy it takes, to be Buck?

So, let us do our math, gals: Let's say that he brings home $6K a month. He religiously pays $5 per espresso to all the *other* seven baristas; I've seen 'em all, met a few. If he gets three of these drive-thru-flirtation-drinks-a-day, that's $450 a month right there. We all know he pays $200-$500 per sex session. I will be frugal and say they average $250. Imagine that three times a week. Total per month for sex then $3,000. Gas money spent for covering all the pit stops equals $900. Booze is at *least* $300. Groceries purchased, where one of his seven works, comes to $600. Child support for all his children, *out of wedlock*, equals $450. So far, girls, we are at $5,700! And that is without any sex-sessions with me - which would take him far and beyond his wallet! And do you remember the anti-harassment? So, if any of you are falling for his crap, you are still as fucked up as I have been my whole life...until now! Who are ya foolin' Christy?

1:57 P.M. I got another email from Sex Swing. He asked what I was doing for Thanksgiving. "Not swinging!" And did hit-the-"send" button this time!

Here is another cardboard letter from Buck: "Ya can git a feel for the land wen ya work it. Ya feel wen things dy. It's part of ya. You, Christy, don't need me. You don't need nobody. If ya luv me, prove it (where did he get that horse-shit idea?). Ya still got it and I'm gonna grab it before someone else takes it away. Ya R gorgeous, sinsasonal, fantastik. Ya'r to gud to be tru or too clever or smart. I don't like that eether. I'll fight for ya. Not too many guys will. Anyway ya lik ta fight. We see guys get killed. It ain't nothin'. The rich and famous ain't nothin' either. I like my peece. Anyway, yu'r a good, hardworkn gal. Bless yo'r hart. Yu'r the nicest person I ever met. When yu'r only half of somethin yu'r reelly only half a nothin'. We make mistakes even in the best a faith. P.S. Nice firm rump."

Bullshit, I tell ya! Remember, folks, cardboard boxes come with eight flaps, top and bottom. My letters are written on *one* of these flaps. He probably copies the same words onto the other 6-7 flaps.

4:45 P.M. Scanner: A structure fire in Crag Rock. Fire trucks will come from all four surrounding cities.

5:00 P.M. I'm leaving to go get more milk.

8:45 P.M. Bye…

11-23 27° Clear.

Crème Fraiche: A shot of buttermilk and vanilla Syrup, espresso shots, steamed Half & Half.

8:55 A.M. Hopefully, snow arrives tomorrow night. Our resort needs it. *I* need it.

No. 5 called and said he was coming here on Thanksgiving. I can't go there, so I said no. I can't do the reminisce-thing on holidays. I'd rather be alone. I need a peaceful day in my store. The heavy load of customers will really be all I can handle.

Here is Harley Dennis's email: "Happy T-Day. I know you'll be working as usual. I'll honk from the train if I go up your way. I hope you are busier than a one-legged man in a butt kickin' contest!" Thanks, Dennis, you too. A seven-engine train passed! That is *gigantic* for this route!

1:51 P.M. Buck found himself an old growth, dry tree in the woods that he can saw into about eleven cords of wood. That is like finding a vein of gold.

I had an SUV stop that contained six very charming men. They all ordered hot chocolates and one of the passengers was trying to pass me the driver's ten-dollar bill – for a tip. We all laughed as the driver yelped, and my hands snatched it up.

3:00 P.M. Andrew called while stuck in traffic and the sec I took my first huge bite of Buck's mama's macaroni salad, I mumbled, swallowed and coughed. "Christy, you'd love this new Lake Union view condo that my rich live-in girl-friend from New York and I bought. It is fabulous – feels like we are rock stars, right in the heart of Seattle. But, the state-of-the-art oven is not working, the sub-zero frig makes ice cubes at a snail's pace, we can't get the damn place warm with all the glass, and that gigantic whirlpool bathtub, where we were going to make mad passionate love, runs out of hot water before it ever fills." After investing $600K, basically, buying a view, he's missing the simple life in the woods.

4:59 P.M. I think I'm gonna sit tight for a while. My equity is increasing…

11-24 27° Mostly sunny.
-Thanksgiving Day.

Thanksgiving Tea: Mix in a mug, 2 black tea bags, fill with hot water, and a splash of each: cinnamon, lemon, and orange syrups.

8:57 A.M. It is a blast to work on holidays. Gobble, gobble, gobbling with family and friends, on the phone, between customers. Happy Holiday everyone.

10:59 A.M. Buck came and looked at my new generator; it won't start for some reason. Then he said that he wanted to clear something up: "I did have dinner at a gal's house awhile back and then watched a movie. But I left without eating because it felt too weird there." Here we go again…Now, girls, let's really listen carefully to this. Aren't movies watched AFTER dinner? Did he actually storm off in his panic without eating, then went back just in time for the movie? Or was there more than one night with this gal? He only claimed once, period. It did not fit. Plus, he knew too much about her to have only seen her once! Liar!

But Buck said that his mama's turkey dinner would be ready by 4:00 P.M. and I would get a care-package. I'll find some yummies to give them in return!

That part of the fam-damily is super.

3:03 P.M. Scanner: A wild turkey in the median on I-5 at milepost 186. That is funny as hell on Turkey Day! Even the dispatcher had to hold back her laugh.

3:45 P.M. Scanner: A twelve-year-old female with a back injury. She was still on the slopes and they were working on transporting her down. That's too young! Dispatch called thirty-five minutes later and they still didn't have her in transport! Maybe she was on the backside of the mountain.

4:50 P.M. Buck brought dinner. It was such a huge plate, full to the brim – it could feed me for days! *Thanks, Mama!* I am eating right now and will roll around in pain shortly from being too full. My drive thru is still open…what else is there to do?

5:13 P.M. Scanner: A motor vehicle accident just east of Treetops Loop. I went out to look and could see flashers on one car. I will wait to put out a flare when I get more facts. A male and female rollover. She had cuts to her head and face, and he had neck pain. They were headed to the hospital. They both worked for Microsoft.

Buck delivered pumpkin spice lattes to a few homes for me. I love to *Holiday-Gift* to some of the older people that hand me fresh-picked asparagus and tomatoes during the summer.

7:55 P.M. Again, Happy Thanksgiving to all…

11-25 34° Mixed rain and snow.

After Dinner: A shot of Amaretto liqueur, espresso shots and top with whipped cream.

8:00 A.M. What a white weekend this will be! It is dumping snow at the pass and all the way to Sunbird! My plow is ready to go. This weather will be hazardous for Thanksgiving travelers, however.

My first customer in handed me a $50 bill. I sent him out to dig in his truck for something smaller and he found it.

Well, I'm back to those $20 cars full of skiers! Totally slammed! I stocked my ice chest with extra ice, milk, eggnog and Half & Half. When I got behind, I just reminded customers that my *machine* can only go *so* fast. We baristas always try *our* best!

11:12 A.M. Scanner: Seventeen-year-old female with a possible jaw fracture at the resort.

11:53 A.M. Scanner: Sixteen-year-old female with a hip injury at the resort.

A couple came in with their punch card. The wife told the husband, in no uncertain terms, that he was *responsible* for keeping an eye on the damn card. I punched it and made their lattes. He left the perforated card on the counter and headed for the car. The wife saw it lying there and said, "I can NEVER trust him!" I asked her, "Which ones can we trust?" "None of them," she claimed, "And if I trip over one more pair of shoes on the stairs in my home, I'm going to give them all to Goodwill!" She was ramrod straight, heading back out to the car. Poor guy…

I just got super slammed and sometimes it sure was tempting to announce that my little *whirligig thingy (blender)* was broken – just no time for blended drinks! Cars whizzing by had at least four inches of snow on their roofs.

1:11 P.M. A guy in a Subaru flew in super-fast, parked and grabbed his little boy out of the back seat and ran in the rain to my park. The poor kid was puking. Then dad put the boy back in, lifted his hatchback and grabbed a rag. Puke all *over* the car. Been there, done that. Shall I lock the doors?

1:33 P.M. Scanner: A nineteen-year-old male with a spinal injury, may have lost consciousness - along with a twenty-one-year-old female who had a concussion and was delirious. They collided on the slope.

Oh God, I think my mystery emailer with the niece just walked in. He bought tons of shit to impress me. He also gave me *that* look when he left, those bugged eyeballs that lasts seconds too long. Gag!

Boone from Grotto stopped and gave me some ground deer meat straight from his hunt in Montana. Venison meatloaf? Meat or no meat, boots stay on, dude.

4:44 P.M. A blocking car injury accident on Mountain Peak Highway at mile-post 25. That was "down-below" but it would still affect our ski traffic. The medics were all starting to get confused about which call each of them were on. Too many injuries at once.

I just ate my last ¼ portion of my T-Day meal, washed it down with one of my own decaf pumpkin spice lattes. I only took three sips. Harley Dennis called. He was eagerly happy during his recent colonoscopy. The same nurse that took care of him the first time assisted on this one. "It felt like minutes - compared to hours! We chatted about life, while the camera was doing its work, up my ass, five feet or so!" He was going to be passing in the train in a couple of hours and would honk. If I were a guy, or gutsier, I'd go out and B.A. him. In honor of his recent procedure.

6:05 P.M. I'm getting silly, gotta go…

11-26 32° A touch of white.

Honeycomb Latte: 2 shots of honey, 2 shots of espresso, steamed whole milk.

9:44 A.M. I have never sold so many 32-ouncers to one party! Seven in one car! Wow think of how many stops there will be, between here and home, every 10-minutes for one or the other.

A gal came in who claimed to be a part of the entertainment at the White-Water Hotel in Saratogan. Entertainment? Holy shit! Up here? I guess it's true; they will be here once a month and she wanted me to come down and listen to the rock-'n-roll. Did I dare go into a local bar? Buck would slash my tires!

I guess her and her boyfriend, the other musician, played backups for Bonnie Raitt and Nancy Wilson, when they did a benefit concert here in Seattle. Nancy Wilson of Heart went to my rival high school in Bellevue. That is almost *too* hip for Saratogan. She said, "People stumbled back and forth from the Train Blow Tavern to the White Water Hotel to get variety." Lady, they have been doing this for a hundred years, with or without music. They *are* the only two *joints* within fifty miles and Saratogan is known to be, one big *stumble* after dark.

3:19 P.M. Scanner: A back injury at the resort. Male snowboarder.

Christmas trees were rolling down the highway on the car rooftops. 'Tis the season…

3:23 P.M. Scanner: Twenty-seven-year-old female skier with back injury.

3:35 P.M. I needed to pee. I was only able to go once in twelve hours! Not yet… Some Asians crashed their rental car in the snow and then got a lift down to my place. They were just thankful to be in one piece.

Before I knew it, there were at least twenty of their friends assisting them for two hours! I called a tow company and visited with the folks, as they continually drank lattes.

This has been the busiest day in at least a year. I did hundreds of drinks and sold gobs of junk food. Someone even bought a fur Navajo parka and some other gift items for Christmas. Business was divine – but not quite as well as *finally* getting two minutes of peace-on-the porcelain!

Rude awakening found me cleaning appalling *handfuls* of toilet paper hanging out of the Porta Potty, along the parking lot and the entire length of the landscaping. I was so busy; I had not caught the rascal that did the 'T.P. Job'. Maybe the other end of the roll was accidentally stuck up their butt?

My birds were a hit all day. Angel seriously believed she was "on a pedestal" and showed off for hours. Mister must have said every word he ever knew. They liked the business as much as I did!

Nine prisoners escaped from a Yakima jail, so my doors were locked a tad early…my ear was practically *attached* to the police scanner!

4:45 P.M. Tick-A-Lock. Only window service. I was so tired, and my feet throbbed; right then I'd have shot those escapees for sure, and without much justification.

Main drinks of the day were peppermint hot chocolates. Pink frost cookies were the most popular junk food.

6:27 P.M. I had an incredible tipping day. Three times I was handed over $5 in tips! That is *big* for a grandma…

11-27 29° Cloudy and white everywhere!

Orange Spice Breve: A shot of orange syrup, a shot of cinnamon syrup, espresso shots, steamed Half & Half.

6:45 A.M. Open

7:57 A.M. Not one espresso junkie.

8:37 A.M. My first two guys. Good tippers! I'm amped again…

A barista is guaranteed no tip if customers hand her their money folded. $8 in folded ones feels nice and thick but there is *never* a tip in that neat little package. That is the customers' way of hiding their shame. The non-tipper who does not give-a-rip either way, just hands it over as a mess of bills, but does not do the eye contact. They must feel a *tad* guilty.

The resort had forty inches of snow, with six inches of new flakes since last night. It was 25° up there. A flocked beauty. It began to snow here, and Angel sang and danced to it. She thought the flakes were a zillion tiny cockatoo feathers. It was just too cute!

10:03 A.M. Scanner: A twenty-nine-year-old female with a possible fractured clavicle at the resort.

Well, two of the nine prisoners were still at large. The one in for murder was caught early on. Thank you.

10:35 A.M. Scanner: Twenty-three-year-old male with a head injury and trauma to the face.

1:31 P.M. A sweet Thanksgiving story: A couple went to spend Thanksgiving weekend with grandma and grandpa. Grandma wouldn't let anyone help her carve the turkey, mash the spuds, doctor the sweet yams, bake the homemade rolls, prepare the pies, or set the table with her finest china. If anyone got near her out of pity, she'd aim her cane at them! Grandma did poke grandpa in the ribs a few times when she caught him doing chores around the house without his walker. "That's a no-no," she'd say. The meal was ready. As in all the years past, the guests chanted in unison, "That was the best meal in the whole wide world!" Grandma and grandpa were ninety-four years old!

Speaking of age. I do realize I am getting older. I can no longer hold my bladder for ten hours straight, after two 24-ounce teas, water, and some food. Dang...I used to! My drive thru is still open and I thought I could hold "it" for a few more minutes. I ran back to my commissary to fill up all the ice trays from the espresso cart. The *moment* I turned the sink on, I suddenly had to use every "hold it" muscle known to man. I was barely succeeding. I started stacking these trays and just as I put number 10 on top, they all toppled over. Cold water went everywhere, including all over me! My bladder was tested beyond capacity and joined in this wet tee shirt and pants party! Just then I heard honking at the espresso window. Did I have time to finish peeing? Hell no! And therefore, I didn't have time to change my pants either! I grabbed a big towel and tied it around my waist. How many baristas suffer like this, stuck in their cubicles for hours on end? When was I going to risk disturbing those rusty old pipes and fix my fucking toilet? As it was, I had to walk a couple hundred feet to the bathroom upstairs and miss out on five to ten customers. Let alone tips! Peeing can get expensive!

4:44 P.M. I finally got back to the commissary to mop up the water. Most of it already soaked through to the storage, spiders, and bats basement. Oh well. My flippin' jeans were really soaked now because I just knocked over my

24-ounce water cup at my cart! I will deal with the water under all the syrups later. Lost a whole roll of paper towels and 8,000 straws! Oh God…it was not water; it was my bleach cup! The chlorine scent confirmed my suspicion. Oh no…my new $45 jeans! How many hundreds of dollars' worth of clothes were ruined in these business, and cute clothes for tips! It added up to millions across the country. Up to the washing machine – before my skin got burned raw. I found tiny holes in the denim. Shit!

6:30 P.M. I just checked to see if DSL was available up here yet. Nope. I couldn't face my snail computer tonight, but I should order some aprons. Maybe this whole Starbucks apron thing *was* the way to go. Men seemed to love fantasizing about the little woman being subservient and all. Maybe more tips. What a concept – and I'd been fighting this to the death…

11-28 24° Clear with high clouds.

Cabin Splendor: A shot of B-52 and cherry syrup, triple shot of espresso, steamed Half & Half.

8:50 A.M. I had a big sale on gifts before I even opened all the way. Then another couple came in and purchased eight gifts. Super nice for a Monday!

A truck stopped in my drive thru and locked-her-up. I asked him to pull out and park on the side of the property and explained what *drive thru* meant. With that, he got out and started checking the air in his 63 tires! "Pull the hell up, Trucker!" He finally got it.

2:02 P.M. A man walked in who lived here in Treetops Loop back in the '60s. His mother was one of the investors who had originally started our Treetops Loop! He went to our dinky school his junior and senior years. Ten kids in a class, maybe less. He was going to take a spin through there after I finished making his flavored latte. He wanted to see if he could find the old place. He returned to inform me, "Your town is in some weird time-capsule. Nothing has changed!" He shuddered…

Second day with no Buck. He was *really* pouting this time. Or a terribly busy boy...

5:53 P.M. Scanner: A fire alarm at Mountain Peak Ski Resort. Probably a false alarm.

5:57 P.M. Scanner: A vehicle injury accident at milepost 61.

6:02 P.M. I'm going to get out of the line of fire...

11-29 29° Snowing!

Fruity Irish: A 1/2 shot of Irish cream and strawberry syrups, espresso shots and steamed milk.

9:09 A.M. It was absolutely dumping snow! I woke to six inches and rising. I plowed first thing this morning once I got the lights on and the birds fed. I will plow again tonight after closing.

Angel thought she died and went to heaven with those white fluffy flakes. But she jumped a foot every time a chunk of ice fell off the roof.

11:30 A.M. More customers in and most were skiers. One gal described the snow up at the resort as "Champagne Powder." Sounds lovely, cushiony for the falls...and thirst quenching!

The snow was not stopping. I could expect another six inches tonight. Thank you, you beautiful full fat juicy clouds up there!

5:08 P.M. A lady walked up to the drive-thru with her two wild monkey sons. Thank God I don't have to let those three in. Doors were locked and this was her only choice. Those boys climbed over every snow bump, tripped off my new landscaping lumber, threw snowballs, and screamed for a soda. Just then, a guy also walked up to get a root beer and she explained that she and the kids just got back from Krispy Kreme. She may as well have shot them up with a syringe full of purified sucrose. She opened the car door and offered this guy a squashed flattened circle of dough, which impersonated a deflated, dirty inner tube. He had never seen her before in his life and he passed on the offer. She didn't offer *me* one, the bitch!

Buck just walked up to the window. He cocked his head to the left so I would see the bandage on his temple. What happened, did the husband of one of your chippies come home unexpectedly early? He mistakenly thought his wound would make me feel soooooo bad for him that maybe I would fuck his brains out. I shut the window on him without mentioning his owie and he left.

The snow was falling in gigantic flakes. I swept my cars off, so I don't wake up to six inches of ice.

7:37 P.M. And I am walking out the door...

11-30 29° Snowing.

Kahlua Cream Americano: A shot of Kahlua liqueur and Irish cream liqueur, 2 shots of espresso, fill with hot water.

8:08 A.M. The forty-nine inches of snow up at the resort was causing plenty of ski-addicts to call in sick. They were coming in bragging about the "story" they told the boss.

I had my 32-ounce crowd of snowboarder dudes in again! Those were $6.50 espressos and yes, they downed them prior to hurling themselves off mountain peaks.

1:31 P.M. Mr. Hunk Wyatt's stepdad came in. Hunk was still in jail and they had no idea how long this was going to last – they hoped to have him home by Christmas? I heard that Wyatt's neighbor happened to be another wife beater, adding to our local list of wanna-be jailbirds. He was an *old* geezer now but still a bastard. His wife probably looked 100-years-old by now. What a life! This social parasite once drove her up into the high country on Barklett Road, forced her to strip naked, and made her walk all the way back home. Why do those women stay? Why don't their relatives and friends hog-tie them and get them the hell out? A FEW FUCKING FAT FELT-TIPPED POINTS OFF THE MALE COLUMN!

2:40 P.M. Scanner: A two-car injury accident at milepost 61. An adult male was complaining of a head injury.

Plowed and shoveled the white stuff, until I felt twice my age. It was slow and seemingly worthless. Another storm is hitting tomorrow anyway.

I am heading out for "something." Didja ever have an "itch" and didn't even know what to scratch? Did not know what would quench it? Chocolate, fresh flowers, a thousand calories, flirt session, new CD, trouble…or just a drive to the local craft store?

5:40 P.M. Back and on my way to the dump. No. 5 called me with "a good tale!" He had his semi at a shipping terminal today. A beautiful lady walked in and explained that she needed to ship her car full of Costco stuff to her husband in Alaska. She asked the dispatcher if there was anyone who could help her unload. "Oh, no problem, ma'am. We will get your assistance right away," he said, drooling. He got on his radio loudspeaker, "A 99 on the deck, please." Three guys rapidly appeared *out of nowhere* for aide. As those guys followed cutie pants out to her car, the dispatcher said to No. 5, "We have a code here. We are all on a *rotating basis* for helping good-looking women and we call them 99's. We used to fight over these pretty little things, so now we take turns. In the past we used '69 on deck' but got into some trouble and changed *that* code." The gal just thought they were being extremely helpful – it's amazing they could even *walk* with their hard-ons. I asked No. 5, "How many of these guys were married?" He replied, "Well, at least half of them were. They make the homely ones lug their own heavy freight merchandise." I hate men! Another point off for those married freakazoids!

6:28 P.M. It is definitely time to close. Even my male *birds* are seeking cover…

DECEMBER

Twinkles' and coffee call for eggnog,
bringing us joy

12-01 27° Overcast. Christmas is in 24 more days!

Shirley Temple: Ice, ginger ale with a shot of grenadine.

8:05 A.M. This is June *Cleaver* month. And poundage! The *"aprons"* in all of us. Most of us have played this scene, every December, every year. We start baking and gain ten pounds *before* the holidays even get here. By the time food hits the oven, it is half the size.

10:00 A.M. Just heard it is snowing in parts of Seattle! That means we are in for it!

1:12 P.M. An old guy I knew in high school, who dialed me twice a year max, called yelling with excitement because it was snowing in Bellevue! That is a rare happening these days! He is taking pictures with his cell phone and going to email them to me. He has now joined the internet dating scene. Took a gal to the ocean last weekend. On their first blind date! Sleazy! Scary! Stupid!

4:00 P.M. One of my regulars came in with his gay buddy from the ski resort today. I could tell his buddy was gay, even before he spoke by the way he was dancing around my gift store like twinkle-toes. But for the life of me, I never could read my regular's sexual preference. The buddy wanted to know if he could pet my macaw, Mister. He had fond memories of French kissing one in Mexico! I asked their preference, meaning drinks. They fell to their knees roaring in laughter. They were fun!

Some poor old ladies were skating around on the ice rink of my parking lot.

Mrs. Periwinkle Luggage stopped wearing her new blue UGGS. Her moods arrive in colors.

6:04 P.M. I was soooo bored – I sat here and created a Christmas lit pink flamingo for the edge of the highway. A Flamingo Rudolph...how flippin' festive!

No. 1 Bachelor, with that sexy cabin, emailed me asking if I would use his hide-a-key and close his fireplace hamper. I told him it would have to wait till morning – too many *trolls* up here after dark. And he had a cozy fire with whom?

7:34 P.M. Over and out...

12-02 27° Snow.

Eggnog Shot: Triple shot of espresso with an inch of eggnog.

7:43 A.M. I got a whole foot of snow last night! I headed up to that chic alluring male pad, to tend to the fireplace. I took one look at his spread and knew I would never get my Jeep back out. Not a bad thought, though - stuck up here with No. 1 Bachelor till spring! Yummmmy. I called and gave him his choice. A built-in Ms. Maintenance with pay or cold digs.

1:05 P.M. I have been plowing the snow, dodging all the clueless drivers. Scared the hell out of one car as I headed right for it like I was going to scoop it up in the bucket. I am finally inside as a female barista, not she-male manual laborer.

1:43 P.M. Scanner: A thirty-seven-year-old female, up at the resort, with a shoulder dislocation and tingling in her fingers.

1:54 P.M. Scanner: A suicidal patient in a white Expedition near the Old Mountain Peak Highway. A mile from me! Thank God the sheriff and aid were now on the scene. If it were one of our locals, I'd hear about it within two hours. They were requesting a fire truck. Weird.

2:00 P.M. Mr. No. 1 Bachelor just came in. I am glad I didn't kill myself over a damper! His visits always brighten a gal's day. He caught me outside installing my huge, heavy, rusted old truck chains! I was on my back *under* the truck; I lost the first set, buried somewhere in a snow berm. My second, and only one left, wrapped itself onto my axle and I had been dragging it around the lot. I got up and tended to his drink order. Of course, he didn't offer to help. He would get wet. Creep.

Night skiing starts again this evening and Icicle Town is also having their first Christmas Lighting Festival. A "hooray for business" weekend!

4:06 P.M. My phone rang. "A free call from an inmate, at *So-And-So* Jail." Hunk Wyatt was on the other end of the line! He sounded dreadful and miserable. He asked if I would like to wipe his tears. I told him to try and chin-up. Just *maybe* a good *lesson* this time.

No. 1 Bachelor came in again. God, he is a beaut! He needed kindling so I gave him three bundles of Buck's crap. Too bad I couldn't get up the nerve, guts, daringness, and confidence to offer to stoke his fire…but then he was selfish to not help me with my chains.

6:46 P.M. Bye…

12-03 29° Snowing.

> **Espresso in Roma: Straight shots of espresso with an orange or lemon peel.**

7:29 A.M. It had been years since we had seen such snow! Another fresh foot to deal with this morning! Personally, I have not had this much in all my years here. I got the one pair of chains off my plow truck's axle with my bolt cutters, shoveled the bed out so I would have room for my garbage, swept off both cars and all walkways. I even unlocked the *emergency* second Porta Potty. They lied and didn't show up yesterday for cleaning. One stinky, smelly, full pot – my customers deserve better than that! Had to dig out both sides of my double gates so I could get Butch into the back forty. I'm exhausted already!

Now I must plow. I almost got stuck but realized that would mean a call to Buck. No bitchin' way! I revved it up, rocked the machine back and forth, and recovered. I was about halfway done when another Microsoft cabin owner pulled up. "Hey, could you pop up to our road and plow it real fast? I can't get in there with my sports car." "Do I look like you're *on call* Guardian-Plow-Angel, bucko?! I have got a business to run. Go ask Sir Gates!" He wasn't amused. Yeah sure, Dude…pull in all my signs, the Christmas lit flamingo, lock a frickin' dozen doors, put time clocks up and for what? To make a couple of swipes for a top dog, rich computer nerd? Forget it, you are in "these-thar-hills" now. Get used to it.

9:53 A.M. Another yuppie bitch, who was a new proud owner of a lovely cabin up here, huffed in asking, "Where is Weston, my plow man?" "Now how the heck would I know?" Just another dissatisfied panicked "city slicker." She snarled, "He is supposed to plow our driveway when it snows this much! Can you tell the guy with the plow out front to come and do it for us?" "Honey, you're looking at HIM and NO I won't do you! I'm workin'!" And then, an hour later, one more Microsoft geek tried plowing with the brush-guard on his new SUV. Oh well, they can afford to repair or replace…

12:02 P.M. Scanner: Three-car injury accident one mile west of the summit. One car was engulfed in flames. It took twenty minutes for the first sign of help to get there. Apparently, no state troopers had made it up here yet today, in all this snow! They had to be dispatched out of Alpine, a good forty-five minutes away, while the metal was being french-fried and glass was exploding.

12:36 P.M. The ski resort in Sunbird was also now open. That was the earliest for them since 1996. Our resort now had a fifty-four-inch base, with thirty-three inches of new snow in the last seven days. I whispered a soft "thank you" as my eyes scanned the skies.

4:04 P.M. Jack and Pete came in. Jack's ex-wife was coming on strong again. He was still tempted – tempted to get squeezed into her clutches once more. Older men were such a sorry lot – just can't be alone!

8:22 P.M. Two guys pulled up to my drive thru and asked for Americanos with cream, "But please leave a lot of room so I don't spill it." I had no-spill lids, as did most baristas, for hot drinks. So, he fell under the *Bailey's Driver Category*. If I don't fill the cup, he would - from under the driver's seat!

No one seemed to have any answers about the suicide situation the other day. Must not have been a local, and hopefully not successful!

8:32 P.M.

Scanner: A two-car accident, one mile west of the summit. One car rear-ended the other and caused it to do a somersault in mid-air.

9:00 P.M. It's snowing and I'm closing...

12-04 23° Overcast.

Original Eggnog Latte: Heat 2 cups of eggnog in saucepan to a simmer. Put in blender with 1 tbs. of rum and bourbon, 1 cup espresso. Blend until frothy. Top with whip and nutmeg.

3:50 A.M. It was the middle of the fucking night and I was so fucking frozen that I had to *get* up and *get* dressed to *get* warm. Remember the "no heat" and 1-inch gaps in windows! My body pillows, that are my bedpartners, were cold as corpses – my hot water bottle was a *stone*. And then I also realized that I had forgotten to *drip* some of my faucets. I threw on three sweaters, sweats over jeans, and silk ski liners, wool socks, and UGGS. Then I had to go *outside* to get to my store and drip my espresso cart lines. If I hadn't remembered, I'd be out of business. Thought maybe the birds would be ready to "*stuff*", but they were okay.

8:45 A.M. Not enough new snow today to worry about clearing. A couple and a teenager came in for drinks, "A hot chocolate for our son, a triple 20-ounce eggnog latte for my wife, and a triple Americano, please." The punk kid walked over to Mister's area and challenged him by sticking his finger inside the wire hole. There were 13-signs in the immediate area that read: I BITE! Mister gave him a warning nip. It smarted a bit and the kid said, "He *does* bite." So, he *can* read!

11:06 AM. Scanner: Twenty-two-year-old male with a direct impact injury to his spine. He may have a fracture in the lumbar region and was in the aid room at the resort. They requested an airlift because his airways were closing. He could be close to death and it will take 1 1/2 to 2 hours to reach a damn hospital bed.

11:16 A.M. Scanner: A twenty-year-old male had lost consciousness for some time, was alert now and was complaining of back pain.

12:00 Noon. I went out back to play with Butch and saw that my grandpa tree had dropped three gigantic branches! More like three small whole trees! Thank God they only partially crushed my old cottage instead of my neighbor's nice cabin. I'm glad Butch didn't get squished. No wonder he was barking – those were *intruders*.

2:33 P.M. Scanner: A twenty-six-year-old male with a possible injured spleen.

I could hear a train coming s-l-o-w-l-y up the tracks. I thought it would be *loaded* with engines, but it only had two! Just one tuckered out, little ole train.

4:14 P.M. Was an exceedingly busy day with constant people at a nice pace. A lady came in wanting an owl item for a friend. I searched in between three more sets of espresso addicts while she waited. No can do, but I know it was here somewhere… Drats! She settled on a $28 painting. She turned it over to look at the back and there was not one, but two, Goodwill stickers reading $5.95. Greeeeeaaaaaaat! I pretended not to be dying of embarrassment and then I suddenly spotted the missing owl sculpture! I got her mind quickly back to owls, instead of preposterous price mark-ups. Whoo-Hoo! After she left, I ripped those blasted Goodwill stickers off and re-hung the painting for its $28 price tag. And that is RETAIL, gang!

5:23 P.M. I just had to wheel and deal with a vanload of teens wanting hot chocolate. Dad sat there counting his money. He was playing poor-me. I discounted this rate and he tipped me a couple of bucks from his loose change. He was a good actor; I'll grant him that…

6:07 P.M. I'm going home. The fifty-three steps and nineteen stairs…

12-05 30° Snowing.

Brandy Cappuccino: Combine 2 cups espresso, 3 cups very hot milk, 6 tsp. sugar. Pour into 8 tiny (demitasse) cups. Garnish with 1 tbs. brandy or 1 tsp. ground chocolate.

9:09 A.M. Scanner: A forty-eight-year-old male suffered a fifteen-foot fall on the back slopes and may have a spinal injury.

12:01 P.M. I just did a quick job of plowing, only four inches of fresh snow. And now it is raining. Whaaaaaat's going on around here?

The local who leased some space for a sign on my fencing brought the finished product. It was half-covered by the snow berm, but he was so proud, he didn't seem to notice. He invited me to his house party tonight. I believe I will pass. That was going to be one of those shindigs where I would not know the men from the women - the males were masculine; the females were masculine!

1:04 P.M. Only two customers! I will run errands later.

Two of my regular forty-eight-year-olds came in for drinks and told me that some guy was lost up at the resort and it has been twenty-four hours! So that was why the Search and Rescue guys were there. Now an hour later, the lost skier was found in someone's bed "down-below"! There went more taxpayer dollars – on a goof ball.

Hunk Wyatt has court tomorrow to determine if/when he will no longer be incarcerated. He says that he will be in an ankle bracelet for a while. Handsomeness will decrease.

1:56 P.M. Scanner: A twenty-seven-year-old male fell while snowboarding. He had decreasing motor functions and they were requesting an airlift.

5:47 P.M. All finished shopping, put it all away, ate, showered, and watched the news. I decided to torture myself and take a drive "down-below" again, just to listen to classic Christmas music, at full volume! Christmas is never the same when you have an empty nest - and I do mean *empty*! I hadn't put up a tree in years and now who cared. My kids were long distance, Alaska to California, so Christmas became a trip to the P.O. for me. But I could not help thinking of all the mothers who were missing their children, for various reasons. Losses to abortion, abandonment, divorce, drugs, murder, illness, accidents, war – and just grown up and leaving. We moms will never forget the days of sifters and Crisco. Today we have pre-sifted flour and non-stick Teflon.

This time of year, I reminisce about one of my son's favorite holiday treats. I remember all the years we picked blackberries and the branches would poke and scratch both of our arms until they bled. I would freeze them, and it was our *annual treat* to pull them out and bake "our" pie, together. Seems like just yesterday…

I would like to dedicate one of my poems to all mothers that miss their children, so painfully and deeply, during the holidays:

LAST PIE

As I wait for preheating
I will now take a seat
Close my eyes ever so tight
To remember the sun
As we picked all our blacks
Discarded the browns
Filled all our buckets
Mother and son on their day

Years later to dare
Pull the fruit from the ice
Mix memories with tears
Sift snow with late summer
Cry softly in vivid dreams

Close tight the oven door
Wash up to hide joy
That once warmed this room

Now is dead for the old
Throw the pans behind doors
Shred the sponge soaked in daydreams

The house was alive
In the days filled with family
My dog cannot reach
These counters with pie crumbs
Apron starched for my banquet
Smells overpower the mind

Why bake in reflection?
Our sunny day in the weeds
As my son with his mother
Once here and now gone

I slice oh so thinly
Last piece devours loss
The bread knife now ponders
As my breast does give in
I lie on my apron
Safely left to my days...

12-06 30° Overcast.

Café Coconut Delight: In an 8-ounce cup combine a shot of chocolate syrup, 1/2 shot canned cream of coconut, 1 shot espresso. Fill up with steamed milk. Garnish with toasted coconut.

8:44 A.M. A short train carrying *huge* airplane fuselage just tooted by – GO BOEING!

12:08 P.M. A barista who had a hut down in the valley stopped by. And while she was here, lots more customers walked in – and pulled up in the drive thru. This sure made an impression and made my joint and me look damn good.

We laughed over some typical stories, colored them up for even more giggles. She planned to get a gun and a panic button, like I wear. She calls her hubby "Rooster" (*isn't that every man's name?*) and he wants her to be protected.

2:22 P.M. Ms. Gossip No. 1 came in for her triple caramel mocha. Today she wanted to gossip about our sheriff. She had heard from legitimate sources that lots of townspeople wanted him gone. I had heard the same. I would venture to guess that since he's worked up here, he has the goods on too many people - enough years to know who's who, who's involved in wheeling and dealing, and he may be getting in the way of some drug deals. Go sheriff!

4:38 P.M. A van full of family members stopped for a ton of drinks. The male driver (dad) asked, "Now this bill *will* stay under $5 won't it?" I looked at him in disbelief. We both laughed at his joke. The total came to $19.18 and he gave me $22, closed it in my hand with a smile. Thank you for nice customers like this!

Hunk Wyatt called from jail again. He gets out tomorrow and wished I could visit and drive him home to his stepdad's – not too far from here. My heart went pitter-patter just imagining a 2- hour drive with this Hunk! I declined, as he knew I would.

Rosie snuck up for a visit today. I don't think she'd seen the light of day for a month.

Her asshole husband was pulling a Saratogan-Old-School-Controlling-Bullshit act on her. Things were getting bad in the house, for her and her little girl. So bad that her dad may come and get the two of them – and get them the hell outta here! I hope to God he would. They *needed* to be rescued. I don't sleep well when children are involved.

By the way, the suicide situation the other day in the Expedition went through as planned. He blew his brains out. No wonder it required fire trucks.

8:01 P.M. Heading upstairs to be educated by Oprah…

12-07 26° Overcast.

Espresso Bubble Tea: Place 1/2 cup chilled, cooked bubble tea pearls in a parfait glass. Combine 1 cup crushed ice, 1 cup espresso, 1 cup whole milk and some honey in a cocktail shaker and shake until frothy. Fill parfait glass with mixture and insert wide straw.

8:30 A.M. It was very icy out. An SUV pulled up to the drive thru and the father's teenage son stepped out and instantly went down, right on his backside. Awkward age for embarrassments and his face registered a rosy veil.

I had three ladies in earlier who said they couldn't shop because it was so darn cold back in my gift shop. My one pellet stove just wasn't cutting it for three huge rooms. Maybe next year…

A pushy gift salesman came in and tried to get me to place an order with his company. I forced myself to be polite, but firm. He ordered an Americano and then left without paying. "Be careful on my icy walkway." He glared back at me, saying that he had driven and survived in these hills for over 20-million miles. *Well, if you're so dang worldly, then why didn't you pay for the espresso you ordered?*

Our power guy came in and asked if Buck had looked at my generator. I told him, "Yes, he did, but that he also wanted sex for his time and that's *exactly* why I don't like *asking* Buck for anything, *anymore!*" He just shook his head. "Yeah, he's known for just wanting a little tail and not carin' much whose back seat it's in…" Buck, your reputation precedes you, big time!

1:11 P.M. Today, I learned some things about jail I never knew before, from a guy customer who just got out! For instance, a lot of holding cells had just one toilet, for a minimum of at least twenty guys. It sat right in the middle of the room for everyone's viewing. And if you had to go number 2, you had better flush that turd down the second it hit water, or you'd get beat up. "No poopin' and takin' your jolly ole time wipin' while the room stunk up," he said, while he was sipping on his mocha. "It ain't worth the broken nose." T.M.I.!!!

3:46 P.M. A truck was sitting forever out in my parking lot completely blocking my landing strip for customers to pull in. It was almost dark out and after twenty minutes I couldn't stand it any longer. I popped my pistol into my pocket and grabbed the flashlight, to go deal with this stranger. I always shone the flashlight in their eyes first, and then walked to the driver's side window, keeping about six to eight feet from the vehicle. They *always* rolled it down to hear me ask, "Can I help you?" This particular driver told me he was on his phone. "Talk elsewhere." He turned the key...

6:29 P.M. I just cradled Angel for an hour. Nitie-nite...

12-08 18° Sunny.

Peach Berry Latte: A 1/3 shot of peach, raspberry and blackberry syrups, espresso shots, steamed milk.

6:00 A.M. The *cold* wasn't funny. I awoke to seeing my breath, ran out of bed to turn on the floor heater in the bathroom so my buns wouldn't stick to the toilet. Jumped back in bed for fifteen minutes.

7:33 A.M. Open. My Espresso rags in the bucket were a chunk of ice – *inside* the back room. The gate was frozen solid, and I couldn't budge it. Pole-vault anyone? Butch's water was one great big cube! I fired up the pellet stove and we were anxiously waiting for it to get to a balmy (*for us*) sixty degrees.

2:02 P.M. I salted the walkways and put hot water in Butch's bucket. My pipes didn't freeze, because I remembered to drip, so it's a damn good day.

Andrew called all paranoid about the possible bird flu epidemic. He wanted to know that if corporations started shutting down their businesses, would he still be responsible for his $60K a year lease? I said yes. He then stopped at Denny's to have a huge steak and eggs breakfast to ward off his panic (No worries about heart failure?). "If we die, Andrew, we die."

5:45 P.M. A lady pulled up and parked in the drive thru. It was dark; she walked up to the window and did not think I could see her dump out her dirty cup. She asked me to fill it up with hot water. Is this a free service, people? Is this a non-profit organization? Did they know how much one of these miniature water heaters cost? I smiled and poured. Just wanted to bitch a minute...

6:34 P.M. Crawling out of here...

12-09 21° Clear with high clouds.

Grasshopper Jumper: A shot of vodka, crème de menthe, crème de cacao, 2 shots of espresso, shot of Half & Half, a cup of ice, blend until smooth. Pour into glass and top with a spot of whipped cream and a mint leaf.

6:42 A.M. For the first time ever, I checked a thermometer *inside* my upstairs house. It read 39 degrees. No wonder I could see my breath! Could this *house* give me arthritis?

8:37 A.M. Scanner: An eighteen-year-old male fell while snowboarding and they didn't know the extent of his injuries at that time. However, he was on a respirator, his body was twitching, and he had a *strong* pulse of *sixteen.*

10:10 A.M. The Porta Potty guy is here. He is claiming that the sewage is *almost* frozen solid. Not *this* again! Cameras! Lights! Action! Taking Christmas Photo Card Orders! He is trying to knock it loose with his vacuum hose end. Suck, knock, suck, knock! I told him, "Someone needs to invent a gargantuan ice pick for you poor guys." With sad eyes, "I'm considerin' quittin'."

2:52 P.M. No. 2 Bachelor emailed for a lunch date. Maybe he thinks I am only avoiding *dinners.* He is misguided. I'm avoiding the whole male population.

3:43 P.M. No. 5 called to get a west side weather report, so he would know whether he had to chain up or not.

4:00 P.M. Ms. Gossip No. 1 came in and said that she and hubby got into a big-fat-juicy-fight yesterday over the heating bill. "He went out and bought a $400 goddamn mower and we don't even have a fuckin' *lawn*! And he's bitchin' at me over a $12 eBay purchase and heat!" If the truth were known, I think he is getting crazy over the change and paper bills she manages to steal out of his pockets. He will have to start showering with his pants on…

I told her about my customer yesterday, who stood here bitching about his wife's addiction to eBay - buying up every single, solitary, Christmas house they had. Following World-War-Four, she agreed, no more spending on the net! The very next day this hubby jumped on the computer while his wife was at work, logged on to her eBay account and saw that the same night of her promise, 11:59 P.M. to be exact, she was at it again! He called her at work and informed her that the item she was bidding on had only 18 minutes left to bid! She hung up.

5:56 P.M. The cold is getting old. I've decided that the cold up here is a perfect excuse to binge and get fat! I just ate my normal chocolate bar with almonds and a hot chocolate…and am thinking of more. Winter blues crave chocolate.

I was sitting here thinking of Hunk Wyatt, those dreamy lips, and wondering why he hadn't contacted me again. Was it because I didn't go and pick him up from jail?

6:50 P.M. I shall retire to my thirty-nine-degree living room and hug my dog…

12-10 21° Clear.

Coffee Bubbles: Mix 3 cups espresso, 1 tbs. sugar, 1 cup Half & Half. Fill four glasses half full. Add 1 scoop of ice cream to each glass and fill with soda water. Top with whip.

9:35 A.M. An old guy stepped in with wide, bright suspenders on. No. 1 Gossip was here and asked him where he was from. He said Seattle and we both mentioned that he didn't look like a Seattleite! Don't think he even realized we were referring to his dress code – white bushy beard and a five-inch red belt to boot. He told us that he grew up in Icicle Town and lived right here, in Treetops Loop, back in '47 and '48. He definitely had that "these-thar-hills" look.

Bossy Blue is after Missy Green. I believed my parakeets were doing it.. I'd never really seen birds getting-it-on before, but I will put a nest inside the cage, and we will see. I also surrounded their cage with oodles of newspapers.

All that flapping around, on the bottom of the cage, was sending too many feathers flying. New drink? Fluffy Feathered Frappuccino!

1:48 P.M. Scanner: A spleen and kidney injury at the resort. A fifty-four-year-old male was now on oxygen.

A local came in again. He was becoming a regular, who liked to talk for a *minimum* of thirty minutes, while his wife waited *out in the car*. I had not met her yet but from here, she looked like hell. He was asking why I liked birds so much. He didn't have any *live* pets, but he did have his seven stuffed teddy bears. Oh boy, here we go… "They all have names and outfits to match. On Mr. Drunk, I put a cute flask in his underwear, and he carries it around. (*Carries!!??*) Mr. Golfer has a dimpled white ball necklace. My Army *friend* is dressed in camo and he is the mischievous one. (*Oh my!*) 'Fatso' is really in bad shape. I got him at a garage sale for $2 and he has to wear a wide collar around his neck, otherwise he wouldn't be able to hold his poor floppy head up." This sixty-year-old man cooed and cuddled them.

That flipping nutso reminded me of the doll lady from last year! Her loads of dolls each with their own personality that argued for her attention. *Get-me-outta-here!!!*

3:03 P.M. Scanner: A fifteen-year-old male lost consciousness on the hill. He was awake now and complained of hip pain.

3:29 P.M. Scanner: Another fifteen-year-old, female this time, with a cut above her eye and in and out of consciousness, at the ski resort.

Just had a fifth guy needing windshield cleaner. I asked if he was driving the rig that was parked in my drive thru. He said, "Oh…sorry…I'll move it right away." He hurried out, for my sake, and couldn't find the lever to open his hood. So…he is still not moving. Why did he have to fill the damn reservoir, right in the middle of the drive thru? I stuck my head out, "Can you please move your car forward a wee bit?" He said, "Oh sorry!" (again!) A wheel did not roll a full three minutes.

5:20 P.M. I was too pooped to pop anymore. I had had a nasty kink in my neck all day. It's been *more* than irritating.

Boring day for this barista. My whole life was boring too! I supposed I *could* juice it up. Nope…not worth it! It was the weekend and TV sucked, so I would sit here for a bit longer. Buck sure had been quiet as a mouse lately. I hadn't really missed him either…

Amtrak whizzed by all lit up and loaded with folks headed to Icicle Town for the Christmas Lighting. Looked very "*merry*"!

7:10 P.M. Just made myself one of *my* famous *wholesome* dinners – sliced bananas with gobs of chocolate syrup and whipped cream - on a paper plate. Fine dining…plus…potassium and calcium galore…

12-11 20° Clear.

Black Forest Surprise: A shot of cherry brandy, rum, crème de cacao. Top with whip and a cherry.

7:44 A.M.

It feels colder than 20° this morning. I feel hormonally unbalanced. My kink is a tiny better. I am getting closer to that ugly age. The fucking "M" word! Women get a bad break. Periods are disgusting, having babies hurts like shit, and we feel like crap during menopause. Men just seem to travel through life at a pretty constant clip. They go from hard-on – to – hard-on.

10:33 A.M. Scanner: A fourteen-year-old male with a left shoulder fracture.

12:06 P.M. Scanner: A twelve-year-old snowboarder crashed and burned and has back pain.

3:31 P.M. Rosie came roaring in for *food*. She quickly demanded *it*, no money in hand. Her shitty husband has not let her go to the grocery store for a couple of weeks. Mother Hubbard's Cupboards were completely bare. Give me a fucking break! Another *two* points off the male column this time! She stuffed food into her mouth and jacket pockets, while I watched, dumbfounded. She still waited for her car to get repaired and she would make her break. If she didn't leave the bastard, I'll never speak to her again!

6:06 P.M. Sad ending to a nice day…

12-12 22° Clear.

Mint Lemonade: Heat 2/3 cup fresh/chopped mint leaves in 2 cups water to a boil. Turn down and simmer for 5 minutes. Let cool, then strain out mint leaves. Mix this mint liquid with a can of frozen lemonade and 4 cups of water. Refrigerate or serve hot.

8:43 A.M. I had an *epic* moment as I headed back up the highway from the post office. A beautiful American bald eagle headed right towards me as we closed in on each other, he went up, circled, and flew along the highway line, as if my escort. It was inspiring!

I had to leave the pellet stove running, 24/7 for as long as this cold snap lasts. I don't care anymore about the cost, I'm sick of freezing. And I'm drained from waking up every night, worrying about my birds. My whole parking lot is white with frost, which hurts business. The customers driving by think it looks too slippery to stop and satisfy.

1:58 P.M. "Are the Porta Potties out there your only bathroom?" a husband asked. I recited the usual shtick. "Yes." "But my wife needs to go, bad, and she's funny about such things." I wanted to admit, I wouldn't go in them either, on a bet – I'd rather shit in the woods like a bear! Same story, different day. "She has three choices as I see it: she can *get over it*, or do the hike, up the hill, across the RR tracks or be in pain all the way home." Maybe BOO had a hole, with a platform, in his camp. But I just smiled – sadly – for the news this husband had to deliver back at the car.

Dark clouds had suddenly filled the skies. Warmer? A nice thought, anyway…

5:13 P.M. Well, move over Microsoft! I just spent the evening in Bellevue at "The Dive", a fun happening joint for the older crowd for mom's birthday bash. Lots of these friends went back forty-plus years. Back when *they* all necked in the back seats of Chevy's, out on the undeveloped 80-acres in Redmond. Now the beautiful, proud, high-rise buildings of the Microsoft Campus covered that ground.

There was Maria, whose number of marriages rivaled mine. She said that of her five trips to the altar, and three times living in sin, she should have stayed with that architect! She said that none of these chaps were too bad compared to the men she dated now. "All the decent ones these days are wilting-on-the-vine and can't keep up with me!" Maria was eighty-seven years old!

Next was Betty, who remembered the real Bellevue, and she still dressed the part! She lived part-time in Arizona, with summers and holidays back up north. She had dated every single 'eligible' bachelor in Seattle and they all still loved her to death. What the hell was her secret?! Maybe the newer guys down in the southwest will give up the info…

Then there was Bobby-Baby, the lovable, cuddly, sweet friend. He looked ten years younger since the last time I saw him. He had a back fusion a while ago and the doctor hit him with a stringent diet and exercise routine.

Jane and Harry were there and still dating. They told the whole room about their recent weekend fling to Icicle Town and the visit to my store. All about the best espresso ever and the special gifts they bought.

And the last couple was Jewels and Albert. I had known them for eons through mom. They'd been more *than just friends* for twelve years now. She would like a ring and a house. So far, the big guy had gotten away with *skating*…

The aging ex-Mariners pitcher still sat on the same bar stool, barking orders at the *subordinates*. "Shut up –– Turn up the damn volume on the TV – Can't ya see I'm trying to watch the football game – My drink is empty – This food is cold!" Or "Can't you see I'm trying to yell into my cell phone?" This phone never rang. No one ever saw him dial out. But it was always attached to his ear. He relived his ivory-tower-days verbally, every night, to anyone who would lend an ear. Mostly only strangers now… or to whatever recording he listened to on his little silver flip box…

This table was where the *true* Bellevue history lies. From the early '60s on… The Bellevue before it was the exciting, state-of-the-art, influential, wealthy place it is now. There was a lot of laughter and love at this huge table. I enjoyed sharing my evening with them, listening to their days of wine and roses, hot pants, and go-go boots. That was a special *circle of friends.*

10:33 P.M. Tucked in…

12-13 34° Clouds.

Cafezinho Brazil: A shot of espresso with a 1/2 cup of sugar and a slice of lemon.

8:00 A.M. I had to run back to Bellevue to get my spine adjusted. Well, since I was having that winter-blues-chocolate-thing going on, I stopped at See's and scored two free truffles. I bought six candy bars, a bag of molasses chips, and some English toffee chunks. The toffee was almost gone by the time I hit the car door!

12:56 P.M. Scanner: A seizure in progress at the Saratogan School.

I couldn't even get the doors unlocked and the scanner went off, the birds screamed, the pellet stove wouldn't start, and customers waited to be served. Turned out our *local* fifteen-year-old girl was our seizure patient once again.

A man stepped up and needed paper towels for his sick dog that had eaten *the* fruitcake. No kidding!

Here is a little lighthearted fruitcake fun for this Holiday Time: Charles Jackens said, "A fruitcake is a geological homemade cake." What is that all *about*? I mean, everyone seemed to hate it, but it always, ALWAYS, seemed to be around! I checked and the first record of fruitcake dated all the way back to Roman times. The first mail-order business for that inedible heavy lump, which most people considered a *perfect* doorstop, or bird food, dated back to 1913. It was a proven fact that people never actually *bought* fruitcake for themselves; instead, they bought it to send to others…they dislike…

12-14 21° Clear.

Beer Buzz: Pour your favorite beer in a glass and add a shot of iced espresso.

8:46 A.M. Ugh cold again.

12:41 P.M. Scanner: A female skier with a back injury. Aid room E.T.A. was twenty minutes.

Well, shit, I needed the aid room! For the fucking third or fourth time, I'd left my hammer on top of the fucking ladder while hanging some fucking rugs! You know the rest of the story… BANG, right on top of my head! The claws not only sliced my head open, they lopped off a chunk of hair! I stood there, next to my espresso machine disoriented, with one of my rags held up against the bleeding. "I want my Mommy!"

An old logger happened to stop for an espresso. I asked if he would *please* assess the damage. In his opinion, stitches were not vital. He coughed and excused himself without an espresso – don't blame him with all the blood lying about.

Automatically, my fingers *did-the-walking*…I dialed Buck. I had always called him with big problems and for sure, injuries. His cell did not accept any incoming calls! With those huge wads of cash, always, why in the hell didn't he pay his bills? Because he was stupid and that was a stupid move on my part. Thank God he would never know that I called!

5:30 P.M. No. 5 called to remind me that we were married tomorrow, umpteen years ago. I told him on days like this, I wished I were still married.

7:52 P.M. I deserved to get out of here and *nurse* myself. Treat myself, but to… what? A drink? No thanks! A man? No *fuckin'* thanks! Guess it must be Dr. Phil, a long bath, and back to the chocolate…

> **NOTE:** I am changing the format a little. During the Christmas holidays, for two weeks, I will be serving up Espresso Food Recipes. So, unearth those *insipid* aprons!

12-15 21° High clouds.

> **Espresso Macaroons:** In a 2-quart heavy saucepan over low heat, heat 2 ounces unsweetened chocolate. Remove from heat. Stir in a 14 ounce can condensed milk, 3.5 ounces flaked coconut, 3/4 cup chopped walnuts, 2 tsp. espresso instant powder, 3/4 tsp. almond extract, 1/4 tsp. salt. Preheat oven to 350°, 2 greased cookie sheets, and drop by tbs. 1" apart. Bake for 12-minutes.

8:22 A.M. My bloodied, matted hair is in a ponytail today. Ms. Gossip No. 1 came in for two caramel mochas this time. "I'm surprising our postmistress with one. What the hell is in your hair? You know, Christy, everyone up here is so happy you have joined our hill. But what the hell happened to your hair?" Does that mean everyone is going to think I am a dirty slob? "It's an owee, I had a hammer claw rip my head open and even took a batch of precious hair." No response…she started to get queasy from my description. "Okay, now you take care of you, but I really meant it when I said how thankful we are to have gotten you, and not only for the espresso, but also for the chitchat." Had she switched sides? Her middle name had always been back-stabbing-bitch! Christmas spirit?

9:39 A.M. La-dee-da…

2:03 P.M. The fighter jet just flew by. Came lower and lower, till all my windows rattled. I pretended that it was Bill Gates' Lear, and he was flying to New York for lunch and swooped down to invite me, but saw I was much too busy… *I must get a life!!*

I just got an email from Clint 15 from "down-below." I dated him long before I started my diary. Seemed like another life. He was a real looker, gracious, and a blast in bed. But just another fine-looking-dickhead! I could add a new chapter! But then again, it would have to take place in a bedroom, which would mean shaving, putting on perfume, taking the lingerie out of mothballs…then endure the mental hell for a couple of weeks once more. Another See's candy bar. Dammit, not quite like getting pounded against his headboard. But tastier.

5:31 P.M. Two male skiers just came in for lattes. They told me that Santa was at the resort handing out candy canes. *Santa* happened to live in Stonewall.

I just got off the phone with Clint 15. He was now a grandpa and wanted to stop and show off pictures and visit. At least we had *that* in common – not much more though… He was also banging his ex again. That had been going on and off, for nine years. He said he had to reassure himself one more time that she really *wasn't* the one. And this *stripper* had been hoping for nine *long* years that *this* time would be *it* and he would stay home for good! He bragged, "She told me that you, Christy, have slept with that whole mountain. Apparently, she knows someone up there." "Sorry…in her dreams." Slut!

6:46 P.M. I took my pure-self upstairs to shower off the gossip…

12-16 16° Clear.

Cappuccino Ice: Combine 3 cups espresso, 1 cup Half & Half and 1 cup sugar into a saucepan on medium. Stir until almost boiling and sugar dissolves. Cool to room temp, pour into an 8-inch square pan and freeze (3-6 hours). To serve, warm in refrigerator for 30 minutes.

7:44 A.M. It is soooooooo cooooooold! The Porta Potty man was due today and I am afraid all that hideous human waste was frozen over again.

11:11 A.M. Mr. Mercury Poison stopped. Did I, or did I not, ask him to stay away? He and his car were both *challenged*. He needed to buy as many cans of car oil as I could spare, just to get down the hill to civilization. He tried to deliver a present to his daughter and stopped because he was having one of his mercury attacks again and was about to pass out. Was he trying to buy a couple of hours of rest here? He looked healthy as a horse, so it was all very strange. A lot of caretaker gals would fall for his looks alone. He would have to be given mouth-to-mouth, before *and* after sex I'm afraid.

2:11 P.M. Damn...here came a high school acquaintance I had not seen since 1976! And my hair was again in its proverbial on-top-of-the-head-hammer-mess! Fuck it! Why would I bother to explain myself to the jock...that still *was*! Even if it had been thirty years! The description would fly back to Bellevue faster than through a carrier pigeon! And I could tell he knew all the beautiful people! He was in a new BMW! Dressed fit to kill. My saving grace was that he came up skiing twice a week and I would make damn sure I looked more presentable next time. Thank God I have a tight ass. Please tell all the folks about that! Priorities!

5:55 P.M. *Over...*

12-17 26° Clear.

Espresso Mocha Marshmallow Treat: Put 8 ounces marshmallow, 1/2-pint milk and 1 tbs. instant espresso powder into a bowl and dissolve over a pan of hot water. Set aside to cool, then stir in 4 ounces cream liqueur. When beginning to set, fold in half of the 1/4 pint of whipped cream and 1-ounce chopped walnuts. Spoon into serving dishes or glasses. Garnish with remaining whipped cream and nuts.

7:00 A.M. The moon was still out when I opened. I always glided in the doors very optimistically, only to get thrashed down. I had only a drop of customers and its 10:03 A.M. What the hell! Get out of bed at the crack of dawn Christy, for what may I ask?

12:05 P.M. Some young teens came through the drive thru and the *young* one in the back asked, "Are you single?" I replied, "Yes, sonny, and I'm a grandma." He persisted, "But you are single?" I said yes again. He then told me that he would be back when he was finished skiing. I said, "In your next life, kiddo!"

Hunk Wyatt was supposed to get out of jail tomorrow. So, that is why he'd been a no-show around here.

1:33 P.M. Rosie and her daughter came by, to hide out for about three hours. I felt like I ran a women's shelter. Her dad was coming to pick them up and take them to his home. She was finally leaving her husband Ex-Con – for good! That wicked, evil man could finish off the men's column of demerits, single-handedly. Rosie pulled a black gadget out of hiding. "I stole this, and this is my way of killing him legally." She had stolen the couch potato's remote control! She planned to chuck it into the nearest receptacle on their trip "down-below" to dads. And she finally relaxed into a *good* sigh.

No. 2 Bachelor came in with his arms full of gifts for me! A big Christmas cookie tin and a huge assortment of candles. What a doll! I will have to bake him one of my blackberry pies. This happened to be the first time I had ever seen the man in a suit and tie. He looked *very* elegant.

A local *hotheaded* guy just called and asked me to the dance up at the ski resort tonight. Ick! No way! You stoned, halitosis, horn-dog freak!

Rosie's dad arrived. Goodbye Rosie, for now…

6:54 P.M. Scanner: A twenty-year-old male with a fractured collarbone at the resort.

7:00 P.M. Just closed, as my Christmas wattage light bill overtook my income, and a car pulled up and they wanted two doppios. *Fuck doppios! Fuck expanding my already jumbo repertoire!* That Italian for "double", meant a 2-shot espresso drink, made with the *oiliest* dark roast beans, ground fine, making sure a nice layer of crème forms on the top, and finished up with a perfect curly-Q. I don't *do* curly-Qs.

7:43 P.M. And I cannot look at another face!

8:03 P.M. The espresso machine and cart are cleaned, the computer is defragging, the pellet-stove hopper is full for the night, and the espresso cart sink put on its slight drip, so the pipes don't freeze. I took a seat at my desk, alongside my sleeping birds, closed my eyes, and thought back on today. I examined the shitty things I did and thought, along with the thankful and happy moments.

9:09 P.M. A prayer for all my family – Rosie and hers too…

12-18 27° Clear.

Cappuccino Parfait: Dissolve 1 tsp. of instant espresso powder into 1/4 tsp. water. Stir this into 1 cup whipped topping. Prepare one box of chocolate or vanilla pudding or pie filling using whole milk. Let stand 5 minutes. Spoon pudding and whipped topping alternately into six dishes. Refrigerate until serving.

8:22 A.M. A super-duper windstorm last night! I woke up several times and heard my big sign whip against the building while all its hardware squeaked. Thank goodness for the tie-downs or it would be in another county by now. Ex-Con took off early in his sports car. Probably headed down to haunt Rosie. He was *not* that puritan description, *early to bed and early to rise, keeps a person fit, healthy and wise.* That heinous beast sells drugs instead!

12:15 P.M. Some of my regular granita lovers stopped. I said, "This is way too early to see you guys off the ski slopes; it's just a little after noon!" She said, "I got blown right off the mountain and pushed down the hill. Never skied so fast in my whole life!"

3:49 P.M. My credit card machine just quit. I have people waiting! Shit, shit, shit! I took it apart and put it back together and amazingly, it was humming along. Thank God for small favors.

Another couple chowed down on some of my holiday cookies. "Are these homemade?" They asked. I just start howling. Me? The apron-hater? With *zero* time on my hands? "I must confess, Costco."

5:43 P.M. Scanner: A fifty-one-year-old male with a hip fracture at the resort.

Hunk Wyatt had not been by yet. I dolled up, just in case, but only to *fuck-with-him*, of course. Female-tease...

6:42 P.M. I was still selling espressos. I had even had a few families walk up from Treetops Loop today. They were the cabin owners, who left their commanding 7,000 sq. ft. homes in the city, to spend a festive weekend roughin' it in the mountains. Yeah...right! Those expensive little cabins were nicer than most middle-class homes!

6:59 P.M. Scanner: A twenty-five-year-old male lost consciousness.

8:07 P.M. Twelve hours non-stop is more than sufficient...

12-19 34° A touch of snow and hail.

Espresso Tuile: Combine 1/2 tsp. salt, 1 cup brown sugar, 1 cup corn syrup and mix. Add in 1.25 cups flour, 6 ounces soft butter, 1/2 tsp. vanilla and mix well. Add 2/3 cup crushed espresso beans and 1 cup chopped pecans. Drop heaping tbs. onto a non-stick cookie sheet, three at a time. Bake at 350° for 8-10 minutes.

7:44 A.M. Rosie's Horrible Husband came in my drive thru. He knew better than to darken my doorway! He asked me to pass along a message to her, "Could you tell her to call me?" Fuck off!!!!

10:42 A.M. Ms. Gossip No. 1 invited me over for their *big-ass-turkey* dinner. (*Her* words!). I was politely passing along my regrets when Ms. Gossip No. 2 pulled up and we began our tattle-tale triangle. They wanted every last detail regarding Ex-Con and his battered wife. They came to the right place! I could spew *venom* over *that* situation! Maniac Ex-Con came by again, so now it was time to email the sheriff. I do not like him putting one toe inside my property line!

5:58 P.M. Scanner: A twenty-four-year-old female with a dislocated elbow at the resort. Also, one person was being rushed to the hospital from a car accident.

9:18 P.M. Accomplished all. What a great day. How time flew. More of these, please…

12-20 34° Rain.

Cappuccino Sundaes: Combine 1/2 cup espresso, 1/2 cup whipping cream, heaping 1/4 cup packed brown sugar, 1 tsp. cinnamon into a saucepan. Simmer until sugar dissolves. Remove from heat. Add 8.5 ounces semisweet chopped chocolate and stir until melted and smooth. Scoop coffee frozen yogurt or ice cream into ten bowls. Top with cooked sauce and sprinkle Roca candy on top.

8:55 A.M. Finally, some wet stuff fell from the sky. An eagle scouted the land. I just saw a second one when I put out my signs.

Ms. Gossip No. 2 came by and I caught her up on more gossip – Ex-Con's second visit, the accidents, and the man who just left his wife over burnt Christmas cookies, while she was rubbing his sore back! Men, you aren't doing very well! Another point off the chart!

10:15 A.M. Hunk Wyatt finally stopped in! He was glad to see me, and visa-versa! He was even more buffed-out and chiseled than before – and quite aware of this! How did I know, you asked? He removed his jacket, wearing only a scoop-necked, sleeveless muscle tee shirt. It was frozen-city in here – so you are the judge!

He went on and on about his macho fight behind jail bars. Whatever… now he plans to take on a local male whore, we called One Beer Bob. That bad dude had tried to fuck all our young daughters over the years. Get him and get him good! To the moon with you! One Beer Bob lived above one of our local bars and kept an eye out only for young ones who got one beer down, with their fake I.D. and then he'd nail 'em. The story goes…he had the first female stripper party in our area. Half the males in town showed up and they caved in his floor. Hunk Wyatt could wail on him anytime!

2:02 P.M. I just had two gals stop-to-shop. They had been in several times for espresso. Today they spent $500! Bought gifts for the world! I told them that *they* were *my* Christmas present!

3:00 P.M. Scanner: A thirty-year-old male with a back injury was in the aid room in horrible spasm.

A very masculine – raging bull arrived– you know the kind – the *jock* that seems to just *erupt* through a doorway. He was looking for a gift for his *newish* relationship. "Can you help, little Shoppe Girl? I asked my chick, 'What do you want for Christmas?' She came back with one of those female-isms, 'If you loved me, you'd *know* what I want'! Well, I don't! To either portion of that sentence! So, she is getting an X-Box. Got any?" "No, sorry." As I made his drink and suggested several things, I thought his "honey" might like, I realized he was impossible. "Case closed, sir."

I had two soldiers in for an espresso shot, an iced chai and a mocha. One of them was stationed in Afghanistan, where chai was that country's favorite drink. He explained, "They made it by boiling pure chai leaves, right on the spot. First, they filled the cups halfway up with sugar, then they poured the tea over that. That way they don't have to keep adding sugar, to get it exactly right. And you take it or leave it that sweet. Was delicious." The other soldier was leaving for Iraq in February. He said, "I love to visit Washington, where everyone knows and appreciates espresso! When someone asks for a shot, they get a shot. If you want to spark it up, the baristas know what the hell you are talking about!" I rang them up, gave them a military discount, and told them how much they were appreciated for protecting our wonderful land. One of them got a little teary…

6:36 P.M. Some foreign guys stopped and were shocked that I absorbed their four-drink order. One of them was a caramel macchiato. By now, that recipe was in the mainframe of my brain - could do it in my sleep. That was pounded into *every* barista's head these days.

8:34 P.M. Sleepy java girl…

12-21 33° Raining.

Espresso Soufflé: Melt 6 ounces of semisweet chocolate in a double boiler, stir until smooth. In bowl mix 4 egg whites until frothy. Add 3 tbs. sugar and beat until soft peaks form. Again, beat 3 egg yolks, 1/4 cup warm espresso into melted chocolate. Quickly fold this into egg whites and divide into six soufflé dishes that have been lightly buttered and sugar dusted. Bake at 400° until crisp on top (10 minutes). Serve at once!

9:03 A.M. I just had the most rude, offensive, belligerent blockheads in my drive thru that I've had in a long, long time! I came so damn close to telling him off.

He thought he was gold-plated, and I was just a working stiff! He told me to hurry up, that he didn't have all day, three separate times. He said his drink almost burned his tongue and tasted like hell. He said it was too expensive and he was never going to stop here again. "G R E A T!" I wouldn't last a day if this were the norm! He wouldn't last one more day in this town! And if I had my way, he wouldn't live one more day anywhere!

11:48 A.M. BMW Brian emailed. He just seemed to have to try, about every six months to see if I was ready to take the thongs down to my knees and coax him out onto that balcony under the palms.

2:32 P.M. Boone from Stonewall just drove up to chat. He brought out the worst in me and the first words that flew out of my mouth were, "So, ya got laid lately?" He glanced up at his headliner, seemingly trying to wrack his brain, and came back with, "Not really." "Boone, that's *not* an answer. NOT REALLY means yes but didn't dig it!" He laughed his head off and wondered how I knew men more than men knew themselves. "*That* isn't even a contest!" He admitted that he had a couple of one-night stands. He disgusted me now – he is getting drecky. Don't think he was like that a year ago. He had a few standards then…

4:44 P.M. The sheriff finally stopped for a visit and wished me a Merry Christmas. That was nice. He told me that he had received all my emails regarding the local *insanity* and was keeping them all in the "Christy File," including the ones about my neighbor, the woman-beater, and the wife he was trying to starve-to-death.

5:15 P.M. I am leaving for my early Christmas celebration at mom's house. She knows my very favorite is rack of lamb, with all the trimmings. And scads of presents!

11:13 P.M. Merry Christmas to all and goodnight…

12-22 33° Loads of rain.

Cappuccino Freeze: In a 2-quart bowl, whisk 1/4 cup instant espresso powder into 1/2 cup boiling water. Then whisk in 2.25 cups water and 1 can sweetened condensed milk until blended. Divide this between three ice shaver tubs. Freeze until firm. Remove from tubs and shave using an ice shaver. Garnish with whip.

7:54 A.M. That fucker Ex-Con was at the drive thru again and tried to intimidate me into giving up some info about Rosie. My lips were sealed – cemented shut!

Well, my Christmas dinner was glorious. Gosh we had fun! Now, I needed to find a minute to run upstairs and grab my doggy bag, filled with leftover lamb! I had lived up here on eggs and Top-Ramen for a year…or so it seemed.

10:36 A.M. A train passed that was pretty with all of the engines matching and a honk-honk from Dennis. He called earlier and told me to listen for honk (Merry), honk (Christmas).

Up at the ski resort, the snow level was back down to forty inches. It was raining again, but you noticed, I hadn't been bitchin' about the cold lately. Because it warmed up, they only received one inch of new snow in the last seven days. Oh God, please let this change…

3:49 P.M. Rosie just popped in to let me know that she was headed down to the house to pick up another load of possessions. She wanted somebody to know – who was close. She will check in again on her way out. I almost didn't recognize her with her first haircut in well over a year and color in her cheeks! I'm so happy for her and her little girl!

She thanked me for all my help and said, "Christy, we are now home."

Gave me goose bumps. Her dad had more gunpowder and bullets than blades of grass, so she was in good hands!

5:31 P.M. I hoped tomorrow would be more of a *customer day* than *a local soap opera*…

12-23 33° Foggy rain.

Espresso Pastry Cream Filling: Blend 2 ounces of chocolate powder, 1 cup cream, 1 cup espresso, set aside. Beat 5 egg yolks until light, add 1/2 cup sugar, slowly, and then a dash of salt. Beat until thick. Add chocolate mixer and blend. Mix together 2 tbs. cornstarch and 2 tbs. milk and mix into the other mixed batch. Put whole mixture into top of double boiler and simmer until thick. Cool. Add tsp. rum. Makes 3 cups.

7:47 A.M. Scanner: Security police at the ski resort called for backup. Some joker was dressed up like Santa, begging little kids to sit on his knee. Good! Our pervert-for-the-day was over and done with – early!

Later, another cute mom took one step inside here, saw the birds, and said, "My kids have *got* to see this, if that's all right?" Oh boy, here we go…my birds *love* kids; they had the same reaction that a tiny baby had to seeing youngsters. I nodded and she went back outside to spend ten minutes unstrapping the four car seats to bring them in for a two-minute *bird adventure*. At first, they just stood there in quiet amazement. Then the birds took off! They danced and dangled, screeched and squawked. The kids were laughing so hard, they were almost crying. Would those little ones ever remember those moments?

1:44 P.M. It was busy as heck with anxious, road-weary holiday travelers. I was splurging on my wattage. This joint was lit up like a Christmas tree, from one end of the property to the other. Oh, those infamous caramel macchiatos again! A gal asked, "Can you make one of those?" "Sure!" (Smarty britches!) She said, "You know what those are way out here?" I cleared my throat, "Even we *country-bumpkins* have to make a living, so we try to stay *on-top-of-our-game*! But I've decided to only serve them to people who can spell it." She blanched. And couldn't…as she left, she paid my concoction the highest compliment, "Waaaaay better than Bellevue Starbucks!" Yeah team and which flavors did I guess on this time?

2:00 P.M. Our newest cabin owners who were yuppies from the city just jogged by. In the visors atop their streak-jobs, blinding diamond studs and tights. Quite a sight up on this mountain highway!

3:29 P.M. Scanner: A nineteen-year-old with a hip fracture had been upgraded to a medic with a possible C.B.S.

I just had three carloads of families stop for drinks. $25+ orders in each car! My cash register loved sounding like a slot machine with three cherries!

3:58 P.M. Scanner: Skier ran into a tree. The twenty-two-year-old female, who was responsive, had been upgraded to a cardiac arrest and still *up on the snow* where they were performing CPR! Merry frigging Christmas! People! Helmets, dammit…or body armor!

My place should be renamed: Drop Off Site for Children! My parking lot had become the swap point between eastern and western Washington. Divorced couples throw children and suitcases from one car to another, always in a gigantic rush to get away from each other. I had about a dozen regulars now. You can imagine the bitching and tales of woe I heard on a weekly basis. Men were the most miserable, with their two-day visit limitation. Women were just sick of the drive, but needed the break from the little darlings.

The twenty-two-year-old has died.

4:59 P.M. I cannot be here anymore. I feel sick...

12-24 35° Pouring. Christmas Eve.

Cappuccino Truffles: Mix 2 tbs. instant espresso powder, 2 tbs. orange juice, 2 tbs. brandy. Slowly add to 7 oz. of marshmallow cream with mixer. Add in 3 cups crushed chocolate wafers, 1 cup chopped pecans, 2 tbs. orange peel. Shape into 1-inch balls; roll 1/2 of the balls into 2 tbs. cocoa and 2 tbs. sugar mixed together. Roll remaining balls into coconut to coat. Makes 5 dozen.

9:40 A.M. Buck just came in wanted to take back all the campfire wood bundles he gave me last spring. He desperately needed them for his mom and dad's Christmas present. So much for *thinking ahead* – their exchange would be in a couple of hours. He was not dressed or showered or shaved, but that's our Buck too! As this may be the highlight of his sweet mom's Christmas, I told him to take the flippin' sticks. He threw $100 at me and left.

12:00 Noon. A few locals came in with invitations to their homes tonight.

Ms. Gossip No. 1 asked again, "Do ya wanna come over for some *big-ass-turkey*, Christy?" She was a heavy smoker, so when she laughed at her own joke, she coughed her head off. Customers on either side backed way off.

My buddy with Lou Gehrig's disease stopped and asked me down for prime rib with his family.

Denny next door wanted to feed me too. He told me if Trucker Bitch's boy toy happened to be there, he would tell him to get lost for a few minutes so I could have a bite with no jail time.

Mom called and begged me to come down for dinner – or close tomorrow and meet her at my brother's for a family celebration. A minimum of a six-hour roundtrip drive and that was just the *travel* portion.

I declined all those invitations. I really needed to work – wanted to work. But I felt so loved and thankful for everyone's kindness.

1:17 P.M. Buck was back – just could not stand a visit without a confrontation, I guess. He wanted to know how my *sex-sessions* were going with Boone from Stonewall, Hunk Wyatt, Gorgeous 15, and No. 7. I told him to relax, I could French braid my leg hairs. "And by the way, my dog died," he said. That dog had one miserable thirteen years! Buck never paid him no mind; he had such matted hair; it had become part of its skin. Buck said, "I came home and found him dead, hangin' over the edge of the couch. At least he didn't make a mess. My dad told me ta go bury him but I was too bushed, so he went swimmin'." "What! You threw him in the river?" "Yep," he admitted. *Boy*, do I still had personal growth to attend do! Until lately, I had him pegged as a soft-spoken, caring, misunderstood, sex maniac, mountain man. I handed him a white mocha since, "Tis is The Season', and I was trying to hang on to my holiday mood. Then I told this non-caring abusive animal jerk to get the hell outta my sight! And never darken my doorway again!

My hammered-head-wound was starting to itch. I keep forgetting and scratching. Ain't too bright!

2:41 P.M. It was a revolving door around here with all the people buying last minute forgotten gifts for forgotten folks. I just had two guys knock on my door. I had to come out of my cage and physically open it for them. I said, "It was unlocked, it's still light out, what's the problem?" They said, "There were so many signs on the building, we didn't know where to look first: no phones, no restroom, no overnight parking, use the Porta Potty, drive-thru only after dark, doors locked…" Apparently, that is the only one they read. But they ate and drank and bought lots of gifts for the family.

Holy shit! Mountain Peak Ski Resort was closed! A customer just told me that insane news. I had been oblivious to it all day long. Freaking closed for three days! Period! Even then, it would open weather permitting. More snow or else! All the ski resorts were suffering, just like last year. Dang snow gods! I set my primroses outside right then! How could this *happen* again during Christmas vacation. Maybe *we'll* all go swimmin' and drown our sorrows!

3:54 P.M. Scanner: The fire distress bell at the ski resort was ringing off the wall. It was locked up *tighter 'n a virgin*, so it must be a false alarm. Or some pissed-off snowboarder just torched the damn place for being sealed shut. Just confirmed – faulty wiring.

Buck came by again and dropped off a large Christmas present. A squishy stuffed dog. There were NO stores open within twenty miles and he sure as hell didn't purchase it beforehand. Wanted to ask him if he'd been to the local dump again but refrained. Then he slipped a couple of notes with two $100 bills paper clipped to each. I took the notes only. Nothing new and exciting in the notes, but the stuffed dog was cute. Thank you.

A couple came in who loved my birds. The husband had a close friend who had to move out-of-state and reluctantly gave her bird away to some loving neighbors. Seven years later she went back for a visit. The moment the bird heard her voice from the entry hall, he flew over to her shoulder and snuggled in her neck! You may eventually hear that elephants are suffering from an identity crisis and have fallen from their claim-to-fame perch.

5:12 P.M. I'm giving it till 6:00 P.M. I'm like…*daring* the people to just *try* and get an espresso… Then I'm going to close and head up and try to make my living room cozy and warm.

A nice but distraught family that lived down south, about eighty miles away, came by whimpering over their ruined holidays up here. They were staying at the White Water Hotel in town and the restaurant was closed again

– indefinitely. Only the bar was open. "I guess we'll just have to get *Merry* at the bar and exist on booze and *pickled pig's feet!*" A resort town with no resorts...

6:32 P.M. Bye, Christmas Eve...

12-25 40° Rain. Merry Christmas!

Espresso Cream: Combine 2 cups water, 2 ounces semi-sweet cooking chocolate, one cinnamon stick, 2 tbs. sugar into saucepan. Heat slowly until chocolate melts. Stir in 4 tsp. instant espresso powder. Discard cinnamon stick. Pour into demitasses (tiny cups), top with whip and cinnamon.

7:22 A.M. I can't wait to greet everyone with a giant, warm, HO HO HO and MERRY CHRISTMAS! Of course, my regulars will think I had hired a replacement...

10:12 A.M. Boone from Stonewall came by for a holiday mocha and little smooch on the cheek.

A lady from Canada about kissed me when she saw chai and soymilk on my menu board! She ordered a 32-ounce, thinking she probably won't score again for days! She and her son were driving to San Francisco for the holiday vacation, just to see the Golden Gate Bridge and Castro Street, with its rainbow flags flyin' proudly.

My truck's chain, lost in the heavy snow that day, just reappeared! The snow berms were melting – fast! So now both sets were back in service. *Winter* needs to get *back in service!* Rats-o-Frats!

1:16 P.M. The father of one of my daughter's best friends, whom I had not seen for about eight years, just brought me a huge box of Frango Mint Chocolates. Frango has maintained a fiercely loyal following through seventy-five years of creating their seductive taste. This man was into *enticement!* By the time he left, we were both in stitches, although I hated to do this on Christmas... The men's column will be losing a point. Same shit, different day! I had to help him shop for at least three different girlfriends. He had been busted this morning by one of them, who called his cell to wish him a *very* Merry Christmas. It wasn't very *merry* when one of the other "ones" answered the damn thing. She said icily, "Well, I guess I'm not the *first* one to send wishes your way!" Oops.

Under my tutoring, he got that pouty little number a couple of extras in the gift shop – a darling circle-of-friends from South America and some yummy lotion for a deserved foot-rub. I told him, "The only reason she's still on the line is because she's the *religious* one." Stuck the last of my recycled bows on the crap and he left with a nasty chuckle. He headed down the road for some more lusty activity – a second Christmas "fuck" with number two. He hollered back, "Thanks for the tip about the rose from an AM/PM." He was safe for the time being, No. 3 was out of town. I liked him much better when he was married!

2:00 P.M. A big-husky-hubby stepped in and belted out, "Meeeeeerry Chriiiiiistmas! We are here to bring you joy!" Then his wife screamed, "Velma Sue, look at that macaw!" Boisterous bunch of hilarious, festive people. Then my first holiday parking lot-puker. A soft pink hue…Velma Sue had her share of cosmos today!

Now, pass my gold leaf truffle…

4:50 P.M. I sent love and hugs to all family members and most friends via the phone's lines.

7:07 P.M. And most everyone I knew. Expectations…

12-26 39° Raining.

Espresso Blackened Beef Tenderloin: A HOLIDAY HANGOVER CURE! Drink several shots of booze while cooking recipe! Season 8 oz. of tenderloin with salt and pepper. Dip both sides in 2 cups of finely ground espresso beans. Sear one side in a cast iron skillet. Turnover and sear the other side. Cook in a 500° oven for 2 minutes (rare) or 8 minutes (well done).

7:49 A.M. Well, I'll be…the ski resort IS open today. I think they may have stretched the yardstick just a tad and a blind eye toward the thermometer. The media said it's snowing and thirty-one degrees. No frigging way! More skiers came down than went up.

3:27 P.M. It was a lackluster, monotonous day, with a steady stream of exhausted customers, not incredibly happy to be going home. Some of the broken families passed the kids off on their Christmas/New Year trade. I remembered those years and years of guilt-ridden shared holidays.

4:47 P.M. And I'm locked up tight. 'Tis The Season when robbers think our cash register is bulging. I'd hate to have to shoot someone on Boxing Day. Some people I knew thought Boxing Day, per folklore, was the day after Christmas when everyone cleaned their houses, ridding them of boxes, crumpled paper, bows, and tags. Or, that first day following the holiday, when everyone dragged their boxes back to the stores for an exchange. And finally…that other myth about the family member who had been waiting a full year to beat the crap out of another family member. Actually, Boxing Day is a *class* thing; Gifts among equals were exchanged on or before Christmas Day, but beneficences, or hand-outs, to those less fortunate were bestowed the day after. Personally, I think it's how re-gifting got started…

I have become a pillar of salt - I've been here all damn day – 12 plus hours!

Mr. Mercury Poison was out front and sent his daughter in to give me a present. He's learnin'! But he had a long way to go – Applets and Cotlets are almost worse than fruitcake! I made her a little drink, gave her a hug, and sent her back out to daddy. Honk honk.

5:55 P.M. Those treats would be in the candy dish tomorrow for the customers who could handle them, if any…

12-27 35° Raining.

Cappuccino Bon Bons: Preheat oven to 350° and place forty 2-inch cupcake liners on to cookie sheet. Combine a 1 pack family brownie

mix, 2 eggs, 1/3 cup water, 1/3 cup shortening, 1.5 tbs. instant espresso powder, 1 tsp. cinnamon, stir until blended. Fill each cup-cake liner with 1 tbs. batter. Bake 12-15 minutes. Cool. Garnish with whipped cream and cinnamon.

8:43 A.M. It snowed again on all of the passes! Skiers were out in force. My espresso machine was slowly breaking down. Hurry-up repairman, before it…r-r-r-spit-r-r-r…and roared to a complete halt. I would have to hand steam the rest of today! I realize this happened every Christmas vacation!

A lady came in and complained about my filthy Porta Potty. Then a guy came in desperately needing a bathroom because his contact fell out of his eye. No… neither of you may go upstairs to my personal Home-Sweet-Home. Sorry…

9:59 A.M. A snapshot: I-80 closed again so we had extra traffic on Mountain Peak Highway, meant a lot more drinks. Today's special request was a caramel chai tea. The most unique name for a female was "Oscar," although it was a customer's story about her bird. I hadn't had one male harassment yet and I spotted three more gray hairs in my long locks this morning.

5:30 P.M. A car pulled up and blocked the drive thru. I asked them to move up, but first, please pick up the trash that accidentally *fell* out of your door. They didn't like the reception, and the fact that the gift store wasn't open. So, what did they do? Tossed out a little more trash, tried to peel out on the icy pavement, and crashed their car into my snow berm. Ha Ha…

I just got my first bare-chested man this winter! Polar bear! He was in the drive thru and sort of looked as if he *did* have clothes on – so many tattoos! Covered! He must be immune to pain or into pills!

7:24 P.M. I stayed open long enough to get my crazy coincidence for the day! My neighbor, Denny, had a daughter who owned a rental house here in town. She came up to the window and asked me if I would possibly post her FOR RENT sign here. I told her I had heard that it was already rented for the season. She said, "Yes it was, but the renter died!" "Literally died?" Her renter was the twenty-two-year-old girl that died last Friday up at the ski resort! This world is as small as a pinhead. The deceased gal's boyfriend had already moved out. He lost his love.

8:04 P.M. Closing on a sad note…

12-28 36° Rain.

> Espresso Marinade: In a bowl, mash 2 large garlic cloves and 1/2 tsp. salt until a paste. Whisk in 1/2 cup espresso, 3 tbs. red wine vinegar, 1 tbs. olive oil, 1 tsp. dried rosemary, 1/4 tsp. pepper. Great for beef, chicken or lamb.

7:38 A.M. Fresh snow and lots of it! Hundreds of cars headed up to the slopes. Mountain Peak Ski Resort had a total of fifty-one inches, with seven inches of fresh powder.

A couple came in, ordered, and paid me to knit them a matching hat and scarf for their son's girlfriend. "She loves green, so you be the judge, Christy." They also bought one of my knitted eyelash yarn purses. Glee!

11:43 A.M. Hunk Wyatt came in to say hi in his sexy painter's clothes. He was headed up to the Microsoft cabin to do some staining on the cabinets. Did Wyatt call on everyone and tell them he was available again cuz he had been sprung? Or had our grapevine up here taken care of his secretarial chores? He looked great today – as I go without!

1:10 P.M. My espresso machine repair guy finally came in, right in the middle of the rush. Thank God, he felt sorry for me and my customers. He let me tiptoe through his tools and mess, to make drinks. When he had to shut it all down, we could only apologize to the desperate people. It's done and humming. I was starved but I'm slammed! Ignored my growling and achy tummy and the fact that I had to go to the pot – the kind that required at least a moment to meditate! And I'm running out of milk! Buuuuuuuuck, could you please pick up around ten gallons of milk on your way home from fuck No. 3 or 4?

2:31 P.M. Scanner: An eighteen-year-old female fell while skiing and had severe neck pain.

4:45 P.M. I had to face facts. I was out of supplies and must go "down-below." That mixing 2% and Half & Half was stupid, time consuming, and expensive. It would never get me through the entire weekend!

5:44 P.M. And I was hallucinating about pizza anyway...

12-29 33° Partly sunny. Happy Birthday, Buckeroo.

Cappuccino Brownies: Preheat oven to 350°. Melt over hot water, 6-ounces semi-sweet chocolate stir until smooth. Set aside. In large bowl combine 1/2 cup sugar, 1/4 cup soft butter. Beat. Add in 2 eggs, 2 tsp. espresso, 1/4 tsp. cinnamon and beat well. Stir in melted chocolate and a 1/2 cup flour. Spread into foil-lined 8-inch square baking pan. Bake 25-30 minutes. Cool. Makes sixteen 2-inch brownies.

8:33 A.M. Last night's shopping spree had an $800 price tag on it! Supplies *only*! And my pizza! I unloaded the two tons in a real downpour! I then finished cleaning the espresso machine.

My mom finally got the scoop on her Senior Cowboy, Rocky. She found out, "He's a gigolo looking for women with money!" I corrected her, "No mom, a gigolo is a guy who is paid for sex." She gasped, "You mean a male prostitute?" She called her gal friend right back to clarify!

Tune in later for another chapter in "The Senior Cowboy who gets paid to take his boots off!"

9:00 A.M. I had a hell of a time getting open today. I wasn't even through the gate when two cars pulled into the drive thru. My doors were not open, the store was dark, and my till was somewhere in the back and all the signs read closed. I got car No. 1 served as he had exact change. Then car No. 2 pulled up and the woman let out a little *snort* with her "iced" drink order. "Sorry, 'Snort', but I'm at least ten minutes away from being open in 'iced mode.' Wanna try something else, or come in for a sec and shop?" She didn't even respond and left in a huff. Guess she didn't *"get any"* for Christmas either. City slickin', impatient snots!

I called Andrew for his birthday and I could tell in the first five seconds that there was a woman under the same sheets! Husky voice, cold as ice, probably *right in the throes of it* and wanted *off* the phone NOW! Ms. New York must be home, because Andrew, with his gift of sexy gab, wasn't playin' around this morning with his barista phone pal. He would call back when he got a minute – probably from the john...

Ten engines went east with no train! That was a first. I am beat today. My hair got soaked last night so it's in a knot up on top...somewhere. Too zonked to wash it this morning. I felt like shit and probably looked like it too. Gonna lock up at 4:30 P.M., close at 6:30 P.M. and go shower. I've *got* to get out of these *stiff* clothes.

10:38 A.M. Scanner: A fifty-four-year-old male with a back injury and left shoulder pain, at the Nordic Center.

10:49 A.M. Scanner: A twenty-four-year-old female with a back injury at the ski resort. She's confused.

12:22 P.M. When I was driving back home last night, there had been a head-on accident that I'm sure was fatal. Measuring tapes everywhere and cameras flashing. The car was twisted beyond recognition.

I had been such a little bitch these days...customers griped and begged for an inside bathroom. "Tough luck, folks – even I have to hold my pee for hours! There is *no* bathroom in this building, except upstairs! I wouldn't care if you were Barbra Streisand (well, maybe) you ain't going into my home."

1:01 P.M. Newest update on Senior Cowboy: He hunted for women with money, then coerced them into giving up some of it – for a sure-thing-investment, of course. "Just need some quick cash for a month or so...then it will be back in your account, sweety, lickity-split, and ten-fold!"

It felt sub-zero, but I wanted to hear a funny story from a male customer at the drive-up window. His buddy, in his early seventies, started to have bladder leakage problems. "Who isn't?" "Well, he purchased some of those 'pad-thingies that ladies use.' He can't *see* either, so he ripped the blue strip off the pad and put it inside his Size 40 Jockeys – accidentally upside down." My customer was almost laughing too hard to finish. "He started bragging about how those pad things were enhancing his bulge and he was positive women were noticing! He was *immensely proud* – until it was time to replace and – YEEEOW – it had adhered itself to his hairy balls! Like a second skin!" Now *I'm* howling...

4:01 P.M. Scanner: Loss of consciousness at the resort (night skiing). A thirty-two-year-old female.

4:32 P.M. Mr. Rancher-Dad, with all the girlfriends, including the bible-thumper, came by for the second time in eight years. Couldn't believe I didn't scare him off with my male-bashing tirade last time! He brought his youngest daughter, that also knew my daughter, and together they bought gifts for grandma. I was too darn busy before to notice, but this guy was enticing, trouble, and feisty – the exact ingredients I used to look for, ensuring a wild and fun time! He owned a mini ranch on the east side of the summit. I reminded myself, he was just another female poacher with persuasive, potent drawing power! I slapped myself up-side-the-head! I was acquainted with one of his past screws – measurements of 38-24-36, so dream on, Christy! He paid again with another $100 bill, the braggart! "By the way," he asked, "how many times have you been married?" N-E-V-E-R MIND! We had a mutual acquaintance from Icicle Town who moved to Alaska to tie-the-knot for the fourteenth time! "He figured he was gonna keep doin' it till he got it right." Isn't it our responsibility to learn some lessons in this life, and not continue to just run around half-cocked (excuse the pun) forever?

7:44 P.M. Still have to go get some (fucking) ice and wash my (fucking) hair and my (fucking) body and my (fucking) clothes. And I'm (fucking) exhausted...

12-30 35° Raining.

Espresso Spread: Blend 4 ounces of soft cream cheese, 1 ounce grated semi-sweet chocolate, 1 tbs. sugar, 1/2 tsp. vanilla, 1 tsp. instant espresso powder. Serve immediately.

8:20 A.M. The snow level definitely came down last night, but it still hadn't reached me, or the highway or the post office that I had visited this morning. Within the last hour, I heard on the news that snow chains were now required at the summit. There had already been a rollover and numerous fender-benders.

Hunk Wyatt came flying through my door, looking for some heat. The Microsoft cabin was almost too icy to even apply stain. Especially without his hot cup of Americano. The dance lessons had begun. He was now hangin' with the low life, the cowboys in Pacifica. He had hired a private dance teacher and set up cozy lessons in her private studio, in the back of the cowboy bar.

Slammed! Busy! Served! Talked and stocked! It was a blast!

"Is that r-e-e-a-a-a-l-l-y-y-y-y-y-y the only bathroom you have?" in that pathetic, whiny voice. "Yup!" She tentatively headed for the *can* – two steps forward, one step back. "They even installed these outside at our brand new trillion-dollar stadium in downtown Seattle – so get over it!" Of course, I wouldn't use them on a bet – I'd be playing *camp-out* and use the woods. Her boyfriend hung around inside and waited for her to come back and place their espresso orders. She never came back in. She had walked straight back to their car with her nose in the clouds…still pissing her pants.

No time for eBay today, let alone greet my birds. I wished I had chains to sell; I could double my investment and still be much lower than the places that gauge those unprepared city folks.

11:13 A.M. Scanner: State patrol is requesting that all the minor-car-accident vehicles, on the west side of the summit, be removed immediately. They were blocking the highway.

12:15 P.M. Scanner: A vehicle collision at the summit. Another one to tow!

An older lady stopped in for a regular cup of coffee. She said she would not know how to order anything else. She had owned a river cabin, just a mile down, for forty years. She bought it for $5K. Her next-door neighbor in the big city had one of those Seattle historic classics that were headed for demolition or relocation when the crews took a wide swath through the center of town to broaden I-5. They had it trailered up here in sections and it went on the market today for $380K!

12:57 P.M. Another lady, practically airborne, rocketed through the door, yelling, "Oh my God! Oh my God! The Porta Potty is a disaster! Someone thought the sink on the wall with the white frisbee thingy was a urinal! And someone stole the sink's handles!" "It is a urinal, lady. And that's why the handles are missing..."

Some women from Florida came in for espresso – but first, "Can we beg, borrow or steal some more toilet paper, napkins, newspaper – *anything* for that nauseating box outside. We know it's the only bathroom for miles and we thank God for small favors!" People were becoming frantic. Even I was excited for them now!

4:53 P.M. Had another chocolate-covered espresso bean grabber. He laid down thirty-five cents and grabbed four beans. First, ya two-fisted-ape-man, "They are ten cents each! And your paws just touched the whole batch. You almost got your hand slapped!" And "This barista handles the food around here. Not you!" He slunk out after he forked out $3.30...

The Doors are Slammed and Bolted! I'm done with inside people. Our tow-truck driver dragged to the door, exhausted, so I let him in. He stopped for a break and a huge mocha. He needed some heavy duty caffeine, intravenously if possible, for the twenty-five or so cars that still waited to be removed off the highway. His new teeth were Paid-In-Full. "So, what's your next purchase, money-bags?" I said brightly. He wasn't paying a bit of attention to me – he just kept muttering under his breath, "DUMBELLS – DIMWITS – DUNDERHEADS!" I popped a few extra chocolate-covered espresso beans on his lid. He held his hand up, "Nope. Can't eat those anymore. See..." "Oops, I forgot!" And he grinned for the first time since I had known him. He must have gotten them from Santa!

I just lent one of my regulars some of the extra chains I found lying around (Buck's?). He just wanted to be able to show the state patrol that he was *carrying* some. Another new business: RENT FAKE CHAINS HERE! $19.95 PER DAY!

5:05 P.M. I've needed to pee since 2:22 P.M. and I'm still hangin'! I think my bladder is sick of waiting these days and just disperses it through my system.

Okay, who done it? Who stole my paper dollar tip that a customer accidentally dropped at the drive thru window? Finally got a minute to go searching. Probably someone walking to the porta potty, head bent down, in pessimistic anticipation of its condition. Thought they deserved to pluck it. Baristas have a small bank that collects below their drive thru windows, that slip through customer's fingers. We collect it all at the end of the day.

7:47 P.M. Getting about ready to sign off. What a day and it was only Friday.

7:58 P.M. Scanner: A car was driving very slowly through a residential area "down-below" and it appeared that there was a foot sticking out of the trunk.

8:15 P.M. Goodnight…

12-31 34° Cloudy. New Year's Eve.

Cocoa Cappuccino Mousse: Combine 14 ounces of sweetened condensed milk, 1/3 cup cocoa, 3 tbs. butter, 2 tsp. instant espresso powder (Dissolve in 2 tsp. hot water), in saucepan over low heat. Stir until butter melts. Remove from heat and cool. Fold this into 2 cups cold whipping cream. Spoon into dishes and refrigerate for 2 hours.

8:06 A.M. Ms. Gossip No. 1 was my first customer. She claimed, "A man over fifty who owns a Corvette up here purchased a dick extension." We both broke up and tried to rack our brains of who the hell that could be? That was our important quandary of the day!

9:00 A.M. Scanner: Respiratory distress at the ski resort. A thirty-two-year-old male. Airlift on the way! It made you wonder if those six shots of espresso, chased down by Red Bulls, followed by strenuous exercise might be killing our young men these days.

10:00 A.M. Scanner: A walk-in patient at our fire station needing a medic. Deep cuts and bruises. Domestic or auto accident? He wasn't saying...

I just cleaned my peppered parking lot: tire-squished beer cans, straws, candy wrappers, empty cigarette packages, gum, lids, cups, bottle tops, and lots of dog poop. Good-fer-nothin' slobs!

3:09 P.M. Four young men came in for espressos. At least I *thought* they were all together. So, the guy with the wallet got charged for all four drinks. Shit happens! The fourth guy was laughing and lovin' it!

Two men came in. One of them was a contractor and built a house for a client who was a bit peculiar in the head! He referred to his parrot as his best friend – constantly! That bird shot rubber bands at people and he wouldn't have believed it if he hadn't seen it for himself. The bird sat on the edge of a bowl of rubber bands, picked one up with his beak, then took a claw pulled it back and shot! I keep telling ya – very amazing pets! I am peculiar in the head!

A kid puked outside, and a separate car overheated. The mom came in and described her kid's sickness. I subconsciously lathered the hand sanitizer.

Another person needed a home for a huge parrot. Did I dare? I did not think the Health Department would be too pleased about me adding an *Avian Adoption Center* to my espresso location!

5:55 P.M. A truck full of wired, young boys stopped. Probably middle teens. I disliked this age anyway! Every other word out of their mouths was "fuck." Even when they ordered, "Make it extra sweet, but don't put a fucking lid on it. What are those fucking round things you put on top?" Then one of the jackasses wanted to know what kind of panties I was wearing. Now it was my turn, "Fuck You and Get the Fuck Back On The Highway!" He apologized and his pimples instantly glowed a ruby-red. He winced when I said, "How dare you talk to a grandma like that!" I am sure it brought to mind vivid pictures of someone verbally abusing *his* favorite granny! They paid. They left. Happy New Year, boys!

I sure was hoping that Treetops Loop didn't set off the usual firecrackers tonight. Scared the hell out of all the animals!

A guy drove up. "Do you have any baking soda for sale?" Sure, mister…does this look like a bakery? Is my apron on? "NO!"

My hammerhead scab just fell off. Yes!

9:48 P.M. Hope you all have a safe, festive, time tonight! Ring in the New Year for me. This Cinderella won't be seeing the bewitching hour! Tomorrow was another day, and a busy one at that. Must be armed for the hangovers…

P.S. How are my exes celebrating New Year's Eve, you ask?

No. 1- is home with his ton of kids and third wife.

No. 2- is trying not to fall off a bar stool somewhere, toasted out of his mind.

No. 3- is braving the huge rains, camping in a trailer in California with his wife.

No. 4- is probably dead.

No. 5- is somewhere in his semi.

No. 6- is at a poker game – and losing as usual – and fuming.

No. 7- is reading his Playboy.

10:00 P.M. See you next year…

JANUARY

Our end is together as we pour just one more

1-01 33° Cloudy. Happy New Year!

New Year's Day Pick-Me-Up: Use blender (earplugs are optional) and mix 1-cup whole milk, 1/4-gallon vanilla or coffee ice cream, 1/4 tsp. cinnamon, 1/2 cup Kahlua. Blend and pour into glass, topped with whipped cream.

7:43 A.M. A *non-drinker*, the only kind of human that could face the light of day at this hour, was in here bright and early this New Year's morning. It was my daughter's friend from Alaska; he lived in Crag Rock and wanted to tell me about the outlandish experience he had last night, taking his wife to an *authentic* Saratogan New Year's Eve event, at our Train Blow Tavern. He hadn't been inside the *joint* since high school and he was still wide-eyed relating his evening, "It was jam-packed, just like in the old days. I used to hear about it when I was a kid, eavesdropping from the top of the stairs. The only difference between then and today is the whores were missing from out on the banisters. I guarantee you, there are *major* hangovers up here today! Toilets were ripped off walls; a bottle *flew through the air* and broke the beautiful, beveled back-bar mirror. Bodies were sailing through the void between our heads and the ceiling – and right out the front door. It was utterly amazing! It was a real 'John Wayne' movie! My wife said if I didn't get her the hell outta there, she was filing for divorce!" He and I were rolling!

10:10 A.M. Scanner: Motor vehicle accident at milepost 69. Seven passengers involved and there was a language barrier. A four-year-old female ejected from the vehicle! Her forehead was swelling. How DARE they do not have the child belted in a car seat!

As I look back over this last year, I think I have *grown up a bit*. My fear level has diminished, and I can handle just about anything here on this property now. I am experiencing change, both physically and emotionally and it feels so *darn* good to be stronger. I may still get mad, sad or even lonely, but I am *less afraid!* I have been running *from* my fear, *toward* men and interdependency, all my life. Abandonment issues *they* say. Now I'm only calling guys "fuckers" once per sentence, instead of three times a-split-second. I am still tempted to fall into my old habits – all the damn time! But I'm learning that men were my *poison* all along, which just magnified the fear…starting with my father. This writing has also allowed me to see my *own* light. My hope for this New Year is that *all* women, everywhere, eventually see their *own* personal brilliance. *Our very own…*

11:16 A.M. Our tow guy had been back twice for raspberry mochas, flashing his radiant, new *ivories*. He is headed home to catch-a-catnap. After drinking that 20 ouncer? Don't *think* so!

To be gay or not be gay is the question. Is he, or isn't he? I still can't tell and I'm dying to know! My regular in question came in and mentioned that he couldn't believe I lived here. He spouted, "I have to be in a clean, warm, cozy, beautiful home!" He continued, "How can you stand the loneliness and isolation up here with all those weird people?" "Yes, we have your average trolls, murderers, hillbillies, ex-cons, militias, freaks, and definitely un-biblical breeding going on, but no one will ever say my life wasn't filled with color!" When I described my BOO, with his bird's-eye view of my place and how he talked to me in "flashlight Morse Code," he couldn't stand it anymore. He grabbed his caramel macchiato and walked out, shaking his head. "This is like a bad dream! Thank God I get to go back to the city!" Bizi, bizi all day! Mostly happy holiday folks and very few poopy, shaky, hangovers. A few *re-stoned* however!

7:33 P.M. Draggy. But people still laid down $20 right and left, so I stayed. Greedy? No…needy! Until I drop.

11:12 P.M. I will say a silent prayer for the little four-year-old, as I drift off…

1-02 32° Icy rain.

Espresso Corretto: A shot of espresso with your favorite coffee alcoholic spirit. Lots of people's holidays are extended through today.

8:13 A.M. My first customers were such a nice family. The dad was a spittin' image of that pretty boy super-star in the fifties, Tony Curtis. He had those curly lips, brilliant blue eyes, heavy browed and that raven hair, with a curl right in the middle of his forehead. The wife was striking too, and the kids were all super behaved. It was a rare pleasure to chat with and serve.

Hundreds of cars headed to the slopes.

A full train passed with ten engines! My male wide-eyed customers headed to the window and started to count.

9:14 A.M. Scanner: A sixteen-year-old male with an arm fracture at the resort.

1:30 P.M. Scanner: An eighteen-year-old male with a decreased level of consciousness.

5:04 P.M. I had no clue where the day went. I was so tired! That was when I could weaken, let down all my guards and either get drunk or arrange some sex! Got man? At least I recognize those trigger points now… Gosh, no groupies, exes or past screws have stopped by this whole Christmas season! Buck does not count.

Jack and Pete dropped in today for drinks; they needed caffeine to help them get psyched for their pending chores. They drove sixty miles one-way to bitch about their trailers.

6:05 P.M. Scanner: A twenty-year-old female with a severe spinal injury. That's messed up!

6:14 P.M. Next, a drive-thru customer wanted *me* to read the ingredients off every single candy bar on my shelf. Dream on! "Sorry! There are too many. But I *will* tell you, sir, some facts I can guarantee. They are loaded with sugar, other disgusting combinations of trans fats, carbohydrates, cholesterol, calories, corn syrup, and caffeine and do the *job* nicely! Extra benefits include zits, sugar highs, a possible launching of diabetes and heart disease. Immediately upon passing the lips, they put inches on the hips! And all that for only a buck-twenty-five. So, sir, how many would you like?" Besides that, he just butted out a weed, right there at my window and was obviously not adhering to the new twenty-five-foot stay-away-law. I smelled it in my hair for hours. I'm not going to allow that anymore! Besides, I could get ticketed to the tune of $100! This bitch has a new rule and a new sign: SMOKE BY MY WINDOW AND *YOU* PAY DOUBLE THE FINE! I'm calling it a *Sin-Tax!*

6:30 P.M. My murderous side was beginning to emerge. I was beyond sick of the whole human race! That would be my very last car. The bucket-of-bolts broke down and the bag-of-bones druggie driver was clueless. I guarantee I'm turning off every damn light in this joint, the very moment they are out of sight!

7:53 P.M. When I think of the hundreds who have stopped here today, it ain't so bad. And the masses were good, fun customers – families, elders, singles, soldiers, friends, law enforcement, employees, tow truck drivers, volunteer medics, Good Samaritans, children, and animals. They have all been *part of my own personal path* this Holiday Season! Thank you...

1-03 30° Partly sunny.

The Latte Shake: Combine and blend until thick! 1 cup espresso, 1 cup Half and Half, 10 ice cubes, 1/3 package of chocolate pudding mix, 2 tbs. cocoa powder, a shot of hazelnut creamer, 3 tbs. sugar. Top with whip!

7:47 A.M. It was 24° with three inches of new snow and a total measurement at sixty-six inches at Mountain Peak Ski Resort. I heard the various sports stores in the city had long lines at the cash registers and were selling out of ski equipment, fast.

I stopped at our local gas station to get milk just in case I got slammed. I could always rely on them to be open. It was a small family-owned business and they worked ghastly hours also. The cashier, whom I had never seen before asked, "So how are yaw guys doin' up there?" Guys? I told her that it was just me and I was still doing my 70–90-hour weeks. She gasped, "You are the only person runnin' it?" I shook my booty and yelled over my shoulder, "ANYTHING IS POSSIBLE IF YOU ARE A WOMAN!"

9:15 A.M. I finally opened and a young guy walked in, who instantly reminded me of my son in height, stature, and dry humor. I became almost teary and definitely homesick for another visit from "my kid!" He asked how my New Year's Eve went. He was visiting from across the country and expected Saratogan to be a quaint, quiet, old-world railroad town. His vacation was booked exclusively for skiing and some small-town ambiance. So, while he was here, he thought he'd take in some local color and step into the Train Blow Tavern on New Year's Eve, for a few beers. Because the Alaskan had preceded him with the story, I knew what was coming. "I never envisioned such *insanity*. I huddled in a corner like a coward, but figured it was my only option for self-preservation. Then I ran for my life, wrote down some license plate numbers, and hustled back to my motel. The sheriff didn't even show up till 9:00 A.M. the next day! Even then, he didn't *want* my information!" I explained that this was the norm and it hadn't changed in a hundred years. The "Law" waited till the next day to arrive on the scene – didn't take any chances with their own life-n'-limb either.

Both Gossips showed up. Ms. Gossip No. 2 was in the drive thru with a car full of flu-infested rug-rats. Ms. Gossip No. 1 stood near the window talking to them. Let *her* inhale all the germs! I'm *lathering* again…

A man came in for a drink, who I'd never seen before in my life. He started venting about how horrible it had been, being stuck under the same roof during the holidays with his girlfriend, her two mermaids and gnome. "Her daughters are bearable, but that son of hers is truly a leprechaun. I swear to God, I'll *never* marry her!" Oh sure, mister, just go and stick that thing in once in a while and eat *her* holiday feast, let *her* buy the candles and CDs, use *her* electricity and heat, then run away with no responsibility or commitment. And then complain to strangers!

It was quiet today, but I guess I didn't mind. It was a nice break and I was able to put oil in my Jeep, fill my pellet-stove hopper, clean up dog-doo, vacuum the store, and pick up the outside never-ending residue of rubbish.

12:47 P.M. Scanner: Ski injury. Thirty-five-year-old male was unconscious for an unknown amount of time.

Oh my…I just had lunch. First time in three weeks. It was a lovely and forgotten experience.

5:18 P.M. My drive thru only was open. A couple drove up, ordered drinks, and the lady asked if I could warm a bottle in my microwave. We were talking a miniature doll-sized bottle. She was raising an inherited baby Chihuahua. The mama booted this poor pup right out of the basket at birth. The head was only the size of a quarter! Cute as a bug! I zapped the bottle for twelve seconds. The caretaker claimed that it was more work than all three of her human newborns, *combined.*

I just opened a belated Christmas card from an old neighbor, who lived in this building twenty-five years ago with No. 1 and me. We both remembered our bikini-clad days, in our separate apartments, way back then. I was married to No. 1; she was a darling cheerleader who was barefoot, pregnant, and single. We were both grandmas now. Some of her relatives still lived in Saratogan and visited for drinks. This was the gal who grew up in a barn, her bedroom literally being a stable with an old straw and mud floor. Her own dad banged her against the wooden boards, nightly. She triumphed and she was one of my favorite *survivors. Successful too!*

Plow trucks headed up the pass. More snow expected!

9:39 P.M. I must get upstairs and turn on my tiny heater…

1-04 29° Sun and high clouds.

Hungarian Coffee: A pint of very strong coffee with a 1/4 shot of almond syrup, strain and place in double boiler. Right before boiling point add in 2 beaten eggs, 2 tbs. sugar, 4 tbs. of thick cream. Cook until custard coats back of spoon. Cool. Then fold in 1 cup of sweetened whipped cream. Top with whipped cream.

11:02 A.M. Zero customers so far. I was tempted to leave but I heard on the news last night that the Barista Bandit was still on the loose. He had robbed drive thru espressos in the Seattle area for days! The last one hit was up north, near the entrance to the highway that headed in this direction. I decided to stay and Man-The-Fort! He brandished a pistol and the poor gals handed over all the ready cash. Heard he even emptied the tip jar. How rude!

After going online for the local news, it turned out the HE was a SHE and this brazen hussy's been caught! She wore a cap, suspenders, and glued-on goatee. Good target practice, I say!

A big, pink-faced guy came in. He was staring at my body parts, so I may have to poke his eyes out. He asked if I had any clothing for sale. I pointed back to the gift shop and there was *no way* I was going to assist *that* one. He rifled through my baskets of flamingo tee shirts and lingerie for twenty minutes. And then it dawned on me - he was one of those "FREAKY UNDERWEAR SNIFFERS!" I glanced at my gun for confidence. What in the hell was this big, pig-ass-pervert going to do with a flamingo thong? It would never make it up past his calf!

11:55 A.M. Russ just called. Who is Russ? Hell, if I even know! He said that he and his gal friend were in yesterday on their way to Icicle Town. They had been admiring my Mt. St. Helens ash glass ornaments. OOOOhhhh, you are that Russ. Now I recall…he came in yesterday with that cold, jealous gal who had fake red hair and hung on him like glue. I asked him how their trip went. "Oh, real nice, but we didn't stay long. She's visiting from Texas and she is just an old friend. I was wondering if you'd like to hook up sometime. You seemed like such a genuine (barf bag, anyone?) person and it would be nice to get to know you better. Are you married?" NO and NO and NO! "Okay, well, um, if you ever want to even just talk, my number is in your Caller I.D." Don't push it, buddy – you and I both know the just a friend was a screw of some sort. And I could tell she thought/hoped it is more than that. And we don't have fucking Caller I.D. up here! Now SCRAM!

4:26 P.M. I'm leaving! Just because I want to!

8:52 P.M. I enjoyed the road rage all the way down the hill behind two trucks that went 35 mph in a 60-mph zone. I felt sorry for Nos. 1 through 7, for all the months they survived my pre-menstrual-period. Nasty woman, I was! But women are also amazing when they got fired up. We can look at maps, change stations, chat on phones, jot down shopping lists, and honk, through the entire road-rage experience, all the while hanging on to the steering wheel. I didn't *say* it was safe! Multi-tasking tigresses!

I was almost home when Buck passed, in the opposite direction. He was headed "down-below" after dark? Uh huh. I knew his routine: He rushed home from work in time to eat everything in mama's refer, took a shower, combed his mop, grabbed the K-Y jelly, and beat it out the door.

This waiting for the perfect guy was torture. Maybe I had to conclude that it was all a big, fat, fallacy.

9:55 P.M. Or maybe it's just that time of the month. This too shall pass…

1-05 35° Raining.

Moon Chai: Combine ten 1-inch pieces of ginger, 4 broken cinnamon sticks, 1 tsp. green cardamom pods, 2.25 tsp. black peppercorns, 1 tsp. whole cloves, 1/2 tsp. fennel seeds, 1/2 tsp. licorice root, 1/2 tsp. allspice, 5 cups water in a saucepan. Cover and simmer for 45 minutes. Remove from heat, let sit for 35 minutes, covered. Strain out spices; add 3 tbs. honey and milk to taste.

8:42 A.M. First laugh of the day. Two macho skiers pulled up by the Porta Potty. One did the "I gotta go! I gotta go!" shimmy, through the rain, all the way to the can. He bolted back to their rig, grabbed some paper towels and danced the jig, back to the hut. Then, a few minutes later, his buddy, with a cell phone attached to his head, rushed more wadded-up paper to the hut's door, in that "He needs more - He needs more!" dance. Cheap entertainment!

12:04 P.M. An old guy who lived here in Treetops Loop called me for Buck's phone number. Apparently, Buck's parents didn't even have it. How could that be? What a creep! Buck will find them one day, hanging over the edge of his couch, and having not a single spare moment, will toss them into the river too!

Guess who pulled up? Mr. Dad Rancher. He told me that I looked *hot* today, as we both chuckled over such obvious B.S. We both know who *he* is. He's just another player *royale*.

12:50 P.M. Scanner: A driver for a company "down-below," in charge of shuttling patients back and forth from hospitals, stopped the van on I-205 and called 911. He no longer felt safe in the vehicle with his patient. She was stabbing herself with a pen.

3:15 P.M. Some regulars came to the drive thru. This was the very first time their son had worked up at our ski resort. What an experience! Both my kids had done it and afterwards, neither of them was ever the same. Sharing a house with twenty-plus kids, going from bed to bed, couch to couch, with the rest of the employees, and begging for the one shower. Included was the smorgasbord of drugs, sex, and parties nightly.

7:22 P.M. Traction tires were advised on Mountain Peak Pass. Why was I still down here at my desk?

7:32 P.M. I headed upstairs to *surf* through my *eight* television channels, I was still unsatisfied...

1-06 36° Slight rain.

Double Vanilla Power: 2 shots of vanilla powder, 3 shots of espresso, steamed whole milk, and top with whip.

7:47 A.M. "Knock-knock." I woke with a start! "Hi, little girl. Do you *realize* it's our Anniversary?" It is two months to the day that Cowboy left us alone. I just wanted to say that I am finally singing again…and so should you." It was my heart…

9:02 A.M. The river was brownish today from heavy, warm rains. Mother Nature must be *dating*, or off somewhere otherwise occupied. She had forgotten about the north westerners who needed colder weather!

My period started, so every male was now safe from my wrath. One of our tow guys and his wife came by for their lattes. I told her about the creeps I got in here occasionally. She gave me her phone number, as she had a concealed weapon permit also. She loved entertaining the idea of a dual, blow-them-away afternoon. Ya don't mess with The Mountain People. They were the proud owners of pit bulls, guns, knives, machetes, dynamite, tools, trucks with extra gas cans, ski masks, and warped minds. They will bury you deep! Then, they'll get curious and dig ya up, just to make sure you're still dead, probably have their way with you and let their pit bulls go at ya for a while. Next, so as not to waste a perfectly good pine box, most likely they'll lob the remains into the river.

I emailed Mr. Rancher to ask him one simple question. "Why do you choose to have more than one girlfriend at a time?" I awaited his response, like a cat waited for nip, anxious to rip his lame excuse to threads.

Oh my…Hunk Wyatt came in for forty-five minutes! He needed me to fax something for him. He was either polite or blind-as-a-bat because he did not hand me a napkin for the drool. "Wanna hear the latest on 'Sugar-Puss' and my dance classes?" I tore myself away from those astonishing eyes, "Sure, give me the scoop on the *Britches* and *Bitches*!" "My ex-wife, who has already spent double my children's inheritance on lawyers, wants me back on the other side of the bed, hoggin' covers. She is flipping mad over my new private boogie-on-down lessons with that adorable lesbian dance teacher of mine, who now also wants me to do a threesome with her and a girlfriend!" I will bet he's already done them both! "I just can't go back to the ex – she is full-on abnormal! By the way, I'm entering an arm-wrestling tournament tomorrow and I'll bring you the trophy." He is too much for me and most gals! Not a *healthy* choice!

12:36 P.M. A car's tire just blew out on the highway, not a hundred feet from me. It sounded like a bomb. Thus, I had a car full of new expectant customers – everyone thought I would have all the answers. Did I have that super-intelligent look about me, or was it because they were hoping I would do anything to get rid of them? Their spare was flat and the other three tires were bald.

8:40 P.M. Obviously a slow Friday. Let's eat and sleep while we can, girl! What's for din-din? Scrambled eggs and smoked oysters again! And a breath mint…

1-07 40° Rain.

Chocó Kahlua: 2 packs of cocoa, 2 shots of espresso, hot water within an inch and fill with Half & Half.

8:33 A.M. It was too warm out, but skiers still headed up for a hopeful run. I called Buck. I needed to harass him. He started first, "I ain't called ta say hi, cuz I figure yer gettin' serviced by *someone!*" "Okay, fuck-wad, when in the world am I not visible?" He continued this stupidity, "Yer visible in the days, cuz I check in 'n I see ya workin', a lot! Must be doin' shit at night. I ran in ta Boone from Stonewall and he's with some crack head bitch, so I know it's not him. I seen Brent to. I stuck ma fist in his gut 'n tol' him ta stay away from ya. He knows I'd like ta sok it to the asshole, so jus' give me 'n excuse, bub. So, who's layin' ya, innneeewaaaaa?" I told him to come by, pick up his damn ring, and give it to his latest. "Ya called ta harass me, didncha, Christy?" Yep! "Well, ol' Roger wants some trees down. That's why he's been callin' ya for ma number. But Jug Head got the job instead, the bastard." I hung up; those conversations were imbecilic.

10:03 A.M. Not a customer and, yes, it is Saturday!

Finally! My first was a regular drive thru gal but this time she walked in. Something was up. Out it came: She had a boyfriend and he stayed in the car. They'd dated for five years and it was not going, even just okay. "He has a lot of baggage. It was my own fault, I know, cuz I could date those nice halitosis ones with great careers – the guys my mom is always trying to fix me up with. And he's such a cheap bastard too! Almost wouldn't stop here for my latte. 'Idling uses too much gas' he said. And you can see, we are in my car." She headed back out, drove up with her punch card and realized, "Oh, a freebie next time, Christy. Goody!" He did speak now, "Yeah, hon, maybe I will have that latte after all!" On her freebie! If they were sharing, he'd be the kind that would hand it back with eight of the ten ounces – gone. He's no more than a bargain basement find, girlfriend. He's stingy and tight and should be depreciated – turned in for a new model! It's another case of a woman with no self-esteem. Damn.

11:19 A.M. Scanner: A clavicle fracture at the resort. It was a seventeen-year-old male.

11:27 A.M. Scanner: A sixteen-year-old female fell while snowboarding. She was stable with a pulse of one hundred but had dizziness.

12:03 P.M. Ms. Gossip No. 2 stopped with her hubby to get drinks. They were headed to the big city to hit all the sales and do their *Christmas shopping*. "We finally have the money for presents, so we've decided to shop, wrap, and have another big feast. We are calling it 'The After-Birth', ha ha ha ha." Some people are just plain *tacky*.

1:44 P.M. I had four customers at the same time. I may wet my pants with excitement as I had already sullenly watched at least thirty cars stop – *just* to use the john. A very strange Saturday, indeed!

I called Rosie's dad. She was safe and fine, and her daddy bought a nice travel trailer for her to call home. Her very own pad, for the first time since she'd left the nest, an eternity ago. They had parked it out in back of her brother's residence, hidden from sight. I asked him if Rosie had gotten the restraining order against Ex-Con. Apparently, she told them so, but they hadn't seen the court papers. I wouldn't bet on it.

2:22 P.M. Scanner: An eighteen-year-old male with left abdominal pain from a ski fall.

I just finished wrestling a two-hundred pound, paid for, antique sewing machine and cabinet through my entire three-room store and out to the front. I have smart customers – pant-pant, they don't arrive a second too soon. I had diligently rearranged the back room to fill the hole. Moving furniture, re-hung pictures, and juggled heavy ceramic pots. Wow, secret treasures – well, *actually*, a hodgepodge! Behind every large piece of furniture were numerous telltale dismemberments – fragments of something a customer found and *once* had a hanker'n for. I could just picture it: Customer grabs gem, and while engrossed in trying to find even a *better* bargain, oopsy... They quickly tallied the situation - no secret camera, thank God, no other customers, and owner is up front. Should I play let's show- 'n-tell or ditch-the-shit? Hide the evidence and run like hell! Wine glasses, picture frames, candles, and endless figurines, lie in repose, severed and shattered. Thanks, y'all – sleep well!

Another first: A guy in my drive thru asked if I took pesos. "Sorry, you are in Washington, not California." Whine, "They won't take 'em there either anymore!" "So, there's your answer!"

A snappy little twit pissed me off! She gave me shit about paying for her eggnog latte. She wanted to take it into the gift shop and pay later, "I don't want to use my credit card for a measly $3.00, and then have to use it again if I find something in your store that I can't live without!" I grit and said, "Does Starbucks make your drink and then let you go for a nice stroll around the block before collecting?" No. You pay first, then you can go off and fuck-the-dog, for all they care. She understood and closed the first transaction.

4:31 P.M. Scanner: A fifteen-year-old female fell thirty feet down off the ski chair lift.

6:15 P.M. I just had two old coots in my drive thru. Today had been full of Biddies and Buzzards. I thought I started the day in quite high spirits, but it's waning fast to melancholy. Buzzards are cadavers and Biddies are backstabbing scorpions. Those guys were super pissed that my doors were locked. "It's pouring buckets and its pitch black out. And those conditions can be dangerous for me." "Get *over* yourself!" Fuck off…in a whisper. This troll-land *is* filled with rascals, rogues and hellions.

People have been more on edge today than through all the days of my holiday season, combined. Has the *whole world* turned bipolar?

6:50 P.M. I sat here and imagined this place as a restaurant. The Menu Board reads: Buzzard Burgers, Will's Tooth Sundae, Logger's Links, Ben's Fries, RR Bum Spaghetti, Mountain Peak Highway Roadkill Steak…just to name a few. Speaking of Ben, I hadn't caught one in ages. Smart little buggers lately.

8:00 P.M. Opposite extremes today…

1-08 35° Some rain.

Orange Caffeinated Americano: My original! One cup hot water, 1 orange tea bag, let steep for 5 minutes. A shot of espresso, cream and sugar to flavor.

7:47 A.M. Punks called me Senorita. Whew…not quite ready for Senor, especially when this was my long day in front of the mirror! And some more fun regulars. And there went our new yuppie joggers. Today she wore a fluorescent orange jacket, bright enough to scare eagles!

I will want to explain why I keep in touch with Buck. For a couple of reasons, really. First of all, just in case I need some emergency muscle. He would always play friend if I needed him – and vice versa. Even with all our nonsense. And secondly, I need to keep up on all the hillbilly news around here. Also, there is no worry of us getting snuggly since I believe I have been afflicted with *Congenital Hyper Trichinosis*. I haven't shaved for so long, trying to keep out of trouble, so I've decided to invent a special leg 'n pit conditioner, or minimally, a new name for *French-Braiding*! Trifold, Sailor Knot, Corkscrew Coil, Spiral Snarl, Whorl Weave?

10:00 A.M. Buck, in his dump truck, finally paid a physical visit. And sure, as hell, Hunk Wyatt's stepdad came in at the same time. Introductions. Buck immediately took a dislike to the old gent; I just might have gotten a tad too close to Mr. Hunk and his family. They inched away from handsome-step-son-talk and both started bragging about how many cords of wood they had cut in a day. "I did five before." "Well, I did six." "Oh yeah, I forgot about *that* day; me too and I even had a hurt shoulder..."

One of Bill Gate's engineers, that owned a cabin up here, came in also. Buck got a shitload of gravel work out of him! Pays to visit Christy! When the engineer went back into the gift shop, Buck said, "It's getting around town that you are a P.T." "Thank you. Much preferable to a whore!" He left and tossed the usual scrap-of-a-cardboard note at me: 'Wil' ya cut ma hair 1 a theeze daz? No strings attach'd. How cum we've gon from 80° to 18°. Here's a kis, jus cuz.' Yes, I will cut your hair – and yes only during daylight hours. I know I'll need help with my plow, crazies, or something. Tit-for-tat, as they say – just don't take that too literally, Mr. Impassioned Logger.

2:33 P.M. Scanner: An eighteen-year-old female had lumbar pain from an extensive fall.

3:20 P.M. Scanner: A forty-eight-year-old male with a concussion at the resort. They requested an airlift.

3:29 P.M. Scanner: Another person with a concussion. The Saratogan airport was setting up for an airlift for both.

5:05 P.M. Finally – what a rush! I had absolutely no idea how many cars were lined-up. I knew there were eight people in front of my counter. That broke my record! I worked as fast as my little fingers would go – with crazy *impatient* skiers, lead cars honking, spilled drinks, and dropped money at the window! "I'm giving you the freakin' fastest service *possible* and the speediest *you'll* ever see! Give me a break..."

6:50 P.M. Scanner: Blocking car accident in Alpine (twenty miles west of me).

7:10 P.M. Scanner: A thirty-nine-year-old female had a spinal injury at the resort. They requested an airlift in the dark. She was alert times four.

I got an email from the negative BMW Brian. I now shred a very unflattering light on this twerp since he always complained about something. The sky could be blue, and it would ruin his month! Today, it was the corporate life – again. And worried about planning his second trip to Hawaii: "It's tough to spend the money, after last year's bad experience, with my high veranda and rain and all…but I'm going to brave it and give it another try." Told you he was a dweeb – a dolt! Backatcha: "Golly gee-whiz Brian sweetie, are you sure this is wise? What if they get a tsunami this year?" Response: "If I give you their weather report every day, can you help me predict something like that?"

God help me…no him!

8:05 PM. Scanner: Traction tires were advised on Mountain Peak Pass. Translation: Chain the-hell-up or get-the-hell home if you know what's good for you!

Next. Skiers still stopped. They were out-of-shape this early in the season and needed to replenish the old bod – salt, sugar, caffeine, and liniment. And if *one* more of those restless people lay on their horn, wouldn't give me a sec or two…and then not know what the hell they wanted anyway, I'd scream – in their ears!

Next. A lady I had never seen in my life, and probably will never see again, stopped for a rice latte. "You are so lucky – I'm practically on my last drop. And I won't be carrying rice milk anymore." She begged me to keep selling it. "Sorry, miss, but it just doesn't sell, and I don't think you can find it in any other barista location – including Starbucks." "That's why you *have* to!" "Where do you live, I haven't seen you before?" "Montana." "Subject closed."

8:17 P.M. Scanner: Head injury at the resort. I had been told that we have the busiest volunteer fire department in the state. That didn't surprise me a bit.

What did surprise me, on the other hand, was why we were still stuck in the 19ᵗʰ century – with *volunteers*?

8:41 P.M. A prayer for the injured, middle finger for the crazies today, and at least I get a *hot* meal tonight...popcorn...

1-09 33° Pouring.

Cheetah Latte: My original! A shot of real caramel, a shot of real fudge chocolate, a shot of white chocolate powder, espresso shots, steamed whole milk.

8:00 A.M. Scanner: A Mountain Peak Ski Resort employee bus went off the road. No injuries. Our buses are very old...so are most of the drivers.

One of my regulars came in without his wife. "She isn't my *wife*. She is still married to her husband next door. We sorta have this co-habitation thing going and we've lived next door to her *lawful* husband for years. But now she is going through some kind of shit, like you see on the crazy afternoon talk shows. I feel like I'm raping her every time we have sex these days. She is dreading every second of it. Doesn't she remember that's exactly what *got* us together – wearing a trench between the two houses! Christy, you know that look when a wife wants sex? Well, me neither, these days! Her doctor says its menopause. We are on the rocks and I'm taking my whiskey that same way these days!" Now, that is a mouthful to say to another woman! He finished, "Yeah, I went back with my old band, just for something to do. You wouldn't believe all the women wanting us, wherever we go. Play music and ride a Harley and you're all set." "Okay, my friend, I've heard enough. Go suck your thumb someplace else!" Frigid! Sounds like she was right on schedule! Point off the men's column. He should be more intelligent than that.

Bear's parents came in shaking. It was dumping snow at the pass and they almost rearranged a snowbank, again! She was driving the last time too when they did a pirouette and sustained injuries; maybe she should let him have a crack at spinning the steering wheel.

My brother called me with his weekly reminder that relationships suck. He nominated himself the *"Crier of Critical Companionship Communiqué."* "Why are relationships so *damn* terrific for about three and a half days?" He and my girlfriend have called off all contact including the sex sessions every 17 days. They decided to bypass all the head games.

1:00 P.M. I just had a lesbian couple in to change their clothes, "Where's your bathroom?" I pointed outside to the Porta Potty, which in that downpour was practically treading water. Without a second thought, the first one removed most of her clothes and they were now drying on my pellet stove. Was this an old Western rerun? Her partner followed suit and now the wet clothes have converted my stove to a humidifier. Ski clothes off and civvies on, right in the middle of my store…if you please. I was too flabbergasted to speak – my other customer counted the grains in the sugar bowl. Even Angel stretched her eyeball to get a better view. I believe there should be a half of a point deducted from both the men's and the women's column, if I read their situation correctly…

Another Ms. Menopause, the wealthy New York psychologist – coupled with my friend Andrew and you have another relationship in trouble. He called just now, "I'm positive I never knew women before and now I'm convinced I ain't interested in learnin'! My gal, you know Christy - the rich, classy one from New York that bought our view condo? Well, this morning one of the plates still had dried food on it, after a full cycle in the dishwasher. It sent her to the floor, crying. No, let me re-phrase, not crying – kicking and screaming and hurling insults at the entire world, including appliance manufacturers, builders, and realtors. She's going to sell the condo, today! She's threatening to make me homeless over a fucking dish!" This woman is a psychologist for Social Services? "Andrew, she needs major meds, or its menopause, or both." He panicked, "If I knew what to order from the pharmacy, I'd lace her tofu with it!"

3:45 P.M. Business was slow – had enough drama - I left to get supplies…

1-10 38° Rain.

Thai Tea: Boil 6 cups of water. Add in 8 black tea bags and 4 tsp. cardamom. Steep for 5 minutes. Strain out tea bags and let cool. Pour into 4 mugs 3/4 full, then add to each 1 tbs. sugar, 1 tsp. cinnamon, 1/4 cup milk. Also, great iced!

8:40 A.M. It poured kitty-cats 'n puppies all night and it was also raining at the ski resort. Bummer.

Espresso made the news again! A clerk served up the customer with his fresh latte and the customer threw the hot brew into the clerk's face, then grabbed the cash register tray and ran! Slimebucket! Then…a Starbucks location in San Francisco got a bomb planted inside their restroom. That is another good reason for *not* having *indoor* facilities. Bomb the Porta Potties! Who cares!

I found out from a Mountain Peak Ski Resort employee that the resort had to turn back two hundred and eighty-eight cars. The parking lots were full. And that was the beginning of the day!

I have been told that by the twentieth of this month, Seattle may break an all-time record for the most consecutive days of rain. Well, that alone will keep the influx of new residents down to a purr!

I began to understand the sport of the French kissing parrot from Mexico. Mister made me an offer – I *can* refuse! Maybe I truly have become a mountain woman!

11:47 A.M. I did get supplies last night and survived the blinding, torrential rains. Home again for at least a week.

Our new school superintendent's husband brought me our school's sports schedule calendar. He was a retired pilot and now has become a "house mom" for two sons. He had them late in life with a much younger wife. The family arrived here from Huntington Beach, California, and settled down in Olympia – then relocated once more to Saratogan. Apparently, their sons wouldn't get out of the car when they first arrived at their free, school-supplied home.

Hubby described their new digs as sub-standard housing in the military. "I haven't lived in a house with only one bathroom since junior high! I swore I wouldn't live in these conditions ever again, after boot camp - and here I am! My wife is at the lowest end of the totem pole for superintendent jobs. I try and remind my kids that this is great! They can go skiing constantly, raft in rivers, have a dog, and enjoy all the beautiful scenery. But it ain't working. They hate Saratogan. They've heard lots of creepy stuff about this small town." As he left, almost immediately, "Will they ever adjust...will I..."

Hunk Wyatt came in. Yes, the lesbian wanted his flesh. He said that he was not sure if he would go for it. "She talks about women constantly and *I'm* the one that is supposed to be hot for that sex." "Oh hell, men have been fantasizing about women with women for centuries. You'll *do* her. By the way, you still haven't walked in with the fancy gold arm wrestling trophy, but I'm sure you don't want me to remind you of that fact..." Dig – dig!

3:36 P.M. Scanner: A semi-truck spun out at milepost 63, blocking eastbound lanes on Mountain Peak Highway.

Something juicy was going on in town. Three sheriff cars and our local cop was all at the "drug house" across from the fire station. Some gal was screaming and lying in the middle of the street. They had to strap her to a gurney. Slipped her a bit too much, boys? The ambulance rendezvoused with the "crazy" van, down in Snow Peak Mine.

3:52 P.M. Scanner: Saratogan will be delivering mental patient to the Snow Peak Mine station. ETA is approximately fifteen minutes.

8:52 PM. I'm locking up and done for the day before I end up at the funny farm...

1-11 35° 25th consecutive day of rain.

Iced Chocolate Milk: Put 2 packs of cocoa in 2 inches of very hot water. Stir until dissolved. Fill cup with ice to the top. Pour cold milk over ice within 2 inches then pour warm mixture into cup and stir.

8:31 A.M. Shall I start the day off with National News? Our Seattle area, with the longest number of consecutive days of rain, made Good Morning America and The Today Show! But I would be willing to bet no one coveted our notoriety. And I am going to have to start serving *cheese* to go with our resident's *whines!*

Our biggest town know-it-all totaled his rig last night only two miles from town. I waited for the facts on whether it is DUI related. Took wagers…

We had three separate car accidents blocking Mountain Peak Highway at mileposts 62, 63, and 69.

Buck just did a spy-drive again in his truck that only gets five miles to the gallon. He probably heard "down-the-line" that Hunk Wyatt was hangin' here for over an hour this morning.

10:18 A.M. My God! This place got busy already. Happy barista time.

Buck popped back to grill me. The more he grilled, the more I clammed! Why didn't men get it? He claimed that he had to drive past my place just now, "Becuz a logg'r bud a mine got his truck stuck on a loggin' rode 'n I was gonna pull the guy out." Yeah right! "You were only spying Buck, admit it." Big pout.

2:48 P.M. Looked like a bit of snow on the car roofs again. It was mixed rain/snow here, which meant that the snow level was only a couple of miles up the road. Will be big business later so I'm going to hit the fridge. Ahhhhhh, two pieces of pizza, downed, without interruption. Utterly amazing.

An elderly skier came in, "I about drowned in the deep snow, cuz they haven't graded some of the lifts in three days; it was the worst two runs of my life! I fell twice and lost a ski both times. I thought they'd have to come and find me with a metal detector!"

I always loved it when Very Important People came in my drive thru and could not *possibly* verbalize their order because they were involved in a Very Important Phone call. He covered the mouthpiece and silently gestured for me to just be patient. Slam went my window! Honk-Honk. I took a break and put that V.I.P. on hold. When he finally ordered it was incomplete. Boy, did he get pissed when I bothered him again, for the size, flavors, and condiments. He thought *he* was irritated! I should just make some half-ass, something or other, and grab the dough. "Just doin' my job, sir!" And all the driver could see were my teeth!

Two ladies with six soggy kids wanted nothing more than a bathroom, use of my hand sanitizer, and some shelter. Everyone was standing, dripping, shaking, and steaming up my whole store with their body aromas. I cracked my window and stood near it, breathing in the cool, fresh air. Germs…

3:20 P.M. Scanner: A twenty-four-year-old male with an arm fracture at the resort.

3:56 P.M. Scanner: Our sheriff called in a non-injury, blocking car accident at the summit.

Snow was a foot high on the cars coming down off the mountain pass, just like the old days!

Another local cabin owner, who happened to be a multi-millionaire, came in complaining about his twenty-year marriage. What's new? "I'm divorcing her for a few reasons. No. 1. Money! She has run up four credit cards lately, to the tune of $11K each and there's nothing visual to show for it." I said, "So… did she run out and buy a new Mercedes-Benz 380SL?" He blabbed, "I'm worth zillions and I'm slightly afraid she may *Butter the Bough of My Boat* and one day, headlines will read, 'Prominent Seattle Sportsman Drowns in Puget Sound – No Known Cause'! And No. 3. I don't want to live in Seattle anymore and she won't join me up here. No. 4, she's going through that 'change' and she is getting very unresponsive – if ya know what I mean!" "Excuses, excuses, funny man. You are just one of the thousands, who are leaving your wife of many years, so you don't have to watch, or help her, age gracefully. And this is starting to sound like a broken record at my counter! We are not pleased." Stunned, and out the door. Then…I screamed to nobody in particular, "Holy shit, men suck!"

Did we *really* change *that* much? Didn't he? Where had these husbands been for twenty-plus years, while we *lived* to make *them* happy? *Oh no…they only* noticed the negative side today; the positive past was long forgotten as if they were suffering from Alzheimer's! And their loving wife had suddenly become *undesirable* and they were not *fulfilled*! So they traded their fifty-year-old in for two and a half twenties year olds. POINT OFF! Men, you are falling behind fast! Shit…*you* are the ones that have huge bellies, baldheads and are grouches cuz you didn't measure up to your imagined potentials!

7:45 P.M. To change this subject: There is something serene about seeing a train coming from afar on a foggy night. The headlights filter through massive space, far beyond its designated beams. It appears a full moon is in motion. Then, as it draws closer, the train *watcher* realizes that this nearing light is indeed a train, with its three eyes guiding the way. The beam dances upon the trees and the night-lights glow from its faithful, following engines. Then, the only sound heard in the pitch-black night is the moment of the train's passing.

8:01 P.M. Maybe it will lull me into slumber land…

1-12 32° Overcast. 26th consecutive day of rain.

Raspberry Espresso Granita: In blender combine: 1 cup full of ice, 1 pack of fake sugar, 1.5 inches of raspberry daiquiri mix, 2 inches of Half & Half, one shot of espresso. Blend and top with whip.

7:59 A.M. Lots of skiers flew *up* the highway, anxious for a cold run and right back *down* a hill.

Another two-minute necessity break upstairs, rudely interrupted by a repeating car horn. Two impatient, indecisive ladies lying on the steering wheel, as I ran down, zipping and buttoning. They still had no clue what to order. "Honk again when you are ready!" Loosely interpreted, this meant Christy was pissed! They honked again shortly, and I strolled to the window. I've decided that their $5.95 was not worth all of the blood pressure – or the wish of death as I flew down those damn nineteen, two at a time. Oh God…now they were dilly-dallying with loose change, lipstick, and seat belts and two more cars, filled with snowboarders, waited impatiently behind them, honking out a tune.

Calm Down, Christy – it's too early in the morning to start pulling hair out – yours or theirs! Hunk Wyatt was in here two days in a row and saw the same clothes, so I felt inclined to change into a new color for the top sweater layer. For what?! Why did I give a damn? Then again, maybe he would start to wonder if I changed my undies and that could get around town. Could they revoke my health license over that? Maybe I would just play 'The Nun' or 'Barbie' and just tell everyone this was my new uniform!

10:33 A.M. Buck called and still didn't have the scoop on whether our local know-it-all plowman got a DUI in that crash report. Darn.

My Mount Manning was all white today. I have seen four eagles already! They were really in high numbers this year.

1:01 P.M. The rain is almost here. Oh joy…

A lady popped in who remembered me from my Parkston store. I reminded her that No. 5 and I had two stores at the same time – one downtown and the other on Highway 10. She flipped, "Have you heard about the owners of the other store you had?" No. "The husband committed suicide." I suddenly want to close for the day, since I sold that property to this nice couple and knew them well. More, "Well, long story short, this is her second husband to commit suicide! Is she a Black Widow or what?" I am taking a point off the women's column, just because of the odds…

Denny next door called, "I need one of your new canes. Mine broke this morning and that basically cripples me. And don't say it was under all the strain of the extra poundage!"

2:12 P.M. Scanner: A non-emergency response to the Mountain Peak aid room for a knee injury. A sixty-three-year-old female.

2:55 P.M. Scanner: Original knee injury patient now had a head injury. That escalated from a non-emergency to an airlift. Someone was not paying attention.

I totally forgot it was Buck's birthday. I soothed my guilt immediately as I remembered he missed mine a couple of months ago too. We got talking about birthdays…birth…death. I was curious about what they did with all the dead bodies from this mountain area in the old days. He knew: "They brought the dead ones down on a train car to the private mill, west 'a town. Then ole Marcus, 'r undertaker, handled his end 'a things. He bleeds 'em 'n runs pickle juice thru 'em. Then they tak 'em down ta Alpine, where another box car takes 'em ta the funeral home." "Sorry I asked Buck… Go away."

6:51 P.M. Scanner: A thirty-four-year-old with a shoulder injury at the resort.

7:51 P.M. Enough of the glorious - exciting - festivity. Upstairs for more intoxicating hilarity. Keep your sense of humor, girl…

1-13 34° Rain.- 27th consecutive day of rain for me! Seattle's record only tied 1961. They cleared up for just one measly day.

Original Outpost Espresso Homemade Granita Mix: This is the 'best'! Combine all into 4 buckets outside, preferably under cover and high in the mountains: 1 whole can of vanilla cappuccino powder, one 12-ounce jar of instant coffee, 5 pounds of sugar, 46 ounces of powdered creamer, 46 ounces of hot chocolate powder, 46 ounce can of mocha frappe powder mix. Put 1/4 of each of these in each bucket. Now the fun part! Take turns pouring this heavy stuff into each bucket until they all appear mixed. Then store all of this delicious powder in the cans and jars you just emptied. Next, how to make the drink recipe? For example, use a 16-ounce cup: Fill the cup with ice and add to blender. Put a full shot glass of this powdered mixture in. Pour 2 inches of Half & Half into the cup. Separately prepare your shot of espresso with a shot of chocolate syrup and pour this mix into the Half & Half. Stir. Then pour cup into blender. Blend and ENJOY!

8:35 A.M. It had not rained this many days in a row since 1961. Seattleites were freaking out, between being excited to see our area all over the TV news channels, and unhappy with their Vitamin D level. Light Therapy Machines were flying off the shelves. Even Costco carried this item in the Northwest now! Californians, who relocated to Microsoft – or for our real estate prices, were in major depression. Shrinks were over-taxed!

11:11 A.M. Denny picked up his new cane. Limped in, strolled out. He felt confident again.

Mr. and Mrs. Periwinkle Luggage stopped. It had been a while. A semi-truck up on the pass just about killed them both a few minutes ago. It jackknifed right next to them! She was still shaking. They were starting to stress me out. Their home life was super dysfunctional, and I wouldn't make it inside those four walls with them for even two minutes. *She* needed meds and he needed her *on* meds. I was exhausted after only fourteen minutes of her rambling on about the family's problems – alcoholism, surgeries, drugs, babies, teenage tribulations, etc.

Buck called, "Mary Jolene in Stonewall told me there's a new gal livin' on Center Street. Boone 'll be doin' her soon. Geez, Mary Jolene is crippled and never gits out and knows more'n we do." Okay Buck, "Have you done newbie yet?" "Yep, an' Boone'l get'r too. She's forty-seven, so either Boone or Brent'll get'r. I hear Hunter'll be breakin' up with his gal too, so look out." "Thanks for the warnings but I don't fancy toothless, unhealthy, perverted, alcoholic, degenerate swingers, thank you very much!" Buck continued, "Well, just hearin' all this shit pisses me off, so my engine I'm wurkin' on shud pop right out and it'll be swingin' in the trees, I'm so fuckin' strong right now.These fuckers 'round here, fuckin' make me mad." "Why, Buck, because they'll get to the chicks before you do. This Mary Jolene must have one powerful telescope… her only entertainment?"

5:02 P.M. The naturalist I served said, "Oh my…your chocolate-covered espresso beans are way toooo expensive. I'm not a Bellevue girl, so I won't be buying any." Frankly, hippie, I don't give one shit, one way or a-tuther. I sell hundreds a week to Bellevue and non-Bellevue people, plain Jacks and Janes, and finicky four-eyes. "Do you have a sink where I can wash my hands? And there are no seat covers in your portable toilet," her bitching continued. I gave a curt reply, "Ma'am, I have no sink for public use. I refuse to pay extra for seat covers that would eventually carpet my parking lot and I will give you a squirt of my hand sanitizer, since you failed to see the container inside the Porta Potty." Now beat it!

6:00 P.M. My skiing firefighters came in again. I told them my two-firefighter tales. The one who pulled my hair out and the other who had stripped in my store. They seemed a bit uncomfortable listening to these tales. True to Their Brother Act, eh? Sorry…authentic!

7:02 P.M. All she wrote…

1-14 35° 28th consecutive day of my rain.
-Happy Birthday, Hunk Wyatt.

> Cider Floater: Combine 2 packs of hot apple cider powder, hot water within 2 inches of top, a splash of cream, then float an espresso shot on top.

8:00 A.M. I am open and made $20 right off the bat. I am organized and ready for bear! I was an early bird and even got ice at 7:00 A.M. The gossip, new news, at the gas station is that Ex-Con *already* had a main sleaze moved in. What a pig – but that's *not* new news!

9:03 A.M. Scanner: A cardiac arrest outside of the Mountain Peak aid room. It was a male patient in his forties. CPR in progress.

11:24 A.M. Scanner: A domestic near Saratogan, in Stonewall. An injured female was in the house and two males were outside. She refused aid. Too late, lady, cops of all varieties were on their way.

12:00 Noon. Mr. "20" came in. Remember him from over the summer? He was going skiing with his two young kids. He was surprised that I remembered him. Crap, who wouldn't?!

Well, ladies, Mr. Rancher from the east side of our hills is '*bi*'. He sent me another warped email that was hard for me to digest. I thought he was just a charming, rough 'n tough "breeder" rancher. I have decided I can't judge for shit!

3:00 P.M. Scanner: An eleven-year-old male with a concussion. He was stable but nauseous and vomiting. Pulse at 103.

So, Buck has had a girlfriend this whole absent period. He said, "Women r' a pain 'n da ass 'n r bitches. They complain that they can't make their mor-gage (hint, hint). They don't know whin ther support payment is comin'. All they want is money, money, money. I think wer havin' slop-over from 'da full moon. Bunch-a weird shit goin' on today." Did you think they were hangin' on cuz you are so suave and debonair?

Bill Gate's engineer came in again. He and his wife were also getting hooked on my scanner info and wanted to know last week's happenings.

3:20 P.M. Scanner: A thirteen-year-old female with a concussion.

The cardiac arrest this morning did die but was revived – info from the Forest Service cop that stopped here, "Yeah, the guy had already been roto-rooter'd. The whole thing was a bloody miracle!"

6:18 P.M. And still got business. Lattes, espressos, cappuccinos, and gifts. And a $4 tip.

8:30 P.M. Another twelve-and-a-half-hour day. We can do it! We can do it! Nighty-nite…

1-15 30° Dumping snow. 29th consecutive day of moisture of some sort here.

Zap: A shot of espresso with a shot of Cola.

8:33 A.M. Scanner: Two pigs grazing on shoulder of Mountain Peak Highway, at milepost 17. I could hear some of the dispatchers making *oink* noises in the background and the relay dispatcher was having one heck of a time holding back her laugh.

Boone from Stonewall called to clear his name on the domestic. I guess every-one was still unclear as to which local was involved. Buck?

Buck called when he was drunk last night, describing his girlfriend and their activities, all in one breath. And in the next, "I luv ya!" I let him ramble as I sat here in my store, closed signs up and alone in the dark. It was company…

10:24 A.M. Scanner: A fire in unit 29 at the Saratogan River Bend Motel! A fan was on fire in the bathroom. They had extinguished it, but the fire spread inside the wall. Ten minutes had passed, and the fire was capped off, but an additional unit was still responding. A *hot* day!

10:40 A.M. Scanner: A blocking injury accident up at the summit at milepost 60. Tow was in route. Chains were now required eastbound.

"Where do we *get* chains?" "Where is the bathroom?" "Need caffeine!" "Help…we need food!" "Any suggestions?" "We don't want to go back home!" All morning long…

It was beyond a chaotic zoo-ville driving up to the resort. Trucks, cars, and buses had all gone astray. Then, if you just happened to bumper-car all the way up to the resort, you would find out that their parking lots were now full. I could not even describe the pissed off moods coming through my doors – screaming for quads and stocking up on candy.

2:08 P.M. Scanner: A twenty-nine-year-old male with a spinal injury at the resort. He was alert times four.

Our tow guy stopped for his chocolate-covered-bean-*less* raspberry mocha, "How do they expect me to tow three cars at once? I'm not a mule-train!"

2:10 P.M. Scanner: A fifteen-year-old-female with an arm fracture and a pos-sible C-spine injury.

A panicked lady came in and she was not dressed warm enough for our area or weather, "Is that the bathroom?" She was holding my entrance door open and frantically waving a painted nail at the "huts". "Yes." "But it's waaaaaaaay too cold in there for me!" Plus, she saw there was now a waiting line for the icy relief. Her husband, acting protective, told her to get back inside their warm car. I don't know what she eventually did – there were no public toilets within fifteen miles westbound or thirty-five miles eastbound (that were clean). Maybe…at the ski resort, but that would require a small hike to even reach the lodge. Too cold to head to the woods. A bucket of some sort in the trunk?

2:21 P.M. Scanner: An accident at the summit. Driver went into a snowbank and was slumped over the wheel.

Some skiers just stopped. This had been *their* hill, *their* preferred resort, for over thirty years and they had never seen chaos like on today's highway. Two-hour car rides to go the last ten miles. Traffic stopped dead. People were told that they would be arrested if they didn't get back inside their cars. Ain't this sport a blast, folks!

3:36 P.M. Scanner: Traction tires were now advised. Chains required had been lifted.

3:40 P.M. Scanner: Injury car accident in High Valley.

3:52 P.M. Scanner: A truck ran out of gas at milepost 52 and was partially blocking.

6:37 P.M. Scanner: A deer/car collision on Mountain Peak Highway. Aid was in route. The injured deer was on the side of the highway.

Two parties asked me today if I had seen the Flamingo Hotel in Vegas. "No. I only get married there. I have never had time to squeeze in a honeymoon or even a tiny tour. Sex, then marriage, then the mad dash back home to tell poor mom! And almost that quick, got the divorce papers." They stared.

7:56 P.M. Scanner: A twenty-eight-year-old male with a hip dislocation at the resort.

8:39 P.M. And I'm closing for good. I honest to God can't take another *nano-second* with customers.

8:45 P.M. Scanner: A twenty-year-old male with a dislocated shoulder.

8:56 P.M. Scanner: A broken bone at the resort. It was a nineteen-year-old male with a broken clavicle, and he had two male friends with him, who also needed to ride in the transport. "Our ambulances aren't a taxi service!" I said to myself out loud to my scanner which became my guest now. Maybe they were drunk.

9:00 P.M. All I'm going to risk is a trip upstairs...

1-16 31° 30th consecutive day of rain for us in "these-thar-hills"!

Brown Snow: Fill 8-ounce cup with steamed Half & Half. Pour a shot of espresso over the top.

8:42 A.M. My cabin owner yuppies jogged by, this time they wore very classy black outfits. First time they hadn't impersonated my neon signs.

10:33 A.M. Scanner: A non-injury car accident at milepost 60.

12:06 P.M. It was snowing.

12:21 P.M. It was now a blizzard. Blowing and raging white.

I played helpless and a guy just did me a huge favor. He put a new roll of toilet paper on the correct rod inside the Porta Potty. He said, "I even put it in with the paper rolling over the top. I've been trained!"

1:24 P.M. Scanner: A fifteen-year-old female with a C-spine injury.

3:00 P.M. Scanner: A non-injury car accident at milepost 61.

3:41 P.M. Scanner: Possible head-on accident at milepost 37. It was still a blizzard out.

4:06 P.M. Scanner: A tree down, blocking both lanes on Mountain Peak Highway, between mileposts 52-54. DOT said it would be some time before they could get there.

4:21 P.M. Travelers were taking their own chainsaws to the tree, to free up the highway.

I'd been so busy, and I was bone tired. Yesterday was a killer too. I had better pop some caffeine beans! Day after day with this nutty public will eventually drive *me* nuts and I will end up just like 'em. I need to get out of here occasionally. I need some fun!

5:58 P.M. Another high school classmate stopped by. I will probably run into all of them eventually now that I am sitting still in one place.

Buck called with a new offer: "I'll marree ya before we make out." So, the past didn't count and now you saw me as a virgin? Who's kidding whom?

Our tow guy came in for another raspberry mocha and gave me a bunch of new frequency numbers for my scanner. He said, "Do ya want the suicide channel?" as he chuckled. Definitely!

An older guy stopped in my drive thru to take his chains off. "Sir, could you please pull up? This is a drive thru." He sped off pissed, tires and metal ripping up the road. I just realized the lighting in that spot is spectacular for those types of jobs…but tough titties!

6:41 P.M. I was suddenly slammed at my window! I heard that they closed the highway because of the tree blockage. Two hours or more. Well, they were all here now! People were frantic, over-it, and miserable. And that new roll of toilet paper was gone again!

7:24 P.M. Scanner: A semi-truck and four cars were blocking the highway up a little further from me.

No. 1 Bachelor called. He must have liked my ponytail and zit yesterday. "Christy, how about that Argentinean dinner, since I know you probably wouldn't want to spend an evening with me at my new cabin? At least until we eat out first." Holy crap…caught me off-guard. I reply, "I think I may be ready for a real meal." He continued, "I have to go back to Mexico to check on my development until the 18th, so how about Friday the 20th?" (You are too fucking busy for my taste, but good boy, at least you asked me out for a weekend evening. I'll give you a point for that!) "Sounds great!" Although I don't feel so sanguine right about *now*…immediate nerves set in! Done deal, gals, but I'm not mentioning it again until that day or I'll chicken out! Do I have to lop off these leg hairs? How many razors will that dull…?

8:59 P.M. And still here. Absolute exhaustion has broken down my barriers and I can't believe I accepted that dinner *date*. But hell, if I'm gonna do it, what a neat guy to do it with! All of you Seattle women out there, eat your hearts out. I ain't missin' *nothin'* up in "these-thar-hills" …

1-17 33° Rain, sun and clouds.
31st consecutive day of rain.

Ski Lodge Madness: My original! 4 shots of espresso, a shot of drip, a pack of cocoa, fill cup full of hot water, stir, then top with Half & Half. Whipped cream of course!

8:44 AM. Today has already been one of *those* days. *Those days from hell, for absolutely no-good rhyme or reason!* I am not aware of any lessons I need to learn, and I haven't taken life for granted…so why?

A thirsty lady stopped, and I told her that I was not open yet - and wouldn't be for a long, long, long while! I explained to her that I had zipped to the dump and my truck wouldn't re-start for home as my Jeep was full of dairy products that needed to be refrigerated, like an hour ago, according to the Health Department, and I just couldn't deal with customers at the moment. The stubborn bitch followed me into my dark store anyway! She lived in this building twenty-three years ago and only wanted to see the inside. Yack yack yack, "I remember the building being the coldest place on creation," she said cheerfully. Well, I'll guarantee, she was the only one around here with a decent attitude! "It's still fucking cold in here, lady, now what do you want?" "Ummmmmm…. I guess a mocha and I'll look around." She had not listened to one damn thing I'd said for fifteen minutes. The ears that stuck out of the sides of her head were only used for hanging ornaments! The store was dark, and I didn't give a damn anymore. She stayed for thirty minutes! Then as she left, "I'll let you unload your groceries now." They were not fucking groceries – they were fragile supplies and half of them were probably gone by now, you moron!

10:45 A.M. The supplies are put away. I've plowed. I've fed all of the animals. I am sitting.

2:33 P.M. Scanner: A male in his thirties was having a cardiac arrest up at the resort. CPR was in progress. Airlift was requested at the summit. His ETA to the Nordic Center was ten minutes. I just REALLY realized that I am blessed. I am done whining and back to espressos.

6:02 P.M. To recap the day: The truck/dairy situation. The electricity went off for 20 minutes, Butch attempted to bite a teasing customer's finger, two men got in a fistfight outside in the parking lot...

7:00 P.M. Today is over, as far as I am concerned, it's too late to think...

1-18 30° Clouds. 32nd consecutive day of fucking rain!

Hot Peanut Butter & Jam: My original! A shot of smooth peanut butter, a shot of raspberry or strawberry syrups, then pour over 2 shots of espresso, stir together until smooth. Add steamed milk and stir.

9:02 A.M. I overslept. A full ten hours of much needed sleep! I had a shocker when I finally got down to the store; I thought Angel had turned green. My heart skipped a beat. But it was Mister sitting on *her* outside perch. A first! How did he get his big body over there? He doesn't fly! I wonder if they kissed.

I've gotten used to these constant days of rain. Boy Christy, your attitude has much improved! Everyone in the Northwest was complaining bitterly about this torrential winter. Does it seriously cause the blues?

Ms. Rachel Welch Five-Carat stopped by. She takes my breathe away. Simply gorgeous.

I just gave some guys crap for not waiting the fifteen seconds in my drive thru before honking for service. The driver said, "Oh…sorry. I didn't see the fine print." Good comeback, had to admit, the sign was about 20" x 20". But they were polite.

Andrew called to talk business and sex. Both were at an all-time low.

No. 5 called and had parrot stories for me.

Three lone train engines passed.

No. 5 called again and said, "Women are aliens in human form, because you never know where they are coming from." He was growing up!

10:47 A.M. Apparently, a skier died today at the resort. He crashed down a hill and into a tree well. By the time the buddy and others pulled him out, he had stopped breathing. He was only nineteen years old.

1:46 P.M. Buck stopped in. He is actually kinda cute when he is dirty. I always did like a man who wasn't afraid to *work*! He looked like a raccoon with his piercing blue eyes and shimmering silver hair, against brown, dirt-stained skin. He finally admitted that he and his latest gal were kissing. "You are getting a tad closer to the truth, Buck, but still a long way to go!"

3:55 P.M. The rain arrived. Again. Tirelessly. Our earth was soaked, and like a sponge, there *is* an end to how much more it could hold. Puddles filled every dip and trough. The dirt was turning to bog. Trees were falling over at the roots. It's been a month of constant typewriter tap-tap on my metal roof. It's cold and wet and cheerless.

4:12 P.M. He appeared out of nowhere – like a *vision* dropped right out of my new ceiling insulation. This clean-cut, brunette gentleman was *at* my friggin' *counter*. The chime on the door did not ring. My dog didn't bark, and he was only 4 feet from the damn serving area! His arrival was engulfed in complete silence. "Excuse me, sir! What can I do for you, and how in the hell did you get in here?" "Hi, Christy. I'm Cody. BOO to you from what I have been told." After I picked myself up off the floor and got some color back into my cheeks, "Um, nice to meet you. Where do you live now? Did you really camp for years above me, over the railroad tracks? Why are you here? What are you doing now?" My questions came like a machine-gun, but I could not help it. "Relax, Christy, I promise I'm a nice guy, and very normal…today. I am sure the sheriff had told you that. You need not be afraid. I have moved back to Saratogan… thanks to you." Oh sure, buddy, now I *am* worried as hell! He continued, "My wife died some years ago and I had to leave this world for a while. But I have to tell you, that I've watched you over the last few years…daily…and your untiring, friendly, exasperated, ferocious, persistent workaholic traits gave me the will to live with humanity again. You may be *solo;* I have been hermitic. No more. Now, may I please have a double espresso?"

Ohmygod, my mind was whirling. I wanted to know everything – and now! We chatted while he sipped. Cody was a true gentleman and quite striking, I might add. He had an athletic frame, probably kept fit by the challenges of his outdoor elements. As he left, "One last thing, Christy, I will be embarking on a new venture and lifestyle - both will include you. More will be revealed soon. Thank you for the long-awaited drink. And finally, *cat is not my cuisine."* And he was gone…

I'm not known to be speechless. I don't get goose bumps often. And I'm practically teary for some unknown reason? But damn if he could get back on the horse, so could I! Mark my words – read my lips – I will be dining in an Argentinean restaurant, two nights from now! I will not cancel. It is time to live…

5:10 P.M. And will life also include Cody? Wow – what dreams I will experience tonight…

1-19 31° 33rd consecutive day of rain.
What's new?

> **Sugar-Free Zebra:** A shot of sugar-free chocolate and sugar-free white chocolate syrups, espresso shots and steamed whole milk.

8:38 A.M. The resort was 26° and now had a total of 110 inches of snow! It was trying to snow here but I understood it is like an explosion at a talcum powder factory up at the pass. Dry, soft, beautiful snow is spreading over the entire area, and halfway down to me.

Ms. Gossip No. 1 came in and we somehow got on the *apron* subject. I shared with her my opinions on that particular 1950's dress code and she replied with the best description I've heard yet. "Christy, those aprons were women's tool coats! The pockets were where she stored various utensils and tools for inflicting injury. Just in case a hubby or the children got unruly! A wooden spoon, a bar of soap for potty-mouth…"

10:01 A.M. Scanner: Hip injury at the resort.

5:00 P.M. No. 2 Bachelor came by for some sanity. Business had been hectic for the workaholic lately. He stood there while his cell phone went off every twenty seconds…no lie. Those guys didn't become millionaires twiddling their thumbs! They talked to me, but their brains were clicking back to business every two seconds! Imagine making love to that… "Hon, tell me again where that G Spot is? Er…excuse me, I must take this call." They drove nice cars, lived in luxurious homes, looked terrific, were dynamic and ambitious, took you to fundraisers, loved to travel, but had to ask what the word feelings meant. Guess you can't have it all…

5:59 P.M. No. 2 Bachelor was still here when Bobby the Braggart walked in. I just let these two go at it – they *polished* off a good thirty minutes, taking turns puffin' out their chests while I polished the espresso machine. They did touch on the "M" subject. Both had gotten rid of their "getting-old-and-bitchy" wives. Menopause strikes again! Bobby said, "I didn't want to stick around and end up being her caretaker. She was still on her damn cane from a surgery *months* ago. God…I'd be jogging by then if I had gone under the knife!" Guys don't become millionaires by having big hearts either. These two were swiftly losing their complimentary *bachelor* titles. I stood back and really gave them both a good looking-over: they looked like workaholic, multi-tasking, cold-hearted, sons 'a bitches. I patted myself on the back for such clarity. I don't date 'em…I just berate 'em!

6:34 P.M. Rain, rain go away, definitely come back another day, and in another state! I'm going to relax now…

1-20 29° Snowing. 34ᵗʰ consecutive day of rain. This would be comical if it weren't so incredible.

The Frigging Macchiato Thing: Layer a shot of vanilla syrup, then 4 ounces of steamed milk, then the shots of espresso (however many the dearest customer requests), whipped cream, and then those damned swirlies (in a circular motion), then swirl back in a woven motion. Damn, I'm too busy to bother! Course if they want to pay $15 for a double tall, I'll give it a go…

7:48 A.M. The air was white, the ground was white. It was beautiful. I had to plow, first thing. Then some rough, fairly dirty gal walked up to me. "Can I check out your store?" "Well…where are you coming from?" She replied, "Ex Con's house." "Absolutely, for sure, don't even take another step – NO! Now scram and you can tell him to fuck himself for sending his new sleaze up here!" He had better keep his "its" away from me. Email to the sheriff is in progress.

No. 5 just pulled up in his semi to remove his chains. I made him a large mocha and we talked for a while and it was really a treat. He pursed his lips at me for a kiss as he left but backed down immediately – he knew better. I can't go there…

11:24 A.M. I-80 is closed again, so I will get some of their spillover. More customers are always wanted, just so long as nobody gets hurt in the process. Avalanche control is their excuse this time.

Denny called and his opinion: "When the river rises, which it has, the rats come running out of their pipes." He must have eyed Ex-Con's new flea.

12:07 P.M. Scanner: Medic response to the Saratogan train station on Main Street. I didn't know they actually had a *station* up here…where in the hell is Main, anyway?

12:16 P.M. Scanner: A westbound train had a burn patient onboard and needed a medic. A thirty-five-year-old female burned her face with hot soup and the skin on her face was already peeling off.

4:53 P.M. I said that I wouldn't mention The Date until the day! I had better get my butt upstairs and get dressed up. Not used to that drill! (Ugh) I crammed my ice-cubes-for-toes into frozen stilettos, pinched my cheeks a tad more and drove myself down to Tillamuk. He will pick me up there and take me down to the 'Big City' of Seattle. A real date with No.1 Bachelor!

I left my Goldie-locks intact, including armpit mania. Why shave? He's seein' nothin'! *And ya just can't carry too much insurance!* Argentinean food, here we come! I would not mention my white-trash-toothless-trolls-and-flea-infested day. I'd keep it a tad more lady-like. Wish me luck, girls, cuz it's been 451 days since I've had a *real* date with an eligible bachelor. Cowboy didn't count – he was married. And Buck's roll-in-the-hay wasn't even *close* – it was strictly a fuck. Neither was a bona fide date at all! I was *finally* learning this difference… Which fork again do you use for the salad? Talk to ya all later, cuz I don't do goodbyes well.

I'm shaking…